THE CAMBRIDGE CC
TO J. M. COE1

C000199531

Nobel Laureate J. M. Coetzee is among the mo
contemporary authors. *The Cambridge Com*
a compelling introduction for new readers, as well as fresh perspectives and
provocations for those long familiar with his works. Coetzee's previously published novels and autobiographical fictions are discussed at length, and there is
extensive treatment of his translations, scholarly books and essays, and volumes
of correspondence. Confronting Coetzee's works on the grounds of his practice,
the chapters address his craft, his literary relations and horizons, and the interactions of his writings with other arts, disciplines, and institutions. Produced by
an international team of contributors, the chapters open up avenues of discovery,
and explore Coetzee's undiminished ability to challenge and surprise his readers
with inventive works of striking power and intensity.

Jarad Zimbler is Senior Lecturer at the University of Birmingham and former
Marie Skłodowska-Curie Global Fellow at the University of Illinois at Chicago.
His book *J. M. Coetzee and the Politics of Style* (2014) was shortlisted for the
2016 University English Book Prize. He is editor, with Ben Etherington, of *The
Cambridge Companion to World Literature* (Cambridge, 2018).

A complete list of books in the series is at the back of this book

THE CAMBRIDGE
COMPANION TO
J. M. COETZEE

EDITED BY

JARAD ZIMBLER
University of Birmingham

CAMBRIDGE
UNIVERSITY PRESS

CAMBRIDGE
UNIVERSITY PRESS

University Printing House, Cambridge CB2 8BS, United Kingdom

One Liberty Plaza, 20th Floor, New York, NY 10006, USA

477 Williamstown Road, Port Melbourne, VIC 3207, Australia

314–21, 3rd Floor, Plot 3, Splendor Forum, Jasola District Centre,
New Delhi – 110025, India

79 Anson Road, #06–04/06, Singapore 079906

Cambridge University Press is part of the University of Cambridge.

It furthers the University's mission by disseminating knowledge in the pursuit of
education, learning, and research at the highest international levels of excellence.

www.cambridge.org
Information on this title: www.cambridge.org/9781108475341
DOI: 10.1017/9781108623087

© Cambridge University Press 2020

First published 2020

Printed and bound in Great Britain by Clays Ltd, Elcograf S.p.A.

A catalogue record for this publication is available from the British Library.

Library of Congress Cataloging-in-Publication Data
NAMES: Zimbler, Jarad, 1980– editor.
TITLE: The Cambridge companion to J.M. Coetzee / edited by Jarad Zimbler.
OTHER TITLES: Cambridge companions to literature.
DESCRIPTION: New York : Cambridge University Press, 2020. | Series: Cambridge companions to
authors | Includes bibliographical references and index.
IDENTIFIERS: LCCN 2019028804 (print) | LCCN 2019028805 (ebook) | ISBN 9781108475341
(hardback) | ISBN 9781108623087 (epub)
SUBJECTS: LCSH: Coetzee, J. M., 1940 – Criticism and interpretation.
CLASSIFICATION: LCC PR9369.3.C58 Z6364 2020 (print) | LCC PR9369.3.C58 (ebook) |
DDC 823/.914–dc23
LC record available at https://lccn.loc.gov/2019028804
LC ebook record available at https://lccn.loc.gov/2019028805

ISBN 978-1-108-47534-1 Hardback
ISBN 978-1-108-46673-8 Paperback

CONTENTS

Contents

CONTRIBUTORS

DEREK ATTRIDGE is the author or co-author of fifteen books on poetic form, literary theory, and South African and Irish literature, including *J. M. Coetzee and the Ethics of Reading: Literature in the Event* (2004), and has edited or co-edited eleven collections on similar topics, including *The Cambridge History of South African Literature* (2012) and *Zoë Wicomb and the Translocal: Writing Scotland and South Africa* (2017). His most recent publication is *The Experience of Poetry: From Homer's Listeners to Shakespeare's Readers* (2019). He obtained degrees from the Universities of Natal and Cambridge and taught at Southampton, Strathclyde, and Rutgers Universities before moving to the University of York, where he is Emeritus Professor of English and Related Literature.

DAVID ATTWELL is Professor of English at the University of York and Extraordinary Professor at the University of the Western Cape. He was educated at the University of Natal in Durban, the University of Cape Town, and the University of Texas at Austin. He has published widely in postcolonial studies, specializing in South African literature. With Derek Attridge he co-edited *The Cambridge History of South African Literature* (2012). His previous books include *J. M. Coetzee: South Africa and the Politics of Writing* (1993), *Rewriting Modernity: Studies in Black South African Literary History* (2005 and 2006), and *J. M. Coetzee and the Life of Writing: Face to Face with Time* (2015).

RACHEL BOWER is a poet and Leverhulme Research Fellow at the University of Leeds, researching the links between poets in Leeds and Nigeria in the 1950s and 1960s. She is the author of *Epistolarity and World Literature, 1980–2010* (2017) and *Moon Milk* (2018). She is the co-editor of two special issues: 'Tony Harrison: International Man of Letters' (*English Studies*, 2018); and 'Crafts of World Literature' (*Journal of Commonwealth Literature*, 2014). She is also the co-editor of the *Verse Matters* anthology, with Helen Mort (2017), and her poems have featured in *Magma, Stand, New Welsh Review, The Interpreter's House, Frontier, Popshot*, and many other places.

List of Contributors

ANDREW DEAN is Junior Research Fellow at the Institute of Advanced Studies at University College London, where he is researching 'laughter'. He is currently working on a monograph on post-World War II metafiction, examining the works of J. M. Coetzee, Janet Frame, and Philip Roth. Previous work on Coetzee has appeared in *MFS: Modern Fiction Studies* and *Beyond the Ancient Quarrel: Literature, Philosophy, and J. M. Coetzee* (2017).

BEN ETHERINGTON is Senior Lecturer in the School of Humanities and Communication Arts and a member of the Writing and Society Research Centre at Western Sydney University. His recent monograph *Literary Primitivism* (2017) argues for a global conception of primitivism as a utopian reaction to the apotheosis of European imperialism. He is currently a Chief Investigator on the three-year Australian Research Council project *Other Worlds*, for which he is working with eminent Australian writers, including Alexis Wright and J. M. Coetzee, to explore the idiosyncratic ways in which writers create literary worlds. Another project is a history of creole verse in the Anglophone Caribbean from slavery to decolonization.

PATRICK HAYES is Associate Professor of English Literature at Oxford University, and a Fellow of St John's College. His research focuses on debates about the nature and value of literature, from the Romantic period to the present day. He is the author of *Philip Roth: Fiction and Power* (2014) and *J. M. Coetzee and the Novel: Writing and Politics after Beckett* (2010), and co-editor (with Jan Wilm) of *Beyond the Ancient Quarrel: Literature, Philosophy, and J. M. Coetzee* (2017). He is currently working on a history of life-writing in the period after 1945.

DAVID JAMES is a Professorial Research Fellow at the University of Birmingham, before which he was Reader in Modern and Contemporary Literature at Queen Mary University of London. His most recent books include *Discrepant Solace: Contemporary Literature and the Work of Consolation* (2019) and *Modernist Futures* (2012), along with edited volumes such as *The Legacies of Modernism* (2012), *The Cambridge Companion to British Fiction since 1945* (2015), and *Modernism and Close Reading* (2020). For Columbia University Press he co-edits the book series *Literature Now*.

MICHELLE KELLY is Departmental Lecturer in World Literature in English at the Faculty of English Language and Literature, University of Oxford. Her research focuses on South African and world literature, on the intersections between law and literature, and on literature and other art forms. She is completing a monograph on Coetzee and confession, and co-editing a book on prison writing to which she is contributing an essay on PEN International and the figure of the writer as prisoner.

List of Contributors

SUE KOSSEW is Chair of English and Literary Studies at Monash University. Her research is focused particularly on the work of J. M. Coetzee and on contemporary Australian and South African women writers. Her books include *Pen and Power: A Post-Colonial Reading of J. M. Coetzee and André Brink* (1996) and *Writing Woman, Writing Place: Australian and South African Fiction* (2004). She has edited *Critical Essays on J. M. Coetzee* (1998) and with Chris Danta and Julian Murphet *Strong Opinions: J. M. Coetzee and the Authority of Contemporary Fiction* (2011). With Melinda Harvey she has also edited the collection of essays *Reading Coetzee's Women* (2019), as well as a special issue of *Australian Literary Studies* (2018), 'Thematising Women in the Work of J. M. Coetzee'. She is concluding a research project funded by the Australian Research Council entitled 'Rethinking the Victim: Gendered Violence in Australian Women's Writing' with Anne Brewster (University of New South Wales). She is a Fellow of the Australian Academy of the Humanities and has held the position of Distinguished Visiting Chair at the Universities of Copenhagen and Cologne.

MEG SAMUELSON is Associate Professor in the Department of English and Creative Writing at the University of Adelaide, Australia, and Associate Professor Extraordinary at Stellenbosch University in South Africa. She is the author of *Remembering the Nation, Dismembering Women: Stories of the South African Transition* and has published widely on African and South African literatures; on Anthropocene thought and the environmental humanities; on coastal and maritime literary and cultural studies; on the global south, southern hemisphere and world literatures; and on women's writing and theories of gender.

JAN STEYN is a translator and scholar of literatures in Afrikaans, Dutch, English, and French. He teaches Literary Translation and French at the University of Iowa and is the editor of *Translation: Crafts, Contexts, Consequences* forthcoming from Cambridge University Press.

ANTHONY UHLMANN is Director of the Writing and Society Research Centre at Western Sydney University, Australia. He is the author of *Beckett and Poststructuralism* (1999), *Samuel Beckett and the Philosophical Image* (2006), and *Thinking in Literature* (2011). From 2008 to 2013 he edited the *Journal of Beckett Studies*, and he is co-editor (with Jennifer Rutherford) of *J. M. Coetzee's 'The Childhood of Jesus': The Ethics of Ideas and Things* (2017). His most recent book is *J. M. Coetzee: Truth, Meaning, Fiction* (2020).

ANDREW VAN DER VLIES is Professor of Contemporary Literature and Postcolonial Studies at Queen Mary University of London, and Extraordinary Professor at the University of the Western Cape in South Africa. He has published widely on South African literatures, print cultures, art, and sexuality, including in *The Cambridge History of South African Literature* (2012) and *Oxford History of the Novel in English* (2016). His books include *Present Imperfect: Contemporary*

South African Writing (2017), *South African Textual Cultures* (2007), and, as editor, *Print, Text & Book Cultures in South Africa* (2012), Zoë Wicomb's *Race, Nation, Translation: South African Essays, 1990–2013* (2018), and *South African Writing in Transition* (2019, with Rita Barnard).

JARAD ZIMBLER is Senior Lecturer in English Literature at the University of Birmingham. He is the author of *J. M. Coetzee and the Politics of Style* (2014) as well as several articles concerned with Coetzee's work and with South African literature more broadly. With Ben Etherington, he is also editor of the *Cambridge Companion to World Literature* (2018).

ACKNOWLEDGEMENTS

I am extremely grateful to all of the contributors for their patience and their assiduousness, and especially to Derek Attridge, Ben Etherington, David James, and Michelle Kelly for their advice and encouragement. I am grateful also to Ray Ryan, Edgar Mendez, and Sharon McCann at Cambridge University Press, to Benjamin Madden for his assistance compiling the chronology, to Caroline Howlett for her copy-editing, to the several anonymous readers for their reports on individual chapters, to Ulla Montan for permission to use her photographic portrait, and to J. M. Coetzee for permission to quote from the Coetzee Papers, at the Harry Ransom Center, University of Texas at Austin.

CHRONOLOGY

This chronology is divided into three parts. The events under 'Life and Works' concern Coetzee's biography and bibliography. They include some significant dates in Coetzee's personal life, but have to do mostly with public and professional matters: when and where he studied, worked, wrote, published, and received certain accolades. The list of articles, prizes, and talks is by no means complete.

By way of sketching literary context, the column headed 'Literary Events' identifies works – primarily novels, but also memoirs, poems, plays, and critical writings – which Coetzee names in his published essays, reviews, and correspondence. In each case, the date is that of publication in the language of composition, though, where the work has been subsequently published in English, the translated title is given. Again, the list is not complete, since it does not draw on Coetzee's teaching materials now housed at the Harry Ransom Center. Nor does it make any attempt to specify the date of Coetzee's initial readings. Nevertheless, in eschewing distinctions between influential and incidental peers and predecessors, this portion of the chronology constitutes a resource in its own right, providing a rather striking and perhaps surprising profile of Coetzee's reading habits and regions of interest. It also provides evidence of his assiduousness: tasked with writing an essay or review, he reads extensively, perhaps comprehensively, across the relevant author's oeuvre.

Finally, events in the right-hand column concern conflicts and crises in the political and economic domains which have somehow impinged upon Coetzee's environments and his writings. Broadly, they fall under the following headings: World War II, the Cold War, apartheid, decolonization, the Vietnam War, the War on Terror, and the global financial crisis. They are also delimited geographically and temporally, in line with the periods of Coetzee's residence in South Africa, the United Kingdom, the United States, and Australia.

Date	Life and Works	Literary Events	Social, Political, and Economic Events
1940	9 Feb.: John Maxwell Coetzee (JMC) born in Mowbray, Cape Town, to Zacharias (Jack) and Vera Coetzee.	William Faulkner, *The Hamlet* Graham Greene, *The Power and the Glory* Sándor Márai, *Casanova in Bolzano* Irène Némirovsky, *Les Chiens et les Loups* Ezra Pound, *Cantos LXII–LXXI* Joseph Roth, *The Leviathan* Richard Wright, *Native Son*	10 May: Germany invades Belgium, Holland, and France. 20 May: First prisoners arrive in Auschwitz I concentration camp. 26 May–4 June: British troops evacuated from Dunkirk. 10 July: Battle of Britain begins, followed by the 'Blitz'.
1941	Coetzee family moves to Johannesburg.	J. L. Borges, *The Garden of Forking Paths* H. I. E. Dhlomo, *The Valley of a Thousand Hills* Sarah Gertrude Millin, *The Herr Witchdoctor* C. M. van den Heever, *Gister* Patrick White, *The Living and the Dead*	10 Feb.: German forces begin to arrive in North Africa. 22 June: Germany invades Soviet Union. 7 Dec.: Japan attacks Pearl Harbor.
1942	Jack Coetzee joins Union Defence Force; goes on to fight in North Africa, the Middle East, and Italy.	Albert Camus, *The Outsider* William Faulkner, *Go Down, Moses* Sándor Márai, *Embers* Mikro, *Huisies teen die heuvel*	20 Jan.: Wannsee Conference convened by Reinhard Heydrich to resolve the 'Final Solution to the Jewish Question'.

Date	Life and Works	Literary Events	Social, Political, and Economic Events
		Wallace Stevens, *Notes Towards a Supreme Fiction* Jochem van Bruggen, *Ampie: die kind*	23 *Aug.*: Battle of Stalingrad begins; ends five months later with Red Army victory. 23 *Oct.–11 Nov.*: Allied victory at El Alamein.
1943	8 *April*: David Keith Coetzee, brother of JMC, born in Johannesburg.	T. S. Eliot, *Four Quartets*	13 *May*: Surrender of Afrika Korps and other Axis forces in North Africa. 3 *Aug.*: Bus boycott begins in Alexandra, a 'native township' near Johannesburg. 26 *Aug.–23 Dec.*: Battle of Dnieper concludes with Red Army taking Kiev.
1944	Vera Coetzee returns with her sons to the Cape.	Gerrit Achterberg, *Eurydice* Saul Bellow, *Dangling Man* J. L. Borges, *Fictions* T. S. Eliot, 'What is a Classic?' W. Somerset Maugham, *The Razor's Edge* Mikro, *Vreemdelinge*	4 *June*: Allied troops capture Rome. 6 *June*: D-Day Allied invasion of Normandy. 19–25 *Aug.*: Allied liberation of Paris.
1945	*June*: Jack Coetzee returns from the war and re-joins his family.	C. M. van den Heever, *Kringloop van die winde*	27 *Jan.*: Red Army liberates Auschwitz. 7 *May*: Nazi Germany surrenders, ending war in Europe.

1946	Coetzee family moves to Pollsmoor, a settlement for returned soldiers; JMC begins his schooling at Pollsmoor Primary School. Coetzee family moves to Rosebank, Cape Town; JMC attends Rosebank Junior School.		6–9 Aug.: Atomic bombs dropped first on Hiroshima, then on Nagasaki. 14 Aug.: Japan surrenders, ending war in the Pacific. 10 Jan.: First meeting of the United Nations (UN). 5 March: Winston Churchill delivers 'Sinews of Peace' speech, using phrase 'Iron Curtain' to describe state of Central and Eastern Europe. Aug.: In South Africa (SA), over 74,000 African workers on gold mines strike for higher wages. 1 Oct.: First of the Nuremberg trials concludes.
1947		Saul Bellow, *The Victim* Albert Camus, *The Plague* Naguib Mahfouz, *Midaq Alley* Irène Némirovsky, *Les Biens de ce monde*	12 March: USA commits to assisting democratic nations under threat from authoritarian forces (Truman Doctrine). 5 June: European Recovery Program (Marshall Plan) drafted.

Date	Life and Works	Literary Events	Social, Political, and Economic Events
			22 *Sept.*: Establishment of Cominform, forum of the International Communist Movement.
1948	*May*: Coetzee family re-settles in Worcester, a predominantly Afrikaans-speaking town north-east of Cape Town; JMC attends Worcester Primary for Boys, a parallel medium school, offering classes in English and Afrikaans.	Graham Greene, *The Heart of the Matter* Alan Paton, *Cry the Beloved Country* Ezra Pound, *The Pisan Cantos* Patrick White, *The Aunt's Story*	21–25 *Feb.*: Communist takeover of Czechoslovakian government. 15 *May–10 Mar. 1949*: First Arab-Israeli war, following declaration of State of Israel. 26 *May*: Jan Smuts loses election to D. F. Malan's National Party; new government begins to pursue policy of apartheid in SA.
1949		J. L. Borges, *The Aleph* Naguib Mahfouz, *The Beginning and the End*	4 *Apr.*: NATO formed. 8 *July*: Prohibition of Mixed Marriages Act comes into effect in SA. 7 *Oct.*: German Democratic Republic (GDR) established. 21 *Sept.*: People's Republic of China established.
1950		Doris Lessing, *The Grass is Singing* Sarah Gertrude Millin, *The King of the Bastards*	25 *June*: Korean War begins. 7 *July*: Population Registration Act requires inhabitants of SA to be

1951	Daphne Rooke, *A Grove of Fever Trees*	classified by race; Group Areas Act subsequently divides urban areas into racially exclusive zones. *17 July:* Suppression of Communism Act bans South African Communist Party and any group subscribing to communism.
1952	*Jan:* Coetzee family settles in Plumstead, Cape Town. JMC begins high school at St Joseph's Marist College, in Rondebosch, Cape Town.	Samuel Beckett, *Molloy; Malone Dies*; Graham Greene, *The End of the Affair*; Daphne Rooke, *Mittee*; Samuel Beckett, *Waiting for Godot*; Guy Butler, *Stranger to Europe*; Paul Celan, *Mohn und Gedächtis*	*17 July:* Bantu Authorities Act creates basis for self-government under traditional tribal authorities, within so-called 'homelands' in SA. *6 April:* Van Riebeeck Festival celebrates the 300th anniversary of the arrival of the Dutch in SA.
1953		Gerrit Achterberg, *Ballade van de gasfitter*; Samuel Beckett, *Watt; The Unnamable*; Saul Bellow, *The Adventures of Augie March*; J. L. Borges, *Labyrinthes*; Antonio Di Benedetto, *Mundo animal*	*5 March:* Joseph Stalin dies. *8 April:* Jomo Kenyatta sentenced to seven years in prison for involvement with Mau Mau Uprising in Kenya. *27 July:* Korean War ends. *9 Nov.:* Cambodia achieves independence from France.

(cont.)

Date	Life and Works	Literary Events	Social, Political, and Economic Events
		Alan Paton, *Too Late the Phalarope* Alain Robbe-Grillet, *Erasers* Daphne Rooke, *Ratoons*	20 Oct.–2 Nov.: Operation Castor: French paratroopers take Dien Bien Phu, in order to block Viet Minh transport routes.
1954		Peter Abrahams, *Tell Freedom* Doris Lessing, *A Proper Marriage* Ina Rousseau, *Die verlate tuin*	1 Jan.: Bantu Education Act (1953) comes into effect in SA. 7 May: Battle of Dien Bien Phu concludes with Viet Minh victory over French. 21 July: Geneva Accords establish a ceasefire line, partitioning Vietnam. 31 Oct.: Algerian National Liberation Front begins revolt against French colonial rule.
1955	JMC qualifies for bursary on grounds of Junior Certificate results.	Antonio Di Benedetto, *El pentágono* Vladimir Nabokov, *Lolita* Ezra Pound, *Section: Rock-Drill* Alain Robbe-Griller, *The Voyeur* Patrick White, *The Tree of Man*	9 Feb.: SA police begin forcibly removing Sophiatown residents. 18–24 April: Bandung Conference of Asian and African states. 14 May: Warsaw Pact signed. 26 June: Freedom Charter adopted at Congress of the People proclaims

	commitment to non-racial democracy in SA. 1 *Nov.*: Vietnam War begins. 2 *March*: In SA, Coloured voters removed from Cape voters roll. 23 *Sept.–8 Oct.*: Hungarian Revolution. 29 *Oct.–7 Nov.*: Suez Crisis 5 *Dec.*: SA police arrest 156 leaders of the Congress Movement, including Nelson Mandela, on charges of high treason.	Peter Abrahams, *A Wreath for Udomo* John Barth, *The Floating Opera* Samuel Beckett, *Malone Dies* (in English). Antonio Di Benedetto, *Zama* Naguib Mahfouz, *Palace Walk*	
1956			Poem 'In the Beginning' wins Stuttaford Book Prize for best narrative poem in Cape Town Eisteddfod. JMC matriculates from St Joseph's. JMC passes bilingualism exam of SA Academy of Arts and Sciences.
1957	7 *Jan.*: Bus boycott begins in Alexandra, SA. 18 *Feb.*: Mau Mau leader Dedan Kimathi executed in Kenya. 6 *March*: Ghana achieves independence. 17 *Dec.*: SA government drops charges against sixty-one of the accused in the Treason Trial, including Albert Lutuli and Oliver Tambo.	William Faulkner, *The Town* Ted Hughes, *The Hawk in the Rain* Naguib Mahfouz, *Palace of Desire*; *Sugar Street* Bernard Malamud, *The Assistant* Irène Némirovsky, *Les Feux de l'automne* Boris Pasternak, *Doctor Zhivago* Alain Robbe-Grillet, *Jealousy* Daphne Rooke, *Wizards' Country* Claude Simon, *The Wind* Patrick White, *Voss*	JMC enrols at the University of Cape Town (UCT). JMC begins attending Imaginative Writing Class, run by Professor Guy Howarth (GH)

Date	Life and Works	Literary Events	Social, Political, and Economic Events
1958	'Attic', 'The Love Song', and 'Procula to Pilate' appear in UCT's *Literary Miscellany*.	John Barth, *The End of the Road* Nadine Gordimer, *A World of Strangers* Doris Lessing, *A Ripple from the Storm* Josef Skvorecky, *The Cowards*	17 Feb.: Bertrand Russell launches Campaign for Nuclear Disarmament in London. 13 May: Right-wing coup begins in Algiers, leading to collapse of French Fourth Republic. 2 Sept.: H. F. Verwoerd becomes Prime Minister of SA.
1959	JMC given assistantship by GH. 'Trivial Verses' and 'Three Poems from a Cold Climate', *Literary Miscellany*. 'Truth Lies Sunken' and 'From Act II of *The Last Spring*' appear in UCT little magazine *Groote Schuur*.	Paul Celan, *Sprachgitter* William Faulkner, *The Mansion* Günter Grass, *The Tin Drum* Harry Mulisch, *The Stone Bridal Bed* Naguib Mahfouz, *Children of Gebelawi* Ezra Pound, *Thrones*	8 Jan.: Fidel Castro's revolutionary forces enter Havana. 6 April: Africanist members of African National Congress (ANC) form Pan Africanist Congress in SA; Robert Sobukwe elected first president. 21 June: Extension of University Education Act prevents non-white students registering at SA universities.
1960	JMC enrols in the English Honours programme at UCT, which he completes with distinction.	J. L. Borges, *The Maker* Nadine Gordimer, *Friday's Footprint* Alfred Hutchinson, *Road to Ghana*	3 Feb.: British Prime Minister Harold Macmillan delivers 'Winds of

'The wives of the rock lobster fishermen' and 'Returning from Carthage', *Groote Schuur.*

1961   JMC enrols in the mathematics Honours programme at UCT. 'Five Night-Thoughts of a Loving Sleepless; to which are appended two poems', *Groote Schuur.*

15 Dec.: Having completed his studies, JMC sails from Cape Town for Southampton, UK.

Doris Lessing, *In Pursuit of the English*

Samuel Beckett, *How It Is*
Günter Grass, *Cat and Mouse*
Graham Greene, *A Burnt-Out Case*
Joseph Heller, *Catch-22*
Zbigniew Herbert, *Study of the Object*
Yasunari Kawabata, *House of the Sleeping Beauties*
Naguib Mahfouz, *The Thief and the Dogs*
Claude Mauriac, *The Marquise Went Out at Five*
Arthur Miller, *The Misfits*
Es'kia Mphahlele, *The African Image*

Change' speech in SA Parliament, endorsing decolonization.
21 March: Demonstrations against pass laws end in Sharpeville massacre; SA police kill sixty-nine.
30 March: SA government declares state of emergency.
1 Oct.: Nigeria achieves independence.

4 Feb.: Portuguese Colonial War begins in Angola.
11 April: Trial of Adolf Eichmann begins in Jerusalem.
17–20 April: Bay of Pigs invasion of Cuba, by CIA-backed paramilitary group.
31 May: Following a referendum, SA withdraws from the Commonwealth of Nations and becomes a Republic.
13 Aug.: Construction of the Berlin Wall begins.
11 Dec.: Official US involvement in Vietnam War begins.

Date	Life and Works	Literary Events	Social, Political, and Economic Events
		V. S. Naipaul, *A House for Mister Biswas* Daphne Rooke, *A Lover for Estelle* Patrick White, *Riders in the Chariot*	
1962	JMC is awarded Croll Bursary by UCT, which he uses to register for an MA in absentia, on the novels of Ford Madox Ford. JMC begins working as a computer programmer at IBM in London.	James Baldwin, *Another Country* Anthony Delius, *A Corner of the World* Zbigniew Herbert, *Barbarian in the Garden* Alex La Guma, *A Walk in the Night* Doris Lessing, *The Golden Notebook* Sarah Gertrude Millin, *The Wizard Bird* Vladimir Nabokov, *Pale Fire* V. S. Naipaul, *The Middle Passage* Daphne Rooke, *The Greyling* Aleksandr Solzhenitsyn, *One Day in the Life of Ivan Denisovich* N. P. van Wyk Louw, *Tristia*	7 *Feb.*: US embargo of Cuba begins. 18 *March*: Évian Accords end Algerian War of Independence. 18 *April*: UK ends free immigration of Commonwealth citizens. 31 *May*: Adolf Eichmann is executed in Israel. 5 *Aug.*: Nelson Mandela is arrested. 14–28 *Oct.*: Cuban Missile Crisis. 6 *Nov.*: UN General Assembly passes Resolution 1761, condemning apartheid, and calling on member states to cease military and trade relations.
1963	JMC resigns from IBM and returns to Cape Town, where he renews	Paul Celan, *Die Niemandsrose* Hugo Claus, *Poems 1948–1963*	28 *March*: Publications and Entertainments Act allows for creation of Publications Control

Board and broad powers of censorship in SA.

25 *May:* Organization of African Unity is established.

11 *July:* SA police raid Liliesleaf Farm, arresting members of ANC underground.

10 *Oct.:* Partial Test Ban Treaty comes into effect, prohibiting above-ground test detonations of nuclear weapons.

2 *Nov.:* Coup in South Vietnam.

22 *Nov.:* John F. Kennedy is assassinated in Dallas, Texas.

12 *Dec.:* Kenya achieves independence.

12 *June:* Mandela and seven others convicted of sabotage and sentenced to life imprisonment.

2 *Aug.:* Gulf of Tonkin Incident leads to escalation of US involvement in the Vietnam War.

Nadine Gordimer, *Occasion for Loving*
Bloke Modisane, *Blame Me on History*
Richard Rive, *African Songs*
Alain Robbe-Grillet, *Towards a New Novel*

Saul Bellow, *Herzog*
Breyten Breytenbach, *Die ysterkoei moet sweet*
Antonio Di Benedetto, *The Silencer*
Alex La Guma, *And a Threefold Cord*
V. S. Naipaul, *An Area of Darkness*

acquaintance with Philippa Jubber (PJ).

April: '**Computer Poem**' appears in UCT little magazine *The Lion and the Impala*

11 *July:* JMC and PJ marry in Johannesburg.

Nov.: JMC submits his MA thesis 'The Works of Ford Madox Ford with Particular Reference to the Novels'.

30 *Dec.:* JMC and PJ depart Cape Town for Southampton.

Feb.: JMC begins work at International Computers and Tabulators. JMC and PJ live in Bagshot, Surrey.

1964

Date	Life and Works	Literary Events	Social, Political, and Economic Events
		Lewis Nkosi, *The Rhythm of Violence* Richard Rive, *Emergency*	*25 Sept.*: FRELIMO launches Mozambican War of Independence. *15 Oct.*: Nikita Khrushchev removed from office in Soviet Union.
1965	JMC applies to US PhD programmes. JMC awarded a Fulbright scholarship. *Sept.*: JMC begins PhD in linguistics and literature at the University of Texas at Austin (UT).	Peter Abrahams, *A Night of Their Own* Samuel Beckett, *Proust/ Three Dialogues* Doris Lessing, *Landlocked* Norman Mailer, *An American Dream* Lewis Nkosi, *Home and Exile* Daphne Rooke, *Diamond Jo*	*8 March*: First US ground troops arrive in South Vietnam. *28 July*: President Johnson announces increase in US troops in Vietnam, to 125,000. *11 Nov.*: Ian Smith's white minority government unilaterally declares Rhodesia's independence.
1966	*9 June*: Birth of Nicolas Coetzee, first child of JMC and PJ. *1 Aug.*: Charles Whitman, the Texas Tower Sniper, kills seventeen people on UT campus, whilst JMC is present.	Sydney Clouts, *One Life* Nadine Gordimer, *The Late Bourgeois World* Naguib Mahfouz, *Adrift on the Nile* Patrick White, *The Solid Mandala*	*26 Aug.*: SA 'Border War' begins when SA Air Force and Police attack South West African People's Organization (SWAPO) base at Omugulugwombashe. *6 Sept.*: SA Prime Minister Verwoerd assassinated in Parliament.
1967	JMC awarded a Graduate Fellowship, and appointed	Samuel Beckett, *No's Knife* Paul Celan, *Breathturn*	*15 April*: Spring Mobilization Committee to End the War in

	University Fellow for academic year 1967–8.	Vietnam organizes march from Central Park to United Nations. 5–10 June: Six-Day War, between Israel and allied armies of Egypt, Syria, Iraq, and Jordan. 26 June: Buffalo Race Riot begins in Buffalo, NY, one of dozens of such riots across the USA this year. Ted Hughes, Wodwo Alex La Guma, The Stone Country Gabriel García Márquez, One Hundred Years of Solitude Norman Mailer, Why Are We in Vietnam?
1968	July: JMC officially accepts an appointment as Visiting Assistant Professor at SUNY Buffalo. Takes up post in September, after completing his dissertation. JMC begins translating Een nagelaten bekentenis, a Dutch novel by Marcellus Emants. 10 Nov.: birth of Gisela Gabrièle Coetzee, second child of JMC and PJ.	30 Jan.: Beginning of the Tet Offensive, one of the largest military campaigns in the Vietnam War. 16 March: My Lai Massacre: US troops kill hundreds of unarmed civilians in South Vietnam. 4 April: Martin Luther King Jr is assassinated, sparking riots across the USA. 20–21 Aug.: Warsaw Pact troops invade Czechoslovakia, following 'Prague Spring' of political liberalization. John Barth, Lost in the Funhouse Paul Celan, Threadsuns Aleksandr Solzhenitsyn, The First Circle
1969	12 Jan.: JMC awarded PhD for thesis 'The English Fiction of	12 Aug.: UN Security Council Resolution 269 calls for end of SA Samuel Beckett, Lessness J. L. Borges, In Praise of Darkness

(cont.)

Date	Life and Works	Literary Events	Social, Political, and Economic Events
	Samuel Beckett: An Essay in Stylistic Analysis', at UT.	Breyten Breytenbach, *Kouevuur* C. J. Driver, *Elegy for a Revolutionary* Doris Lessing, *The Four-Gated City* Les Murray, 'Evening Alone at Bunyah' Vladimir Nabokov, *Ada or Ardor: A Family Chronicle* Daphne Rooke, *Boy on the Mountain* Philip Roth, *Portnoy's Complaint* Gary Snyder, *Earth House Hold*	administration of Namibia by 4 October. *12–20 Nov.*: Journalist Seymour Hersh breaks story of My Lai massacre; explicit photographs published by *The Plain Dealer*. *1 Dec.*: First draft lottery in the USA since World War II.
1970	*1 Jan.*: JMC begins work on 'The Narrative of Jacobus Coetzee'. *25 Feb.*: Protests against the Vietnam War turn violent on SUNY Buffalo campus, injuring twenty-seven people. *15 March*: JMC joins forty-four colleagues in a sit-in at the office of SUNY Buffalo President, protesting the continued presence of	Samuel Beckett, *Mercier and Camier* J. L. Borges, *Brodie's Report* Patrick White, *The Vivisector*	*1 March*: Rhodesia declares itself a Republic, severing ties with UK. *5 March*: Nuclear Non-Proliferation Treaty comes into effect. *26 March*: Bantu Homelands Citizenship Act allocates citizenship in Bantustans to all black South Africans.

police on campus. All forty-five are arrested and charged with 'criminal contempt of the law and unlawful entry'.

2 *April*: US Department of Justice turns down JMC's application for permanent residency.

Oct.: **'The Comedy of Point of View in Beckett's Murphy'**, *Critique*.

Dec.: PJ returns to Cape Town with Nicolas and Gisela.

30 *April*: US troops cross border from Vietnam into Cambodia.

4 *May*: During protests against US incursion into Cambodia, four Kent State University students are killed.

15 *May*: International Olympic Committee expels SA from International Olympic Movement.

12 *Oct.*: President Nixon announces that the USA will withdraw 40,000 troops from Vietnam.

Breyten Breytenbach, *Om te vlieg*
Hugo Claus, *Morning, You*
Nadine Gordimer, *A Guest of Honour*
Doris Lessing, *Briefing for a Descent into Hell*
Es'kia Mphahlele, *The Wanderers*

1971

May: JMC returns to Cape Town, lives with his family at Maraisdal, near the Coetzee family farm Voëlfontein.

June: Charges against JMC and his colleagues are rejected by the New York State Supreme Court.

21 *Dec.*: JMC receives news of appointment to temporary lectureship at UCT.

13 *Feb.*: With US air and artillery support, South Vietnamese troops invade Laos.

29 *March*: US Army Lieutenant William Calley found guilty of twenty-two murders in My Lai Massacre.

13 *June*: *New York Times* begins to publish Pentagon Papers.

21 *June*: International Court of Justice declares SA's presence in Namibia illegal, and obliges it to withdraw.

Date	Life and Works	Literary Events	Social, Political, and Economic Events
1972	JMC's appointment at UCT made permanent; completes translation of *Een nagelaten bekentenis*. *11 June:* JMC begins work on 'The Vietnam Project'. *Nov.:* 'The Manuscript Revisions of Beckett's *Watt*', *Journal of Modern Literature*.	Breyten Breytenbach, *Skryt* Nadine Gordimer, *Livingstone's Companions* Alex La Guma, *In the Fog of the Seasons' End* Les Murray, 'Walking to the Cattle Place' Josef Skvorecky, *The Miracle Game*	*26 May:* Strategic Arms Limitation Treaty (START) I is signed by USA and Soviet Union. *12 July:* Black People's Convention is formed in Pietermaritzburg, SA; includes Steve Biko amongst its leadership.
1973	*March:* 'Samuel Beckett's *Lessness*: An Exercise in Decomposition', *Computers and the Humanities*. *Oct.:* 'Samuel Beckett and the Temptations of Style', *Theoria*. *19 Dec.:* JMC agrees contract with Peter Randall, at Ravan Press, for publication of *Dusklands*.	André Brink, *Looking on Darkness* Athol Fugard, John Kani & Winston Ntshona, *The Island* Graham Greene, *The Honorary Consul* Wopko Jensma, *Sing for Our Execution*	*27 Jan.:* Paris Peace Accords end US involvement in Vietnam War. *16 May:* SA Minister of Justice bans protest meetings in Cape Town, following student protests. *6–25 Oct.:* Yom Kippur War in the Middle East; prompts OPEC oil embargo, which leads to 1973 energy crisis.
1974	*18 April: Dusklands*, Ravan Press (Johannesburg).	Nadine Gordimer, *The Conservationist* Naguib Mahfouz, *Al-Karnak*	*18 March:* OPEC oil embargo ends. *25 April:* Carnation Revolution overthrows Portuguese government,

	'Nabokov's *Pale Fire* and the Primacy of Art', *UCT Studies in English*. 'Man's Fate in the Novels of Alex La Guma', *Studies in Black Literature*. *1 Dec.*: JMC begins work on *In the Heart of the Country*.	Daphne Rooke, *Margaretha de la Porte* Zbigniew Herbert, *Mr Cogito* Gerald Murnane, *Tamarisk Row* Doris Lessing, *Memoirs of a Survivor*	prompts Portugal's withdrawal from African colonies. *8 Aug.*: Following Watergate scandal, President Nixon announces resignation. *9 Oct.*: SA Publications Act replaces Publications Control Board with Directorate.
1975	*A Posthumous Confession*, JMC's translation of *Een nagelaten bekentenis*, by Marcellus Emants, Twayne (Boston). *27 June*: JMC writes to Peter Randall, describing progress on *In the Heart of the Country*, and asking about Ravan's practices regarding censorship.	Aharon Appelfeld, *Badenheim 1939* Saul Bellow, *Humboldt's Gift* J. L. Borges, *The Book of Sand* Yvonne Burgess, *The Strike* Guy Butler, *Selected Poems* Stephen Gray, *Local Colour* Harry Mulisch, *Two Women* Aleksandr Solzhenitsyn, *The Oak and the Calf*	*17 April*: Khmer Rouge takes control of Cambodia. *30 April*: Saigon falls to North Vietnamese, ending Vietnam War. *25 June*: Mozambique achieves independence. *14 Oct.*: South African Defence Force (SADF) initiates Operation Savannah, its military intervention in Angola.
1976	JMC appointed to Senior Lectureship at UCT. *March*: 'The First Sentence of Yvonne Burgess's *The Strike*', *English in Africa*.	André Brink, *An Instant in the Wind* Breyten Breytenbach, *A Season in Paradise* Etienne Leroux, *Magersfontein, O Magersfontein!* Amos Oz, *The Hill of Evil Counsel*	*27 March*: SADF withdraws from Angola. *30 April*: Pupils at Orlando West Junior School in Johannesburg strike in protest against use of

(cont.)

Date	Life and Works	Literary Events	Social, Political, and Economic Events
	31 May: JMC accepts offer from Secker & Warburg to publish In the Heart of the Country.	David Wright, A South African Album	Afrikaans as medium of instruction. 16 June: Soweto Uprising: SA police fire on black schoolchildren, killing at least 176. 11 Aug.: Protests spread to Cape Town: black pupils from Langa, Gugulethu and Nyanga march in solidarity with Soweto students.
1977	March: 'Achterberg's "Ballade van de gasfitter": The Mystery of I and You', PMLA. 13 June: In the Heart of the Country, Secker & Warburg (London). 11 July: Copies of In the Heart of the Country are seized by SA Customs on arrival in Cape Town.	Breyten Breytenbach, Blomskryf Charles Eglington, Under the Horizon Naguib Mahfouz, The Harafish Les Murray, 'The Buladelah-Taree Holiday Song Cycle' Josef Skvorecky, The Engineer of Human Souls	6 Jan.: Charter 77 is published by Czechoslovakian intellectuals, calling on the government to implement human rights commitments. 18 Aug.: Steve Biko, anti-apartheid activist and leader of Black Consciousness Movement, is arrested near Grahamstown.

Year	Life	Works	Public events
	Sept.: Following a review by SA censors, the embargo on *In the Heart of the Country* is lifted. *20 Sept.*: JMC informed that *In the Heart of the Country* has been awarded the Mofolo-Plomer Prize; begins work on *Waiting for the Barbarians*.		*12 Sept.*: After being severely tortured and beaten by police, Steve Biko dies in their custody. *4 Nov.*: UN Security Council Resolution 48 imposes a mandatory arms embargo on SA.
1978	*Feb.*: **In the Heart of the Country**, SA edition, with Afrikaans dialogue, Ravan Press (Johannesburg). *March*: *In the Heart of the Country* awarded the CNA Prize. **'Hero and Bad Mother in Epic, A Poem'**, *Staffrider*.	Aharon Appelfeld, *The Age of Wonders* André Brink, *Rumours of Rain* A. S. Byatt, *The Virgin in the Garden* Antonio Di Benedetto, *Absurdos* Graham Greene, *The Human Factor* Amos Oz, *Soumchi* Adam Small, *The Orange Earth*	*8 Jan.*: Rick Turner, former leader of the National Union of South African Students, is assassinated in Durban. *15 Feb.*: Rhodesia announces it will accept multi-racial democracy within two years. *4 May*: SADF raids SWAPO facility at Kassinga, killing 624. *9 Oct.*: P. W. Botha becomes SA Prime Minister.
1979	*Jan.*: **'Surreal Metaphors and Random Processes'**, *Journal of Literary Semantics*. JMC on leave from UCT, spends one semester in the Department of Linguistics at UT, and three	Nadine Gordimer, *Burger's Daughter* Alex La Guma, *The Time of the Butcherbird* Norman Mailer, *The Executioner's Song* V. S. Naipaul, *A Bend in the River*	*20 April*: Federation of South African Trade Unions is founded. *1 June*: Under power-sharing deal, majority-led government is formed in Rhodesia.

(cont.)

Date	Life and Works	Literary Events	Social, Political, and Economic Events
	months at the University of California, Berkeley. JMC explores the possibility of filming *In the Heart of the Country*, and produces a draft screenplay.	Christopher van Wyk, *It is Time to Go Home* Patrick White, *The Twyborn Affair*	*16 July:* Saddam Hussein becomes president of Iraq. *24 Dec.:* The Soviet Union invades Afghanistan.
1980	JMC and PJ divorce. *Jan.:* 'The Rhetoric of the Passive in English', *Linguistics*. *March:* 'Blood, Flaw, Taint, Degeneration: The Case of Sarah Gertrude Millin', *English Studies in Africa*. *23 April: Waiting for the Barbarians* awarded the CNA Prize. Coetzee's acceptance speech is later published as 'SA Authors Must Learn Modesty', *Die Vaderland*. *31 May:* JMC begins work on *Life & Times of Michael K*.	Breyten Breytenbach, *Die miernes swel op* Joseph Brodsky, *A Part of Speech* Nadine Gordimer, *Something Out There* Cees Nooteboom, *Rituals*	*4 April:* Umkhonto we Sizwe (MK) guerrillas attack Booysens Police Station in Johannesburg. *18 April:* Zimbabwe achieves independence, with Robert Mugabe as Prime Minister. *21 April–30 July:* Coloured students in the Cape begin boycott of schools and universities, which soon spreads across SA. *June:* Beginning of Operation Sceptic, a significant SADF incursion into Angola. *17 Sept.:* Solidarity, an independent trade union, is formed in Poland,

16 Oct.: **Waiting for the Barbarians**, Secker & Warburg (London)/ Ravan Press (Johannesburg).

JMC joins Afrikaanse Skrywersgilde (Afrikaans Writers' Guild).

Dec.: JMC begins a relationship with Dorothy Driver (DD).

William Burroughs, *Cities of the Red Night*
Nadine Gordimer, *July's People*
Gabriel García Márquez, *Chronicle of a Death Foretold*
Cees Nooteboom, *A Song of Truth and Semblance*
Alan Paton, *Ah, But Your Land is Beautiful*
Richard Rive, *Writing Black*
Salman Rushdie, *Midnight's Children*
Sipho Sepamla, *A Ride on the Whirlwind*

following successful strikes at Gdańsk Shipyard.
22 *Sept.*: Iraq invades Iran, beginning the first Persian Gulf War.

1981

Jan.: JMC promoted to Associate Professor at UCT.
April: **'Time, Tense, and Aspect in Kafka's "The Burrow"'**, *MLN*.
Aug.: *Waiting for the Barbarians* is awarded the James Tait Black Memorial Prize for Fiction. It wins the Geoffrey Faber Memorial Prize in the same year.
Dec.: JMC approached by Human & Rousseau to undertake a translation of Wilma Stockenström's *Die kremetartekspedisie*; JMC agrees.

30 *Jan.*: SADF raids suspected MK safe area in Maputo, Mozambique.
14 *May*: UN General Assembly publishes list of multi-national companies with links to SA.
25 *Apr.–7 May*: MK undertakes series of attacks on infrastructure.
Aug.: SADF launches Operation Protea, attacking SWAPO bases in Angola.

(cont.)

Date	Life and Works	Literary Events	Social, Political, and Economic Events
		Mongane Wally Serote, *To Every Birth Its Blood* Wilma Stockenström, *The Expedition to the Baobab Tree* Patrick White, *Flaws in the Glass*	
1982	*Jan.*: 'Newton and the Ideal of a Transparent Scientific Language', *Journal of Literary Semantics*. *Sept.*: JMC discusses adapting *In the Heart of the Country* with Belgian film-maker Marion Hänsel. JMC receives Thomas Pringle Literary Article Award for 'Blood, Flaw, Taint, Degeneration: The Case of Sarah Gertrude Millin'.	Aharon Appelfeld, *The Retreat* André Brink, *A Dry White Season* Nadine Gordimer, 'Living in the Interregnum' Harry Mulisch, *The Assault* Gerald Murnane, *The Plains*	*14 March*: A bomb explodes at the ANC headquarters in London. *6 June*: Lebanon War begins: Israel invades southern Lebanon. *17 Aug.*: Anti-apartheid activist Ruth First is killed by a parcel bomb in Mozambique. *8 Oct.*: Poland bans Solidarity. *9 Dec.*: SADF raids ANC houses in Maseru, Lesotho, killing thirty-seven. *18–19 Dec.*: Four explosions cause damage at Koeberg Nuclear Power Station, near Cape Town, in an attack claimed by the ANC.

	1983		
1983	*The Expedition to the Baobab Tree*, JMC's translation of Wilma Stockenström's *Die kremetartekspedisie*, Faber and Faber (London). *1 June:* JMC begins work on *Foe*. *4 Aug.:* JMC promoted to Full Professor at UCT. *Sept.:* JMC joins editorial board of *Standpunte*. *Life & Times of Michael K*, Secker & Warburg (London)/ Ravan Press (Johannesburg). *26 Oct.: Life & Times of Michael K* awarded the Booker Prize. *15 Nov.:* Embargo on consignment of *Life & Times of Michael K* is lifted in Cape Town. English Academy of SA awards JMC prize for creative work; makes him a full member.	Aharon Appelfeld, *Tzili; The Immortal Bartfuss* Breyten Breytenbach, *Eklips*; ('*Yk*') André Brink, *Mapmakers* Hugo Claus, *The Sorrow of Belgium* Antonio Di Benedetto, *Cuentos de exilio* Salman Rushdie, *Shame* Zbigniew Herbert, *Report from a Besieged City* Les Murray, 'Equanimity'; 'On Interest' Josef Skvorecky, *Dvořák in Love*	*20 May:* Pretoria Church Street bombing: MK car bomb outside SA Air Force (SAAF) headquarters kills twenty-one and injures 217. *23 May:* Operation Skerwe: SAAF retaliates, attacking ANC facilities in Maputo, Mozambique. *20 Aug.:* United Democratic Front (UDF), a non-racial coalition of labour unions, churches, student and civic organizations, is launched in Cape Town, opposing the introduction of a Tricameral Parliament representing white, coloured, and Indian citizens. *2 Nov.:* In referendum, white South Africans vote in favour of constitutional reforms, including creation of Tricameral Parliament.
1984	*Jan.–June:* JMC is Butler Visiting Professor in English at SUNY Buffalo.	Breyten Breytenbach, *Buffalo Bill* Sydney Clouts, *Collected Poems* Athol Fugard, *Notebooks 1960–77* Nadine Gordimer, *A Soldier's Embrace*	*16 March:* SA and Mozambique sign non-aggression treaty.

(cont.)

Date	Life and Works	Literary Events	Social, Political, and Economic Events
	26 April: *Life & Times of Michael K* is awarded the CNA Prize. JMC's acceptance speech, which arrived too late to be read in his absence, published as '**The Great South African Novel**', *Leadership SA*. *3 Oct.*: '**Truth in Autobiography**' delivered at UCT as JMC's inaugural lecture, after appointment to full professorship.	Cees Nooteboom, *In the Dutch Mountains*	*5–6 Nov.*: Calls for stay-away in the Transvaal heeded by as many as 500,000 workers, and 400,000 students.
1985	*Life & Times of Michael K* is awarded the Prix Femina étranger. *6 March*: Vera Coetzee dies. *April*: JMC is awarded his first honorary doctorate, from the	Breyten Breytenbach, *True Confessions of an Albino Terrorist; Mouroir; Lewendood* A. S. Byatt, *Still Life* Antonio Di Benedetto, *Sombras, nada mas …* Doris Lessing, *The Good Terrorist*	*11 March*: Mikhail Gorbachev ascends to power in Soviet Union. *20 July*: P. W. Botha declares a state of emergency in parts of SA in response to township revolts.

University of Strathclyde in Glasgow.

July: 'Confession and Double Thoughts: Tolstoy, Rousseau, Dostoevsky', *Comparative Literature.*

Aug.: *Dust,* Marion Hänsel's adaptation of *In the Heart of the Country,* premieres at the Venice Film Festival.

1986

Jan.: JMC takes part in 48th International PEN conference in New York.

Jan.: 'Into the Dark Chamber: The Novelist and South Africa', *New York Times.*

JMC is Hinkley Visiting Professor of English at Johns Hopkins University and Butler Visiting Professor in English at SUNY Buffalo.

A Land Apart: A South African Reader, anthology edited with André Brink, Faber and Faber (London).

Gabriel García Márquez, *Love in the Time of Cholera*
Harry Mulisch, *Last Call*
Gerald Murnane, *Landscape with Landscape*
Caryl Phillips, *The Final Passage*
Karel Schoeman, *Another Country*

Joseph Brodsky, *Less than One*
Breyten Breytenbach, *End Papers*
Günter Grass, *The Rat*
David Grossman, *See Under: Love*
Caryl Phillips, *A State of Independence*

15 Aug.: P. W. Botha delivers 'Rubicon Speech', refusing to make concessions, or undertake reforms.

19 Nov.: Reagan and Gorbachev meet for the first time, in Geneva.

23 Dec.: MK bomb Amanzimtoti shopping centre outside Durban, killing five and injuring forty.

25 Feb.–6 March: 27th Congress of the Communist Party of the Soviet Union: Mikhail Gorbachev speaks of *Glasnost* and *Perestroika.*

26 April: Chernobyl Nuclear Disaster kills at least 4,056.

1 May: More than 1.5 million heed call by Congress of South African Trade Unions (COSATU) for general strike.

12 June: Nation-wide State of Emergency declared in SA.

16 Sept.: European Economic Community (EEC) reaches agreement about imposing sanctions on SA.

Date	Life and Works	Literary Events	Social, Political, and Economic Events
	JMC begins work on *Age of Iron*. *Sept.*: *Foe*, Secker & Warburg (London)/ Ravan Press (Johannesburg). *Oct.*: 'Farm Novel and *Plaasroman* in South Africa', *English in Africa*.		*11–12 Oct.*: Reagan and Gorbachev meet in Reykjavík. *2 Oct.*: The US Comprehensive Anti-Apartheid Act comes into effect, imposing sanctions on SA.
1987	JMC begins, then sets aside, the memoir that will become *Boyhood*. *9 April*: JMC accepts the Jerusalem Prize for *Foe*, and delivers his '**Jerusalem Prize Acceptance Speech**', condemning colonialism and apartheid. *Oct.*: JMC delivers talk at *Weekly Mail*'s Book Week in Cape Town, which is later published as 'The Novel Today', *Upstream*.	Aharon Appelfeld, *For Every Sin* Paul Auster, *New York Trilogy* Breyten Breytenbach, *Boek: Deel een* Zoë Wicomb, *You Can't Get Lost in Cape Town*	*12 June*: SA government renews State of Emergency for two years. *9–12 July*: Dakar Conference: Leading members of Afrikaans community meet seventeen-person ANC delegation. *9 Aug.*: SA National Union of Mineworkers begins a strike, which lasts twenty-one days. *8 Dec.*: First Intifada begins in the Gaza Strip and West Bank; Intermediate-Range Nuclear Forces Treaty is signed by Reagan and Gorbachev.

1988	JMC elected Fellow of the Royal Society of Literature (UK) and Chevalier dans l'Ordre des Arts et des Lettres (France). JMC and David Attwell begin work on *Doubling the Point*. *White Writing: On the Culture of Letters in South Africa*, Yale University Press (New Haven). 30 June: Jack Coetzee dies. 31 Oct.: JMC and Nadine Gordimer have public disagreement at conference organized by COSAW and *Weekly Mail* over decision to withdraw invitation to Salman Rushdie. 'The Taint of the Pornographic: Defending (against) *Lady Chatterley's Lover*', *Mosaic*.	Breyten Breytenbach, *Judas Eye* Joseph Brodsky, *To Urania* Nadine Gordimer, *The Essential Gesture* Seamus Heaney, *The Government of the Tongue* Christopher Hope, *White Boy Running* Jamaica Kincaid, *A Small Place* Gerald Murnane, *Inland* Philip Roth, *The Facts: A Novelist's Autobiography* Salman Rushdie, *The Satanic Verses* W. G. Sebald, *After Nature*	2 Jan.: Soviet Union begins economic restructuring (*Perestroika*). 24 Feb.: UDF banned, and COSATU prohibited from involving itself in political activities. 23 March: SADF makes final assault on Cuito Cuanavale, Angola, but is resisted by the FAPLA, supported by Cuban troops. 29 March: ANC representative Dulcie September assassinated in Paris. 14 April: Geneva Accords: Soviet Union commits to withdrawing troops from Afghanistan. 20 Aug.: Iran-Iraq War ends. 7 Dec.: Nelson Mandela is moved from Pollsmoor Prison to Victor Verster Prison, given his own cottage and allowed visitors.
1989	Jan.: JMC is Hinkley Visiting Professor of English at Johns Hopkins University. 21 April: Nicolas Coetzee dies.	Paul Auster, *Moon Palace*	14 Feb.: Ayatollah Ruhollah Khomeini issues a fatwa calling for death of Salman Rushdie.

Date	Life and Works	Literary Events	Social, Political, and Economic Events
			5 April: Polish Government and Solidarity agree to hold democratic elections.
			4–5 June: China puts down Tiananmen Square protest; Solidarity wins Polish election.
	JMC becomes honorary fellow of the MLA and honorary foreign member of the American Academy of Arts and Science.		*5 July:* P. W. Botha and Nelson Mandela meet for the first time at Tuynhuys.
			15 Aug.: P. W. Botha resigns, and F. W. de Klerk becomes acting State President of SA.
			23 Oct.: Hungary proclaims itself a republic.
			9 Nov.: GDR opens checkpoints in Berlin Wall.
			17 Nov.–29 Dec.: Velvet Revolution in Czechoslovakia.
1990	*May:* 'Censorship in South Africa', *English in Africa.* *13 July:* PJ dies.	Aharon Appelfeld, *To the Land of the Reeds* A. S. Byatt, *Possession* Gerald Murnane, *Velvet Waters*	*2 Feb.:* Bans on ANC, Pan Africanist Congress and SA Communist Party are repealed.

Year		Works	Events
	Age of Iron, Secker & Warburg (London).	Les Murray, 'The Tin Wash Dish'; 'Dog Fox Field' W. G. Sebald, *Vertigo*	11 *Feb.*: Nelson Mandela released from prison; addresses crowd of approx. 50,000 from steps of Cape Town City Hall. 18 *March*: GDR holds first free elections. 21 *March*: Namibia achieves independence. 2 *Aug.*: Iraq invades Kuwait. 6 *Aug.*: ANC agrees to suspend armed struggle. 3 *Oct.*: Germany reunified.
1991	21 *Feb.*: JMC begins work on *The Master of Petersburg*. '**What is a Classic?**' delivered as a lecture in Graz, Austria. *Aug*: JMC visits Australia with DD, as writer in residence at the University of Queensland.	Aharon Appelfeld, *The Iron Tracks* Nadine Gordimer, *Jump and Other Stories* Cees Nooteboom, *The Following Story* Caryl Phillips, *Cambridge* Philip Roth, *Patrimony*	17 *Jan.–28 Feb.*: Operation Desert Storm, the combat phase of the Gulf War, which concludes with Iraq's defeat. 15 *April*: EEC lifts economic sanctions on SA. 14 *Sept.*: National Peace Accord signed in Johannesburg. 21 *Dec.*: Convention for a Democratic SA begins.

(cont.)

Date	Life and Works	Literary Events	Social, Political, and Economic Events
1992	**Doubling the Point: Essays and Interviews**, edited by David Attwell, Harvard University Press (Cambridge, MA).	Harry Mulisch, *The Discovery of Heaven* Les Murray, 'Translations from the Natural World'; *The Paperbark Tree* Cees Nooteboom, *Roads to Santiago* W. G. Sebald, *The Emigrants* Josef Skvorecky, *The Bride of Texas; Headed for the Blues*	*26 Dec.*: Soviet Union is formally dissolved. *1 Feb.*: President Bush and President Yeltsin formally declare end of Cold War. *18 March*: In referendum, white South Africans vote for political reforms and end of apartheid. *5 April*: Bosnia and Herzegovina proclaims independence; Serb troops besiege Sarajevo. *17 June*: Clash between ANC and Inkatha leads to death of at least forty-five in Boipatong.
1993	JMC is appointed to the Arderne Chair of Literature at UCT. '**Homage**', *The Threepenny Review*. JMC institutes honours course in creative writing at UCT, which is eventually expanded into an MA.	Breyten Breytenbach, *Return to Paradise* Gabriel García Márquez, *Strange Pilgrims* Harry Mulisch, *A Ghost Story* Caryl Phillips, *Crossing the River* Philip Roth, *Operation Shylock: A Confession*	*10 April*: ANC's Chris Hani is assassinated. *25 July*: APLA members open fire on congregation in St James Church in Cape Town, killing eleven. *13 Sept.*: Oslo Peace Accords signed. *22 Dec.*: Interim Constitution approved by SA Parliament.

1994			
	Nov.: The Master of Petersburg, Secker & Warburg (London).	Aharon Appelfeld, *Unto the Soul* Doris Lessing, *Under My Skin* Amos Oz, *Panther in the Basement*	*28 March:* Shell House massacre: Inkatha and ANC supporters clash in Johannesburg, resulting in at least fifty-five deaths. *6 April:* Assassination of Rwandan President Juvénal Habyarimana precipitates beginning of Rwandan genocide. *27 April:* In first SA election held under universal adult suffrage ANC wins sweeping victory. *10 May:* Nelson Mandela inaugurated as SA President. *11 Dec.:* President Yeltsin orders troops into Chechnya.
1995	JMC is visiting professor at Texas Center for Writers, UT. *March:* JMC makes enquiries about emigration to Australia. *19 Aug.:* JMC begins work on *Disgrace.*	Joseph Brodsky, *On Grief and Reason* A. S. Byatt, *Babel Tower* Nadine Gordimer, *Writing and Being* Gerald Murnane, *Emerald Blue* Caryl Phillips, *The Higher Ground*	*1 Jan.:* World Trade Organization (WTO) is established. *11 May:* Nuclear Nonproliferation Treaty is extended indefinitely. *11 July:* Srebrenica massacre.

(cont.)

Date	Life and Works	Literary Events	Social, Political, and Economic Events
		Philip Roth, *Sabbath's Theater* Salman Rushdie, *The Moor's Last Sigh* W. G. Sebald, *The Rings of Saturn*	*19 July:* Promotion of National Unity and Reconciliation Act provides for establishment of a Truth and Reconciliation Commission (TRC) in SA, as a means of recording human rights violations during apartheid, and granting amnesty. *30 Aug.:* NATO begins bombing campaign in Bosnia and Herzegovina. *4 Nov.:* Assassination of Israeli Prime Minister Yitzhak Rabin. *14 Dec.:* Dayton Agreement is signed, ending Bosnian War.
	Dec.: 'What is Realism?' delivered as lecture in Amsterdam. *Dec.:* 'Meat Country', *Granta*.		
1996	*Giving Offense: Essays on Censorship*, University of Chicago Press (Chicago). JMC begins regular visiting professorship at the Committee on Social Thought, University of Chicago.	Les Murray, *Subhuman Redneck Poems*	*2 March:* Liberal/National Coalition, headed by John Howard, wins Australian federal election, ending thirteen years of Labor Party government.

March: Théâtre de Complicité mounts a stage adaptation of *Foe* by Mark Wheatley.

11 Oct.: JMC begins work on *Youth*.

Nov.: At Bennington College, delivering the Ben Belitt Lecture, JMC presents **'What is Realism?'**

1997   JMC resigns the Arderne Chair, and becomes a Distinguished Professor in the Faculty of the Arts at UCT.

Sept.: **Boyhood: Scenes from Provincial Life**, Secker & Warburg (London).

15–16 Oct.: **'The Lives of Animals'**, presented as the Tanner Lectures on Human Values at Princeton University.

Les Murray, *Killing the Black Dog*
Caryl Phillips, *The Nature of Blood*
Philip Roth, *American Pastoral*

15 April: TRC, chaired by Archbishop Desmond Tutu, begins hearings in Cape Town.

3 Sept.: USA launches Operation Desert Strike after Iraqi forces attack and occupy Arbil.

27 Sept.: Taliban captures Kabul.

30 Oct.: Colonel Eugene de Kock, commanding officer of a counter-insurgency unit of SA Police, is sentenced to 212 years in prison for crimes against humanity.

4 Feb.: New SA constitution comes into effect.

23 April: Eugène Terre'Blanche, leader of the Afrikaner Weerstandsbeweging, is convicted of attempted murder and assault.

2 May: Labour Party returned to power in UK, with Tony Blair as Prime Minister.

20 May: Human Rights and Equal Opportunities Commission's

Date	Life and Works	Literary Events	Social, Political, and Economic Events
			report, *Bringing them Home*, recommends Australian government apologize and pay compensation for forced removal of Aboriginal children from their families.
			21 May: Australian Federal Government announces further cuts to immigration.
1998	Peter Glazer produces a stage adaptation of *Foe* at Northwestern University.	Nadine Gordimer, *The House-Gun* Les Murray, *Freddy Neptune*	*20 Feb.:* Saddam Hussein and Kofi Annan negotiate deal for weapons inspectors to return to Iraq.
			28 Feb.: Massacre in Likošane sparks beginning of the Kosovo War.
	Oct.: JMC is the only non-US recipient of grant from Lannan Foundation.		*26 May:* First National Sorry Day is observed in Australia, following recommendation of *Bringing them Home*.
	11 Nov.: 'The Novel in Africa' presented at the Doreen B. Townsend Center for the Humanities, University of California, Berkeley.		*7 Aug.:* US embassies in Dar es Salaam and Nairobi are bombed by Islamists linked to Osama bin Laden, killing 224.

1999	*The Lives of Animals*, Princeton University Press (Princeton). *July*: **Disgrace**, Secker & Warburg (London). *Oct.*: *Disgrace* is awarded the Booker Prize. *Disgrace* wins the Commonwealth Writers' Prize, and M-Net Literary Award.	Breyten Breytenbach, *Dog Heart: A Memoir* W. G. Sebald, *On the Natural History of Destruction*	*2 June*: ANC is victorious in second democratic elections in SA. *16 June*: Thabo Mbeki succeeds Mandela as SA President. *24 March*: NATO launches air strikes against Federal Republic of Yugoslavia. *6 Nov.*: Referendum in Australia rejects preamble to constitution recognizing Aborigines as Australia's first people. *23 Nov.*: Australian Government bars refugees from seeking asylum if they have right to live elsewhere. *31 Dec.*: Vladimir Putin becomes acting President of Russia, after Yeltsin resigns.
2000	*5 April*: ANC includes *Disgrace* in its submission to the SA Human Rights Commission's hearings on racism in the media. *Oct.*: **'A House in Spain'**, *Architectural Digest*.	Anita Desai, *Fasting, Feasting* Philip Roth, *The Human Stain* Zoë Wicomb, *David's Story*	*28 May*: 250,000 people walk across Sydney Harbour Bridge in support of reconciliation with Aboriginal people. *12 Oct.*: USS *Cole* is damaged by Al-Qaeda suicide bombers in Yemen, killing seventeen.

(*cont.*)

Date	Life and Works	Literary Events	Social, Political, and Economic Events
2001	*2 Feb.*: Australian immigrant visas are granted to JMC and DD. ***Stranger Shores: Essays 1986–1999***, Secker & Warburg (London).	Nadine Gordimer, *The Pickup* V. S. Naipaul, *Half a Life* Philip Roth, *The Dying Animal* W. G. Sebald, *Austerlitz*	*24 July–9 Aug.*: Tampa Affair: boat carrying refugees refused entry to Australian waters. Australian Government enacts 'Pacific Solution', processing asylum seekers in detention centres on Naura and Papua New Guinea.
			11 Sept.: Islamist terrorists hijack four planes and direct them at the World Trade Center (NYC), the Pentagon, and Washington DC, killing 2,997.
	Sept.: '**The Problem of Evil**' presented in Chicago.		*20 Sept.*: US President Bush declares 'War on Terror'.
			7 Oct.: USA and allies invade Afghanistan.
	Dec.: JMC retires from UCT.		*10 Nov.*: Howard government reelected after campaigning on immigration and war on terror.

2002	JMC and DD settle in Adelaide, Australia. *April: **Youth**,* Secker & Warburg (London). JMC receives Commonwealth Writers' Prize. *A **House in Spain / Een Huis in Spanje**,* Uitgeverij Cossee (Amsterdam).	Paul Auster, *The Book of Illusions*	*19 Jan.:* Seventy asylum seekers in Woomera Detention Centre sew their lips together and begin a hunger strike. *1 July:* International Criminal Court is established. *10 Oct.:* Thabo Mbeki questions link between HIV and AIDS. *12 Oct.:* Bali bombings, carried out by Islamist group Jemaah Islamiyah, leave 202 dead, including eighty-eight Australians and thirty-eight Indonesians.
2003	*June:* 'Fictional Beings', *Philosophy, Psychiatry, & Pscyhology.* *July:* JMC becomes Distinguished Service Professor at University of Chicago. *Sept.: **Elizabeth Costello**,* Secker & Warburg (London).	Nadine Gordimer, *Loot and Other Stories* Günter Grass, *Crabwalk*	*20 March:* USA and allies – including Australia – invade Iraq. *21 March:* TRC releases its final report. *9 April:* US forces seize control of Baghdad.

(cont.)

Date	Life and Works	Literary Events	Social, Political, and Economic Events
	2 Oct.: Swedish Academy announces that JMC has won the Nobel Prize in Literature. 7 Dec.: JMC accepts the Nobel Prize and delivers a Nobel Lecture entitled 'He and His Man'. JMC resigns his professorship at University of Chicago.		11 Nov.: Turkish Kurd asylum seekers sent from Melville Island, Australia, to Indonesia. 13 Dec.: Saddam Hussein is captured by US troops.
2004	Landscape with Rowers: Poetry from the Netherlands, Princeton University Press (Princeton). 15 Jan.: 'As a Woman Grows Older', New York Review of Books. April–May: JMC and DD hosted as Visiting Professors at Stanford University. Dec.: JMC elected to Australian Academy of Humanities. JMC joins Voiceless in Australia.	Gabriel García Márquez, Memories of My Melancholy Whores Irène Némirovsky, Suite Française Philip Roth, The Plot Against America	28 April: Torture of Iraqi prisoners by US troops at Abu Ghraib prison becomes widely known. 6 Aug.: Australian High Court finds that existing immigration laws are valid, and failed asylum seekers can be detained indefinitely. 9 Sept.: Bomb outside Australian Embassy in Jakarta, Indonesia, kills eleven. 26 Dec.: Indian Ocean earthquake and tsunami kills over 200,000; Australia leads humanitarian fundraising to aid its neighbours.

2005	April: JMC begins work on *Summertime*.	Paul Auster, *The Brooklyn Follies*	6 *July*: Palmer Inquiry report is released, identifying systematic weaknesses in Australian Department of Immigration.
	Sept.: **Slow Man**, Secker & Warburg (London).	Gerald Murnane, *Invisible Yet Enduring Lilacs*	7 *July*: Four suicide bombings in central London.
	10 Sept.: Opera adaptation of *Waiting for the Barbarians* with libretto by Christopher Hampton and music by Philip Glass premieres at Theatre Erfurt, Germany.		6 *Dec.*: Australian Anti-Terrorism Act 2005 becomes law, allowing for preventative detention and control order.
	27 Sept.: President Thabo Mbeki confers the Order of Mapungubwe on JMC in Pretoria.		*11–12 Dec.*: Cronulla race riots in Sydney; mobs attack people of Middle Eastern appearance.
2006	6 *March*: Australian citizenship is conferred on JMC in a ceremony at Adelaide Writers' Week.	Philip Roth, *Everyman*	*14–15 March*: SA Students' Congress and ANC Youth League stage violent protests at North-West University, when students are excluded over unpaid fees.
			11 July: Seven bombs in Mumbai kill more than 200.
			30 Dec.: Saddam Hussein is executed.

(*cont.*)

Date	Life and Works	Literary Events	Social, Political, and Economic Events
2007	22 Feb.: JMC delivers 'Voiceless: I feel therefore I am' at Sherman Gallery, Sydney. *1 April*: 'Eden', JMC's translation of poem by Ina Rousseau, *Poetry*. ***Inner Workings: Essays 2000–2005***, Vintage Books (London). *Sept.*: ***Diary of a Bad Year***, Harvill Secker (London).	Norman Mailer, *The Castle in the Forest*	*26 March*: David Hicks, an Australian detained at Guantanamo Bay, pleads guilty to supporting terrorism. *2 April*: New Century Financial Corporation files for bankruptcy, signalling beginning of subprime mortgage crisis in USA. *21 June*: John Howard declares child abuse and domestic violence in indigenous communities a 'national emergency'. *9 Aug.*: BNP Paribas freezes three funds in response to losses in the US subprime mortgage market.
2008	JMC begins a correspondence with Paul Auster. *June*: *Diary of a Bad Year* receives M-Net Literary Award.	Philip Roth, *Indignation*	*12 May*: Riots begin throughout SA, targeting immigrants. *1 June*: Australia ends its combat operations in Iraq.

	Coetzee	Literary context	Historical context
2009	6 Sept.: A film adaptation of *Disgrace* by Anna Maria Monticelli and Steve Jacobs premieres at the Toronto International Film Festival. Sept.: ***Summertime***, Harvill Secker (London).	Gerald Murnane, *Barley Patch* Philip Roth, *The Humbling*	29 July: Immigration Minister announces Australia will reform its policy of mandatory detention of asylum seekers. 15 Sept.: Lehman Brothers investment bank files for bankruptcy, triggering collapse in stock markets. 20 Sept.: ANC recalls President Thabo Mbeki. 26 Jan.: Icelandic government and banking system collapse. 4 Aug.: Members of an alleged terrorist cell in Melbourne are arrested on suspicion of plotting suicide attacks in Sydney. 18 Oct.: Australian customs vessel rescues seventy-eight asylum seekers and takes them to Indonesia, where they refuse to disembark.
2010	19 Jan.: David Coetzee dies. 13–16 May: 'Is dit J. M. Coetzee' festival in Amsterdam; JMC is	Philip Roth, *Nemesis*	27 April: Standard & Poor's downgrades Greek sovereign credit

(cont.)

Date	Life and Works	Literary Events	Social, Political, and Economic Events
	awarded Ridder van de Nederlandse Leeuw (Netherlands). "'Nevertheless, My Sympathies are with the Karamazovs": An Email Correspondence: May – December 2008', with Arabella Kurtz, *Salmagundi*.		rating to junk, triggering decline in stock markets. *15 Dec.*: At least thirty people die when a boat carrying asylum seekers crashes into Christmas Island. *17 Dec.*: Protests in Tunisia mark beginning of the Arab Spring.
2011	*Jan.*: JMC takes part in Jaipur Literary Festival. *June*: JMC takes part in Festival of Ideas at the University of York. *Scenes from Provincial Life*, Harvill Secker (London).		*15 Feb.*: Uprisings against Muammar Gaddafi begin in Libya. *15 March*: Government violence against protesters in Damascus marks the beginning of the Syrian Civil War. *31 Aug.*: High Court of Australia rules that the government's 'Malaysia Solution' for processing of asylum seekers is unlawful. *18 Dec.*: Boat of asylum seekers from Indonesia sinks off coast of Java; at least 160 die.
2012	JMC begins work on *The Childhood of Jesus*.	Gerald Murnane, *A History of Books* Patrick White, *The Hanging Gardens*	

16 Aug.: SA police open fire on striking miners at Marikana, killing thirty-four.

14 Dec.: UN High Commissioner for Refugees criticizes treatment of asylum seekers at Nauru Detention Centre.

21 March: Prime Minister Julia Gillard apologizes on behalf of Australian Federal Government for families affected by forced adoption.

6 June: Edward Snowden discloses US government's mass surveillance program.

21 Nov.: Pro-EU demonstrations begin in Ukraine.

7 Dec.: WTO delegates sign Bali Package aimed at loosening global trade barriers.

24 March: Russia suspended from G8, following its annexation of Crimea.

13 May: Australian federal budget is released, featuring significant structural reform aimed at debt reduction.

---

10 Dec.: JMC delivers address at graduation ceremony of University of Witwatersrand (SA) about importance of teaching young children.

2013

March: *Here and Now: Letters 2008–2011*, with Paul Auster, Harvill Secker (London).

March: *The Childhood of Jesus*, Harvill Secker (London).

June–Nov.: At the invitation of sculptor Berlinde de Bruyckere, JMC curates the Belgian Pavilion's exhibition at the 55th Venice Biennale.

2014

Two Screenplays, JMC's adaptations of *Waiting for the Barbarians* and *In the Heart of the Country*, edited by Hermann Wittenberg, UCT Press (Cape Town).

(cont.)

Date	Life and Works	Literary Events	Social, Political, and Economic Events
	JMC begins biannual visit to the Universidad Nacional de San Martín in Argentina (UNSAM) where he directs a seminar series entitled 'Literatures of the South'.		*5 June:* ISIS militant group begins offensive in northern Iraq.
			8 Aug.: USA begins air offensive against ISIS in northern Iraq.
	*Oct.: **Three Stories**,* Text Publishing (Melbourne).		*14 Sept.:* Australia sends combat aircraft and special forces to Middle East to assist in fight against ISIS.
	24 Oct.: An opera adaptation of *Slow Man,* with music by Nicholas Lens and a libretto by JMC, premieres at the Malta Festival, Poznań.		
2015	*The Good Story: Exchanges on Truth, Fiction and Psychotherapy,* with Arabella Kurtz, Harvill Secker (London).		*11 Feb.:* Australian Human Rights Commission releases report *Forgotten Children: National Inquiry into Children in Immigration Detention.*
			23 Feb.: Prime Minister Tony Abbott outlines plans to strip Australian citizenship from dual nationals involved in terrorism.

2016	*Oct.*: *The Schooldays of Jesus*, Harvill Secker (London)/ Text Publishing (Melbourne).	*17 March:* Group of UCT students demand removal of statue of Cecil Rhodes, prompting campaign for transformation of SA universities. *24 March:* Outbreak of xenophobic violence in SA. *9 Aug.:* Australian Census of Population and Housing is held. *31 Dec.:* US troops withdraw from Afghanistan.
2017	*12–13 Sept.:* JMC takes part in 'The Work of John Maxwell Coetzee in Latin America', at UNSAM. *Dec.:* 'Lies', *New York Review of Books*. *Dec.:* '**The Dog**', *The New Yorker*.	*10 March:* UN warns that up to 20 million people are at risk of starvation and famine in Yemen, Somalia, South Sudan, and Nigeria. *14 June:* Australian government agrees compensation package for asylum seekers held at Manus Regional Processing Centre in Papua New Guinea. *9 Dec.:* Iraqi military announces that all of Iraq's territory has been liberated from ISIS.
2018	*Late Essays: 2006–2017*, Harvill Secker (London).	*12 Feb.:* Royal Commission into Misconduct in the Banking, Superannuation and Financial

(*cont.*)

Date	Life and Works	Literary Events	Social, Political, and Economic Events
	Siete cuentos morales, El Hilo de Ariadna (Buenos Aires)/ Literatura Random House (Barcelona).		Services Industry opens in Melbourne. *19 June*: USA announces it will withdraw from UN Human Rights Council.
2019	Oct. *The Death of Jesus*, Text Publishing (Melbourne).		

ABBREVIATIONS

Works by J. M. Coetzee

AI   *Age of Iron.* 1990. Harmondsworth: Penguin, 1998.

B   *Boyhood: Scenes from Provincial Life.* 1997. London: Vintage, 1998.

CJ   *The Childhood of Jesus.* 2013. London: Vintage, 2014.

DBY   *Diary of a Bad Year.* 2007. London: Vintage, 2008.

Dis   *Disgrace.* 1999. London: Vintage, 2000.

DP   *Doubling the Point: Essays and Interviews.* Ed. by David Attwell. Cambridge: Harvard University Press, 1992.

Dusk   *Dusklands.* 1974. London: Vintage, 1998.

EC   *Elizabeth Costello: Eight Lessons.* 2003. London: Vintage, 2004.

F   *Foe.* 1986. Harmondsworth: Penguin, 1987.

GO   *Giving Offense: Essays on Censorship.* Chicago: University of Chicago Press, 1996.

GS   *The Good Story: Exchanges on Truth, Fiction and Psychotherapy.* With Arabella Kurtz. 2015. New York: Penguin Books, 2016.

HN   *Here and Now.* With Paul Auster. New York: Viking, 2013.

IHC   *In the Heart of the Country.* 1977. London: Vintage, 1999.

IW   *Inner Workings: Essays 2000–2005.* With introduction by Derek Attridge. 2007. London: Vintage, 2008.

LE   *Late Essays: 2006–2017.* London: Harvill Secker, 2017.

LT   *Life & Times of Michael K.* 1983. London: Vintage, 1998.

MP   *The Master of Petersburg.* 1994. London: Vintage, 1999.

SJ   *The Schooldays of Jesus.* London: Harvill Secker, 2016.

SM   *Slow Man.* 2005. London: Vintage, 2006.

SS   *Stranger Shores: Essays 1986–1999.* 2001. London: Vintage, 2002.

Sum   *Summertime,* 2009. London: Vintage, 2010.

WB   *Waiting for the Barbarians*. 1980. London: Vintage, 2000.
WW   *White Writing: On the Culture of Letters in South Africa*. New Haven: Yale University Press, 1988.
Y   *Youth*. 2002. London: Vintage, 2003.

Library Archives

CP   Coetzee Papers, Harry Ransom Center, University of Texas at Austin.

JARAD ZIMBLER

Introduction

J. M. Coetzee is the author of fourteen novels, three autobiographical fictions, and several volumes of translations, critical essays, correspondence,
and short stories. Born in 1940 in Cape Town, South Africa, and resident
there throughout his childhood and for much of his adult life, he has lived
since 2002 in Adelaide, Australia. Claimed initially as a South African
author, and subsequently by a host of other constituencies, Coetzee's career
has been powerfully shaped by his intimate experiences of apartheid's brutality and the demands of decolonization; the twilight of European imperialism
and the persistent inequalities wrought by neo-colonialism and late capitalism; the 'hypercentrality' of the English language and the provinciality of the
two settler colonies in which he has made himself at home.[1] These experiences are at the heart of all Coetzee's writings, as is his commitment to
a rigorous thinking through of literary practice, literary history, and the
horizons conditioning literary forms and their expressive possibilities.

There are certainly continuities across Coetzee's oeuvre, but also striking
shifts in theme, genre, narration, and even syntax. Readers already immersed
in his writings will be familiar with an element of style that first becomes
prevalent only in his middle fictions: moments in which an otherwise unre-
markable word is made the subject of a semantic unravelling, exposing more
of its textures and hues, so that it seems as if Coetzee is indeed using certain
words with 'the full freight of their history behind them'.[2] Frequently, this
unravelling involves a kind of speculative etymology and is conducted by the
concatenation of cognates: once the central term is highlighted (often by
italicization), its meanings ramify by the apposition of phrases or clauses.
*Blessing, care, charity, comfort, grace, gratitude, heart, possession, soul,
stupidity, substance, visitation*: all are amplified in this way, the effects
colouring subsequent as well as antecedent occurrences, both in the works
themselves and across the corpus.

The word *companion* receives this treatment in *The Childhood of Jesus*
(2013): 'Companionable: that is what they have become, over time.

Compañeros by mutual agreement. Companionate marriage: if he offered, would Elena consent?' (*CJ*, 168). Here, the central term is not only italicized, but given in its ostensibly untranslated 'original' (a neat variation on Coetzee's strategy in previous fictions). Imbricated with *companionable* and *companionate*, the word's simplest meanings are brought to the fore by its inflected repetitions – one who often spends time with another, a person with whom one chooses to socialize or associate, a friend (*OED*) – though particular emphasis is given to mutuality and accord. To Simón, the novel's chief focalizer, such an habitual being-together offers ease: 'Living with Elena and Fidel in their flat would certainly be more comfortable than making do in his lonely shed at the docks' (*CJ*, 168); yet it seems also to entail compromise, a relationship of convenience rather than of passionate encounter. We glimpse as much in Simón's previous explanation for visiting the *Salón Confort*, a kind of brothel: 'I am not looking for some ideal match, I am simply looking for company, female company' (*CJ*, 166); but it is especially apparent in a still earlier passage, where he reflects on the forking paths of goodwill and desire: 'From goodwill come friendship and happiness, come companionable picnics in the parklands or companionable afternoons strolling in the forest. Whereas from love, or at least from longing in its more urgent manifestations, come frustration and doubt and heartsore' (*CJ*, 68).

Companionship, then, is a stay to solitude, and may even provide solace and satisfaction, but it is nevertheless somehow deficient. However, as so often in Coetzee's fictions, the focalizer's views are gradually disarticulated. In catching on *companion*, Simón's thoughts do not resolve its meanings, but ask that we put them into question. They ask, indeed, that we consider these meanings in light of words drawn from the same semantic fields, and upon which the novel similarly alights (comrade, friend, brother, guardian, uncle, godfather, father, mother; friendship, family, fatherhood, motherhood, brotherhood); in light of the narrative, which turns on different ways of configuring and understanding the bonds between adults, between children, between adults and children, and between animals and humans; and in light of other stories about companionship, drawn from a repertoire that includes the New Testament and Miguel de Cervantes's *Don Quixote* (1605/ 1615).

While it becomes a central theme and question of *The Childhood of Jesus*, companionship has, in truth, been one of Coetzee's persistent preoccupations. Across the whole of his oeuvre, we find some version of the question: what does it mean to be in the world with others? This concern is played out at the level both of character and plot, structuring relations between the personages of the novels, as well as their tasks and the events they undergo. Journeys in particular seem to demand companionship. This is plainly the case with Jacobus Coetzee and his servants in *Dusklands* (1974); the magistrate and barbarian girl in *Waiting for the Barbarians* (1980); K and his mother in *Life & Times of Michael K* (1983); Susan Barton and Friday in *Foe* (1986); Elizabeth Costello and her son John in *Elizabeth Costello* (2002); Simón, David, Inez, and Bolivar in *The Childhood of Jesus*. In other fictions, it is travel of a metaphysical or at least figurative kind that occasions companionship. Verceuil in *Age of Iron* (1990), Fyodor Mikhailovich in *The Master of Petersburg* (1994), David Lurie in *Disgrace* (1999), Anya in *Diary of a Bad Year* (2007): all are imagined as chaperones or guides for departing souls. And even where the prospect of death is less immediate, as in *Slow Man* (2005), its proximity gives rise to relationships that are as intimate as they are odd.

Of course, there are differences. In the early and middle fictions, companionship is frequently inhibited by brute oppression, while it is merely complicated by those legacies of colonialism, migration, socio-economic stratification, and bureaucratic rationalization that characterize the worlds of the 'South' with which Coetzee's more recent novels have been concerned.[3] Nevertheless, a generalization is possible: no matter how unlikely and ill-suited, companions provide a kind of succour or care; and yet, if the intimacy that arises in getting together from one place to another is essential, it is also uncomfortable, even challenging, something to be endured more than enjoyed. For the match is never ideal, and companionship entails an entanglement with others, obligation as much as assistance. However vital, this entanglement is merely the condition of a sociality whose full realization can only be intimated or intuited in works which confront the truth of a damaged life, a life which denies us a reciprocity for which we must nevertheless continue to long.

You hold in your hands, or otherwise in your gaze, the *Cambridge Companion to J. M. Coetzee*. To whom is such a volume directed? Whom or what does it accompany? Certainly not the author *in propria persona*. John Maxwell Coetzee is unlikely to keep this volume with him, if at all, and its focus is chiefly on his works not his life. Only occasionally do we approach the person of J. M. Coetzee, however refracted by his archive and writings, and by his public performances. For the rest, the materials of his biography (which he has carefully guarded and marshalled) are outlined in this volume's chronology, where they are framed by concurrent events of literary and socio-political significance.[4]

This volume should therefore be thought of principally as an accompaniment to Coetzee's corpus as it traverses the various circuits of the academy; and to its readers, as they pick their paths across its sometimes difficult terrain. In both respects, it seeks to emulate the companions that people

Coetzee's fictional worlds, offering to comfort and discomfit, to console and provoke, through readings that are intimate and careful, partial and probing, and that do their best to indicate avenues of discovery, without attempting or being able to pursue interpretations to their very ends.

Brought together by design and common purpose, the chapters in this *Companion* offer literary critical readings, rather than overviews, and do not aim to be exhaustive or comprehensive, either individually or collectively. In fact, they occasionally cut across and overlap one another, sometimes pull in different directions, and always leave room for the future unfoldings of Coetzee's career, and for readers later to expand upon or qualify their arguments.[5] Nevertheless, the volume is so organized as to ensure that Coetzee's novels, as well as his autobiographical fictions, are discussed at some length; and that adequate treatment is given also to his translations, scholarly books and essays, and works of correspondence. Rather than proceeding thematically or by strict chronology, the chapters repeat at a larger scale the approach of this introduction: they begin immanently, with particular features of Coetzee's practice, and from these starting points chart itineraries across the corpus. In this way, they avoid the routes made familiar in previous volumes of this kind, and reveal continuities as well as discontinuities.

The chapters of Part I, Forms, address Coetzee's fictions from the perspectives of particular elements of technique. Frequently praised for his craft – his spare, taut, and lyrical prose, his narrative and generic inventiveness – Coetzee has from the outset written with an eye to the history of the novel, as well as with subtle appreciation of the subterranean operations of grammar, rhetoric, and narration. Scholars have therefore felt confident emphasizing the importance of questions of form, even if they have often responded by assigning Coetzee's practice to fairly lumpy categories on rather spurious grounds. In contrast, this volume makes some effort to treat Coetzee's works with the same attention to detail and to the practical demands of storytelling that one finds in his own literary criticism.

Coetzee's critical acuity, and his interest in questions of style, are evident as early as his PhD thesis on Samuel Beckett's English fictions, completed at the University of Texas at Austin, where he scrutinized Beckett's manuscripts in the hope of discerning their principles of composition. In his recently published intellectual biography *J. M. Coetzee and the Life of Writing* (2015), David Attwell follows closely in Coetzee's path, making extensive use of his notebooks and drafts in order to reveal the secrets of Coetzee's craft. In his chapter in this *Companion* (Chapter 1), Attwell relies on this

Introduction

research to give illuminating accounts of two of the most celebrated of Coetzee's novels, *Waiting for the Barbarians* and *Life & Times of Michael K*, bringing to light signal features of Coetzee's compositional practice, and reflecting on the reversals, blockages, and serendipitous encounters that have shaped it and that sit alongside and athwart the long-held notion of Coetzee as a highly controlled craftsman. In so doing, Attwell also attends to the sometimes surprising and far-flung intertexts on which these novels draw, even as they respond to the very local political and discursive pressures of apartheid South Africa.

Meg Samuelson, writing about *Foe*, *Boyhood* (1997), *Youth* (2002), and *Slow Man* in Chapter 2, similarly considers Coetzee's awareness that the specificities of locale are always embedded in histories and conflicts that exceed the nation. She does this by exploring why and how setting matters in Coetzee's fictions, focusing on its 'indexical function': the way that narrative, in fleshing out its spatial and temporal dimensions, both invokes a reality beyond the fiction, and makes its own imagined reality more tangible. This is to depart somewhat from Coetzee's own preoccupations. Indeed, he has often disavowed a realism premised on inventorizing reality. But, as Samuelson shows, these disavowals should not obscure his accomplishment in rendering fictional worlds that are vivid and compelling, and which thereby attain their own substance, whilst calling attention to the world outside of themselves, divided and structured by histories of trans-oceanic and trans-hemispheric trade, conquest, and colonization.

My own chapter (Chapter 3) is prompted by Coetzee's longstanding interest in stories and storytelling, an interest that is registered across his critical essays and reviews, and thematized in several of his works. Focusing on *In the Heart of the Country* (1977), *The Master of Petersburg*, and *The Childhood of Jesus*, as well as the computer poem 'Hero and Bad Mother in Epic' (1978), the chapter charts the relationship between the nature of the stories that Coetzee has told – generally limited in the scope of their plots and the number of their principal characters – and the forms of narration he has adopted, which vary from the first-person character narration of certain of his early and middle fictions, to the tightly focalized external narration of many of his later works, to the dialogue-heavy and somewhat affectless narration of the *Jesus* novels. In each case, I suggest that the particular form of narration is related to the particular truth with which the work seeks to confront its readers.

Narrative perspective is addressed also by David James, in Chapter 4, along with other of 'the most granular properties' of Coetzee's style, includ-ing those of rhetoric, syntax, prosody, phonology, and lexis. James tracks from Coetzee's first novel, *Dusklands*, through *Age of Iron* and *Disgrace*, to his very recent work, *The Schooldays of Jesus* (2016). In each he finds evidence of a desire to police the 'grace of language', which he associates with Samuel Beckett's repudiation of 'style as consolation'. Yet, if the strict economy of his prose signals that Coetzee approves of this repudiation, at least at the outset of his career, James is particularly interested in moments in which this economy is disturbed. These moments include the frenzied catalogues of *Dusklands*, which give the lie to imperialism's rhetoric of expansion; but also fleeting passages of 'pellucid and euphonious language', which coincide in the middle and late fictions with efforts to scrutinize the nature of absolution, consolation, comfort, and the self.

Part I is brought to a close by Derek Attridge (Chapter 5), who considers a trio of late works, *Elizabeth Costello*, *Diary of a Bad Year*, and *Summertime* (2009), in light of Coetzee's belief that genres and their conventions can always be creatively re-imagined. Attridge looks closely at the ways these fictions invoke particular genres (novel, short story, lecture, philosophical meditation, diary, opinion piece, autobiography) and then spring surprises. For Coetzee, this makes it possible to keep these genres in play whilst reflecting on how they operate. For his readers, the consequent generic sliding demands that they remain agile and alert, taking the works' lessons, opinions, and reminiscences seriously, even as they recognize that these are not simple assertions of truth, and that their persuasiveness has much to do with the novelist's practice. In this manner, Attridge argues, Coetzee poses questions about the literary writer's tasks and responsibilities, and about the capacity of imaginative fictions to make 'truth claims about the world'.

Chapters in Part II, Relations, range more freely across the oeuvre. They consider Coetzee's endeavours as translator, collaborator, and scholar, as well as the nature of his engagements with fellow writers and critics, and with his environments and horizons. A capacious, avid, even avaricious reader, and a salaried academic for much of his adult life, Coetzee has often seemed preternaturally alive to the late twentieth and early twenty-first centuries' intellectual and aesthetic currents. For this reason, although his own undertakings have seldom been curtailed by the fashions of the moment, his translations, critical writings, works of correspondence, and – since their unveiling – his archive of notebooks and teaching materials, have been grist to the scholarly mill, providing cues and prompts, and confirmation of Coetzee's interest in whichever writer/philosopher/school of criticism has happened to be in vogue. Instrumentalized in this way, Coetzee's non-fictions have had certain of their dimensions distorted.

This accounts for some enduring myths in Coetzee scholarship, including the view that his literary relations and aesthetic orientations were from the outset exclusively and resolutely cosmopolitan. Although clearly indebted to Samuel Beckett and Franz Kafka, to Ezra Pound and T. S. Eliot, to Daniel Defoe and Fyodor Dostoevsky, and to a host of other canonical European and American writers besides, Coetzee's practice was shaped alongside and against those of his South African predecessors and peers, and supported or at least valorized by South African institutions. Since moving to Australia, he has engaged with antipodean authors and problematics (his relationships with the Melbourne-based Text Publishing, the J. M. Coetzee Centre for Creative Practice at the University of Adelaide, and the Writing and Society Research Centre at Western Sydney University are three instances of this), just as he has involved himself, more recently still (2015–18), with the Universidad Nacional de San Martín in Argentina, as director of a seminar on 'Literatures of the South'. He has done all this, moreover, generously and generatively, in that spirit of collaboration which has very often characterized his professional interactions, and which belies another scholarly myth, that of Coetzee as a taciturn and difficult author, resentful of any intrusion. With an eye to distortions of this kind, the chapters in Relations broach several questions that have preoccupied literary critics: what to make of Coetzee's other pursuits and professional activities; how to understand his allegiances and affiliations; and how to determine the proper contexts in which to understand his writings.

In Part II's first chapter (Chapter 6), Jan Steyn gives an account of Coetzee's work as a translator and his views on translation. He reflects on Coetzee's knowledge of the two Netherlandic languages, Dutch and Afrikaans, and gives readings of the poem 'Eden' (2007) and the novel *The Expedition to the Baobab Tree* (1983), translated by Coetzee from the Afrikaans originals of Ina Rousseau and Wilma Stockenström respectively. In both, he finds evidence of a particular attunement to the demands of place, and also of Coetzee's belief (one common amongst translation theorists) that to translate is always to interpret. Lingering on the conditions and challenges of translation, including those which pertain to the hierarchies of the literary world, Steyn concludes by considering and ultimately resisting the claim that the simplicity of Coetzee's prose is determined by a quest for translatability.

Especially when familiar with the target language, Coetzee has often followed his own translators closely, giving advice, making corrections, suggesting improvements. This approach to collaborative labour becomes the entire focus of Rachel Bower's chapter (Chapter 7). Questioning Coetzee's reputation as a reclusive figure, and a reluctant interlocutor,

Bower looks at *Here and Now* (2013) and *The Good Story* (2015) – which record, respectively, his correspondence with the American novelist Paul Auster and with the British psychotherapist Arabella Kurtz – and at how these epistolary volumes explore 'the conditions for dialogue and working together'. Taking the nature of this correspondence as indicative of Coetzee's career-long resistance to banalized formulas of exchange, Bower unfolds Coetzee's conception of collaboration, and then uses it to frame her readings of epistolarity in *Summertime* and *Age of Iron*. In these, she attends to moments of confrontation and even provocation, as well as to slips, errors, and crossed connections, which are understood as essential rather than inimical to dialogue.

Bower concludes by remarking that, in order 'to fulfil our responsibility as interlocutors', we must read both with Coetzee's works and against them – a pertinent reminder, given the extent to which Coetzee has been able to shape the reception of his works, especially through *Doubling the Point* (1992). Until recently, this anthology of early scholarly reviews and essays, accompanied by interviews with David Attwell, the volume's editor, was the principal source of insights into Coetzee's writerly preoccupations, but it also framed these preoccupations in particular ways. This is a point made by Sue Kossew, who focuses, in Chapter 8, on Coetzee's works of criticism, which include the texts collected in *Doubling the Point*, as well as the volumes *White Writing* (1988), a landmark study of South African literary culture, and *Giving Offense* (1996), a series of reflections on the relationship between literature and censorship. Kossew addresses each of these volumes in turn, as well as the three collections of Coetzee's more recent lectures, reviews, and articles, describing their broad outlines, and alighting on individual essays, which, for better and for worse, have proven especially fruitful for critics, including the uncollected though ubiquitously cited 'The Novel Today' (1988) and 'Homage' (1993).

As Kossew indicates, Coetzee's critical writings have been ransacked repeatedly for evidence of influence. This surprisingly durable preoccupation is interrogated by Patrick Hayes (Chapter 9), who begins with several 'influence stories' that Coetzee has told about himself. Hayes observes that the notion of influence is nebulous, and that Coetzee's thinking and writing have been shaped from the outset by wide-ranging engagements of various kinds. More important, these engagements have seldom been uncritical, a point he brings home by addressing Coetzee's response to intertextuality, understood not as a practice of allusion, pastiche, and parody, but as a philosophical notion associated with the decentring of the author and of the human subject. In his readings of *Foe* and *The Master of Petersburg*, Hayes illustrates the use that Coetzee makes of significant literary forebears, such as Beckett, Defoe, and Dostoevsky, to put pressure on this philosophical notion. Coetzee does this, Hayes argues, by revealing the moral costs of celebrating selves and texts as radically ruptured, and of treating this rupture as a condition for powerful imaginative experiences.

In Part II's final chapter (Chapter 10), Ben Etherington steps back from debates between localists and universalists, to explore the horizons of Coetzee's fictions, and the worlds and worldliness of Coetzee's practice. As a way of probing the vision of her creator as an exemplary 'world' writer, Etherington tracks Elizabeth Costello's encounters with the national and international circuits of literary prestige. He then outlines 'the distinctive repertoire of world making techniques' which are characteristic of Coetzee's body of works, and which, shaped in response to the literary and political pressures of apartheid South Africa, have a 'precondition in national circumstances of production and reception'. Finally, in Coetzee's recent efforts to establish literary relations between South Africa, Australia, and Argentina, Etherington finds signs of a Southern horizon and sensibility which have been latent across Coetzee's corpus, and from within which Coetzee's works seek both to evade the limits of nationalism and to enter the world literary market on their own terms.

Throughout his career, Coetzee has responded to film-makers, photographers, composers, and musicians; as well as to works of linguistics, philosophy, anthropology, sociology, psychology, pedagogy, and history. In turn, he has captured the attention of readers and scholars far beyond the confines of literary studies. His fictions seem to be increasingly attractive to philosophers, and recent adaptations have brought them into contact with operatic, theatrical, and cinematic audiences. With these matters in mind, the chapters of Part III, Mediations, consider the exposure of Coetzee's works to other forms, media, discourses, disciplines, institutions, and publics; as well as the intersection of life and art within them.

In Chapter 11, Michelle Kelly begins by asking what Coetzee's interest in 'other arts' contributes to our understanding of his works. She notes that his fictions often attribute to visual and performing arts 'expressive powers' that exceed those of literary art forms: to film and photography a more immediate access to the real; to music the ability to overcome linguistic and cultural differences that otherwise condition aesthetic experience. This, she suggests, is a feature of Coetzee's broader concern with the 'mediated nature' of human language. Indeed, the otherness of other arts has to do precisely with their access to forms of expressivity unavailable to the literary arts, and to the novel especially. Which is why, Kelly argues through her readings of musical experience in *Youth* and *Age of Iron*, and of dance and song in

Disgrace and *Foe*, Coetzee so often turns to embodied art forms when seeking to 'interrogate the bounds of the literary'. Yet, as Kelly explains in her chapter's final section, precisely because they encode visual and performing arts as other to writing, Coetzee's works invite but also challenge adaptations, which must struggle to keep faith both with Coetzee's 'original' and with the 'aesthetic conventions and histories' of their own forms and media. The crux of this difficulty is illuminated in Kelly's reading of *Slow Man* and its operatic adaptation by Nicholas Lens.

In the chapter that follows (Chapter 12), Anthony Uhlmann pursues a related set of arguments concerning Coetzee's encounter with philosophers. After a brief description of Coetzee's formation and institutional affiliations, he turns his focus to the ways in which Coetzee has probed both the capacity of literary works to confront philosophical questions as well as the limitations of philosophy's own embedded disciplinary procedures and approved forms of discourse. Coetzee has done this, Uhlmann argues, by developing provocations: elaborating propositions – about the nature of human language, consciousness, and being; about the nature of truth, knowledge, and existence – that entice and frustrate philosophical readers, asking that they at least consider what their discipline takes for granted or leaves out of account in its framing of these issues.

Several chapters in this volume, Uhlmann's included, draw extensively on the meticulously organized (and carefully curated) Coetzee Papers. Housed in the Harry Ransom Center at the University of Texas at Austin, this archive includes manuscript drafts of Coetzee's novels (formerly available at the Houghton Library, Harvard College), as well as notebooks, correspondence, teaching materials, and photographs. Recently opened, the archive has prompted a new wave of critical studies, only some of which have been sufficiently alert to, or indeed sceptical of, the procedures and decisions involved in its establishment and organization. This is a matter on which Andrew Dean reflects in Chapter 13. He considers the provenance of these papers in light of Coetzee's career-long quarrying of autobiographical materials, his project of self-archiving, his fictions' explorations of archival themes, and his preoccupation with the nature of secrets and lies, of concealment, distortion, and revelation. For Dean, it is vital that critics think carefully about their own purposes in reading the archives; about the writer's purposes in producing them; and about the kinds of truth at stake in the works, the archives, and the literary criticism they occasion.

Part of the story that Dean tells has to do with the institutions of publication, reception and consecration that have mediated Coetzee's work, and that have called on him to perform in public, and to disclose his private

Introduction

views, thoughts or experiences. Coetzee's cooperation with and resistance to these demands, and his appreciation of the costs of entry into various public spheres, is the focus of the volume's final chapter (Chapter 14). Here, Andrew van der Vlies frames his account by considering Coetzee's approach to the problem of cultural capital, that is, the prestige that facilitates the circulation of authors and their works, accorded through reviews, literary prizes, honorary degrees, fellowships, and scholarly citations. Van der Vlies explores Coetzee's scepticism regarding external validation, and his efforts to disrupt those institutions – including the institution of authorship – tasked with performing this validation. In describing the publication history of *Dusklands* and *In the Heart of the Country*, he reveals Coetzee's efforts to balance and sometimes circumvent the desires of editors and publishers, the restraints of apartheid's censorship regime, and the interests and tastes of readers, reviewers, prize committees, journalists, and university managers.

Taken together, the chapters of the three parts of this *Cambridge Companion to J. M. Coetzee* give ample coverage of Coetzee's writings, and so provide a thorough introduction to his oeuvre, whilst offering their own distinctive critical readings. As companion pieces – essays by different authors with different interests, orientations, and preoccupations – they travel together and help one another along, emphasizing certain features of Coetzee's practice; but they are not entirely aligned, and cannot be. In fact, their differences, which are more than methodological, bring to light some of the abiding tensions in scholarship devoted to Coetzee's works, and in contemporary literary studies more broadly. These have to do with disagreements about the use, value, and relevance of archival, biographical, and bibliographic materials; about the relationship between local literary cultures, transnational networks, and global markets; and, fundamentally, about the means by which literary works communicate truths, and the nature of the truths they communicate.

Of course, in plotting their particular routes across Coetzee's oeuvre, these essays necessarily neglect alternative paths. As in his fictions, there can be no corpus, no body of works, without its residual elements. Other features of practice might well have been considered in greater detail; and other relations too, with mathematicians, computer programmers, theologians; with photographers, film-makers, sculptors. And more might have been said about questions of gender, sexuality, and race; or about Coetzee's interests in pedagogy and animal ethics, in the humanities, humanism, and the non-human. These are important matters, and, without being the focus of any single chapter, pertinent remarks do appear across several (and can be found using the index). They are also dealt with substantively in other volumes and articles, some in print, others in production, many included under Further Reading. Finally, it is the fate of any companion – at least of any of Coetzee's companions – to force compromises and curtailments, even in acts of solicitation; and to fall somehow short, demanding that those it accompanies complete their journeys otherwise, or alone.

Notes

1. On this use of 'hypercentrality' to designate the status of English relative to other languages, see Johan Heilbron, 'Toward a Sociology of Translation: Book Translations as a Cultural World-System', *European Journal of Social Theory*, 2 (1999), 429–44.
2. J. M. Coetzee, 'Working with Translators' in Alexandra Lianeri and Vanda Zajko, (eds.), *Translation and the Classic: Identity as Change in the History of Culture* (Oxford: Oxford University Press, 2008), pp. 407–20 (p. 408).
3. 'There are no universals of oppression', Coetzee reminds us, 'in each nation, each culture, oppression has its own historical determinants and its own forms' (*GO*, 81).
4. For more extensive coverage of Coetzee's life and works, readers may consult biographies by J. C. Kannemeyer and David Attwell (see Further Reading).
5. Even as this volume reached its final stage of production, *The Death of Jesus* (2019) appeared in Australia from Text Publishing.

PART I

Forms

I

DAVID ATTWELL

Composition and Craft: *Waiting for the Barbarians, Life & Times of Michael K*

This chapter explores the genesis and development of the two novels that brought J. M. Coetzee significant international success in the early phase of his career. It also locates this account within a broader understanding of Coetzee's creative processes, which can be gleaned from the archive now housed at the Harry Ransom Center at the University of Texas at Austin. *Waiting for the Barbarians* (1980) was awarded the James Tait Black Memorial Prize and the Geoffrey Faber Memorial Prize, and *Life & Times of Michael K* (1983) won the first of his two Booker Prizes. Prior to these came his first work of fiction, *Dusklands* (1974) – less a novel than two linked novellas – and his second, equally experimental *In the Heart of the Country* (1977, 1978), which draws on 1960s French avant-garde cinema and the *nouveau roman*. In the subsequent two novels, *Waiting for the Barbarians* and *Life & Times of Michael K*, Coetzee made peace, to some extent, with more traditional features of the novel as form, a change that brought him a wider range of readers beyond South Africa. My purpose is to describe the composition of these texts, drawing on his notebooks, manuscripts, and research materials. In both works, Coetzee made several false starts as he struggled to find the right story, and to give the right shape to that story.[1]

When Coetzee began writing *Waiting for the Barbarians*, sketching an idea in a notebook on 11 July 1977, the novel's fictional empire – which, for many readers, is its most memorable feature – had not yet materialized. The story he started with was in fact set in a fully recognizable Cape Town with South Africa undergoing the death throes of apartheid, and Robben Island no longer a prison but an embarkation station for white refugees fleeing the republic in UN-chartered ships. The manuscript begins:

From the open window of the guardroom Manos Milis watched the refugees trudge up the road ~~from the jetty to the~~ that led from the jetty to the ~~prison~~ gates. The launch that had brought them was already half-way back to the mainland. It was plain that the crew were not talking to the people they had ferried. Otherwise who would come.[2]

Milis is a middle-aged former history teacher, writing (at one stage in the development of this protagonist) a history of the fall of Constantinople. His intellectual pursuits obviously mirror the world he is caught up in, but Milis is relatively detached from the situation both as an intellectual and, being of Greek descent, as an atypical English-speaking South African.[3] Although in a state of political passivity, an observer rather than participant, he throws himself aggressively into a relationship with a much younger woman and his reckless sexuality begins to take on representative status – as if the random violence around them had begun to shape the couple's despairing erotic lives. Milis's misogyny makes for unpleasant reading in these early drafts, but it is clear where Coetzee is taking us. He records in his notebook that Milis is to be 'an explorer of the vitalities thrown up by the last days of the republic', and that the novel is to be 'Literally a fin de siècle book'.[4]

In the same notebook entry, Coetzee mentions that behind the story lies the influence of Robert Musil. This is a reference to Musil's three-volume magnum opus published between 1930 and 1943, Der Mann ohne Eigenschaften, translated as The Man without Qualities. Musil's novel is set in World War I and charts the last years of the Austro-Hungarian Empire. Like Musil's Ulrich, Coetzee's Milis was to be an intellectual whose irony is a mask behind which churn the political upheavals and moral turmoil of the times. The style Coetzee was developing, judging from the opening paragraphs, was naturalism in the mode of Émile Zola – a mode that fellow-Capetonian Alex La Guma had used in A Walk in the Night (1962), a fiction about District Six. But after weeks of writing and despite having the outlines of a compelling novel, Coetzee was unable to find the momentum that he needed; after several attempts, each false start is marked 'ABANDONED', although elements do survive from one version to the next.

A significant development came with the fifth version, which he calls 'Version E', and which he entitled 'Disposal of the Dead'. Having tried various other titles ('Exile', 'Traitors', 'The Border Guard', and 'Barbarians'), the one he eventually settled on was borrowed from C. P. Cavafy's poem, 'Waiting for the Barbarians.' The Greek connection through Cavafy was one way in which Milis's story was carried through to the final text, although more importantly, his relationship with the young woman would eventually be transposed into the magistrate's relationship with the barbarian girl. These developments were still some way off, however, and behind 'Disposal of the Dead' lies T. S. Eliot, whose The Waste Land (1922) begins with a section called 'The Burial of the Dead'. Through his years of self-imposed apprenticeship, as *Youth* (2002) attests, Coetzee was drawn to T. S. Eliot, along with Ezra Pound, both figures modelling an impersonal modernism that was a place of safety for him. With suitable poetic power, Eliot also enabled Coetzee to register that white South Africa was destroying itself from within.

Coetzee knew, however, that these efforts to launch his third novel were laboured: 'After 22 pages, no liftoff yet', he writes in the notebook. 'It would seem that I can get nowhere unless the whole thing turns into a drama of consciousness a la *In the Heart*. But I cannot face the prospect of writing at that hysterical intensity again. Once is enough.'[5] The problem seems to have been twofold: what he felt he lacked was a credible addressee for the voice that sustained the narrative, what he called 'a credible beloved you'.[6] Already in this uncertainty about the mode of address there is evidence that he was inching his way from third-person towards the first-person narration of the published text. The second problem was that he had no sympathy with conventional realism: 'I have no interest in telling stories; it is the process of storytelling that interests me. This man MM, as a "he" living in the world, bores me. "Creating" an illusionistic reality in which he moves depresses me. Hence the exhausted quality of the writing.'[7]

As he frequently did when he reached an impasse in the progress of a novel, Coetzee went in search of resources. He found inspiration in a poem by Robert Duncan, 'The Song of the Borderguard', in which 'The sound of words waits – /a barbarian host at the borderline of sense.'[8] Whether it was the influence of Duncan's poem alone, or of the poem in combination with other materials, Coetzee began exploring the voice and persona of an officer on an imperial frontier, writing letters to his superiors in a distant capital. This was an important breakthrough: the first-person, epistolary mode of the official's letters (he had not become a magistrate yet) gave him the intimate mode of address that he had been seeking. To create the milieu for this voice he drew on the late nineteenth- and early twentieth-century travel writing about western China and Mongolia of the Swedish explorer Sven Hedin.[9] But he also saw merit in keeping the setting deliberately vague: 'Sometimes it is the Amazonian jungle (Aguirre [a reference to Werner Herzog's film *Aguirre: Wrath of God*, about a conquistador]), sometimes central Asia (Buzzati [a reference to Dino Buzzati's novel *Il deserto dei Tartari*]); other possibilities South Africa, colonial N. America, Roman Europe.' And he added, 'The position is beleaguered. They are forgotten, nevertheless they do their duty.'[10]

The inner voice was as important as the outer milieu, certainly, but the task he had set himself of inventing a landscape enabled Coetzee to draw on all his resources, including, paradoxically, the Karoo. 'Make the desert more like the Karoo', he writes, when the narrative is well under way.[11] There are indeed several passages in the manuscripts where the influence of the Cape's semi-desert is strong and where his love of the family farm, Voëlfontein, is palpable: 'Summer is wheeling to an end', the 'orchards groan under the burden . . . In the sky there are a million stars. We are on the roof of the world. I open my eyes in the middle of the night and lie dazzled.'[12] Coetzee explores this nostalgia with a kind but critical eye in his first volume of partly fictionalized autobiography, *Boyhood* (1997). In *Waiting for the Barbarians*, such inspired landscape description is filled with foreboding, because the magistrate is aware that the life he is leading is coming to an end. The historical research that Coetzee had done before writing *Dusklands*, on the Dutch colonial ethnography of the Cape, also found new uses in *Waiting for the Barbarians*: while the novel is careful not to repeat ethnic typologies, it reconfigures them structurally, in the relationships between the barbarians, the fisher-folk, and the inhabitants of the settlement.

The novel had taken some of the decisive turns that it needed to, by this stage, in order to become the work that we know – except for the most consequential development. Its provocation was local and explosive: in South Africa, the Black Consciousness leader Stephen Biko was murdered under interrogation by the security police. Following his death on 12 September 1977, an inquest was held in open court, which meant that the liberal press could report on it, which they did in great detail, in daily updates. Coetzee kept press clippings from these hearings and used them in constructing his narrative, including the *mise en scène* of the torture chamber.

In 1986 Coetzee published an essay in the *New York Times Book Review* entitled 'Into the Dark Chamber', in which he stated frankly that *Waiting for the Barbarians* was 'about the impact of the torture chamber in the life of a man of conscience'.[13] To Coetzee himself, in retrospect, it seems that the uncertainties around the mode of address and the setting that he had felt in the early stages of writing the novel were resolved by the impact of torture, as a feature of late apartheid, on self-respecting liberal intellectuals. This was the terrain he was to explore through the magistrate's encounter with Colonel Joll's Third Bureau, and through his relationship with the barbarian girl.

Coetzee's notes are remarkably candid about his uses of Biko's murder and related events: 'This may not be entirely honest', he writes, 'but I must make the relation of the story to the Biko affair, the inspiration of the story by the Biko affair, clear.'[14] Most obviously, he uses the political background: Joll's military police resemble South Africa's Bureau for State Security (BOSS), which detained people without trial and frequently tortured them for information. Liberals objected in the press and in parliament, but with little effect, a situation that is registered in the magistrate's distress over the torture taking place under his watch.

When Coetzee worries in the notebook that it 'may not be entirely honest' to signal the relevance of incidents from the Biko affair, the reason would seem to be that he was absorbing these details into a narrative whose composition was already under way, and whose essential structure was already staked out. He had his own purposes, in other words, and was making use of events in order to give his fiction greater weight and verisimilitude. The path he was pursuing, after all, was to write about desire, and the ways in which it becomes malformed when there is endemic political conflict. The Biko affair brought torture into this partly realized fictive situation: the 'you' became the barbarian girl, a torture victim, crippled by blows to the ankles and partially blinded by Joll. The magistrate takes her into his rooms, where the previously imagined sexuality of Milis finds a new, culturally loaded significance.

After these months of composition, the novel gathered momentum. Having written for nearly a year, by late 1978 Coetzee was reading widely to flesh out the themes he was exploring. In the notebook he lists his sources and each of these intertextual connections would merit further research: on cemeteries, rituals associated with death, and despair (Søren Kierkegaard, Henry James, Boris Pasternak); on *Madame Bovary* (1856) and literary art (Gustave Flaubert, with Leo Bersani's commentary); on the pleasure of the text (Roland Barthes); on Tantrism (Octavio Paz); on space (Henri Bergson); on sound (Walter Ong); on dreams (Sigmund Freud); on the body (Paul Ricoeur, Simone de Beauvoir); on fantasies of invasion (George Steiner). He records Simone Weil's aphorism, which finds its way into the text: 'the crime which is latent in us we must inflict on ourselves'.[15] By 1 June 1979 he had a complete typescript, which he continued to revise by hand for another year while visiting Austin, Texas, and Berkeley, California, on sabbatical leave.

The narrative arc of *Waiting for the Barbarians* is shaped by the magistrate's relationship with the barbarian girl. His attentions are confused, both predatory and tender, and the confusion itself fuels the eroticism; but he knows that the relationship will never be reciprocal while she is unable to act as a free agent. This discovery is gradual but decisive, initiating the central action, which is the journey he undertakes with a cohort of men from the settlement to return her to her people. The manuscripts show Coetzee inching towards the magistrate's ethical recovery. The girl's blindness is the result of a hot iron being brought too near her eyes: they are 'dead, flat, like the eyes of a dead fish'. Thereafter his attentions are 'full of nostalgia': he 'watches her jealously when she comes into his room, when she moves, when she undresses, hoping to capture movements of her body that belong to an earlier free state; ~~before she was blind and~~ but everything she does is crabbed, tentative, defensive, the movement of a trammeled body'.[16]

'Somewhere, always, a child is being beaten', Coetzee writes, with reference to Freud (WB, 88).[17] Following these developments, in both the manuscripts and the final text, the magistrate knows that things cannot continue as before. The eroticism gives way to reparation, some tenderness, and although the desires are still mixed, he becomes fatherly. In later reflections he says, 'I think of one who despite her age was still a child; who was brought in here and hurt before her father's eyes; who watched him being humiliated before her, and saw that he knew what she saw.' He realizes that he wanted to take the father's place, but 'I came too late, after she had ceased to believe in fathers. I wanted to do what was right, I wanted to make reparation: I will not deny this decent impulse, however mixed with more questionable motives.' After her father was exposed to her, naked and in pain, 'she was no longer fully human, sister to all of us. Certain sympathies died, certain movements of the heart became no longer possible to her' (WB, 88–9).

On the magistrate's return from the frontier, Joll accuses him of consorting with the enemy and at this point the magistrate himself is tortured, publicly. He is forced to climb a ladder wearing a blindfold, with a noose around his neck and the rope looped around an overhanging branch of a tree. Facing death, he remembers his encounter with the leader of the barbarian contingent that had received the girl on the frontier: 'standing in front of the old man, screwing up my eyes against the wind, waiting for him to speak ... The girl, with her black hair braided and hanging over her shoulder in barbarian fashion, sits her horse behind him. Her head is bowed, she too is waiting for him to speak. I sigh. "What a pity," I think. "It is too late now"' (WB, 131–2). The reciprocity that the magistrate sought as the proper solution to an unsatisfactory relationship proves to be elusive to the end. When given the choice, the girl had decided to return to her people.

Irresolution is in fact a keynote of the novel to the end. As Coetzee observed after a year of drafting, the book would be about 'waiting for a desire which does not come because one is waiting for it. Waiting for Godot is about waiting for a subject.'[18] As he reached the end of the complete first draft he noted, 'the centre of [the magistrate's] bafflement must be that his life has never become clearly emblematic, even at its crisis points. The meeting with the barbarians was vacuous, no words were exchanged, the police are not simply evil, the girl refuses to betray her meaning to him, and finally the barbarians do not come ... <u>This is a novel in which meaning is continually held back</u>' (original emphasis).[19]

The suspension of meaning, paradoxically no doubt, was deliberate and purposeful. At a late stage of drafting Coetzee read Jacques Derrida's *Glas* (1974), a layered commentary on Hegel and on an autobiography by Jean Genet, and considered adding a layer of metafictional reflections. He abandoned the idea, although, embedded in its realism, the text contains passages of self-aware reflection on language and semiotics. The magistrate's 'translation' of the script written onto slips of poplar wood, for example, which he has unearthed in his archaeological diggings, is an illustration of the novel's politicization of language – and as the reference to Cavafy's poem makes clear, the empire itself is an empire of signs. The concluding paragraphs have the magistrate attempting to write a history of settlement, but they are self-interested, self-exculpatory passages and he abandons them. Coetzee had decided that to bring the lines of tension to a neat resolution would be to undo the nuanced ethical positioning of the magistrate towards the end, and possibly, also, to traduce the novel's relation to the history in which it had been written. Coetzee might have shifted the milieu away from Cape Town, but the condition of South Africa facing an indeterminable future, which was important in the novel's original conception, remained influential to the end.

As with *Waiting for the Barbarians*, the provocation behind *Life & Times of Michael K* was largely obscured in the published text. Rather like the magistrate's encounter with Colonel Joll, the new novel was to concern a liberal intellectual shaken from complacency by the latent violence of the culture around him. Having returned to Cape Town from his sabbatical leave in September of 1979, a month later on 17 October Coetzee drew up a rough outline for a novel in which 'a man of liberal conscience' arrives home to find that his house has been burgled and vandalized.[20] The police are unhelpful because they are preoccupied with putting down political rebellion in the townships; believing that he has no recourse to the law, the man abandons liberal decency and mounts a campaign of vigilantism.

Like the unrealized character Milis in *Waiting for the Barbarians*, the man in *Life & Times of Michael K* (still unnamed at this stage) is also working on a literary project: a verse-translation of Heinrich von Kleist's German Romantic novel of 1810, *Michael Kohlhaas*. This is the primary literary reference behind the name Michael K, although Franz Kafka's Joseph K is certainly relevant. In Kleist's novel, set in the sixteenth century, a horse dealer is tricked into giving up his horses by corrupt officials. Without access to the law he leads a rebellion of robbery and murder; he is caught, tried, convicted, and executed, but not before he has demonstrated to the court and to the world at large an innate sense of freedom and justice that embodies the highest ideals of the Enlightenment. In addition to the structure of ideas in Kleist's novel, Coetzee was also drawn to the swift pacing of its prose, in the picaresque style.

By May of the following year Coetzee had given up the idea of basing the novel on the fortunes of a white intellectual. As with the previous novel, he began to explore the narrative potential of a couple and their relationships both with each other and to the times. Although he drew on names from his own family, Albert (a great-uncle and novelist in Afrikaans) and Annie (a great-aunt with literary ambitions who features in *Boyhood*), initially the couple are ethnically marked as coloured, in apartheid-era terms. Albert, who is ailing, is writing a great poem based on Kleist's *Michael Kohlhaas*, while Annie, who takes care of him, is writing a monologue that Coetzee hoped would become the text of the novel.

How this situation would turn into the vendetta that had been Coetzee's basis for choosing *Michael Kohlhaas* was still unclear. Albert and Annie are misfits with literary aspirations, living through a society rapidly deteriorating into a state of civil war. The situation encourages Annie to imagine that if they were to move to the country, specifically to Genadendal ('Valley of Grace'), the seat of an historic mission where they have ancestral roots, she might be able to nurse him back to health (the origins of K's journey to Prince Albert, with his mother in a makeshift cart, lie here). But Coetzee struggled with this material: 'After writing for a few days, I am face to face with the fact that I cannot continue until I clarify my ideas about the historical reality in which this action is supposed to be taking place. All that I have done thus far is to enclose the woman, with a silent partner, in a room in Sea Point in a world in which, it appears, the forms of everyday life have broken down (how? why?).'[21]

Coetzee struggled with the form as much as with the plot: 'But really, for No. 4, there needs to be some <u>inventiveness</u> in form. It can't just be another loony soliloquy, with a corpse rotting in a closed-off bedroom, etc. [referring to *In the Heart of the Country*].'[22] With remarkable frankness, he identified a contradiction – what he called a 'spiritual' problem – that lay at the heart of his efforts to write a novel based on a story of revenge from a position of underclass disaffection:

> I show no advance in my thinking from the position I take in <u>WfB</u> [*Waiting for the Barbarians*]. I am outraged by tyranny, but only because I am identified with the tyrants, not because I love (or 'am with') their victims. I am incorrigibly an elitist (if not worse); and in the present conflict the material interests of the intellectual elite and the oppressors are the same. There is a fundamental flaw in all my novels: I am unable to move from the side of the oppressors to the

side of the oppressed. Is this a consequence of the insulated life I lead? Probably.[23]

The solution that Coetzee found was to turn Michael K into a figure of *absolute* marginality who (miraculously) remains impervious to all the manifestations of aggression and entrapment that are brought on by a civil war. '[T]he only way out', he noted, 'would seem to have to do with language itself'.[24] He consulted Chaucer (the boy in *The Prioress's Tale*), William Wordsworth's Immortality Ode (1807), and Rudolf Steiner's educational doctrine. K was to speak of 'God and the angels and his [fictional] hero, Michael', though Coetzee resisted making him too other-worldly. Instead, he identified a symbolic code in which Michael could be positioned outside the messiness of history, and in this way K was eventually to become a gardener. Given the genesis of this idea, K's gardening should not be seen an ideological alternative to materialism, informed, for example, by ecological consciousness (although it may include that), but as a distinctive mode of being that operates symbolically as an alternative to the predations of history.[25]

In *Waiting for the Barbarians*, Coetzee had become absorbed in the labour of creating verisimilitude for his fictional empire. In *Michael K* he was inventing a South Africa in which the latent conflict would be overt, a forewarning of what was to come; nevertheless, he was frustrated by what he felt was the conventional realism that the task required. He sought ways to address this frustration through changes in point of view: he introduced a second narrator who became the medical officer of Part Two, and a double-voiced form of narration for K's internal consciousness. The 'voice' of *Michael K* is in fact a shifting construction in which different perspectives are played off against one another. For example, in the following sentence it is unclear whether K is remembering the hunger he constantly felt in Huis Norenius, or whether the narrator is commenting on it: 'Whatever the nature of the beast that had howled inside him, it was starved into stillness' (*LT*, 68). This shifting perspective enabled Coetzee to give his reader access to the mind of a simpleton, while also keeping him elusive. A notebook entry indicates that this feature of the narration was hard won and brought Coetzee a sense of achievement:

Sense of elation yesterday for the first time re this project. New idea: to cast the whole as a screenplay, with the addition of (1) passages from a <u>hypothetical</u> novel behind it (set on the page in quote marks), and (2) voice over spoken by K – from his hospital bed to the narrator: only when we get to the hospital sequence do we understand the vantage point. Also perhaps (3) voice over of the narrator (to be called 'my voice').[26]

23

The published text was not so explicitly layered (though the narrative structure Coetzee describes here is clearly relevant to *Foe* (1986), his subsequent novel). Nevertheless, K's elusiveness is fundamental to the work, and becomes apparent in the confusion of the medical officer, who is fascinated by K but cannot understand him. To the reader who witnesses the medical officer's confusion, K's indeterminacy becomes precisely what he is, an escapee from all the camps into which he is thrown, as well as the nets of meaning that are cast over him. The medical officer does give a credible interpretation of K: 'Your stay in the camp was merely an allegory, if you know that word. It was an allegory – speaking at the highest level – of how scandalously, how outrageously a meaning can take up residence in a system without becoming a term in it' (*LT*, 116). But since K also escapes from the medical officer's attentions, even this reasonable conclusion is cast into doubt – K's essence is that he is, 'essentially', indefinable.

Coetzee had transformed Kleist's incendiary hero into a figure who is more ambiguous and indeed metafictional, while still embodying an ideal of freedom. Coetzee knew that this transformation would lead him into political difficulties, so in the process of composition he sought to head off the danger. A critical point in the novel's development is the moment when K has to decide whether or not he will join the guerrillas who have their bases in the Swartberg mountains above Prince Albert. They pass through K's settlement, using the well for water and feeding their horses. When they move on, K decides not to follow or join them, choosing to remain true to his newfound vocation as a gardener.

For some critics, K's decision clarified the novel's politics. When it was published, Nadine Gordimer reviewed it for the *New York Review of Books*, arguing that a 'revulsion against all political and revolutionary solutions rises with the insistence of the song of cicadas to the climax of this novel'. The problem, apparently, was K's indifference to the anti-apartheid struggle and the fact that Coetzee 'does not recognize what the victims, seeing themselves as victims no longer, have done, are doing, and believe they must do for themselves'.[27] On the evidence of the notebook and manuscripts, it is poignant that Coetzee *anticipated* this criticism and sought to negotiate a passage through it, even as he wrote. As if in self-admonishment, he noted, 'The book started with Kleist behind it. Is Michael K– ever going to take to the hills and start shooting?'[28]

K's decision not to join the freedom fighters is narrated with full recognition of the heroic path that Gordimer would have preferred. K imagines himself in the company of the guerrillas, soaking up their stories of 'adventures, victories and defeats and escapes. They will have stories to tell long after the war is over, stories for a lifetime, stories for their grandchildren to listen to open-mouthed' (*LT*, 109). But as he reaches down to check his shoelaces before running to join them, he thinks: 'enough men had gone off to war saying the time for gardening was when the war was over; whereas there must be men to stay behind and keep gardening alive, or at least the idea of gardening; because once that cord was broken, the earth would grow hard and forget her children. That was why' (*LT*, 109). The explanation is credible, but (not unlike the medical officer) Coetzee withholds belief in it by having Michael K realize that it is not entirely true. What the truth *is*, however, he is not sure: 'Always, when he tried to explain himself to himself, there remained a gap, a hole, a darkness before which his understanding baulked ... His was always a story with a hole in it: a wrong story, always wrong' (*LT*, 110).

The effect of Coetzee's metafictional narration (that is, narration that alludes to the ways in which meaning is created) is to keep K ambiguous, and even impervious to explanation in straightforward terms. The position thus crafted for K acquires more authority, because we admire K for his honesty as well as his resilience and autonomy. The metaphor in which this solution is clinched is that of the host and parasite, which Coetzee borrowed from J. Hillis Miller's essay in *Deconstruction and Criticism* (1979).[29] Continually accused of being a parasite, K turns out in fact to be the host, the one who is occupied or taken over both by the authorities and by those who seek even in a benign way to interpret him, like the medical officer.

By implication, the metaphor also applies to readers who might seek to throw their own nets of meaning over the uncontainable protagonist. In her review, Nadine Gordimer proved herself to be stubbornly resistant to the figurations of the novel itself – to the self-consciousness that the text assumes in its readers. In an interview in *Doubling the Point* (1992), Coetzee speaks of the political nakedness of this moment, referring to Gordimer's review. He answers her objection by saying, 'One writes the books one wants to write ... The book about going off with the guerrillas, the book in the heroic tradition, is not a book I *wanted-to-write*' (*DP*, 207–8. Italics in original). He ends by complicating this *wanting*, saying, in effect, that the desire that informs it is inscrutable, even to himself – the distance between Michael K and his author is paper-thin, at this point.

Coetzee had developed a metafictional turn that would challenge the politicization of fiction, but this was also an autobiographical turn. His notes reveal that he did understand K to be an extension of himself: he writes, K's 'not going off with the guerrillas is thematized as a lacuna in his story. It is a lacuna in the logic of his political progression, a lacuna in my own position. It is an unbridgeable gap (and must be so with all comfortable liberal whites), and the best one can do is not leave it out but to represent it as a gap.'[30]

As he had done at a critical stage when writing *Waiting for the Barbarians*, Coetzee explored further cultural resources through which to define K's stature and representativeness. He re-read Kafka's 'A Report to an Academy' (1917) and 'A Hunger Artist' (1922), Fyodor Dostoevsky's *The Idiot* (1868–9), Blaise Pascal's *Pensées* (1670), Friedrich Nietzsche's *Daybreak* (1881), Flaubert's 'A Simple Heart' (1877), and Herman Melville's 'Bartleby, the Scrivener' (1853). He read medical texts on the cleft palate and nutrition, and Marshall Sahlins on scarcity economics. He also read theology: Rudolf Bultmann's *History and Eschatology* (1957), *Theology of the New Testament* (1948), and a commentary on the Gospel of John. Bultmann's existentialist readings of the Gospels sought to explain how the meaning of Christ could be encoded in the reader's experience of the text. Coetzee's is not a religious novel, but it does seek to embed 'meaning' in the experience of reading.[31] In *Life & Times of Michael K*, Coetzee overcame the uncertainties and about-turns that the novel's creation threw in his path, producing a character who is both a resistant textual anomaly and a representative of artistic and intellectual freedom.

The compositional processes that produced *Waiting for the Barbarians* and *Life & Times of Michael K*, as described here, illustrate certain key features of Coetzee's authorship. Chief among them is the paradox (and creative tension) between control and randomness; between self-discipline, organization, preparation, and record-keeping, on one hand, and on the other, absolute faith in the creative process, wherever it may lead. All the manuscript and notebook entries are dated, which is convenient for those who wish to follow the novels' genesis and development, but the purpose of such recording was that it served the creative process because it enabled Coetzee to put down markers of how far he had come, if necessary to be able to return to earlier moments and recover them without losing track of the whole.

Readers have wondered whether the self-archiving is a sign that Coetzee had an eye on posterity; that may be so, but the more important function is that it served the creativity. The phrase 'composition and craft' suggests deliberation, or the skill of the craftsman who understands his tools and realizes a pre-conceived vision. Coetzee's compositional process is far from this model: working his way towards a hunch, an intuition, or a structure of feeling, he surrenders himself to the uncertainties of creation, and only once the structure has emerged will he then hone and shape it with precision. The least stable of the elements that Coetzee works with is the plot, which in some phases of his writing changes daily. The focus more often is on the inner voice and its situation, in a style, a tone, an attitude, and a genre – a prior text, often a canonical one, can provide the model for such a structure – and crucially, a history. Coetzee's self-consciousness as a writer is related to an underlying existential sense that at its most intense, writing is a matter of bearing witness to one's existence in a given historical situation.

Notes

1. This account relies on Chapters Six and Seven of my book *J. M. Coetzee and the Life of Writing: Face to Face with Time* (Oxford: Oxford University Press, 2015), pp. 105–47.
2. J. M. Coetzee, *Waiting for the Barbarians*, early handwritten drafts (20 September 1977–26 March 1978), CP 5.1, 20 September 1977.
3. In some respects, Milis mirrors the sense of being 'alien' that Coetzee describes as his own experience of growing up in South Africa, in *DP*, pp. 393–4.
4. J. M. Coetzee, *Waiting for the Barbarians*, small spiral notebook [1] (11 July 1977–28 August 1978), CP 33.3, 25 July 1977.
5. Ibid., 10 October 1977.
6. Ibid.
7. Ibid., 17 October 1977.
8. Robert Duncan, 'The Song of the Borderguard', *The First Decade: Selected Poems 1940–1950* (London: Fulcrum Press, 1968), p. 135.
9. Hermann Wittenberg and Kate Highman, 'Sven Hedin's "Vanished Country": Setting and History in J. M. Coetzee's *Waiting for the Barbarians*,' *Scrutiny2*, 20.1 (2015), 103–27. See also *DP*, pp. 142–3, where Coetzee remarks that the 'feature of technique on which there is a heavy concentration' in *Waiting for the Barbarians* is 'milieu'.
10. Coetzee, *Waiting for the Barbarians*, notebook 1, 6 November 1977.
11. J. M. Coetzee, *Waiting for the Barbarians*, small spiral notebook [2] (30 August 1978–29 June 1979), CP 33.3, 23 February 1979.
12. Coetzee, *Waiting for the Barbarians*, early drafts, 13 March 1978.
13. J. M. Coetzee, 'Into the Dark Chamber: The Novelist and South Africa', *New York Times Book Review*, 12 January 1986, p. 13. Reprinted in an expanded form as 'Into the Dark Chamber: The Writer and the South African State' in *DP*, pp. 361–8.
14. Coetzee, *Waiting for the Barbarians*, notebook 1, 25 July 1978.
15. Coetzee, *Waiting for the Barbarians*, notebook 2, 27 September 1978.
16. Coetzee, *Waiting for the Barbarians*, early drafts, 4 January 1978.
17. Sigmund Freud, '"A Child is Being Beaten": A Contribution to the Study of the Origin of Sexual Perversions', *International Journal of Psycho-Analysis*, 1.4 (1920), 371–95.
18. Coetzee, *Waiting for the Barbarians*, handwritten draft 'Version G' (28 April 1978–29 October 1978), CP 5.2, 24 October, 1978.
19. Coetzee, *Waiting for the Barbarians*, handwritten draft 'Version H' (1 November 1978–1 June 1979), CP 5.3, 19 February 1979.
20. J. M. Coetzee, *Life & Times of Michael K*, grey casebound notebook (1972–82), CP 33.5, 17 October 1979.
21. Ibid., 9 June 1980.

22. Ibid.
23. Ibid., 16 June 1980.
24. Ibid., 13 December 1980.
25. Peter Horn observed the probable influence of *Michael Kohlhaas* on *Life & Times of Michael K* before the evidence became available in the manuscripts. 'Michael K: Pastiche, Parody or the Inversion of Michael Kohlhaas', *Current Writing*, 17.2 (2005), 56–73.
26. Coetzee, *Life & Times of Michael K* notebook, 19 June 1981.
27. Nadine Gordimer, 'The Idea of Gardening', *New York Review of Books*, 2 February 1984, p. 6.
28. Coetzee, *Life & Times of Michael K* notebook, 8 August 1981.
29. Ibid., 19 September, 1981.
30. Ibid., 23 July 1982.
31. Ibid., undated entry.

2

MEG SAMUELSON

Scenes and Settings: *Foe, Boyhood, Youth, Slow Man*

In poetry the action can take place everywhere and nowhere: it does not matter whether the lonely wives of the fishermen live in Kalk Bay or Portugal or Maine. Prose, on the other hand, seems naggingly to demand a specific setting.

– J. M. Coetzee, *Youth* (62–3)

When the aspirant author of J. M. Coetzee's *Youth* (2002) attempts 'his first experiment with prose', he is disconcerted to find that it takes a South African setting (*Y*, 61). He has, after all, journeyed to the metropolis in a bid to shed his 'South African self', which he considers a 'handicap' (*Y*, 62). Initially, he tries to emulate Henry James, observing approvingly that 'James shows one how to rise above mere nationality': 'it is not always clear where a piece by James is set . . . so supremely above the mechanics of daily life is James. People in James do not have to pay the rent; they certainly do not have to hold down jobs; all they are required to do is to have supersubtle conversations' (*Y*, 64). But *Youth* has, tellingly, opened with a detailed reckoning of how John earns and pays his rent, and the 'price to be paid' for setting is repeatedly calculated across Coetzee's oeuvre.[1] John's attempt to write a story in which his characters are able to transcend place thus proves to be 'like trying to make mammals fly': 'For a moment or two, flapping their arms, they support themselves in thin air. Then they plunge' (*Y*, 64). In a later episode, the gravitational pull of place is no longer experienced by John as failure and elicits instead the affirming sensation of belonging 'on this earth' (*Y*, 117). Through these and other pivotal scenes, Coetzee's *Künstlerroman* asserts that setting matters.[2]

Setting refers broadly to the milieu or socio-historical circumstances of narrative as well as to the particular locations in which specific scenes or sequences of events take place. It both establishes context and provides the space in which the episodes comprising a story are enacted. This space can be either incidental to the action or foundational. The distinction between the two is described by narratologist Mieke Bal as that between 'frame-space' and 'thematized space', or the space 'which allows these events to happen'.[3]

The setting of John's 'experiment with prose' in *Youth* appears to be of the latter order: it is described as both vividly realized and essential to the story's meaning. Setting can also inform narrative while being subordinated to it, such as when it is used to generate atmosphere or to provide a screen onto which the emotion of characters is projected. *Youth* demonstrates these functions in its depiction of a cold and stony London in which its protagonist dwells gloomily on his bleak prospects. But setting also plays a more profound role in *Youth*, as it does elsewhere in Coetzee's writing: it helps to produce what some of his narratives refer to as 'substance' by investing them with 'worldly weight' (*AI*, 110).

Coetzee has expressed disinterest in 'the kind of realism that takes pride in copying the "real" world' and is often received as an anti-realist writer,[4] but he nonetheless maintains that his fictions 'are representations of the real world'.[5] If he has indeed abjured imitating the real, or performing mimesis, he has consistently produced credible, vivid, and authentic fictional worlds that cohere around an often meticulously realized verisimilitude, or appearance of reality.[6] Setting articulates the relation to the real that Coetzee maintains in his fiction and is vital to narrative world-making. Providing the spatio-temporal co-ordinates of narrative, setting performs an indexical function that points to a context outside of the story while rendering the imagined world tangible. This imagined world is assembled out of various *mises en scène* in which the elements that comprise each episode are laid out.[7] Verisimilitude, as Monika Fludernik notes, is often 'conjured up by using clichés to prompt readers to apply schemata already familiar to them'.[8] The protagonist of *Youth* recognizes that the construction of setting through the arrangement of clichéd elements grants credibility to a fictional world when he conceives of a writing project that readers might infer to be the germ of Coetzee's first novel, *Dusklands* (1974): 'If, to make his book convincing, there needs to be a grease-pot swinging under the bed of the wagon as it bumps across the stones of the Karoo, he will do the grease-pot. If there have to be cicadas trilling in the tree under which they stop at noon, he will do the cicadas' (*Y*, 138). These clichéd elements will, he anticipates, situate the story in time and space in ways that both evoke an imagined world and point to the real world.

The locale conjured up by these particular elements is also indicative of which settings come to matter in Coetzee's writing. The real and imagined worlds that they call to mind and bring forth are those of the arid interior region of the Cape Colony in what is now South Africa. John's projected setting thus refers to an area that is both less-than-national (the Karoo) and more-than-national (empire). This is notable because Coetzee's writing has often chafed against the category of a national literature and has sometimes been received as eschewing context and thus evading its responsibility to the real. What this *Künstlerroman* – and his oeuvre – indicates instead is a sustained and deepening sense of situatedness that is both informed by and larger than Coetzee's South African experience. The 'South African situation', he points out in an early interview, is 'only one manifestation of a wider historical situation to do with colonialism, late colonialism, neo-colonialism'.[9] As suggested by the subtitles of his later quasi-autobiographical works, the category he came to favour over a national literature is that of 'scenes from provincial life'. Elaborating provincial settings, his often-episodic narratives observe the local textures that are smoothed out in a national framework while admitting a bondage to the metropole that it denies. More recently, Coetzee has re-directed the category of 'a provincial literature' to that of 'literatures of the South'.[10] Focusing on setting, this chapter tracks a movement through the provincial-metropolitan axis towards what Coetzee calls the 'real South' across four narratives: *Foe* (1986), *Boyhood* (1997), *Youth*, and *Slow Man* (2005).[11]

'Cruso's Island', the House of Foe, and the 'Home of Friday'

> The island was Cruso's (yet by what right? by the law of islands? is there such a law?), but I lived there too, I was no bird of passage, no gannet or albatross, to circle the island once and dip a wing and then fly on over the boundless ocean. Return to me the substance I have lost, Mr Foe: that is my entreaty.
>
> – J. M. Coetzee, *Foe* (51)

Foe's conceit is that the 'female castaway' Susan Barton joined Crusoe (here named Cruso) and Friday on their island sanctuary and later commissioned the writer, Foe, to recast her experience in narrative. The implication is that Daniel Defoe, the author of *The Life and Strange Surprising Adventures of Robinson Crusoe, of York, Mariner* (1719), pillaged Susan's story and then wrote her out of his famous novel. Susan's extra-textual erasure is anticipated in her premonition that Foe might decide the story would be '[b]etter without the woman' (*F*, 72), as it is in her complaint – quoted in the epigraph – that Cruso claims the island as his own. Both are said to deny her 'substance'.[12] That this condition is related to the want of an appropriate setting is suggested by Susan's unhoused and itinerant state throughout the narrative: unlike Cruso, Foe, and even Friday, she has no place that she can claim as her own.

In search of substance, Susan is vexed by the question of how to paint a vivid and authentic picture of the island that will demonstrate that she, too, once inhabited it. When she first decides to peddle her story, she recoils from advice to introduce a 'dash of colour': 'If I cannot come forward, as author, and swear to the truth of my tale, what will be the worth of it? I might as well have dreamed it in a snug bed in Chichester' (F, 40). Susan's commitment to the veracity of experience and her opposition to representational techniques that would lend colour to the island allude to Olive Schreiner's *The Story of an African Farm* (1883), the first novel published by a writer born in what is now South Africa, and one set in the Karoo region of the Cape Colony.[13] In her preface to the second edition, Schreiner issued a much-cited rejoinder to a metropolitan critic who would have preferred 'a history of wild adventure'. 'Such works', she maintains, 'are best written in Piccadilly or in the Strand' from where writers might exercise their 'creative imagination, untrammelled by contact with any fact'; the provincial writer, in contrast, 'must squeeze the colour from his brush, and dip it into the gray pigments around him' in order to 'paint what lies before him'.[14] Far from feeding the metropolitan appetite for local colour, the provincial setting is tendered here as marker and measure of the relation between representation and the real. Susan therefore tries to summon 'a vision of the island to hang before [Foe] like a substantial body' so that he might write authentically of her experiences rather than fall back on the conventional topos of the '*desert isle*' (F, 53, 7).[15] Itemizing the fauna, flora, topography, and climatic conditions of the island, Susan recognizes – as she elsewhere puts it to Cruso – that the credibility of her account depends on the accumulated detail of 'a thousand touches' (F, 18).[16] In thus 'evok[ing] reality by particularizing it',[17] she employs one of the techniques of verisimilitude that Defoe himself helped forge in his account of Robinson Crusoe's calamitous arrival on an island.

It is notable that the catalogue comprising Susan's portrait of the island enumerates the features of the location from which Coetzee wrote the novel: South Africa's Cape Peninsula. Part Defoe's imagined setting and part Coetzee's actual situation, Cruso's island is the ground from which *Foe* addresses its implication in the form of the English novel, and in the context of its own composition. Whereas the latter is often overlooked in favour of the novel's self-reflexive commentary, it is also conveyed through the island setting. Jarad Zimbler points out that 'Robinson's island' echoes the name of the maximum-security gaol in which political opponents of the apartheid regime were imprisoned.[18] The offshore penitentiary of Robben Island has in turn been presented as a microcosm of South Africa's carceral state in works like Athol Fugard, John Kani, and Winston Ntshona's play *The Island* (1973). Cruso's island might be read as similarly expressive of the confining and isolated nature of this state. The setting of Part 1 of *Foe* certainly resonates with Coetzee's contemporaneous commentary on the pressures that this context exerted on literature. The *South African Reader* that he co-edited and published in the same year as *Foe* was tellingly titled *A Land Apart*;[19] in a subsequent address, he bemoaned of South African writing that '[i]t is exactly the kind of literature you would expect people to write from a prison', observing that, for all the expansiveness of the national landscape, its literature 'reflects feelings of entrapment, entrapment in infinitudes'.[20] Such indeed is the feeling evoked by the picture Susan paints of Cruso pacing the cliffs and 'scanning the horizon for a sail' (*F*, 18).

But if *Foe*'s island refers to Coetzee's South African writing context, it is not reducible to the boundaries of that insular state, for this island is also located within a wider context of the Atlantic trade triangle, and might even be read as the earth writ small. The novel presents the 'business of the world' being conducted by merchantmen and slave ships across an arena composed of the nodal points of Africa, Brazil, and England, which are figured respectively in synecdoche as forests, plantations, and properties bounded by hedges (*F*, 23–4). Presenting what Coetzee elsewhere describes as 'unabashed propaganda' for imperial expansion, Defoe's protagonist gainfully transforms 'his' island from a wasteland into a serviceable colony (*SS*, 24). In contrast, Coetzee's Cruso – with the help of Friday's labour – constructs terraces in the absence of seed, converting a landscape of 'pebbles and bushes and swarms of birds' into one of 'bare earth, baked by the sun and walled about' (*F*, 33). Unlike the protagonist of *Life & Times of Michael K* (1983), Cruso is no gardener. As Bill Ashcroft observes, the barrenness of Cruso's endeavour parodies the colonial project.[21] At the same time, it points to the loss of biodiversity on a planetary scale in a geological epoch that some have dated back to the plantations of the 'new world' colonies.[22] The purview of this setting thus extends indefinitely beyond the context of its production – somewhat like the stream that issues from Friday's mouth in the novel's concluding scene: flowing 'through the wreck; washing the cliffs and shores of the island, it runs northward and southward to the ends of the earth' (*F*, 157).

As the action shifts from Cruso's island to London at the conclusion of Part 1, the scene of writing – of the production of narrative – itself thickens into setting. Following an initial disappearance that mimics Defoe's effacement of his authorial presence in *Robinson Crusoe*, Coetzee's Foe later manifests as conspicuously embodied and thus partakes in the condition of habitancy: the primary settings of Parts 2 and 3 are the houses of Foe, which Susan first envisions and then occupies. She imagines his writing room as being 'barely furnished', and later reports that he will find it 'bare' on his return: 'First the bailiffs plundered it' and then she stripped the remaining accessories to 'buy necessaries' (*F*, 49, 93, 88). Verisimilitude, note Leech and

Short, depends on the 'mock reality' being '"well furnished" with data'.[23] In this ransacked structure that begins to teeter like a metafictional house of cards, Susan feels herself reduced to 'a being without substance', which she fears is the 'fate of all storytellers' (*F*, 51). Still in search of her story, she later enters another house to which Foe has repaired. Her knock on the door 'echoed as if on emptiness' (*F*, 113). Inside this dwelling, she and Foe muse on the gaps in the story and seek to extract from Friday the substance with which to fill them by establishing his proper setting. The words Susan tries to teach him are 'house', 'ship', 'Africa', 'mother', which present a sequential chain leading back to what she imagines to be his origins and reiterate her effort to return him by ship to Africa, which she calls his 'homeland' (*F*, 145–6, 107). But *Foe* retorts that the unfathomed ocean is instead 'the home of Friday' (*F*, 157).

When Susan first imagines Foe's writing situation, she thinks of him in his attic 'as a steersman steering the great hulk of the house through the nights and days' (*F*, 50). In the final part of the novel, another narrator enters the house of Foe after both authorial figures, Susan and Foe, have died – and then again some centuries later when he or she now finds a plaque 'bolted to the wall. *Daniel Defoe, Author*' (*F*, 155). Rather than charting a course from the poop of Foe's writing bureau, this narrator slips overboard into the ocean, setting meaning adrift in the 'home of Friday'. This is 'not a place of words'; the inhabitants of the 'deep water realm' are – as Coetzee has suggested elsewhere – 'indifferent' to authorial attempts to 'pin them down' (*F*, 157).[24] Following the poets Adrienne Rich ('Diving into the Wreck') and Derek Walcott ('The Sea is History') into this realm, the final narrator of *Foe* descends into a setting that displaces 'the book of myths' and the demand for 'monuments and martyrs'.[25] This is the domain of what Shakespeare's Ariel describes as the 'sea-change' of base matter into 'something rich and strange', and it is where Prospero would 'drown [his] book' in a disavowal of his use of 'art' or 'magic' to manipulate others and assert power.[26] Materializing the poststructuralist trope of the 'death of the author', the concluding scene destabilizes the authority invested in Defoe and strips away the illusions of verisimilitude. But its earth-encircling setting nonetheless insists on the substantial nature and transformative potential of the represented world.

'Scenes from Provincial Life'

If I am right to say that what we are doing is not building a new national literature, but instead building on to an established provincial literature, then it seems to me that the most constructive way to behave – certainly

*a more constructive way than pitying ourselves for our provincial lot, or
plotting an escape to the metropolis – is to set about rehabilitating the
notion of the provincial.*
— J. M. Coetzee, 'SA Authors Must Learn Modesty'

The first two volumes of Coetzee's 'scenes from provincial life' open by
situating the narratives in locales traversed by an infrastructure of flight.
Boyhood begins: 'They live on a housing estate outside the town of
Worcester, between the railway line and the National Road' (*B*, 1).
A similar scene-setting description introduces *Youth*: 'He lives in a one-
room flat near Mowbray railway station' (*Y*, 1). The trajectory along
which these lines of flight convey their protagonists leads away from their
despised 'provincial lot' to the 'library that defines all libraries' at the heart of
the metropolis (*Y*, 138). But another setting nests inside that of the domed
reading room in the British Museum in which the protagonist of *Youth*
arrives: this is the 'country of his heart' (*Y*, 137). The forsaken place to
which he returns in the pages of a travelogue by the eighteenth-century
British naturalist William Burchell is the Karoo. This is the 'beloved landscape of ochre and grey and fawn and olive-green' that is painted in *Boyhood*
from the same muted palette assembled by Schreiner to assert an authentic
provincial perspective (*B*, 90).

The chapter of *Boyhood* devoted to the Coetzee family farm, Voëlfontein, is
the longest in the book. The clipped plotting of the narrative expands luxur-
iously as the landscape is simultaneously catalogued and rendered immeasur-
able in uncharacteristically effusive prose. Focalized through the child, this
adoration is unreserved. The reader familiar with Coetzee's 'Jerusalem Prize
Acceptance Speech' (1987), the essays in *White Writing* (1988), and the novels
In the Heart of the Country (1977) and *Life & Times of Michael K* has,
however, been cued to receive the boy's expression of love for the land –
along with the references to idleness, labour, fences, and camps – through
a refracted light. *Boyhood* also shows its privileged setting to be shadowed by
the surrounding milieu of apartheid South Africa, just as Schreiner's celebration of the Karoo is qualified by her critique of colonial society.

The farm in *Boyhood* is said to root the boy and grant him 'substance', but
his status on it is that of 'an uneasy guest' (*B*, 79). While this unsettled state
refers to his familial situation (his uncle cannily bought out his siblings'
shares in the farm) it also points to the settler condition: the boy recognizes
that others belong to this land – 'if not to Voëlfontein, then to the Karoo' –
more than the Coetzees ever will; recalling Susan Barton's trope, his family
are like 'swallows, seasonal, here today, gone tomorrow, or even like spar-
rows, chirping, light-footed, short-lived', and Coetzee further underlines the

implication by translating the name of the farm as 'bird-fountain' (B, 87, 80). The point is made more baldly in Youth when a bucolic scene of receiving succour from a horse-drawn milk cart concludes with the recognition that white South Africans 'are here on this earth, the earth of South Africa, on the shakiest of pretexts' (Y, 17).

The boy is also shown to have made a category mistake in his estimation of Voëlfontein: what he receives as expansive veld is actually enclosed property. Earlier, he and two friends climb through a fence on his assurance that 'it could not be a farm, it was just veld', only to be nearly whipped for trespassing (B, 71). Hunting on the family farm with his father, he comes up against another fence, and is 'taken aback', having imagined Voëlfontein as 'a kingdom in its own right' (B, 91). The farm is moreover subdivided into 'camps' for rotational grazing, so that the depleted veld can support ever more sheep (B, 100). Having once sustained a diversity of creatures and crops, it is now an enterprise devoted to the production of wool. The narrative here recalls Susan Barton's sharp remarks about Cruso's terraces in Foe. The enclosure movement and its imperial expansion – of which Defoe's novel presents a 'master narrative' – is instantiated in stark form in South Africa.[27] Commenting on the impossibility of Michael K's utopian project in his earlier novel, Coetzee notes: 'he can't hope to keep the garden because, finally, the whole surface of South Africa has been surveyed and mapped and disposed of'.[28] This act of disposal produces what Coetzee elsewhere presents as the 'dream topography' of the South African pastoral: 'a network of boundaries crisscrossing the surface of the land, marking off thousands of farms, each a separate kingdom ruled over by a benign patriarch' (WW, 6).

While the father in Boyhood is no 'patriarch', the boy does style himself as 'prince' of the household (B, 12). Preceding the chapter on the farm is an episode in which he celebrates his birthday by treating his friends at the Globe Café in Worcester, 'feel[ing] princely, dispensing pleasure'. But the occasion is 'spoiled by the ragged Coloured children standing at the window looking in on them' (B, 72). The cold and brittle pane between them manifests the peculiar combination of proximity and partitioning in the apartheid state. The boy knows, moreover, that all he need do to restore his contentment is demand that the manager remove the children from his field of vision. As Coetzee observes elsewhere: 'The response of South Africa's legislators to what disturbs their white electorate is usually to order it out of sight. If people are starving, let them starve far away in the bush … If the black townships are in flames, let cameras be banned from them' (DP, 361).

Apartheid is thus registered as a spatial project that produces segregated and concealed settings.

In order to summon a scene that the apartheid state has rendered inaccessible, the boy makes recourse to fiction. Only in his imagination can he follow the Coloured youth, Eddie, to his home: 'He thinks of it as a cold, sodden place. In Eddie's mother's house there is no electric light. The roof leaks, everyone is always coughing. When you go outside you have to hop from stone to stone to avoid the puddles' (B, 76). The scene he conjures in that grim setting is a familiar one in writing from this segregated state. Es'kia Mphahlele, in his autobiography *Down Second Avenue*, presents it as an expression of what he calls the 'tyranny of place' and shows how it compels flight only to relentlessly preoccupy the writer in exile.[29] Mphahlele drew inspiration from Peter Abrahams who, similarly, escaped segregated South Africa and its deprived settings in order to 'tell freedom'.[30] The protagonist of the autobiographical narrative that Abrahams produced after leaving South Africa, and which concludes with this flight, first registers his confined situation when looking at the world denied him through a pane of glass – he is, as it were, on the other side of the window of Coetzee's boyhood.

The protagonist of *Youth* also flees the all-absorbing circumstances of South Africa in order to realize his literary aspirations, but Coetzee does not afford him the tragic stature of his black counterparts. Instead, John's callowness is relentlessly exposed. The opening scene after John's transfer to London announces that the would-be deracinated poet has arrived belatedly ('past midnight') in an artificially illuminated city that is 'stony, labyrinthine, and cold' (Y, 41). Committing the pathetic fallacy – or what Coetzee elsewhere identifies as 'the worst excesses of realism' – John's focalization suffuses the city with his 'subjectivity', projecting his isolation and austerity onto the 'objective world' (DP, 358–9). His 'loneliness' is 'indistinguishable from the low, grey, wet, weather of London or from the iron-hard cold of the pavements'; both in turn mirror his cool temperament (Y, 52). Commenting on an essay in which Coetzee criticizes another writer for the failure that John exhibits here, Zimbler notes how it shows 'that one can write explicitly about the world, and nevertheless turn away from it'; Coetzee's prose, he avers, is instead 'oriented ... towards the world'.[31]

This orientation is demonstrated and given direction in *Youth*. Late in the narrative, John experiences an epiphany on Hampstead Heath: 'He used to be impatient of poems about budding flowers and zephyrous breezes. Now, in the land where those poems were written, he begins to understand how deep gladness can run at the return of the sun' (Y, 117). The incident, as María López points out, affirms the 'interrelation between literature and location'.[32] The narrative frames its import as offering John 'a hint that he belongs on this earth' (Y, 117); it provides, in other words, an intimation of substance. A second epiphany occurs in the British Museum, where he is struck by the indexical sign pointing to southern skies in Burchell's *Travels in the Interior of Southern Africa* (1822, 1824): 'real stars glimmered above his head ... It dizzies him even to think about it' (Y, 137–8). Whereas on the Heath he felt 'the steady wheeling of the earth' in his blood, he now experiences the giddy sensation of spinning around on its surface, turning southward (Y, 117).

'Sun Pictures' from 'the South'

> [T]here is only one South – with its unique skies and its unique heavenly constellations. In this South the winds blow in a certain way and the leaves fall in a certain way and the sun beats down in a certain way that is instantly recognisable from one part of the South to another. In the South, as in the North, there are cities, but the cities of the South all have a somewhat phantasmatic quality ... We have troubled histories behind us, which sometimes haunt us. It is nothing like this in the North.
> – J. M. Coetzee, 'Literatures of the South'

Slow Man is the first novel composed after Coetzee's emigration to Australia, and it is the only work to date set in Adelaide, the city where he has since resided (although the imagined city of Estrella in *The Schooldays of Jesus* (2016) resembles Adelaide in the same way that Cruso's island does apartheid South Africa). Through its French-Australian protagonist Paul Rayment and his Croatian nurse Marijana Jokić, *Slow Man* stages the theme of migration, while noting the persistence of the provincial condition – or what Australians call cultural cringe – in the face of the metropolitan presumption that the Antipodes have 'Zero history' (SM, 49). While thus alluding to the provincial-metropolitan axis, *Slow Man* also develops Coetzee's subsequently stated interest in the 'real South' as opposed to the 'mythic South' of the metropolitan imagination – which is notably presented as *setting* rather than geopolitical category in the lecture quoted above.[33] This turn is gestured to in the final scene of *Foe* when the craft that has conveyed the narrator from the metropolitan house of fiction to the 'home of Friday' is '[g]ripped by the current' and 'drawn south' (F, 151). It comes into greater focus in *Youth*, which plots the would-be author's 'escape to the metropolis', but which is published in the year in which Coetzee moves instead along the southern latitude that runs between Cape Town and Adelaide.

The setting of John's 'experiment with prose' in *Youth* is, notably, a Cape beach. It is so distinctive that he does not bother to publish the story as he assumes its substance will be lost to a metropolitan readership:

> For the beach in the story they will summon up an English idea of a beach, a few pebbles lapped by wavelets. They will not see a dazzling space of sand at the foot of rocky cliffs pounded by breakers, with gulls and cormorants screaming overhead as they battle the wind. (*Y*, 62)

Historical content is given to this littoral space when John recognizes the untenability of the claim laid on South African soil by descendants of the 'handful of Hollanders' who 'waded ashore on Woodstock beach' in the mid seventeenth century (*Y*, 121). Soon after, he evokes the beach again when conjuring an image of his homeland as counterpoint to a bitter English winter: 'In South Africa it is summer. If he were there he could be on Strandfontein beach, running over mile after mile of white sand under a great blue sky' (*Y*, 102). Whereas John's appreciation of the poetics of place on Hampstead Heath is brought forth by the sun-deprived nature of the north, the sun-drenched settings that he evokes reference an antipodal position. The expansive release that they enable stands in contrast to his anxiety that his provincial beginnings are a 'handicap', as well as to his dreary tramps through the labyrinthine streets of London. But they are also edgy, threshold spaces that convey the 'troubled histories' of the peninsular town at the tip of Africa from which he hails as well as the wider context of the settler South that now concerns Coetzee.[34] The reference in *Youth* to Hollanders arriving on the Woodstock beach is thus echoed in *Slow Man* when Paul describes how his stepfather, the 'Dutchman', delivered his family to 'the sunny land of opportunity' at 'the ends of the earth' (*SM*, 66, 156). The same light floods across this setting, and it is burdened with a related history of colonial invasion: the Dutch explored parts of the Australian coast in the same century that they settled the Cape; and the colonization of Australia by Britain begins in 1788, followed a few years later by the British occupation of the Cape.

There is of course also disjuncture between these southern lands. The opening scenes of *Slow Man* seem teasingly to invite an allegorical reading of an author addressing himself to the new setting in which he has alighted. Flying through the air and landing on the bitumen, Paul is transported to hospital where he awakes surrounded by 'whiteness unrelieved', asking '*What is this place where I find myself?*' only to be greeted by the ubiquitous Australian colloquialism: 'No worries' (*SM*, 3–4). Rather than homing in on its exceptionality, however, Coetzee again situates the national within a wider context: the laid-back attitude resonates more unpropitiously with a laissez-faire neo-liberalism that is eroding the welfare state referenced in the hospital and private homecare sequences and which is the latest chapter in the long history of commerce and rationalization that *Foe*, *Boyhood*, and *Youth* address.

Other scenes in *Slow Man* gesture to the gracious city that Coetzee has admired in his public pronouncements: there is a pedestrian mall monitored by solicitous police; a conveniently situated pub and café are within easy reach of Paul's apartment; and Elizabeth Costello haunts the encircling parks through which the River Torrens meanders, feeding the ducks. But the sense of place presented in the novel is otherwise sparse: the setting is much curtailed by Paul's accident and his refusal to be fitted with a prosthesis, which – in another nod to *Robinson Crusoe* and John's sense of himself suffering a 'handicap' – confines much of the action to his apartment in Coniston Terrace. One of the few occasions on which Paul ventures beyond his immediate surroundings is to visit Marijana in the new development of Munno Para (the 'dark continent', Costello quips, alluding to Mungo Park's travels in the African interior) (*SM*, 241). The Jokićs live in 'a colonial-style house with a green lawn around an austere little rectangular Japanese garden', which elicits from Costello the response 'So real! . . . So authentic!' (*SM*, 242). Melinda Harvey notes that this 'draws our attention to the fact of it being the very opposite, an ersatz reality'.[35] The scene has indeed been read as realizing an earlier prognosis Coetzee made after asserting that 'people can only be in love with one landscape in their lifetime': 'I would probably feel a certain sense of artificial background construction if I were to write a fiction set in another environment', he concluded in 1982.[36] However, his more recent statement that cities of the South share a 'phantasmatic quality' suggests that the illusionary likeness may rather be received as authentic to the 'real South'.

The faux-real can thus be said to convey the substance of the South in ways that reflect the novel's ability to render a credible and authentic fictional world capable of both indexing the real and pointing southward. *Slow Man* develops this idea through the theme of photography. Reprising and elaborating the encounter John has with Burchell's *Travels* in the British Museum are the scenes in which Paul presents to Marijana and her son Drago a collection of old photographs that he has bequeathed to the State Library of South Australia and which he stores in 'two old-fashioned cedarwood cabinets' in his apartment. Included in his fictional collection of 'the early mining camps of Victoria and New South Wales' are two actually existing images that were taken by the French prospector-turned-photographer Antoine Fauchery, who in 1859 co-published the first series of Australian photographs under the title *Sun Pictures of Victoria* (*SM*, 47–8). The scenes framed by the setting of the mining camp are thus the product of a northern gaze, but they index the southern sun. Paul observes how the silver albumin print 'records the way the sunlight fell, one day in 1855, on the faces of two long-dead Irishwomen', proclaiming: '*I was here, I lived, I suffered*' (*SM*, 177). His appreciation of analogue photography's procedure of 'taking in light and turning it into substance' owes much to Roland Barthes, for whom the photograph 'is literally an emanation of the referent' to which it is joined by the 'umbilical cord' of 'light' (*SM*, 65).[37]

Paul shuns the digital turn, which he describes as 'a *techne* of images without substance, images that could flash through the ether without residing anywhere' and which are possibly 'doctored, untrue' (*SM*, 65). The depiction of his aversion to digital manipulation – like that of his refusal to be fitted with a prosthesis – can be received as a mockery of the old-fashioned belief in unmediated access to an unadulterated real. But it is rewarding to read it as also commenting on how the novel uses setting to establish a relation to the world that is simultaneously fictitious and true. Like the image in analogue photography, narration must reside somewhere if it is to attain substance. Elizabeth Costello may thus be rendered homeless in pursuit of her subject, but she must still find alternative habitation in Paul's apartment or 'suffer the heat of the sun' in the public spaces of the city when he turns her out to accommodate Drago (*SM*, 142). Costello's eruption into the narrative of *Slow Man* is certainly a striking manifestation of Coetzee's impatience with mimesis, but it is at the same time an indication of the ontological reality attained by his fictional creations: this character will simply not be contained within the covers of the eponymous book in which she features.[38] Though her appearance on Paul's doorstep recasts the opening scene of *Slow Man* as metafiction, the 'sun's touch' on Paul's prone body – like that 'on the faces of two long-dead Irishwomen' – nonetheless maintains the substance of the external world in even this most self-consciously fictional reality (*SM*, 1, 177).

When Drago digitally adapts Paul's Fauchery prints and inserts his Croatian family members into these proto Anglo-Irish Australian scenes, he raises significant questions about who is included in the Australian national community. But it is notable that he does not question the frame itself. On the contrary, both his adaptation of the mining-camp scenes and his desire to join the navy suggest a commitment to the borders of the nation-state whose anthem proclaims: 'With golden soil and wealth for toil/ Our land is girt by sea'. When Paul declines Elizabeth Costello's closing invitation to tour 'the whole of this wide brown land, north and south, east and west' on the recumbent bike that Drago has built for him, and thus to become a 'well-loved Australian institution', he once more displays the peevish conservatism that makes him the butt of the joke (SM, 263).[39] But he also represents a critical refusal to endorse the frame of Australia as 'island-continent' – that is, as yet another manifestation of Cruso's island, whether like the 'fortress state' of apartheid South Africa deplored in Summertime or the defensive frontier town of Waiting for the Barbarians (Sum, 5).[40] At the same time, the narratives that represent Coetzee's land of birth, whether mimetically or analogically, show up the limits of Paul's preoccupations. The collection that he declares 'a genuine national treasure' contains only one of the three constellations of subjects and settings that comprise the Sun Pictures: Anglo-Irish immigrants in the mining camps. Fauchery's images of Aborigines in the bush and of Melbourne's European burghers are not mentioned by Paul, whose interest is entirely absorbed by Anglo-Australian settler histories.[41] Paul and Drago's attention to the scene composed within the frame can be contrasted with Mrs Curren's perusal, in Age of Iron (1990), of photographs of a colonial childhood that feature herself and her brother (also named Paul) but excise those to whom the setting 'rightfully' belonged, only to find that these photographs 'have become negatives again, a new kind of negative in which we begin to see what used to lie outside the frame, occulted' (AI, 111–12).

Slow Man takes an Australian setting while flagging its disinclination to trace the borders of this southern land in ways that would contain it entirely within the national frame.[42] Instead, the novel is part of an ongoing project of writing the 'real South' in which setting is neither trompe l'oeil nor exotic local colour, neither blank screen nor empty frame, but instead that which conveys the very substance of the real: the sun that 'beats down in a certain way' on Paul, Elizabeth Costello, and the miners arranged before Fauchery's lens, as it does in Coetzee's subsequent narratives such as Summertime and the Jesus novels.[43] The South emerges in these works as an alternative centre of gravity that generates its own deictic markers. Here the condition of being 'on this earth' remains unsettled, haunted as it is by dispossession, erasure, and exclusion, but Coetzee's writing nonetheless takes its direction from this bearing, however shaky it may be, and finds in it a true line leading to the 'real world'.

Notes

1. See, inter alia, J. M. Coetzee, 'Jerusalem Prize Acceptance Speech' (1987) in DP, pp. 96–9.
2. On the importance of place in Youth, see under Further Reading for books by Rita Barnard and María J. López, and Kai Easton's article.

3. Mieke Bal, *Narratology: Introduction to the Theory of Narrative*, 3rd ed. (Toronto: University of Toronto Press, 2009), p. 139.

4. Tony Morphet, 'An Interview with J. M. Coetzee', *Social Dynamics*, 10.1 (1984), 62–5 (p. 62).

5. 'I am enough of an Aristotelian to believe that fiction, or my fictions at least, are representations of the real world.' J. M. Coetzee, 'Lectura John M. Coetzee en Malba', *Museo MALBA*, 11 September 2017, www.youtube.com/watch? v=U5Ms65oo2wI

6. For a convincing rebuttal of the critical orthodoxy that claims Coetzee as an anti-realist writer, see: Jarad Zimbler, *J. M. Coetzee and the Politics of Style* (Cambridge: Cambridge University Press, 2014). Zimbler draws on Geoffrey Leech and Mick Short's *Style in Fiction: A Linguistic Introduction to English Fictional Prose*, 2nd ed. (Harlow: Pearson Longman, 2007), which helpfully identifies five aspects of realism: credibility, verisimilitude, authenticity, objectivity, and vividness (p. 148).

7. As M. H. Abrams notes in *A Glossary of Literary Terms*, 7th ed. (Boston: Heinle & Heinle, 1999): 'The French *mise en scène* ("placing on stage") is sometimes used in English synonymously with "setting", though it refers more precisely to the arrangement of props, actors and other elements of a play on the stage (p. 285).

8. Monika Fludernick, *An Introduction to Narratology* (Abingdon: Routledge, 2009), p. 54.

9. Qtd. Stephen Watson, 'Colonialism and the Novels of J. M. Coetzee' in Graham Huggan and Stephen Watson (eds.), *Critical Perspectives on J. M. Coetzee* (Basingstoke: Macmillan, 1996), pp. 13–36 (p. 13).

10. J. M. Coetzee, 'SA Authors Must Learn Modesty', *Die Vaderland*, 1 May 1981, p. 16; and J. M. Coetzee, 'Literatures of the South: Introductory Remarks', *Literaturas del Sur*, Universidad Nacional de San Martín, 2016, qtd. in James Halford, 'Southern Conversations: J. M. Coetzee in Buenos Aires', *Sydney Review of Books*, 28 February 2017. See also J. M. Coetzee, unpublished address in 'Cultural Musing: The South', 'Other Worlds' ARC Project, Adelaide, 2017.

11. Coetzee, 'Literatures of the South'.

12. For a resonant analysis of 'substance' in *Foe*, see Zimbler, *Politics of Style*, pp. 159–69.

13. On the allusion to Schreiner, see David Attwell, *J. M. Coetzee: South Africa and the Politics of Writing* (Berkeley: University of California Press, 1993), pp. 105–6.

14. Olive Schreiner, 'Preface to the Second Edition', *The Story of an African Farm* (London: Little Brown, 1888), p. 9.

15. On the 'fixed combination' of 'space and event' that constitutes a topos, see Bal, *Narratology*, p. 141.

16. See Fludernick, *Introduction*, pp. 54–5.

17. Leech and Short, *Style in Fiction*, p. 136.

18. Jarad Zimbler, 'Under Local Eyes: The South African Publishing Context of J. M. Coetzee's *Foe*', *English Studies in Africa*, 47.1 (2004), 47–59.

19. André Brink and J. M. Coetzee (eds.), *A Land Apart: A Contemporary South African Reader* (Harmondsworth: Penguin, 1987).

20. Coetzee, 'Jerusalem Prize Acceptance Speech', p. 98.

21. Bill Ashcroft, 'Silence as Heterotopia in Coetzee's Fiction' in Chris Danta, Sue Kossew, and Julian Murphet (eds.), *Strong Opinions: J. M. Coetzee and the Authority of Contemporary Fiction* (London: Bloomsbury, 2011), pp. 141–57.

22. The relocation of 'plants, animals, microbes, people' for the purposes of 'extraction' might be taken as a 'key transition' into a planetary condition that could thus be described as the 'Plantationocene' rather than the 'Anthropocene'. See Donna Haraway, *Staying with the Trouble: Making Kin in the Chthulucene* (Durham, NC: Duke University Press, 2016).

23. Leech and Short, *Style in Fiction*, p. 126.

24. J. M. Coetzee, Launch Address, *Borderlines*, University of Adelaide, 8 Nov. 2017.

25. Adrienne Rich, 'Diving into the Wreck' in *Diving into the Wreck: Poems 1971–1972* (New York: W. W. Norton & Company, 1973), p. 32; Derek Walcott, 'The Sea is History' (1979), in *The Poetry of Derek Walcott: 1948–2013* (London: Farrar, Strauss, and Giroux, 2014), p. 253.

26. William Shakespeare, *The Tempest* 1.i.401–2; 5.i.57; 5.i.50. On the allusions to *The Tempest* in this scene, see Derek Attridge, *J. M. Coetzee and the Ethics of Reading: Literature in the Event* (Chicago: University of Chicago Press, 2004).

27. Robert P. Marzec, 'Enclosures, Colonization, and the *Robinson Crusoe* Syndrome: A Genealogy of Land in a Global Context', *boundary* 2, 29.2 (2002), 129–56 (p. 139).

28. Morphet, 'J. M. Coetzee: An Interview', p. 456.

29. Ezekiel Mphahlele, *Down Second Avenue* (London: Faber and Faber, 1959).

30. Peter Abrahams, *Tell Freedom* (New York: Alfred A. Knopf, 1954).

31. Zimbler, *J. M. Coetzee and the Politics of Style*, p. 42.

32. Maria J. López, *Acts of Visitation: The Narrative of J. M. Coetzee* (Amsterdam: Rodopi, 2011), p. 241.

33. Coetzee, 'Literatures of the South'.

34. Ibid.

35. Melinda Harvey, '"In Australia you start zero": The Escape from Place in J. M. Coetzee's Late Novels' in Chris Danta, Sue Kossew, and Julian Murphet (eds.), *Strong Opinions: J. M. Coetzee and the Authority of Contemporary Fiction* (New York: Continuum, 2011), pp. 19–34 (p. 24).

36. Coetzee in Folke Rhedin, 'J. M. Coetzee: Interview', *Kunapipi*, 6.1 (1984), 6–11 (p. 10).

37. Roland Barthes, *Camera Lucida: Reflections on Photography*, trans. Richard Howard (New York: Hill and Wang, 1981), pp. 80, 81.

38. On the 'ontological weight' and reality of fictional characters, see Stephen Muecke, 'An Ecology of Institutions: Recomposing the Humanities', *New Literary History*, 47.2 & 3 (2016), 231–48.

39. The allusion is to Dorothea Mackellar's nationalistic poem 'My Country' (1908).

40. See Suvendrini Perera, *Australia and the Insular Imagination: Beaches, Borders, Boats, and Bodies* (Basingstoke: Palgrave Macmillan, 2009).

41. See Catherine De Lorenzo, 'French Photographic Constructions of Australia Paradis Primitif', *History of Photography*, 21.4 (1997), 319–29.

42. The name of Australia is derived from 'Terra Australis' or 'southern land'.

43. Coetzee, 'Literatures of the South'.

3

JARAD ZIMBLER

Stories and Narration: *In the Heart of the Country, The Master of Petersburg, The Childhood of Jesus*

Towards the end of *Here and Now* (2013), a surprisingly poignant moment arrives in Coetzee's description of his afternoon naps:

> I nod off during the day, sometimes sitting at my desk – little fugues from the world that usually last no more than a few seconds but sometimes extend to five or even ten minutes.
>
> I've taken to having the most interesting dreams during these escapes: episodes with believable little plots, acutely realistic in their situations, their dialogue, the look of things. They don't seem to be based on memories at all, but to be pure invention. Nothing fantastic in them, nothing menacing. I think of them as finger exercises of the imagination, the improvisations of a mind with something like forty years of practice in conceiving situations. They are of no use to me – they don't fit into what I am writing – so there is no point in noting them down. I am pleased with them, I enjoy them while they are running, but they leave a residue of sadness too. It seems a pity to have built up, over the decades, this particular little skill, and to think that it is going to be lost, eclipsed, when I go. (*HN*, 227–8)

As so often across Coetzee's writing, a quiet lyricism is threaded through an account of otherwise prosaic events. Related in a manner at once immediate and reserved, the anecdote brims, unexpectedly, with the promise of meaning. It thereby provides evidence of the skill it describes: a capacity for using even the unlikeliest materials to conceive situations with narrative potential.

To those familiar with Coetzee's reputation, what may seem especially striking about this anecdote is how it characterizes his craft. More than an art of writing, or, indeed, of language, it becomes one of imagination, of invention; an art of thinking up plots and settings and characters with speaking parts. Alongside the vision of Coetzee as austere master of prose it gives us Coetzee as creator and maker of stories. In this respect, the anecdote chimes with a tendency, intermittently visible across Coetzee's writings, to attach himself to the figure of the storyteller.[1] What is at stake in this attachment? To begin with, it may be Coetzee's way of connecting his craft with the deep

45

time and broad expanse of verbal art, by invoking practices that seem distributed universally amongst human cultures and communities. But he may also be pushing against or away from other appellations, including that of 'novelist'. And if it seems that his attachment to story and storytelling has only grown over time, this may be related to the expansion of his oeuvre into genres that are non-novelistic, even non-fictional. Story becomes a useful catch-all, allowing us to gather together Coetzee's novels, autobiographical fictions, and even works of correspondence.

Coetzee's investment in story is relevant to the principal aim of this chapter, which is to address the nature of the stories he has told, as well as his approach to telling them. Here, story means something like the basic elements of event and character – what is done, and by or to whom – and is distinguished from narration, which has to do chiefly with the way these basic elements are arranged and how they are recounted. This is a common enough distinction, and one fundamental to most theories of narrative, whether it is described by the opposition of fabula to syuzhet, or of récit to discours, or in some other terms; though it should also be kept in mind that, when asked what a story is about, we tend to say not only what happens but also what it concerns.[2]

This chapter will focus on three fictions: In the Heart of the Country (1977, 1978), The Master of Petersburg (1994), and The Childhood of Jesus (2012). Each wrestles with particular varieties of story and of narration, and in each the nature of the story and of its telling are mutually determining. This will become clear, as the chapter proceeds from describing the novels' story-elements (characters and plots) to reading their narrative techniques, via an extended reflection on the peculiar challenges posed by familiar fictions.

'Little Plots'

The novels on which my discussion pivots effectively span the breadth of Coetzee's career, and the stories they relate are quite different. In the Heart of the Country, the second of Coetzee's fictions, tells of a woman, Magda, who lives on a farm in the Karoo, struggling to establish relations of reciprocity, or at least intimacy, first with her father and her father's second wife; next with two farm-servants, Hendrik and Klein Anna; and, finally, with the airmen (or sky gods) who fly above the farm. These efforts end in catastrophe: Magda kills her father, is attacked and raped by Hendrik, and is ignored by the airmen. She remains, at the end, trapped and isolated on the farm. Or so it seems. For Magda's account is often contradictory, not least in describing two distinct occasions of her father's death (murdered with a hatchet in the first, accidentally shot in the second), before presenting him in the final pages as an old man in her care. If this suggests that Magda is delusional, or prone to fantasy, we come to understand that her struggle and failure to escape her confinement are the consequence not simply of a poisoned mind, but of social relations corrupted by histories of colonial domination.

The Master of Petersburg, Coetzee's seventh novel, relates the story of a Russian man who returns to St Petersburg in October 1869, to claim the belongings of his adult stepson, Pavel, who has fallen, or been pushed, to his death. We soon discover that this man is the writer Fyodor Mikhailovich Dostoevsky, who immediately moves into his son's former lodgings and becomes entangled in a relationship with his landlady, Anna Sergeyevna, and her daughter, Matryona. Whilst mourning Pavel's loss, Fyodor Mikhailovich also becomes embroiled in the machinations of a young nihilist, Sergei Nechaev, to whom Pavel had grown close, and who wishes to draw the famous writer into his efforts to foment revolution. Seeking to evade the police and to resist Nechaev's zeal, Fyodor Mikhailovich battles to understand where and how salvation might be achieved, for himself, for Pavel, and for Pavel's generation, even as he finds ways to turn his pain to the profit of storytelling. To these ends, he must take possession of, or allow himself to be possessed by, Nechaev's spiritual derangement.

Finally, *The Childhood of Jesus* offers the story of a man, Simón, and a child, David, who arrive by boat in an unfamiliar land, washed clean of their memories. Trying to establish new lives, they settle in Novilla, a coastal city, where Simón finds work as a stevedore while searching for David's mother. He discovers Inés, whom he believes is the boy's true if not his real mother, and does what he can to care for them both. David, however, is a gifted, wilful, wildly imaginative child who resists any kind of instruction. This makes confrontation inevitable when he is sent to school. After David becomes difficult and disruptive, Novilla's authorities resolve to remove him to a facility for children with special needs, and, ultimately, from the care of his guardians. Refusing to abandon David to an education whose rationality threatens to designate him deficient, even delinquent, and wary of a bureaucracy which is revealed as inhumane, perhaps violent, the unlikely family flees Novilla, seeking a new life in Estrellita.

Different as they are, these stories share certain features. Before turning to these, however, it is worth reflecting on my use here of paraphrase. A tool of criticism often deemed inadequate to the complexity of literary writing and experience because it abstracts only certain elements – especially characters, events, and settings – on its way to delivering judgements on themes and meanings, paraphrase seems to short-circuit plot and point, and to flow counter to the movement of reading. After all, recognizing which characters and events are important requires interpretation; we interpret as we read; and our experiences of reading are shaped by elements that paraphrase tends to ignore, including elements of style, and the horizons of possibility from which works emerge and which shape their effects and meanings.[3] On the other hand, the use of paraphrase is something most readers take for granted. A review without a synopsis would seem deficient, and even scholarly essays, which presume greater familiarity, frequently give summary accounts. Coetzee's critical writings are exemplary: even where he recognizes its limitations – as when he notes that his summary of C. M. van den Heever's *Somer* (1935) deprives 'the characters of the moral colouring the author has given them' – he deploys paraphrase in his reviews and essays as a means of examining, evaluating, and comparing the structure of each 'particular plot' (WW, 84).

We can certainly do something similar with Coetzee's own oeuvre, for even works as different from one another as *In the Heart of the Country, The Master of Petersburg*, and *The Childhood of Jesus* have story-elements in common. In fact, a number of these may be crucial to the sense of Coetzee as a narrative minimalist. To begin with, each is sparsely populated: *In the Heart of the Country* has at most six recurring characters with speaking parts, *The Master of Petersburg* seven, and *The Childhood of Jesus* eleven. Each novel, moreover, revolves around unlikely and somewhat provisional three-person family units (Magda with her father and Hendrik; Fyodor Mikhailovich with Anna Sergeyevna and Matryona; Simón with David and Inés) which are put under pressure by the arrival of ambivalent figures (Magda's stepmother, Klein Anna, Nechaev, Daga) who seek to enter the family, but also to destroy it, if only by supplanting one of its members. In addition, outside the family, there is a threatening institutional presence – neighbours, the police, the educational authorities – sometimes instantiated in a particular character (Maximov, Señor León), and standing in for the power of a coercive community or state.

Without taking this kind of functional analysis too far, it is enough to show that one consistent feature of Coetzee's novels is their relatively small cast. Another such feature, which goes hand-in-hand with this limitation on characters, is a limitation on events. This expresses itself in several ways. First, the stories are simple ones, without parallel or subordinated plots; they follow the actions and interactions of a single set of characters rooted in a single place and time. This is true even of *In the Heart of the Country*, which merely makes explicit the different possibilities that fork from its several junctures, but which, in marking them as mutually exclusive, ensures that we follow only a single track at a time. For example, rather than sustaining parallel plot-lines in which two new wives return simultaneously to the farm (a version of the upstairs/ downstairs narrative), the story of Magda's stepmother must be terminated before that of Klein Anna can begin. Events are limited in another sense too. 'Nothing happens or can be made to happen', Magda complains, and she is right (*IHC*, 78). These novels are hardly chock-full of dramatic incident. Although Fyodor Mikhailovich is pursued by revolutionaries and watched by the police, his story is dominated by the motions of his own consciousness and his interactions with others. Even his confrontations with Nechaev consist mostly of talk. As for *The Childhood of Jesus*, much of the novel is taken up with discussions between Simón and his several interlocutors; or otherwise with Simón's accomplishment of fairly run-of-the-mill tasks: finding an apartment; having a picnic; watching football; visiting the grain store; clearing a blocked toilet; attending a parent-teacher meeting. Which is to say only what readers of Coetzee's novels will already know: that if the question 'what happens?' is challenging, it is not because we struggle to enumerate their significant events. Nor are his stories ones of suspense, sudden revelation, happy coincidence, or mounting drama. They trace arcs of shallower peaks and troughs, which terminate in irresolution and ambiguity, and never in success, rapture, release.

Since both his characters and plots seem curtailed, impressions of Coetzee's narrative minimalism appear well founded. His stories are *little*, however, not in any absolute sense, but against the background of related works and practices. Against the background, that is, of novels on proximate themes by familiar peers, such as Etienne Leroux's *Seven Days at the Silbersteins* (1967 [1962]) and A. S. Byatt's *Possession* (1990), with their troupes of characters and complex plots.[4] This kind of relationality is essential also to the *meanings* of Coetzee's minimalism and to the unsettling power of his fictions, though in both respects we ought to begin by addressing a more immediate factor: the nature of those few events in Coetzee's fictions that *are* dramatic, or which constitute what Roland Barthes and Seymour Chatman call the stories' 'kernels' – 'nodes or hinges in the structure, branching points which force a movement into one of two (or more) possible paths'.[5]

Frequently, these are acts of violence, as is readily apparent in the story of *In the Heart of the Country*, where the killings and rapes constitute the principal incidents. But even in those fictions in which violent acts are somewhat displaced, because they concern peripheral figures or happen out of sight, they remain important to the plot's development. Thus, in *The Master of Petersburg*, the story begins with Pavel's death, and proceeds via Ivanov's murder and Katri's capture and suicide, before it ends with the distant vision of the city aflame. In *The Childhood of Jesus*, death again appears to be the premise of the story (several passages indicate that Simón and David are recently deceased), and the dramatic incidents affecting the characters and their trajectories include Daga's attack on Álvaro, Marciano's fatal and Simón's near-fatal accidents, and David's removal to and escape from the reputedly brutal Punta Arenas, with its barbed wire, beatings, and boys carrying knives.

When something finally happens in these fictions, then, it often entails violence or the threat of violence. This continuity in theme makes Coetzee's writing not only spare but stark – strong, powerful – and is related to his persistent preoccupation with bodily suffering and death. As far as his broader orientations are concerned, however, it is significant that in each case the particular moments of violence that drive and punctuate the stories are conditioned by and symptomatic of environments that are somehow repressive, or in which social relations have been damaged or made inhumane. That is, these acts testify to worlds from which something has gone missing or been liquidated.

This is all too clear with *In the Heart of the Country*, which addresses a context of colonial domination, and also with *The Master of Petersburg*, whose violent events are directly related to a contest between an oppressive imperial regime and revolutionaries who act without regard for their own lives or those of others. In *The Childhood of Jesus*, Novilla may seem a model city, providing all of its citizens with their essential needs – shelter, food, transport, entertainment, education, medical care – yet, apart from the fact that inequalities persist (life in the Blocks is different from life at La Residencia) it is precisely its rationalized, bureaucratic character that makes the city inhospitable to exceptional children and unsanctioned desires. It is a world at once orderly and insensitive, in which civility masks an apathy regarding human suffering, and frustrated libidinal energies threaten to spill out and over.

In spite of their obvious and great differences, then, these several fictions exhibit both structural and thematic continuities: a tendency to make stories that are relatively simple and compact, and that are nevertheless concerned with substantial and difficult matters: the causes and consequences of a damaged life; the possibility for and means of recovery; the meaning of care and the nature of need and its place in a properly human society. If we are again prepared to risk exorbitant abstraction, we might even say that each of these stories turns on the desire for recognition and salvation, the desire to be seen and to be saved, or, rather, to be saved by being seen.[6] And that, in each, this desire is stifled by conditions of existence which give rise to passages of violence that are always of dramatic significance, but never cathartic.

Familiar Fictions

Coetzee's anecdote in *Here and Now* eulogizes the inexorably eclipsed craft of the storyteller, but also expresses ambivalence about this craft: since the realm of 'pure invention' is entered in a sleep-state, and thus shadowed by automatism, the work of the imagination seems habitual rather than deliberate. A related tension runs through Coetzee's fictions, which frequently characterize storytelling as a valuable means of self-formation, even salvation; and stories embedded in a literary culture as vital resources for such projects. Yet stories of this kind are also marked as potentially restrictive and damaging, because of the meanings they encode or because their deeply worn grooves prove difficult to escape.

This ambivalence is apparent in all three narratives we are considering, though it is most extreme in Magda's. Determined to find stories that will save her, Magda is hemmed in by those which, while freely available, seem familiar and therefore predictable. The most pressing, and the stories to which she is most resistant, are associated with the 'pastoral' (*IHC*, 77). 'I am not a happy peasant', she insists, 'I am a miserable black virgin, and my story is my story, even if it is a dull black blind stupid miserable story' (*IHC*, 5). Yet even this 'miserable story' is compromised by its predictability:

> The story of my rage and its dire sequel: am I truly going to climb into this vehicle and close my eyes and be carried downstream . . . ? What automatism is this, what liberation is it going to bring me, and without liberation what is the point of my story? (*IHC*, 5)

In the end, however, to complete her tale, Magda cannot help but concede. She surrenders initially to roles offered by the most foundational fictions – the 'castaway', the 'ugly sister in a story in which only Cinderella is saved' (*IHC*, 143), 'the witch of fable' (*IHC*, 146–7) – and ultimately to a variant of precisely that 'bucolic comedy' she had most wished to evade, the version of the pastoral which leaves her guarding her father in 'his dotage' (*IHC*, 46).

The challenge for Fyodor Mikhailovich, who identifies himself not as a novelist, but as a writer of 'Stories', of 'Story-books', is somewhat different, though it also turns on the ambivalent character of familiar fictions (*MP*, 144). Believing it his task to find 'the true words' with which to give Pavel a voice, he has an intimation that these 'may be waiting for him in one of the old ballads' (*MP*, 111). He is therefore pleased to discover that 'the old stories are coming back, stories he heard from his grandmother' (*MP*, 126). But not all tales are worth telling or keeping. He distinguishes, for example, between stories and 'parables', because 'Stories can be about other people: you are not obliged to find a place for yourself in them' (*MP*, 183–4). Life-giving stories, he implies, must have autonomy, something lacking in both the 'Siberian story' Pavel has written, and the 'story' of the 'spread of the spirit among the servants' which he has merely outlined in his diaries (*MP*, 216, 218). Fyodor Mikhailovich longs 'to breathe life' into the former (*MP*, 194), and declares of the latter that it is not 'a story' at all, but 'a fable, an allegory', precisely because it has 'No life of its own, no centre. No spirit' (*MP*, 218).

In *The Childhood of Jesus*, Simón is similarly sceptical of stories that are either dead and deadening, or which frame David's sense of himself in ways he finds troubling. He is dismissive of the inane classroom tales favoured by Señor León – 'Stories about vacations' (*CJ*, 255), and 'about Juan and María and what they did at the seaside' (*CJ*, 294) – and upset by the 'Third Brother stories' that Inés relates at bedtime (*CJ*, 173–5). But Simón does not outlaw storytelling. Rather, he encourages David's enthusiasm whilst trying to give a different shape to the boy's self-conception, by telling stories of his own choosing (including that of the mythical twins Castor and Pollux), and by presenting him with *An Illustrated Children's Don Quixote*.

In all three novels, then, stories promise liberation but threaten to constrain. They may be enlivening resources for understanding the self and the world, but they may also obscure the world and deprive the self of autonomy. This ambivalence, which is especially acute when stories are in some sense foundational to a literary tradition or culture, makes it especially striking that Coetzee draws heavily on stories of precisely this kind in conceiving the situations of these three novels. He cannibalizes story-elements from the South African genres of the farm novel and *plaasroman* in the case of *In the Heart of the Country*; from the life and oeuvre of Dostoevsky in the case of *The Master of Petersburg*; and from the Gospels in the case of *The Childhood of Jesus*.

These borrowings are clearly signalled by Magda, in her references to the pastoral. Fyodor Mikhailovich is less aware of his origins – he is confused, for example, by the familiarity of a scene drawn directly from *Crime and Punishment* (1866)[7] – but *The Master of Petersburg* openly re-frames the source and composition of an especially significant episode in Dostoevsky's *Demons* (1872; also translated as *The Devils*, and *The Possessed*), whilst alluding to other yet-to-be written novels, especially *The Brothers Karamazov* (1880). Likewise, in *The Childhood of Jesus*, although the inhabitants of Novilla seem wholly ignorant of the Bible, the novel's language, characters, and episodes recall the New Testament. The 'family of David' (*CJ*, 309), for example, consists of a small boy, a man who is not his father, a woman turned 'from virgin into mother' (*CJ*, 109), and an 'unwashed young man' named Juan (*CJ*, 322); and their 'flight' to Estrellita parallels that of the Holy Family into Egypt (*CJ*, 312).[8]

These novels thus confront structurally the questions they pose thematically: how does one respond to the demand for stories as well as the demands of stories? How does one exploit the semantic richness of the most familiar fictions, whilst evading their confinements? In all three, this confrontation revolves around particular features of narration, and around style more broadly. Before considering each case, however, it is helpful to frame a general principle underpinning Coetzee's conception of narration. To do this, we turn not to his critical writings, which, in spite of their tremendous scope, tend to address these questions only obliquely or in passing, but to 'Hero and Bad Mother in Epic', a computer poem Coetzee began composing in the late 1960s, and completed by the mid 1970s.[9]

The poem consists of lines that initially seem inventively metaphorical, even surreal. This is its opening stanza:

> dusk seeps up the entrail of the seaborn nude
> the vegetable sleeps in its circle
> the bedroom drowses
> the casino is swathed in tidal melancholia
> the nude awaits the hero (ll. 1–5)

These lines, however, originate in a random process: a program designed by Coetzee to generate sentences by combining terms from a limited lexicon. This randomness becomes apparent as we read the poem and notice the repetition and recombination of particular words (in subsequent stanzas, for example, 'tidal' qualifies 'nude', 'goose', 'entrail', and 'casino'). But if this prompts a diminished hermeneutic investment in its striking phrases, the work itself does not collapse into nonsense. On the contrary, we remain able to discern its story, which is simple enough: the hero of the title sets off on adventure; seeks out a villain; acquires a magical agent; vanquishes the villain; and returns home.

How is this possible? For three reasons: first, because the title provides important information about the central characters (Hero, Bad Mother) and about the nature of story (Epic); second, because, no matter the confusing and to some extent meaningless noun phrases, the poem's verb phrases – and thus the story's actions or events – remain clear, distinct, and coherently arranged; third, because the pattern of the story is deeply familiar, even paradigmatic. We might identify it, indeed, as a version of the folktales analysed in Vladimir Propp's *Morphology of the Folktale* (1928), a text Coetzee read whilst working towards his PhD and later used in his teaching; or of the 'monomyth' described in Joseph Campbell's *The Hero with a Thousand Faces* (1949).

One of the poem's insights, then, is that when story-types are deeply embedded in a culture, their underlying structures can be elicited by the subtlest promptings of a fragment, even a rhythm. These are the kinds of stories we tell and hear without thinking, the kinds that might well seem as if they had been produced by a machine. But 'Hero and Bad Mother in Epic' is also something of a riposte to structuralist accounts such as those offered by Propp and Campbell. For it ultimately lays bare the necessity of an organizing narrative consciousness. Such a consciousness is implicit in the coherent, prosodic arrangement of the verb phrases and lines, since this exceeds the capacity of the program, but the moment of its true revelation comes at the poem's climax, where we suddenly encounter a new arrangement – three rows and three columns – at the centre of which, capitalized, is the single and singular occurrence of the word MOONBURST:

the philatelist	the bedroom	the spider
the casino	MOONBURST	the goose
the matriarch	the sword	the fiction (ll. 58–60)

In this moment of orchestrated semantic density the opaque surface of the poem is pierced. For the studied meaningfulness of this composition is impossible without the intervention of a narrative consciousness which is both aperture and source of illumination, both a window onto the poem and the light shining through it, a narrative consciousness whose appearance throws into relief the automatism as well as the purposeful design of its preceding parts, making this a poem *about* the mechanics of storytelling, and not simply *of* them.

Stepping back from 'Hero and Bad Mother in Epic', we might say that it attests to an awareness that narration itself can become automatic, falling 'into the rhythms of storytelling. Like a piston-engine, incapable of any other motion' (*MP*, 72). We might say that it attests also to a conviction that the appropriate perspective on and arrangement of even the most familiar, clichéd story-elements can free itself of such rhythms, and thereby liberate the meanings of these stories. No less important, such a perspective and arrangement can also liberate the meanings of these stories' *constraints*, revealing what it is that familiar fictions necessarily efface, and why.

In these respects, the poem is something of a companion-piece not only to early novels such as *Dusklands* (1974) and *In the Heart of the Country* (which thematize the mechanical unfolding of particular generic plots), but also to Coetzee's early critical remarks regarding the absence of a central narrating intelligence in the novels of South African contemporaries, whether by accident, as in Yvonne Burgess's *The Strike* (1975), or by design, as in the naturalist novels of Sipho Sepamla and Mongane Wally Serote.[10] But, without being made so explicit, this same awareness and conviction are also apparent in several of Coetzee's more recent critical writings, such as his review of Philip Roth's *Nemesis* (2010), or his account of W. G. Sebald's *Austerlitz* (2001), where the (question of the) narrator is given the last word (*LS*, 43; *GS*, 190).

Decisions about narration have also been central to the ways in which Coetzee has drawn on the resources of familiar fictions whilst evading their limitations; central, moreover, to his own evolving practice, and to the changing inflections of his spare lyricism. His novels therefore demand a peculiar alertness to the entanglement of story and storytelling. This is not simply a matter of identifying the narrator with a set of norms and positions likely to influence the account; but of attending to the subtle means by which features of narration – the extent and frequency with which events are recounted; the person, proximity, and epistemic character of the narrator; its relationship with the work's central consciousness – interact with one another, and with the story.

Storytelling

In the Heart of the Country is oppressively claustrophobic, an atmosphere which speaks of entrapment in a brute reality and in a local variety of the pastoral. This is Magda's experience as well as our own, and conditions her anxiety that she 'will dwindle and expire ... unless she has at least a thin porridge of event to live on' (*IHC*, 25). Prompted by this anxiety, she is compelled to 'pluck the incident after incident after incident whose little explosions' will sustain her (*IHC*, 46). And though she occasionally protests ('I do not see why the story of our lives should have to be interesting' (*IHC*, 64)) and doubts her capacity for narration ('Lyric is my medium, not chronicle' (*IHC*, 77)), she ultimately recognizes what is required: 'through the agency of conflict with my father I hope to lift myself out of the endless middle of meditation on unattached existence into a true agon with crisis and resolution' (*IHC*, 67–8).

Why this agon must entail the most exorbitant acts of violence lies beyond Magda's ken, an ignorance which itself ensures that she remains trapped, along with her readers. Indeed, the oppressive atmosphere only intensifies over the course of her narrative. How and to what end is this achieved? On both counts, the work's repetitiveness is important, a characteristic discernible at the level of words and phrases, but especially at the level of events. Even a minimal account of the novel's action-sequences would have to include two occasions on which a new bride arrives on the farm (Magda's stepmother, Klein Anna); two occasions on which Magda kills her father (murder, manslaughter); and two occasions on which she seeks unsuccessfully to establish reciprocal relations with others (Hendrik and Klein Anna, the airmen). Within these action-sequences, moreover, events are narrated several times over. Sometimes this is because the action in question requires several attempts, as when Magda tries to rouse Hendrik from his drunken stupor, or when she struggles to bury her father. At others, the events themselves appear to be singular, but are described repeatedly, as with the scene of Magda's rape.

The first and third forms of narrative repetition, coupled with Coetzee's odd use of numbered passages (266 in total), have led to the impression that either Magda is mad or the novel anti-realist. There are indications, however, that the narrative is often merely considering its rather limited stock of options ('Or perhaps' is one of its chief refrains). In other moments, it indulges in stories of the future (Magda's visit to the seaside) and past (Magda's siblings) whose grammatical mood is subjunctive or conditional. We might therefore think of the novel as an experiment in modality, or the different gradations of fictional irreality. But whichever way we interpret the ontological status of the novel's repetitions, we cannot escape their effect, which is to reinforce the sense that its repertoire, and thus its world, are narrowly enclosed.

Narrative repetition is also a means of disclosing the meaning of this narrowness. For the singular events that are recounted several times, and on which the novel's unfolding therefore seems to catch – the death of Magda's father, Magda's discovery of Jakob and Anna's absence, Magda's rape – speak directly to the origin of her solitude: a world laid bare by violence and domination, in which the possibility of relations of reciprocity has been extinguished. This is the truth that the novel forces us to confront, but which is kept from Magda precisely because she remains a creature of the kind of story from which she emerges, and thus of its limitations. As In the Heart of the Country reveals, these limitations include a blindness to those systems of racial and economic exploitation that ground the stories of South African farms and their 'happy peasants'.

Yet, if it is the achievement of the novel's style to make us feel the truth of this bare world, and of the constraints of the plaasroman, story and narration are only two elements of this style, and repetition only one aspect of narration. Other features contribute to the novel's taut intensity: its pacing; the way its narrative is tightly packed into its numbered sections; its rhythmic modulation between stark and lyrical passages; and its enclosure within a single consciousness – a character narrator who speaks in the first person and, for the most part, in the present tense, as if relating experiences as they occur. It is the interaction of all these features that is essential (if not sufficient) for producing the particular effects and meanings of *In the Heart of the Country*.[11]

This is worth keeping in mind when thinking of Coetzee's other novels, where the use of a first-person character narrator has different consequences; or which make use of external narrators who speak in the third person but whose focalization, or point of view, is closely tethered to the work's central consciousness. In *The Master of Petersburg*, Coetzee uses this kind of third-person narrator for the first time. The focalizer here is Fyodor Mikhailovich, though the narrator is so exceptionally close to him that it seems as if we are reading a first-person narration that has simply undergone a grammatical transformation. This proximity begs the question: what is gained by so limited a shift in perspective?

To begin with, the use of the third person is vital in characterizing the distinctive structure and motions of Fyodor Mikhailovich's consciousness. This is clear in passages such as the following, which narrate the aftermath of his epileptic seizures:

> When he wakes it is into a darkness so dense that he can feel it pressing upon his eyeballs. He has no idea where he is, no idea who he is. He is a wakefulness, a consciousness, that is all ... Be calm, says this consciousness, addressing itself, trying to quell its own panic. (*MP*, 69)

> When he comes back he has again lost all sense of who he is. He knows the word *I*, but as he stares at it it becomes as enigmatic as a rock in the middle of a desert. (*MP*, 71)

These passages describe and produce the effect of a bewilderment that is experienced by a vacated consciousness returning to itself as a self. It is an effect almost impossible to achieve if narrated in the first person. We see this if we consider the following hypothetical sentences:

I have no idea where I am, no idea who I am.

*When I come back I have again lost all sense of who I am. I know the word *I*, but as I stare at it it becomes as enigmatic as a rock.*

Quite apart from the oddity of saying 'I' whilst denying knowledge of its meaning, such instances of the first person convey a confident singularity that belies any sense of the self's incoherence.

Fyodor Mikhailovich's fits may be extreme, but they are not different in kind from other motions of his mind that entail the unbidden appearance, as if from elsewhere, of thoughts, moods, memories, and fantasies.

A substantial portion of the narrative is taken up with such experiences. They include the 'Memories like wisps of smoke ... Visions that come and go, swift, ephemeral' which make Fyodor Mikhailovich feel that he is 'not in control' (MP, 53), as well as such imaginings as his pornographic fantasy of Anna Sergeyevna, in which he is split into both actor and observer, becoming an object of his own voyeurism (MP, 131). Collectively, accounts of these mental occurrences produce the effect of a consciousness entered, taken over, or ruptured, and this effect very much depends on the narrator's avoidance of singular pronouns in the first person (I, me, my, mine), as much as on its use of singular pronouns in the third (he, him, his).

The link between Fyodor Mikhailovich's fits and his disorienting memories and visions is made explicit towards the novel's conclusion, when he wonders 'whether seizure is any longer the right word, whether the word has not all along been possession' (MP, 213). For the novel uses 'possession' to designate the kind of unboundedness and displacement of the self that is necessary for both writing and reading, and also to figure the moral derangement and psychic damage caused by oppression and resentment, that is, by the violence one suffers as well as the violence one inflicts. Ultimately, possession will also be used to understand how this damage might be redressed. It is by inhabiting Pavel, and by allowing Pavel to be inhabited in turn by the 'dull, resentful, and murderous spirit' of Nechaev (MP, 44), that Fyodor Mikhailovich attempts to realize the task to which he ultimately accedes: 'To live where Pavel died. To live in Russia and hear the voices of Russia murmuring within him. To hold it all within him: Russia, Pavel, death' (MP, 235).

By this late stage, the form of the novel's narration has itself produced a powerful sense of what it means to live with a consciousness that is intimately layered, and at once opaque to itself and open to the occupation of alien thoughts and ways of being. We know also that the notion of such a consciousness is anathema to Nechaev, and, indeed to Maximov, for the same reason that both insist on treating Fyodor Mikhailovich's stories as parables: a certain literal-mindedness and gross materialism that are themselves consequences of their society's psychic derangement, and which make both men resistant to Fyodor Mikhailovich's talk of spirits and possession, as well as to 'Pavel's ... old-fashioned language of the heart' (MP, 196). And it is precisely because they refuse to contemplate possession that they must remain possessed.

The use of a tightly focalized third-person narration is thus central to the meanings of The Master of Petersburg, though other features of style are also significant, not least its own use of a language of the heart and the soul.[12] But if Fyodor Mikhailovich is aware of the necessity of conceiving a self more complicated than the one permitted by Nechaev and Maximov, there is something important that he does not know, and cannot know, precisely because, like Magda, he remains a creature of the stories from which he is derived, and of their limitations. He is, after all, a version less of the real-life Russian author than a kind of back-formation from his fictions (something indicated by Coetzee's distortions of Dostoevsky's biography, the most striking of which is the invention of his stepson's violent death). And while Dostoevsky's fictions certainly provide resources for conceiving the damage caused by manichean struggle, they also ensure that the character Fyodor Mikhailovich cannot explain this struggle otherwise than as a symptom of an inherent Russian illness, or the inexorable conflict between generations. It is why he cannot see, ultimately, where Nechaev's 'lines of force' lead: to the material, structural conditions of inequality, poverty, and violent domination (*MP*, 181).

Turning to *The Childhood of Jesus* allows us further to clarify the extent to which narration achieves its effects in relation to the other features of a work's style. For this very recent fiction uses the same strictly focalized third-person, present-tense narrator that we find in *The Master of Petersburg*, but with quite different results. This is for at least two reasons. First, more than in any previous fiction, the narrative of *The Childhood of Jesus* is dominated by dialogue. Second, and relatedly, it keeps its focalizer's mental and emotional terrain largely out of sight. We occasionally glimpse Simón's doubts and reflections, but his memories, dreams, and fantasies remain mostly hidden. Indeed, if the narrator of *The Master of Petersburg* traverses the layers of Fyodor Mikhalovich's consciousness in a way that produces the impression of total possession (whilst also giving those layers articulation), the narrator of *The Childhood of Jesus* seems to be perched on Simón's shoulder, seeing what he sees, hearing what he hears, occasionally knowing what he knows, but never being able to experience his innermost moods and longings.

This lack is not entirely unmotivated. New arrivals in Novilla have been 'washed clean' of their memories (*CJ*, 116), 'appetites', and 'desires' (*CJ*, 36), and learn to conduct 'all human relations' in a 'beginner's Spanish' which inhibits the expression of their 'heart's feelings' (*CJ*, 127). They are therefore deprived of much that is essential to a complex internal life. On the other hand, Simón views himself as 'the exception' precisely because his own appetites and desires remain urgent (*CJ*, 77). He is dissatisfied with the 'diet of bread and water and bean paste' (*CJ*, 36–7), and a philosophy concerned only with 'tables and chairs' (*CJ*, 283). Simón, therefore, seems to retain the materials for a rich inner life, but as to its actual existence, this is something we are told about, rather than shown, inferring it mostly from what he and others say. It is Simón, for example, who describes to Ana and Álvaro respectively his longings for 'beefsteak with mashed potatoes and gravy' (*CJ*, 36–7) and a philosophy that 'shakes one' (*CJ*, 283). Elsewhere, it is left to Ana to make explicit his sexual desire (*CJ*, 37), Elena to express his need for 'storms of passion' (*CJ*, 75), and Álvaro to remark his 'bad mood' (*CJ*, 128). When the narrator *is* permitted to describe Simón's feeling-states, this is often in retrospect, as with 'the reckless, bitter mood that has plagued him since he gave up the child' (*CJ*, 162).

This narrative strategy – indicating the existence of Simón's more visceral affective and reflective states whilst denying access to them – makes his consciousness seem blocked off, occluded. More even than this, it communicates Simón's own experience of Novilla, his sense that 'things do not have their due weight here', that the

> music we hear lacks weight. Our lovemaking lacks weight. The food we eat, our dreary diet of bread, lacks substance – lacks the substantiality of animal flesh, with all the gravity of bloodletting and sacrifice behind it. Our very words lack weight, these Spanish words that do not come from the heart.   (*CJ*, 77)

For, by giving prominence to dialogue that is itself cool and rational, and by depriving us of more immediate access to Simón's moods, feelings, fantasies, and visions, *The Childhood of Jesus* compels us to inhabit a strangely flat, 'bloodless' world, an etherized world, deficient in feeling (*CJ*, 36).

Oddly enough, this sense is compounded by an occlusion that works in the opposite direction, blocking from its characters what the novel's title calls to the attention of its readers: the many biblical phrases and episodes that echo across the narrative. These echoes create the impression of hidden depths, of that 'doubleness' (*CJ*, 182) that Simón associates with stories, and with *Don Quixote* (1605/ 1615) especially, as well as with human nature (*CJ*, 157), but which he believes is missing even from Álvaro and Elena, who do 'not see any doubleness in the world, any difference between the way things seem and the way things are' (*CJ*, 76).

To be clear, this narrative 'doubleness' is not the kind of one-to-one correlation with the Gospels that would convert the novel into a parable. It draws as much on non-canonical accounts of the life of Jesus (such as the Infancy Gospel of Thomas) as on the canonical Gospels, and the sources of resonance are often multiple and contradictory. For example, Simón's relationship to David may parallel that of Joseph to Jesus, but his words and actions also recall the apostle Simon Peter, as when, apologizing for allowing David to be taken to Punta Arenas, the novel alludes both to the apostle's failure to watch over Jesus in the Garden of Gethsemane, and his subsequent confrontation with the Temple guards: 'I slept while I should have watched', says Simón, and 'I will borrow a sword' (CJ, 287).

This doubleness throws into relief and thus intensifies the sense of Novilla's flatness, by emphasizing the richness it lacks. It also communicates the truth of what is at stake in Simón's desire to cling to 'the memory of having a memory' (CJ, 117), 'the feel of residence in a body with a past, a body soaked in its past' (CJ, 169). Some of these effects can be illustrated if we look again at Simón's use of the words *substance, flesh, bread, blood-letting*, and *sacrifice* to designate Novilla's weightlessness. These words may seem airy and ephemeral to him, but, for any likely readers of the novel, their concatenation is peculiarly resonant and charged, recalling the story that is most foundational to all literary cultures originating in Europe, and one through which profound suffering comes to be understood as profound passion. This invests Simón's declamation against Novilla's bloodlessness with sudden and massive weight.

Both occlusions – of the focalizer's 'inner voices' for readers (CJ, 125) and of the narrative's 'double nature' for characters (CJ, 157) – thus contribute to a style that passes judgement on a certain notion of the good life, and indeed of salvation, as a rationalized, bureaucratically managed existence in which the needs for survival are met, but those of a fully human life are ignored. A salvation, in other words, which misrecognizes the absence of desire as its sublation, and the termination of appetite as the negation of suffering. For the style of the novel itself reveals that the costs of such an existence include the liquidation of the passions and thus of a certain form of unreasonable, devotional love; and the loss of that doubleness which is vital to an enlarged notion of ourselves, to our capacity for imagining the world other than it is, and to storytelling.

Another cost of this existence is the effacement of deeply embedded stories, whose resources cannot be tapped unless they are first acknowledged. In this regard, it is important to understand that Simón's total ignorance of his own fictionality and of the story whose elements resonate with his own is not incidental, but a necessary consequence of that story's constraints. That is, Simón cannot suspect his origins because, inasmuch as the farm novel is blind to black labour and Dostoevsky's fictions to the material conditions of social antagonism, it is in the nature of holy writ to deny that the power and even truth of stories may be a matter of rhetoric rather than revelation. Scripture and its creatures (now including Simón) cannot know, therefore, how much of the richness of the Gospels' story is acquired precisely through its many repetitions and amplifications, however contradictory, apocryphal, or heretical; through its being a story, in other words, that breeds other stories, rather than putting them to an end.

What each of these novels makes apparent, then, is that, though certain of the materials of story and of storytelling might certainly be carried across the bounds of time, place, language, and literary culture, they remain inexorably subject to that process of thickening that David Lurie bemoans in *Disgrace* (1999): through long and repeated use they lose 'their articulations, their articulateness, their articulatedness' (*Dis*, 117). To be made newly supple and dynamic, they must be freshly exercised, their elements and joints exposed and re-articulated. And this requires an awareness not only that a story and the manner of its telling are mutually determining, but also, crucially, that the meaning of any given feature of narration, indeed any feature of style, is highly localized and relational, emerging always within a particular horizon of possibilities, and in the course of a particular work and of its truth's conveyance.

Notes

1. It chimes also with the compositional practices that have been revealed in Coetzee's notebooks, now at the HRC. I am grateful to Michelle Kelly for pointing out that, unlike the manuscript drafts previously available at Harvard's Houghton Library, these attest not only to Coetzee's assiduous revisions, but also to a play of imagination and invention.
2. These terms originate, respectively, in the work of the Russian formalists Viktor Shklovsky and Vladimir Propp, and of the French structuralist Gérard Genette (see Further Reading). It is having a 'point', according to Ruth Ronen, that 'turns an action-structure into a *story*'. 'Paradigm Shift in Plot Models: An Outline of the History of Narratology', *Poetics Today*, 11.4 (1990), 817–42.
3. The critique of paraphrase is associated with New Critics such as Wayne Booth, Cleanth Brooks, and John Crowe Ransom. For recent ripostes by Helen Thaventhiran and Patrick Fessenbecker, see Further Reading.
4. The former re-works the South African tradition of the *plaasroman*. The latter uses 'possession' as a means of reflecting on what it means to inhabit, and to be inhabited by, the minds and voices of others. Of Byatt, Coetzee has remarked that she 'aspires to a large canvas, wide cultural relevance . . ., and, by no means least, plenitude of characters' (*SS*, 186).
5. Seymour Chatman, *Story and Discourse: Narrative Structure in Fiction and Film* (Ithaca: Cornell University Press, 1978), p. 53.
6. This means of salvation needn't be limited to human interactions. In his overview of Juan Ramón Jiménez's *Platero and I* (1914), Coetzee writes that the donkey 'Platero comes into existence as an individual – as a character, in fact – with a life and a world of experience of his own at the moment when the man whom I call his owner, the crazy man, sees that Platero sees him, and in that act of seeing acknowledges him as equal' (*LE*, 131).
7. Margaret Scanlan identifies a number of occasions on which Coetzee's novel reveals that his fictional Fyodor Mikhailovich is only vaguely familiar with works which the real Dostoevsky had completed by 1869 (Further Reading).

8. For helpful discussions of the novel's biblical allusions, see Urmila Seshagiri's review and J. U. Jacobs's article (Further Reading).
9. J. M. Coetzee, 'Hero and Bad Mother in Epic, a Poem', *Staffrider*, 1.1 (1978), 36–7. Extended reflections on narration can be found in Coetzee's essays on Beckett's *Murphy* (*DP*, 31–8), and on Kafka's 'The Burrow' (see *DP*, 210–32).
10. For Coetzee's review of *The Strike*, see *DP* 91–3. His remarks on South African naturalism can be found in J. M. Coetzee, 'Grubbing for Ideological Implications: A Clash (More or Less) with J. M. Coetzee', with Alan Thorold and Richard Wicksteed, *Sjambok* [1981], 3–5.
11. I give a more detailed account of repetition and these other aspects of narration in *J. M. Coetzee and the Politics of Style* (Cambridge: Cambridge University Press, 2014).
12. This language of the heart and soul is analysed in Chapter Five of my *J. M. Coetzee and the Politics of Style*.

4

DAVID JAMES

Styles: *Dusklands, Age of Iron, Disgrace, The Schooldays of Jesus*

'Style here is style as consolation, style as redemption, the grace of language' (*DP*, 47). The 'here' in Coetzee's cross hairs happens to be Flaubert, who famously envisioned the ideal novel as 'dependent on nothing'. Buttressed by aesthetic integrity alone, such a work would be 'held together by the internal strength of its style'.[1] Flaubert's vision of style as fiction's essential, binding element is nothing if not consoling; in this idealist vision, the novel's formal physiology becomes virtually self-sufficient. For his part, Coetzee approves of the fact that Beckett seemed suspicious of such compensatory ideals. But might this vaunted circumspection, this vigilance toward style's mitigating or substitutive effects, become in itself a comforting if not self-satisfying attitude for a writer to adopt? Is there not something reassuring about rejecting the allure of rhetorical finesse, particularly when this rejection – as a conscious, creatively sober act – also promotes the novelist who dodges the decoys of adornment? After all, Beckett would gain plenty of prestige as a master chronicler of disconsolation, precisely through his 'repudiation' of the allegedly redemptive proceeds of expressive elegance and semantic transparency (*DP*, 47). What could be more self-affirming, then, than the novelist's dignified veto of style's myriad 'temptations'?

Even though Coetzee doesn't entertain this paradox, it's one that nonetheless shadows his own career-long wariness of the magnetism of style. Committed to economy, the renowned leanness of his language underwrites his continued notoriety. Dedicated temperance has supplied Coetzee's fiction with creative energy and cultural capital, even though aspects of what some critics have seen as the aridity of his later prose – and, recently, of his settings too – have come to divide opinion.[2] If anything, he has found a good deal of sustenance in what he calls an ethos of 'thrift': austere though this sounds, over the years his fiction has attracted considerable praise for its lissom alliance of tonal poise and rhetorical parsimony. 'Spare prose and a spare, thrifty world', admits Coetzee: 'it's an unattractive part of my makeup that has exasperated people who have had to share their lives with me' (*DP*, 20).

While expressional thriftiness has become an iconic feature of his fiction, it's worth recalling that Coetzee was himself an exacting scholar of style well before he started writing novels. Rigorously systematic in its microscopic commentaries on discrete syntactic components, Coetzee's brand of 'stylo-statistics' combined 'two of his academic interests', as David Attwell points out, namely 'Beckett and mathematics (or computer science)'.[3] With this approach, Coetzee could inspect 'rhythmic groups', 'phonological or syntactic equivalences', or 'the structure of couplings underlying' a given paragraph (*DP*, 46, 47). Such were his subjects in the 1973 essay with which I began, where Coetzee observes *Murphy* 'repudiating the religion of style'. Warding off the 'seductions' of gracefulness, this 1938 novel entered a 'battleground' with rhythm, cadence, and euphony; some fifteen years later, *Watt* would fall prey (according to Coetzee) to style's 'lulling plangencies', as though Beckett's resistance to 'the grace of language' had buckled under the weight of 'narcissistic reverie' (*DP*, 47). The early Beckett's prudence, then, receives a firm endorsement. Yet these qualitative observations from Coetzee sit side by side with the more impartial job of grammatical classification and description. Taking our cue from this kind of approach, we could set about anatomizing clausal patterns with analytical exactitude and dispassion; or we might go systematically in search of some compositional logic in a writer who, in Coetzee's phrase, 'uses the same syntactic operation again and again', thereby 'signaling a particular habit of making sense of his [*sic*] material' (*DP*, 147). But the method has its drawbacks. Whatever insights we glean about a work's 'logical or epistemological matrices' or 'underlying' rationale are obtained at the risk of circumventing less quantifiable features of, and reactions to, literary expression (*DP*, 147, 151). This captures something of the critical double-sidedness of our affective involvement with any style, of course, be it spare or convoluted, lean or ornamental: a type of involvement whose effects remain elusive and unpredictable, resistant to stable classification, though not, in the end, completely inimical to qualitative judgement or aesthetic evaluation.

Such is the slipperiness of style itself as an object of study – if indeed we can see it as an 'object' to be caught in critical pincers at all. Perspectives on what style is and what the term covers will always differ, depending on whether we're speaking about the reception of a work (the impression we form of a style through our affective involvement with expression) or its imaginative production (what specific stylistic innovations or recurrent configurations disclose about a writer's commitments and artistic aspirations). As a result, from a reader's perspective we may legitimately wonder how our variable *experience* of style can be pinned down, elucidated, still less explained, by the methodical procedures of stylistics. And from the writer's perspective, style's unpredictable repercussions may not be the result of deliberate planning, despite what novelists themselves claim about the correlation between conscious designs and finished works. Yet the opposite may also be true: though it seems too fuzzy for meticulous dissection, too mercurial at times to be aligned with authorial motives, style is nevertheless bound up with the aesthetic *identity* of a piece of writing, including the kinds of reaction – whether strenuous, sumptuous, arid, or disturbing – we might expect writers we know well to provoke in us. Which doesn't mean that style has consistent habits or other behavioural norms. What could be further from the truth for a writer as wily in his creative departures as J. M. Coetzee? But despite his variety, for want of a better term – a variety in tenor and topic that will become apparent as this essay arcs across his career – it would be odd to dismiss the extent to which our admiration of Coetzee's work may be enhanced by our attention to microelements of his prose that we come to recognize over time as quintessentially his own. Indeed, recognizing our recognition of his radically metamorphosing style is all part of the critical pleasure of working through his sizeable oeuvre.

Furthermore, precisely because we now have a whole corpus of formal features and transitions to survey in retrospect, it seems impossible to dissociate entirely what Coetzee does as a stylist from how we understand his ethical, literary-historical, and philosophical sensibility as a writer. In what follows, I don't suggest that we try to fasten down such correlations between artist and attitude, or assume that we can use style as a reliable compass of Coetzee's priorities for envisioning alternative destinations for the novel as a cultural form. Rather, I will take a somewhat pragmatic view: particular moments in Coetzee's career can reveal facets of technical development, adjustment, and renovation, without in any sense inhibiting our interpretive freedom when encountering his work's affective impact and politico-ethical consequences. To consider these moments chronologically, texts from my title will each serve not only as apposite examples for unpacking Coetzee's style, but also as critical levers for shifting gear from one level of stylistic analysis to the next. As we do so, we'll break down 'style' into various subunits, in order to consider how it informs the social efficacy and emotional potency of these striking texts: rhetorical aspects of narration that facilitate the critique of imperialism; relations between mode, metre, and genre at the tumultuous crossroads of personal loss and racial violence; the manipulation of perspective, together with the moral reverberations of seemingly incidental modulations in focalization; and strange discrepancies between the damage of events and the graceful language of their expression, offering aesthetic amnesty to the very lyricism from which Coetzee has at times distanced his writing. As the list here suggests, this coverage will inevitably be incomplete. But it will hopefully give some account of the stakes of attending to the most granular properties of Coetzee's prose, even as we grapple with the most philosophically and morally demanding implications of his plots.

The Rhetoric of Imperialism

Coetzee himself is a sober guide to the challenges and opportunities of reading for style. In an essay from 1980, he observed that a 'crucial step' for stylistics is the very 'act of interpretation that allows us to move from the habitual ... pattern to the meaning it signals': from objective, ponderous classification, in other words, to semantic connotation; from anatomizing a work's verbal engineering to accounting for its sensuous impact, even if systematic examination is ultimately one component of a full series of experiences solicited by that work (*DP*, 148). Undoubtedly, Coetzee's enthusiasm for the systematicity of stylistics – in its most pragmatic, taxonomical form at least – did eventually wane. David Attwell remarks that 'over time' Coetzee became 'less and less confident about what kind of knowledge the field's scientific methods could deliver about a text, over and above what we might already know intuitively'. And it was this gradual move against critical rationalism that complemented in spirit Coetzee's 'entry into fiction' the year after his 1973 Beckett essay with the publication of *Dusklands*. In this structurally arresting, emotively disturbing novel, Coetzee integrates 'anti-rationalism' into the text's formal 'revolt', as Attwell describes it, 'against ... realism's unadventurous epistemology'. Dramatically too the narrative participates in a critique of colonial expansion, domination, and possession as rational, self-legitimating virtues of efficient imperial progress. Across this frequently traumatic and rebarbative debut, Coetzee initiates what would become a lasting 'connection between writing and self-confrontation'. *Dusklands* turned out to be uncompromisingly personal to the core: a fundamentally 'angry work', in Attwell's phrase, the book bore the signature of 'a young author who is angry about his origins, and angry about the role that his origins have assigned him in the world'.[4]

Anger certainly drives the novel's 'The Vietnam Project', written by a specialist in psychological warfare, Eugene Dawn, who we soon discover is psychically dissolving. Brutal testimonies to marital estrangement and professional competition braid with unrelieved self-excavation. Dawn considers himself to be 'an up-and-coming subordinate who will not follow the slow, well-trodden path to the top', flouting in private the managerialism of a 'threatened' 'bureaucrat' named Coetzee (*Dusk*, 5). Yet Dawn does 'not underestimate Coetzee' (*Dusk*, 2), conceding that he would 'prefer his love to his hatred' (*Dusk*, 5). In one of the novel's early instances of textual self-referentiality, this observant supervisor tries to quell Dawn's ambition by lending advice on his prose as a ruse for ensuring his 'proposals will get a hearing' by the military, recommending that Dawn should give the impression, 'through the very genuflexions of your *style*, that you are merely a functionary with a narrow if significant specialism, a near-academic with none of the soldier's all-round understanding of the science of warfare' (*Dusk*, 4. Italics in the original). Such moments capture what Jarad Zimbler calls 'the mild reflexivity of *Dusklands*', drawing our attention to style's work in mediating the transmission and manipulation of knowledge against the backdrop of a politically arrogant justification of US force.[5] Mildly metafictional though the novel may be, the exertions of its style are more aggressive. In sequences of quite relentless self-immolation, Dawn taxonomically dissects his working demeanour in creaturely, anatomical terms:

> I read, my face starts to lose its life, a stabbing begins in my head, then, as I beat through gales of yawns to fix my weeping eyes on the page, my back begins to petrify in the scholar's hook. The ropes of muscle that spread from the spine curl in suckers around my neck, over my clavicles, under my armpits, across my chest ... My eyeballs ache, my mouth constricts. If this inner face of mine, this vizor of muscle, had features, they would be the monstrous troglodyte features of a man who bunches his sleeping eyes and mouth as a totally unacceptable dream forces itself into him. From head to foot I am the subject of a revolting body. (*Dusk*, 7)

Indeed he is; but by virtue, at least in part, of this stylized self-portrait, with its sinewy, paratactic grotesquerie of body parts, whose verbal vigour seems, weirdly enough, to counter Dawn's drooping face and enervating yawns. All the more animated when describing these contortions, style performatively enacts the revulsion Dawn histrionically indulges. Pornographic in its denigrations, this ghoulish species of characterization peaks early in Coetzee's career, contiguous with his critical work on Beckett. Raw and plosive though nonetheless propulsive, the percussive phrases in this depiction of monstrosity pay homage to the 'energy of quite a savage order' that Coetzee discovered in Beckett, a force that Beckett nevertheless managed to bring 'under the control of syntax of the utmost lucidity', just as Coetzee himself would find more explicitly controlled, formal correlatives for the 'spare, thrifty world' of his later fictions.[6] Here in *Dusklands*, the savagery remains in full swing. Taking the form of an all-consuming anatomy lesson, Dawn's catalogue of disgust anticipates that mode of self-scrutiny – at once ethically compromised and emotionally uncompromising – which would become a hallmark of several of Coetzee's subsequent narrators.

If 'each narrating subject' of *Dusklands*, as Dominic Head points out, 'is exposed as a product and perpetrator of colonial projects', then much of the work of exposure is undertaken by imperious styles of narratorial self-explication.[7] As a 'memoir' of sorts, the novel's second and tumultuous part, 'The Narrative of Jacobus Coetzee', only intensifies this mode of self-revelation, while simultaneously insinuating and counterfeiting the participation of the historical Coetzee as a purported 'translator' of this explorer's 1760 transcript. The novel formally dramatizes through its forged documents ('Translator's Preface', mock-scholarly notes, an Appendix) the fact that 'the fortunes of the Hottentots', as Coetzee reflected in a 1984 essay, were recorded 'in a history written not by them but for them, from above, by travelers and missionaries, not excluding my remote ancestor Jacobus Coetzee, *floruit* 1760' (*DP*, 52). Distortions of colonial history are precisely what the novel critically emulates through the stylized presentation of fake documents and the equivocal authority they represent. Because *Dusklands* affectively involves us – experientially, through style itself – in the obscenities of imperial aggression and dehumanization, the novel's critical purchase on its late twentieth-century moment seems in retrospect all the more tangible, a moment when policies of enforced segregation and relocation in South Africa were being brutally implemented. In place of the bare historical facts of racial subjugation, the novel formally instantiates the force of colonial atrocity, bringing the physical brutalities and psychic consequences of imperial domination not only into diegetic close-up but also allowing them to be 'manifested', as Derek Attridge observes, 'in the rupturing of narrative discourse'.[8]

Lists contribute vividly to this ruptural aesthetic: 'I am a hunter', declares Jacobus Coetzee, 'a domesticator of the wilderness, a hero of enumeration' (*Dusk*, 80). And enumerating is indeed this character's grim forte. As they did for Dawn, ferocious catalogues take centre stage. The list especially suits Jacobus's run-on fantasies, including his daydream of ceremonial execution by the Hottentots, which he itemizes as an

Arcadian ordeal of losing toenails, toes, fingernails, fingers, nose, ears, eyes, tongue, and privates, the whole performance accompanied by howls of the purest anguish and climaxing in a formal disembowelling, I might, yes, I might have enjoyed it, I might have entered into the spirit of the thing, given myself to the ritual, become the sacrifice, and died with a feeling of having belonged to a satisfying aesthetic whole, if feelings are any longer possible at the end of such aesthetic wholes as these.

(*Dusk*, 82)

DAVID JAMES

In a perversion of the Flaubertian dream of novelistic autonomy, of a work sustained only by the cohesion of its own style, Jacobus Coetzee takes masochistic solace in the 'aesthetic whole' of ritualistic sacrifice. Luridly, the language of aesthetic integrity seems primed for this vision of Arcadian oblation, whose seamlessly vicious 'performance' only complements the ferocity of imperialism itself. 'Do aesthetics make empire seem beautiful?', wonders Russ Castronovo.[9] For Coetzee's imagined ancestor, they surely do: elegant logic is discerned in brutal domination, in 'the effective meaning of savagery, which we may define as enslavement to space', just 'as one speaks obversely of the explorer's mastery of space' (*Dusk*, 80). And to this merciless and self-sanctifying prospector, mastery is itself another testament to jurisdictional wholeness, to the 'satisfying' reach of imperialism's planetarity. Incessant though Jacobus's self-aggrandizement is ('My Hottentots and my oxen had given me faithful service; but the success of the expedition had flowed from my own enterprise and exertions' (*Dusk*, 64)), it's the same egomania that breeds devotion to imperial design, a design that proves 'while empire may be fundamentally an unequal relation of power', in Castronovo's phrase, 'it cannot be conceived or imagined without aesthetics'. If Jacobus rehearses this aestheticizing substrate of colonialism's self-definition – the 'poetic circle' of a totalizing 'organic whole', with that circle itself offering 'an analogue for the globe' – then he does so in the very process of envisioning his own violent demise.[10] Consequently, as narrative action aspires for the wholeness of domination, narrative style unravels and captures mounting dissolution. The novel thus contains, exploits even, a counterpoint between diegetic catalogues of rapacious colonial ambition and a mode of expression that soon becomes deranged. Style's abrasiveness instantiates the viciousness underlying such self-exalting, globalizing ambitions.

Elegy in Apartheid

No wonder Coetzee was apprehensive as a young novelist about the tacit occlusions, sanctions, and self-justifications of expressive 'grace', when European imperialism historically represented one of the most efficient articulations of geopolitical administration and self-consolidation. No wonder too that his fiction has often guarded against its own complicity with organic wholeness, poetic fulfilment, or structural resolution. What's more, his vision of worlds marked by the shame of colonialism and its legacies allows few opportunities for characters themselves to escape their often-visceral entanglement in the 'bare life' of racial conflict and disenfranchisement. In 1990, Coetzee published his most explicit engagement with such conditions, confronting the immediate political upheaval and violence of

South African apartheid in the late 1980s. He did so through a distinctly private narrative of confession – but confession less as the archaeology of past misdeed than as an apprenticeship for oblivion. Terminally ill with cancer, Mrs Curren writes an extended letter to her emigrated daughter about the horrors of police brutality and about an unlikely companionship she finds in the homeless Vercueil who accompanies her dying days. Yet despite the directness with which the novel addresses the social conditions and costs of apartheid, Coetzee's archive also reveals that he felt '[t]his book represents my farewell to realism and to a duty to the South African scene',[11] repeating a sentiment that was already brewing in the years leading up to Foe: 'I have always written best out of an adversary position'.[12] Coetzee's clear sense of resolve here emphasizes for us today Age of Iron's double vision – looking into the private self, looking out, though often intermittently, at immediate atrocity – which is also the culmination of a complicated trajectory in his method through the 1980s. If the spatio-temporal anonymity of Waiting for the Barbarians solicited allegorical readings, and if Foe's audacious experiments in metafictionality and transpositions in narrative voice solicited postmodernist ones, then Age of Iron extends a somewhat more fraught critical invitation. At once socially referential yet graphically interiorized, the novel seems to want to debate its own responsiveness to a political context which its very genre (in the form of a personal elegy) confronts only obliquely. Elegies have traditionally revolved around subjective renditions of sorrow, articulating the laments of a single speaker/narrator consumed by loss and meditating on the possibility or implausibility of working through grief toward some quantum of consolation. As such, the genre offers an ambivalent model for a novel framed by social cataclysm and its systemic ramifications for collective life.

As we would expect, Coetzee embraced the challenge. Age of Iron configures loss in terms of what one anticipates as much as what one no longer possesses, departing from elegy's familiar preoccupation with regret, mourning, or other triggers of retrospective contemplation. A notebook entry from 1988 reveals that Coetzee took great care in synchronizing the novel's perspective and register:

> Rewrite from the beginning in the first person (woman's point of view), past tense, with that *elegiac tone* that comes from something irreversible having happened between the time of which is being written and the time of writing.[13]

He created a narratorial standpoint that could bear the weight of witnessing a history of apartheid leaving irreparable scars on the nation's future – the past an anterior wound of still-unfolding damage. Alongside its retrospective mode, the novel develops another temporal orientation, a *prospective* one:

'in looking forward to the end', he records in the same notebook, 'one begins to cut one's ties with the land, one begins to die away from it'. In this observation lies the germ of what Coetzee considered to be the novel's 'necessity' of including 'someone who is in fact dying and comes to welcome death', even if that person then reaches 'a point of conversion at which hope is explicitly abandoned'.[14]

Expecting no reply, the novel's style thus arises from what Andrew van der Vlies calls an 'impossible occasion', one that reinforces Mrs Curren's enunciating authority even as her own narrative revolves around ontological self-dismantlement.[15] 'I write', she insists, 'I follow the pen, going where it takes me. What else have I now?' (AI, 108). Yet it becomes apparent that her letter is more than a futile substitution, more than a means of expending time till oblivion: 'Death may indeed be the last great foe of writing, but writing is also the foe of death' (AI, 115–16). A means for 'holding death at arm's length', writing consoles not through self-delusion or distraction, but because it invites her to find some reassurance in 'follow[ing] the pen' into the unknown – where the letter alone, its materiality, will remain (AI, 116). As she insists at one point: 'The comfort ... should flow forward, not backward' (AI, 73). Age of Iron pivots on this axis between 'irreversible' loss and the letter's potent afterlife, a prospect that also serves to counteract precisely the question Coetzee posed in his notebook to the novel: 'Have things come to such a state that one may not prepare one's soul for dying?'[16] While finding in writing an equivalent for that preparation, Mrs Curren 'uses her body's breakdown', as Justin Neuman suggests, 'as a heuristic device to help her understand her own ethical place within a disintegrating apartheid system'.[17] Yet she also recovers from this breakdown a language of the soul that elevates her letter, turning it into something other than a factual record of the system she describes in horror. Voicing Coetzee's 'farewell' to the sort of ideologically instrumentalized fiction that succumbs, in his words, to the 'pressure for so-called relevance to SA' in contemporary letters,[18] Age of Iron's 'uncontestable lyricism', as critics have noted, 'cuts against any reductive claims regarding its political realism'.[19] Stylistic felicity becomes in itself a form of resistance, carrying out Coetzee's insistence that it's 'hard for fiction to be good fiction while it is in the service of something else'.[20]

Which by no means implies that the novel tries to cultivate a Flaubertian dependence upon nothing but its own style at the expense of social turmoil. Rather, Mrs Curren's elegiac address to an 'only child thousands of miles away' is as ethically ensnared as it is rhetorically energized by her witnessing the nation's ravaging 'time out of time' (AI, 50):

In every *you* that I pen love flickers and trembles like Saint Elmo's fire; you are with me not as you are today in America, not as you were when you left, but as you are in some deeper and unchanging form: as the beloved, as that which does not die. It is the soul of you that I address, as it is the soul of me that will be left with you when this letter is over. Like a moth from its case emerging, fanning its wings: that is what, reading, I hope you will glimpse: my soul readying itself for further flight.

(*AI*, 129)

The repeated pronoun 'you' builds into a reparative refrain about her daughter's 'unchanging form', a form preserved in the present tense, then perpetuated, with the help of auxiliary verbs, in future predictions. Writing in this vision reaches beyond physical oblivion, toward a daughter who appears (as Mrs Curren will too) not as she was but as she might spiritually remain. This prophetic succour is amplified through analogy, as she pictures the letter's provenance as a moth-like soul, 'glimpse[d]' and retained even when her daughter's reading of it 'is over'. For Mrs Curren is adamant, wishfully so, about her daughter's immutability, insisting 'you are' 'not as you were' but 'as that which does not die'. The punctuation, too, heightens the denotative character of what is otherwise a conjectural sequence of claims. Each colon signals the cementing of the image or action that follows on from it in an elaborating clause: the daughter *will* remain 'the beloved'; Mrs Curren's soul *is* something she 'hope[s]' her daughter '*will* glimpse' in the warp and weft of the letter. Colons typically prepare us for further information, of course, through catalogues with consecutive definitions or qualifications. Here they visibly distinguish and affirm Mrs Curren's restitutive, if perhaps futile, prospect of love's legacy inscribed by the 'ghostly passage' of her own 'pen', projecting an era that could be better equipped in 'trying to keep a soul alive in times not hospitable to the soul' (*AI*, 130).

If theological aid isn't something Mrs Curren foresees or even desires in an age 'not hospitable to the soul', then hospitality is nonetheless what Mrs Curren in the end receives. The homeless man, Vercueil, on whom she has become increasingly reliant, becomes her final 'carer' and dubious palliative. Events surrounding this unexpected relationship are quite delicately choreographed, albeit disturbingly so. What's unsettling is the way Coetzee's spare, declarative present tense enables prosody to confront plot, as though rhythm itself initiates its own risky form of redress. 'Now I put my life in his hands instead', she confides: 'This is my life, these words, these tracings of the movements of crabbed digits over the page. These words, as you read them, if you read them, enter you and draw breath again. They are, if you like, my way of living on' (*AI*, 131). The robust alternation of iambic and anapaestic phrases here counterweighs her seemingly exhausted self-surrender to Vercueil, their pressing rhythm complementing her investment

DAVID JAMES

in words as tools of spiritual continuity. Metre itself shifts athwart the imminence of her ultimate diminishment. Although they're mere 'tracings' and 'crabbed digits', her phrases survive through their very tempo of enunciation, the surefooted vigour of her final belief that 'they *are*, if you *like*, my *way* of *liv*ing *on*' carrying out the promised endurance they declare. In circumstances where solace – traditionally one of elegy's profits – seems unlikely if not desperate, narrative's rhythmical 'movements' thus engender their own comforting preservations.

The seemingly implausible sustenance Mrs Curren finds in Vercueil as an unreliable chaperone for her final days affects the very structure of her explanations, which successively counterpoint each other: 'I give my life to Vercueil to carry over. I trust Vercueil because I do not trust Vercueil. I love him because I do not love him. Because he is the weak reed I lean upon him' (*AI*, 131). By moving the conjunction to the head of the clause in that final sentence, Coetzee shifts the register from self-disputing justifications, toward a firmer acceptance of Vercueil's dependability as Mrs Curren's 'weak reed'. Beyond her uncertain stating and negating of 'love' and 'trust', Vercueil is nothing other than what he is – and, in the end, becomes the subject of her conviction: 'When it comes to last things, I no longer doubt him in any way. There has always been in him a certain hovering, if undependable solicitude for me, a solicitude he knows no way of expressing. I have fallen and he has caught me' (*AI*, 196). 'Solicitude' comes from the Latin *sollicitudo*, from *sollicitus*, which itself is linked to 'solicit' from the Latin *sollicitare*: to agitate. *Concern* thus coincides with 'hovering' *agitation*, something manifested in Vercueil's own bouts of irritability and self-destructive inebriation. In characterizing Vercueil's 'solicitude' as 'hovering, if undependable', Coetzee redoubles Mrs Curren's earlier image of him as a 'weak reed' that she must somehow depend on.

Vulnerable in his own disquiet, then, the 'solicitude' Vercueil is barely able to communicate cannot be self-administered either. That he is deprived of the very solace he seems, however oddly, to supply is something Mrs Curren recognizes in the mutual company they keep:

> I need his presence, his comfort, his help, but he needs help too ... He does not know how to love. I speak not of the motions of the soul but of something simpler. He does not know how to love as a boy does not know how to love ... The nearer the end comes, the more faithful he is. Yet still I have to guide his hand.　　　　　　　　　　　　　　　　　　　　　　　　(*AI*, 196)

Clutching at the 'comfort' Vercueil habitually conceals, she welcomes the concern 'he knows no way of expressing'.[21] At the same time, she elegizes Vercueil's untimely return to pubescence through a touching, forgiving

74

analogy – mourning his arrested development in ways that momentarily stave off her own physical demise. This makes her the novel's belated site of assuagement, compelled as she is 'to guide his hand'. Knowing there is little more than this, that there is little left, she nonetheless stands as witness, *through* the process of writing, to a bare act of faith that may or may not be reciprocated. Cold comfort may be what Vercueil's embrace finally holds, but it does nothing if not allay utter loneliness. Whatever its haptic inadequacy or disappointment, the embrace's 'mighty force' remains (*AI*, 198). In a disturbing tableau that abruptly ends the novel, the image of this clasping couple resonates on – as elegiac laments are traditionally supposed to do for the living – an image that commemorates a macabrely consoling intimacy born out of accelerating violence.

Stylish Souls

Both 'chaste and lyrical without being self-conscious' – Paul Bailey could well have been talking about *Age of Iron*. In fact this was his critical assessment a decade on of *Disgrace*, the novel he deemed to be 'quietly stylish', a phrase that offers a neat way of characterizing the implicitly frictional priorities of Coetzee's prose: verbally bridled yet affectively potent, unembellished yet athletic, displaying a knack for what we might call virtuosic restraint.[22] The sheer agility with which Coetzee guards against adjectival excess and sonority sails close to performative contradiction, offering an exhibition of dexterity that his own sense of economy seems otherwise to dispel – a contradiction that continues to remain remarkably generative. Where the reader is concerned, apprehending Coetzee's style thus means negotiating a (seemingly) conflictive aesthetic, inasmuch as his fiction's ethical ambitions find expression in a language that often behaves with the utmost reticence, when the philosophical gravity of thematic concerns coincides with formal self-denial. But stylistically speaking, his writing more often than not has it both ways. Monitoring its own phrasal exertions without dispensing with vivid symbolism; chiselling itself down to bare syntactic components while still showcasing the rhythmic potential of grammatically simple sentences; finding in the very 'barrenness of narrative', in his terms, an unlikely sense of melody and 'inspiration': Coetzee's prose has managed to police its own lyricism though without forgoing the very gracefulness that piqued some suspicion in his early essay on Beckett.[23]

By the time Coetzee reached *Disgrace*, this grace was clearly surviving the onslaught of his idiosyncratic self-control. Rare though they remain in the fabric of this novel's tightly executed use of free indirect discourse – focalized as it is by David Lurie's taut yet lacerating self-examinations – intermittent moments of pellucid and euphonious language play a dramatic role in their own right. As we've already seen in *Age of Iron*, suddenly elegant expressions often coincide with severe episodes of self-scrutiny, as though stylistic verve emerges from the very recognition of disgrace. And in his novel of that name, this discrepancy between what style effectively does and the situations it conveys warrants a closer look, when Coetzee's orchestration of uncommonly melodic moments becomes especially poignant. As someone for whom shame has become a whole way of being, a world view, Lurie is beset by 'listlessness, indifference', along with the sensation that 'he has been eaten away from inside and only the eroded shell of his heart remains'. Ultimately he wonders whether 'a man in this state' can 'find words' to offset 'the feeling wash[ing] over him', let alone 'find music that will bring back the dead' (*Dis*, 156). We have to wait until the final pages of *Disgrace* to discover what Coetzee will do to redress Lurie's ignominy and yet still deny him redemption. Both the scenario and its style grant some reprieve, as Lurie approaches his daughter unawares as she works on her plot:

> Softly he speaks her name. 'Lucy!'
> She does not hear him.
> What will it entail, being a grandfather? As a father he has not been much of a success, despite trying harder than most. As a grandfather he will probably score lower than average too. He lacks the virtues of the old: equanimity, kindliness, patience. But perhaps those virtues will come as other virtues go: the virtue of passion, for instance. He must have a look again at Victor Hugo. Poet of grandfatherhood. There may be things to learn.
> The wind drops. There is a moment of utter stillness which he would wish prolonged for ever: the gentle sun, the stillness of mid-afternoon, bees busy in a field of flowers; and at the centre of the picture a young woman, *das ewig Weibliche*, lightly pregnant, in a straw sunhat. A scene ready-made for a Sargent or a Bonnard. City boys like him; but even city boys can recognize beauty when they see it, can have their breath taken away.   (*Dis*, 217–18)

This crystalline episode embalms the reader in a 'moment of utter stillness', of respite even, ahead of the more solemn close where Lurie gives over the 'young dog, the one who likes music' and whom he has befriended, to lethal injection (*Dis*, 219). By specifying the moment's discrete components, Coetzee's descriptions acquire conspicuous functionality (what could be more clichéd, arguably, than picturing bees as *busy*?); and while 'stillness' isn't an easy noun to replace, its repetition evinces his idiomatic refusal of elegant variation. At the same time, however, the episode's alliteration (*sun, stillness, field, flowers*) counterbalances this undecorated depiction of scenic elements, as though style acoustically compensates for its own frugal diction – recouping in enunciation what's withheld in vocabulary. In one sense, then, Coetzee's straightforward wording is altogether apposite for the 'ready-made' appeal of this scene, which, in its combination of figure, landscape, and light sits (for Lurie at least) somewhere between Sargent's realist portraiture and Bonnard's post-Impressionism. But in another sense, flutters of sibilance allow Lurie's envisioned state of grandfatherly tenderness to gain some level of credence in this present instant, as it connects across phrases 'kindliness' with 'stillness', thereby linking an alternative way of being with his surrender to what he now sees. Lexically spare yet also euphonic: what seem like contrary properties of style may also provide its dramatic charge. For in this instance style has a plot of its own to impart, not a plot of successful repentance (what reader would expect Coetzee to grant such amnesty to someone who has behaved so unconscionably?), but merely one of self-effacing kindness, as the awed 'city boy' replaces himself with Lucy 'at the centre of the picture'.

One could argue that this kind of reading is perversely affirmative, all-too enthused by spotting a level of sonic springiness normally screened by Coetzee's sparseness; a reading that asks us to acknowledge, perhaps against our better judgement, that his seemingly stern frugality can also curate its own remedial effulgence. For even the moment itself doesn't last, as though Coetzee refuses to fulfil Lurie's 'wish' that it be 'prolonged'. What's more, however lightening this painterly scene appears against *Disgrace*'s prevailing backdrop of jeopardy and dereliction, the instant it frames – an ordinary encounter that leads to Lucy welcoming her father afresh, as if this represented a 'visitation' for Lurie, 'a new footing, a new start' (*Dis*, 218) – anticipates the entirely more sorrowful 'moment when, bewilderingly', the dog's 'legs buckle' (*Dis*, 219). Thanks to their striking proximity in textual space, these affectively contrasting moments perform through their juxtaposition the successive insinuation and effacement of redemption that the novel enacts throughout.

And yet, *Disgrace*'s oscillation here between promise and pain reveals something more about Coetzee's stylistic development. It would appear that he came to tolerate in his later fiction lyrical qualities of expression he once collapsed with suspicion into the work of 'style as redemption'. This tolerance reveals something about the journey his writing has made from repelling style's consolatory efficacy outright to viewing it as one of fiction's ethical nodes, a journey that is also part of Coetzee's broader 'movement away from the precipice of late modernism', as Zimbler puts it, 'or at least the radical aesthetics' of Beckett, who became as we know a lodestone for Coetzee's early opposition to style's capacity to somehow redress or resolve what it articulates. In its closing sequence, *Disgrace* brings that movement to poignant fruition. There narrative discourse appears 'to signal an acceptance, perhaps reluctant, of the process of naming' rather than dispelling the operation of recuperation on which its irrepressible lyricism is borne.[24] In spite of the ending's indisputably pathetic tone, Coetzee asserts the potential of style itself for critically contemplating the sense of uplift it produces. To do this, he introduces two vocabularies, spiritual and material, which compete for attention. Refracting these distinct positions, the image of a 'soul' modulates in such a way that unsettles the narration's implied provenance. For as it 'hangs about in the air, twisting and contorting' (Dis, 219), the soul sets in motion an alternation between theological and pathological lexicons. Familiar from Age of Iron, and Mrs Curren's contemplation of her soul preparing itself for flight ahead of the body's oblivion, the trope returns in Disgrace to flag internal discrepancies in the language of its finale. What appears at first to operate as free indirect style contains descriptive inconsistencies that imply another presence, another voice shadowing Lurie's consciousness. And those inconsistencies are nowhere more revealing than in the motivic handling of the spirit. Initially, it is figured in olfactory terms: inside a veterinary 'room' where 'something unmentionable' is performed, Lurie detects 'the smell of expiration, the soft, short smell of the released soul' (Dis, 219). But as the focus turns to the euthanizing procedure itself, the diction becomes more violently compulsory. No longer seen as involuntarily seeping out into the ether, 'the soul is yanked out of the body' (Dis, 219), a verb – deriving from late eighteenth-century Scots, meaning a 'sudden sharp blow' – that starkly reinforces the combination of functionality and violation in a procedure that has nonetheless become routine for Lurie after volunteering at Bev Shaw's animal hospice.

Lurie's responses to the transubstantiating moment where buckling dogs emit writhing spirits seem to shift incrementally. Neither heightened into sorrow nor flattened into dejection, implied reactions are conveyed by a narrative voice whose position and perspective adjust unpredictably in kind. Perspectival manipulations become more complex still when, following the soul's agonizing contortions, Coetzee returns us to the blank presence of the room where it all happens. Though Lurie knows this terminus well, the venue is pictured in prospective terms as an unfathomable zone for the dog; somewhere that 'will be beyond him', the room denotes less a place than 'a hole where one leaks out of existence' (Dis, 219). This enigmatic layering, then, of alternative figurations of the soul – from releasing to yanking to leaking – suggests there's an incongruity between what Lurie visualizes and how his observations are recorded. It's as though these observations don't seem to 'own' the imagery that accompanies them, at least not in a way that would affirm how closely their diction is inflected by Lurie's mentation. Perhaps, however, instead of introducing an ambivalent gap between the narration's derivation and its (sporadically) focalizing subject, this sense of detachment is perfectly apt: Coetzee's retraction of the sort of emotional intimacy and psychological ventriloquism we associate with free indirect style may itself be read as a formal equivalent to Lurie's own growing sense of emotional self-deletion, of inconsequentiality. In a 1998 draft, for instance, he decides that 'what goes on in his heart will be of the utmost irrelevance' when bearing the corpse of his befriended dog to the incinerator.[25] Yet surely it couldn't be *more* relevant to *Disgrace*'s reader at this point. Indeed, Coetzee's deletion of that draft sentence implies that he wanted to keep the option afloat of conveying – even from a distance, even without the penetration of internal focalization – how heartfelt, how *in*consolable, the act of giving up this dog will remain for Lurie, even as he distances himself emotionally from that duty by recognizing its inevitability. The denouement's motile perspective thus embodies through its intermittent exteriority the unsustainable 'irrelevance' of Lurie's 'heart' to an undertaking that clearly disturbs him – a ritual whose routine is far from spiritually serene. Although the diction that apostrophizes the dog's soul morphs in ways that disclose a distinct voice in play with the freedom to inhabit Lurie's interiority and to depart from it at will, by the same token Coetzee's language stays just close enough to Lurie's impressions to suggest that this is hardly a dispassionate task either, a task for which he seeks some rationale in a selfless, unsentimental ethic of justified 'care'.

Late Lyricism

And the soul certainly doesn't go away. Nearly two decades later, it returns as a stylistic catalyst in an otherwise restrained work, *The Schooldays of Jesus*, a novel so devoid of description, so dialogue-driven, that it almost reads like the script for its own stage play. *Schooldays* isn't a complete break, by any means. Along with its 2013 predecessor, *The Childhood of Jesus*, the novel retains the philosophical tenor of Coetzee's postmillennial duo, *Elizabeth Costello* (2003) and *Slow Man* (2005), both of which could be classed as 'novels of ideas' that anticipate the more explicit ruminations on government, terrorism, and public life in the typographically experimental *Diary of a Bad Year* (2007).[26] But in *Schooldays* that level of topical and historical referentiality drops away, along with detailed scenic description and psychological focalization, leaving us with a curious form of naked narration that winds its pedestrian way from one episode to the next. In one sense, *Schooldays*'s terseness perfectly complements the sceptical, unsentimental mood of Simón, a father figure who sees that he needs to protect the adopted boy, Davíd, from pedagogical extravagances promoted by the Academy of Dance, an eccentric school he now attends. One day, though,

Simón lets his guard slip – and Coetzee's style lifts. Usually distrustful of the cerebral claims made for music played in Academy of Dance, Simón finds himself suddenly enraptured by the instructor Arroyo at the piano. Initially he thinks Arroyo might be rehearsing; but when he realizes that what he hears is the process of 'composing', Simón 'listens with a different kind of attention' (*SJ*, 194). Although the music itself 'is too variable in its rhythm, too complicated in its logic for a ponderous being like him to follow', it nevertheless 'brings to mind the dance of one of those little birds that hover and dart, their wings beating too fast to see', an image that prompts Simón first to recall one of the Academy's mottos – '*If we listen with attention the soul will begin to dance within us*' – and then to wonder '[w]hen did his soul last dance?' (*SJ*, 194). This question might seem redolent of the kind of self-scrutiny that Coetzee's characters have often focalized; but on this occasion, the ensuing reflections don't unravel into crippling indictment or self-denunciation, but in fact swell into something like reverie:

> Unable to see his soul, he has not questioned what people tell him about it: that it is a dry soul, deficient in passion. His own, obscure intuition – that, far from lacking in passion, his soul aches with longing for it knows not what – he treats sceptically as just the kind of story that someone with a dry, rational, deficient soul will tell himself to maintain his self-respect.
>
> So he tries not to think, to do nothing that might alarm the timid soul within. He gives himself to the music, allowing it to enter and wash through him. And the music, as if aware of what is up, loses its stop-start character, begins to flow. At the very rim of consciousness the soul, which is indeed like a little bird, emerges and shakes its wings and begins its dance. (*SJ*, 194)

A soul that 'aches with longing' serves in that assonantal paragraph as a personified counterpart to Simón's once dormant and now revived capacity for rapture; in the absence of 'alarm', his soul, like his immersion in Arroyo's melody, begins uncharacteristically to 'flow' – a movement embodied by a sentence whose succinct yet successive clauses resist subordination. By turns fortuitously lyrical and shot-through with pathos, such moments can sound 'lushly autumnal yet edged with irony' (*Dis*, 181), to borrow Lurie's description of the kind of harmonies he envisages for his Byron opera in *Disgrace*: it's tempting to draw from this synthesis of the lush and the ironic a formula for reckoning with Coetzee's career-long developments in style. But the formula would be too inflexible, especially given the direction in which his most recent fictions are moving. For, if anything, *Schooldays* seems to replace irony with declarative earnestness, which has the effect of inviting the reader to entertain, if only for an instant, the sentiments being expressed on their own emotional and evocative terms. To read the scene above 'straight' in this way is not to indulge a naïve appreciation of linguistic effects for their own sake, or to deny ourselves the interpretive opportunities for allegorizing the otherwise 'featureless arena' of *Schooldays*, as one reviewer described it, where 'colossal philosophical questions cast long shadows'.[27] Rather, it is to note that in his late work Coetzee doesn't seem as concerned with upholding an ironic view of his own procedures – however ironically we're invited to view Simón's sudden impulse to dance – nor thereby as adamant as his early and middle fictions perhaps were about sustaining that rueful alertness to 'style as redemption'.

By the lights of this adjustment, we can see how Coetzee doesn't quite chime with notions of 'late style' as antagonistic, volatile, ruptured. Sure, we'd be hard pressed to find 'a new spirit of reconciliation and serenity' in the *Jesus* novels, to borrow Edward Said's terms; but if these later works refuse 'harmony and resolution', they also seem to skirt extravagant displays of 'intransigence, difficulty, and unresolved contradiction'.[28] If anything, the unexpected, mischievous sincerity of the intermittent lyricism of *Schooldays* corroborates Coetzee's own sense of 'late style', which 'to me', he says, 'starts with an ideal of a simple, subdued, unornamented language and a concentration on questions of real import, even questions of life and death' – which may in turn entail repurposing questions about the soul, as we've seen, that have long inhabited more ostensibly violent and socially referential fictions from previous decades (*HN*, 97). 'It is the soul that brings grace to the dance', proclaims Arroyo earlier in the novel, as Simón struggles to understand the baffling 'place of the dances in [Davíd's] education' (*SJ*, 97); and it is the enduring figuration of that soul which continues to bring discrepant grace to Coetzee's fiction.

What's intriguing is the way this grace co-exists with Coetzee's ethos of 'searing self-interrogation', as Carrol Clarkson has called it, a longstanding ethos that continues to spur his 'critical and creative acuity' as a writer and thinker.[29] Moments in his fiction kindled by shame, by the recognition of irremediable limitation, by intimations of personal redundancy, or by sensations of possessing a dry and deficient soul, are also paradoxically moments of great linguistic facility, whose acuity lies precisely in their equivocation over the aesthetic and affective forms of redress such language affords. Out of this eagled-eyed yet enriching aesthetic, where self-examination equals replenishment, comes a lesson for the reader. Which is surely no surprise, for Gayatri Spivak is right to say that in Coetzee's work we invariably find ourselves 'learning how to "read"'.[30] And among the lessons is this. No doubt there's some critical satisfaction to be had in entertaining Coetzee as a stern gatekeeper of his own panache, who refuses in advance his own aesthetic temptations, forestalling the phenomenal pleasures of form by substituting austerity for sublimity. In practice, his language doesn't always behave in this manner, as carefully paced, heightened sequences here from *Age of Iron, Disgrace,* and *The Schooldays of Jesus* attest.

Over time Coetzee was perhaps unable to measure up to that steely repudiation of style's redemptive capacities he once applauded in Beckett. For as we've traced, linguistic grace is everywhere apparent – or at least forever standing by, poised for the appropriate cue – even in narratives backlit by historical trauma or imminent loss whose plots unwind beyond rescue. Hard though it is to predict when these moments of agile yet ambivalent expressivity will turn up, they tend to occur when thematic interrogations of solace, forgiveness, recovery, or spiritual promise solicit our awareness of the ethically freighted nature of style in scenes environed by menace, damage, or desolation. This only accentuates for us the challenge of dealing with Coetzee's limber yet razor-edged prose, as it drills deep into the grammar of moods that look to be self-evident, and defies critical approaches that seem all too convenient.

Notes

1. Gustave Flaubert, Letter to Louise Colet, 16 January 1852, *The Letters of Gustave Flaubert,* vols. I and II: *1830–1880,* ed. and trans. Francis Steegmuller (London: Picador, 2001), vol. I, p. 213.
2. As one reviewer of *The Schooldays of Jesus* put it, the novel's setting is 'eerily stripped down … the 'scenery is so flimsily assembled that it could come straight from Ikea'. Elizabeth Lowry, 'No Passion in an Ascetic Allegory', rev. of *The Schooldays of Jesus,* by J. M. Coetzee, *Guardian,* 18 August 2016.
3. David Attwell, *J. M. Coetzee and the Life of Writing: Face to Face with Time* (Oxford: Oxford University Press, 2015), p. 61.
4. Ibid., pp. 62, 64, 58.
5. Jarad Zimbler, *J. M. Coetzee and the Politics of Style* (Cambridge: Cambridge University Press, 2014), p. 35.
6. J. M. Coetzee, 'Homage', *Threepenny Review,* (Spring 1993), p. 6.
7. Dominic Head, *J. M. Coetzee* (Cambridge: Cambridge University Press, 1997), p. 29.
8. Derek Attridge, *J. M. Coetzee and the Ethics of Reading: Literature in the Event* (Chicago: University of Chicago Press, 2004), p. 30.
9. Russ Castronovo, 'Transnational Aesthetics', in Yogita Goyal (ed.), *The Cambridge Companion to Transnational American Literature* (New York: Cambridge University Press, 2017), p. 82.
10. Ibid., pp. 84, 85.
11. J. M. Coetzee, *Age of Iron,* small red notebook (June 1986–June 1988), CP 33.6, 5 October 1988.
12. J. M. Coetzee, *Foe,* green casebound notebook with gilt edges (1982–5), CP 33.6, 17 March 1984.

13. Coetzee, *Age of Iron* notebook, 9 March 1988.
14. Ibid., 17 March 1988.
15. Andrew van der Vlies, "'[From] Whom This Writing Then?" Politics, Aesthetics, and the Personal in Coetzee's *Age of Iron*' in Laura Wright, Elleke Boehmer, and Jane Poyner, (eds.), *Approaches to Teaching Coetzee's 'Disgrace' and Other Works* (New York: MLA, 2014), p. 104.
16. Coetzee, *Age of Iron* notebook, 20 November 1988.
17. Justin Neuman, *Fiction beyond Secularism* (Evanston: Northwestern University Press, 2014), p. 91.
18. Coetzee, *Age of Iron* notebook, 19 November 1988. In the same entry, Coetzee himself worries that he is 'capitulating before' that pressure to be politically relevant (and therefore 'realist').
19. Kim L. Worthington, '*Age of Iron* (1990)' in Tim Mehigan (ed.), *A Companion to the Works of J. M. Coetzee* (New York: Camden House, 2011), p. 126.
20. Jane Poyner, 'J. M. Coetzee in Conversation' in Jane Poyner (ed.), *J. M. Coetzee and the Idea of the Public Intellectual* (Columbus: Ohio University Press, 2006), p. 21.
21. The stronger nouns *presence* and *comfort* replace the more straightforward desire for 'help', as it appears in a handwritten amendment to draft 10.3: 'I need his help, but he needs help too'. J. M. Coetzee, 'Rule of Iron' [*Age of Iron*], CP 16.2.
22. Paul Bailey, 'Sex and Other Problems', rev. of *Disgrace*, by J. M. Coetzee, *Independent*, 2 July 1999: www.independent.co.uk/arts-entertainment/books/features/sex-and-other-problems-743456.html
23. Coetzee, *Foe* notebook, 5 February 1985.
24. Zimbler, *J. M. Coetzee and the Politics of Style*, pp. 32–3.
25. J. M. Coetzee, *Disgrace*, handwritten early draft (19 August 1995–20 July 1998), CP 35.4–5, 26 January 1998.
26. For a valuable reconsideration of the postwar diversifications of this subgenre, see Michael LeMahieu's 'The Novel of Ideas' in David James (ed.), *The Cambridge Companion to British Fiction since 1945* (New York: Cambridge University Press, 2015), pp. 177–91.
27. Lowry, rev. of *The Schooldays of Jesus*.
28. Edward Said, *On Late Style: Music and Literature against the Grain*, introd. Michael Wood, with a foreword by Mariam C. Said (New York: Pantheon, 2006), pp. 6, 7.
29. Carrol Clarkson, *J. M. Coetzee: Countervoices* (Basingstoke: Palgrave, 2009), p. 2.
30. Gayatri Chakravorty Spivak, 'Lie Down in the Karoo: An Antidote to the Anthropocene', rev. of *The Childhood of Jesus*, by J. M. Coetzee, *Public Books*, 1 June 2014: www.publicbooks.org/lie-down-in-the-karoo-an-antidote-to-the-anthropocene/.

5

DEREK ATTRIDGE

Genres: *Elizabeth Costello, Diary of a Bad Year, Summertime*

J. M. Coetzee's first published work of fiction, *Dusklands* (1974), announced a writer committed to challenging the norms of novel-writing. Its readers encountered two texts: a first-person novella that included a military report written for a supervisor by the name of Coetzee; and what appeared to be a scholarly publication translated from Afrikaans and Dutch by another Coetzee. *In the Heart of the Country* (1977), Coetzee's second fictional work, took the form of a series of numbered paragraphs and a self-contradicting narrator. Later works included a reimagining of the early history of the British novel (*Foe*), and a central character who is visited by his – the character's – own author (*Slow Man*). Genres, for Coetzee, are always open to creative re-engineering. The three works to be discussed in this chapter, *Elizabeth Costello* (2003), *Diary of a Bad Year* (2007), and *Summertime* (2009), are among the most radical of his challenges to generic conventions.[1]

Genre can be, and has been, approached from a number of angles,[2] but for the reader of literary works the chief significance of the concept lies in its relation to *expectation*, and the opportunities readerly expectation offers to the author for creative surprises.[3] Sometimes thought of as a set of limiting conventions, genre is better understood as a vital resource for the inventive writer: the reader who picks up a literary work begins it not with a blank mind but with a rich array of anticipations and assumptions about what is to come, many of which are tied to the work's presumed genre, and which can be exploited by the canny author. These generic expectations are derived from two sources: on the one hand, the information imbibed by the reader from teachers, books, advertising, conversations with friends, and a variety of other external sources; and on the other, previous experiences of reading. And they are activated by a number of cues: what a reader has heard about the work he or she is about to start, how the work is packaged, the work's title and format, familiarity with the author's other publications, and so on. As the reader progresses through the text, these initial expectations are either satisfied or challenged, and new expectations may be aroused to displace those that have proved irrelevant.

Most successful works of literature combine elements of familiarity, providing reassurance, and surprise, providing new ways of experiencing the world and language's relation to it. If expectations are wholly met, the reading experience is likely to be a rather dreary one; if they are challenged on every page, the reader may well give up before getting very far. Readers don't have to start from scratch each time they begin a text; they don't have to rely only on the words before them to deduce how they are to take the language's relation to a speaker, to the world they represent, and to the unfolding thematics of the work. The knowledge (or, rather, the belief) that they are starting an adventure story, or an autobiography, or, for that matter, a sermon or an opinion piece, provides a significant amount of guidance as to how to read the text. Deviations from what is expected will then contribute to the depth and liveliness of the work. (What is called 'genre fiction' hews closely to the norms of a particular genre such as 'science fiction' or 'crime' and thus offers the reader a strong sense of familiarity and the publisher a ready market; however, the very strength of generic expectations makes it easier to spring surprises in such works.) One might think that this play of fulfilment and deviation would not operate when a work is being re-read, but this is not the case: although some surprises may be weakened when we encounter them for a second or third time, generic expectations are so firmly embedded that they can be triggered afresh in repeated readings.

Genres, and the expectations they arouse, are not, of course stable; they alter over time and vary from national tradition to national tradition. Temporal change is not a major issue in reading Coetzee's fiction, although, to take one example, it is possible that many of today's readers of literary novels are less surprised by the metafictional features of *In the Heart of the Country* than would have been the case in 1977. And we cannot know whether readers in fifty or a hundred years will bring to his work mental frameworks similar to those of readers today – and if not, whether the work will require historical excavation for full appreciation, or will find new ways of speaking to its audience, as the work of Sophocles or Shakespeare or Wordsworth continues to do. Geographical difference is more significant for Coetzee's readers: those familiar with the South African tradition of the Afrikaans farm novel, for instance, will register the generic challenge of *In the Heart of the Country* more powerfully than those who aren't. However, Coetzee's allegiance to European traditions, evident in his critical writings as well as his fiction, means that most of the generic conventions he explores will be familiar to audiences around the globe. It's perhaps significant that an early novel, *Waiting for the Barbarians* (1980), has no determinable geographic setting, and that the same is true of his most recent *Jesus* novels.

When, in 1997, John Coetzee, Arderne Professor in English at the University of Cape Town, walked to the lectern to begin his Princeton University lecture, 'The Philosophers and the Animals' (one of the series of Tanner Lectures on Human Values), his audience thought they knew what to expect. With the first sentence of the lecture – 'He is waiting at the gate when her flight comes in' – they were obliged to recalibrate their generic expectations very rapidly: what they found themselves listening to was not the academic exposition of an argument but a fiction – and, it soon turned out, a fiction about an apparently well-known author from the Southern Hemisphere delivering an invited lecture at an American college on the topic of 'The Philosophers and the Animals'. While Coetzee was reading that part of his story that presents his fictional character's lecture, the Princeton audience had to juggle between two sets of generic codes, those pertaining to fiction (treating the lecture in the story as evidence of the character's beliefs, emotions, state of mind, and personality) and those pertaining to academic presentations (treating it as an argument to be assessed on the basis of its plausibility and evidential strength). Some of them, undoubtedly, found themselves wondering about the status and function of the genres themselves: can fiction successfully convey arguments? Is the content of an argument impaired when it is presented as the utterance of a fictional character? Coetzee's exploitation of his hearers' generic expectations enabled him to raise serious issues about the treatment of animals while at the same time offering a moving portrait of the human costs of feeling strongly about those issues – and encouraging reflection on the two genres thus invoked.

Coetzee's two Tanner lectures – the second lecture was called 'The Poets and the Animals' – appeared in print in 1999 under the title *The Lives of Animals* with some of the trappings of an academic treatise: an editor's introduction, footnotes, and a series of commentaries by experts in the field of animal ethics.[4] To some extent, then, this publication produced for its readers the same generic surprise as the lectures themselves: what looked like a scholarly publication turned out to have, at its heart, two fictional stories. Four years later a book appeared bearing the name of the fictional lecturer as its title: *Elizabeth Costello*. Subtitled *Eight Lessons*, it consisted of eight short narratives, all involving the eponymous author, plus a postscript in the form of a letter supposedly written by another E. C., Elizabeth, Lady Chandos. The reader who goes through the chapters in numerical order comes to 'The Lives of Animals: ONE: The Philosophers and the Animals' as 'Lesson 3', after chapters on 'Realism' and 'The Novel in Africa', both of

86

which also include lectures given by Costello (although in these chapters her presentations are less foregrounded than in the case of 'The Lives of Animals'). In its new context, the piece is generically transformed: no longer a lecture in an academic series, it is now a story in an extended fiction. The opening holds no surprises, therefore; it's a rather conventional short story opening, the unidentified pronouns inviting the reader to identify with the focalizer. (John – Costello's son, through whose eyes her visit is presented to us – would not use his and his mother's proper names in his inner discourse.) Instead, the surprise comes when it becomes evident that we are to be given the full extent of Costello's lecture: it occupies nearly twenty pages, with only the sparsest of interpolations (mostly revealing the indignation of John's wife Norma at what she perceives as the lecturer's failures of logic). The reader who is familiar with the short story genre will register this departure from the norm, and, like the initial audience, will experience a mutual – and productive – contamination of this genre and the genre of the academic presentation, together with a reflection on the way these two genres operate.

Intensifying the generic instability further are the content and rhetoric of Costello's lecture. Although I have been describing it as an argument, its (fictional) author is insistent that rational argument is exactly what is *not* appropriate in trying to convince her audience to adopt her way of thinking and, more importantly, feeling. For it is the hegemony of reason, Costello claims, that gives rise to the treatment of animals that she deplores, and in employing the genre of the rational argument – the genre her audience is expecting – she is betraying the cause which she endorses so strongly:

> [A]lthough I see that the best way to win acceptance from this learned gathering would be for me to join myself, like a tributary stream running into a great river, to the great Western discourse of man versus beast, of reason versus unreason, something in me resists, foreseeing in that step the concession of the entire battle.
>
> (EC, 69)

In the second of the chapters on 'The Lives of Animals' Costello suggests two ways in which the views she holds could be more successfully conveyed than by rational argument: 'I urge you to read the poets who return the living, electric being to language; and if the poets do not move you, I urge you to walk, flank to flank, beside the beast that is prodded down the chute to his executioner' (EC, 111).

There has been much discussion about the degree to which we ought to take Costello's views as Coetzee's own, and this is, of course, a debate about genre. If we hold to the view that a genre such as the novel has impermeable boundaries, within which nothing can be taken at face value as an assertion of the author's beliefs, we will say that *Elizabeth Costello* offers no guide to

Coetzee's views on the treatment of animals. The fact that in other genres, such as the newspaper article, Coetzee has expressed views very similar to Costello's, is, the argument would go, irrelevant.[5] On the other hand, if we understand genres as lacking fixed boundaries, and generic expectations as always open to challenge by inventive authors, we might say that 'The Lives of Animals' invites us to consider very seriously the position endorsed by Costello – and that the very vividness with which her distress and exhaustion are conveyed is part of that invitation.[6] In other words, we are not only, or perhaps not even primarily, asked to weigh the rational arguments Costello presents but rather to open ourselves to the experience, at once affective and intellectual, of a work of literature that brings to life one (imagined) person's engagement with this issue. That the stories include powerful objections to Costello's position is also part of the invitation; the outrage at her association of abattoirs with the Nazi death camps expressed by the poet Abraham Stern, for instance, is important not so much for the content of his complaint but for the force with which he, as another singular individual with strong feelings, presents it.

A further effect of reading the two chapters on 'The Lives of Animals' as the work of a novelist and not a philosopher is a strengthening of the alignment between Costello and Coetzee: we are inclined to link the novelist in the text to the novelist behind it. In other words, Costello's emphasis on the greater effectiveness of literature in comparison with rational argument is easy to read as a justification for Coetzee's choice of genre in expressing his own views on human conduct towards animals. And the entire book is, in part, an investigation of the tasks, capabilities, and responsibilities of the literary writer, or, more generally, the artist.

The first chapter of *Elizabeth Costello*, 'Realism' (also a re-tooled lecture Coetzee had given at an American university, in this case Bennington College), recounts Costello's visit to another (fictional) American college, Altona, to receive an award, take part in a couple of interviews, and make a speech, to which she gives the title 'What Is Realism?' (the title of Coetzee's Bennington College lecture, in fact). Her topic is the impossibility of straight-forward realism of the sort she claims could be produced before what she calls the breaking of the 'word-mirror', though she gives no date for this momentous event. But there is another way in which the chapter exposes the artifice of realist fiction: an anonymous author figure interpolates comments throughout the piece, shattering the word-mirror that is the product of generic expectations. The unsuspecting reader who begins the work expect-ing the representation of a fictional world encounters instead the statement, 'There is first of all the problem of the opening, namely, how to get us from where we are, which is, as yet, nowhere, to the far bank' (*EC*, 1). There could hardly be a brasher opening announcement that the genre of realist fiction is under scrutiny. During the course of the chapter several narrative gaps of the kind allowed to pass without comment in realist writing are explicitly signalled, thus suspending the reader's suspension of disbelief. 'Realism has never been comfortable with ideas' (*EC*, 9), we are told at one point: they need to be embodied in characters – which is, of course, precisely what the chapter is doing. Each time the intrusive authorial voice breaks the surface of 'Realism' we experience a shift in genre, from realist fiction (which presents an affecting portrait of the elderly novelist and an absorbing rendering of her interaction with others) to metafiction (which converts those vivid pictures into products of the novelist's art).

Opening the book with this challenge to generic expectations constitutes an invitation on Coetzee's part to read on (at least) two levels at once: to engage with the content, and in particular with the views being presented, and to recognize (and enjoy) the artifice which at once makes that content powerful and renders it other than the simple assertion of truth. It may even be that, at least for readers today, the author's indication that he is aware of the relativity of truth claims of this kind – the fact that they always arise from particular contexts – is a guarantee both of his sophistication and his good faith. The second chapter, 'The Novel in Africa' (another re-worked lecture), eschews metafiction and uses Costello as focalizer for the first time. The setting is a cruise ship on its way to Antarctica, and the long lecture after which the chapter is named is given not by Costello but by an African novelist, Emmanuel Egudu, a lecture in which he makes large claims for a genre foreign to both Costello's and Coetzee's practices: the oral novel. As in many of the chapters, Coetzee gives us opposing positions with no con- clusive privileging of one over the other. Costello's intellectual objections to Egudu's arguments are complicated by her recollection of their past physical relationship – another instance of the embodiment of ideas in realist fiction.

In two more chapters the giving of a lecture is the central event. 'The Humanities in Africa' again features a lecture by someone other than Elizabeth Costello, this time her sister Blanche, a nun working at a mission in rural Zululand. Blanche's attack on the humanities and their championing of the faculty of reason over the revelations of religious truth receives con- crete exemplification when she introduces her sister to a Zulu sculptor work- ing at the mission. His endlessly repeated wood carvings of Christ in agony on the cross constitute an extreme of generic stability, and stand in strong contrast both to Costello's own beliefs in artistic creativity and to Coetzee's creative practice as a novelist. The reader again finds herself sliding between two genres: a fiction about a novelist encountering a powerful challenge to her convictions, which is to be enjoyed for its portrait of a character's mental struggles; and a claim about the world to be judged on its own terms. Against Blanche's thoroughgoing Christian beliefs we are given an anecdote by Elizabeth about providing sexual solace to a dying man – a not entirely convincing counter-example.

'The Problem of Evil' also invites readerly engagement on both levels: Costello faces another crisis in her intellectual and emotional life, and at the same time she offers an opinion we are invited to judge. The crisis has occurred as a result of Costello's reading of a passage in a novel: the events it describes (based on actuality) are so horrible that she feels it should not have been written, and should not be read. Is this Coetzee's view? He gives a measured non-fictional account of the damaging effects of censorship in *Giving Offense*; but here, as in 'The Lives of Animals', the rational argument is less important than the experience – intellectual, emotional, and physical – of his character, whose response we are encouraged to take seriously.

After a short chapter ('Eros') on sex between gods and humans that is securely in the genre of the meditative essay, Coetzee ends the main part of the book with one of his most brilliant inventions: the story 'At the Gate'. Costello, finding herself in some kind of antechamber to the afterlife, is obliged to write a statement expounding her beliefs as a writer. More than any of the earlier chapters, this one reads as a narrative fiction from start to finish, albeit one which again raises issues of central importance to the writing life. Costello's difficulty in stating what, as a writer of fiction, her beliefs are – if, indeed, she has any – returns us to the question of genre: can imaginative fictions assert truth claims about the world or human actions? And if they can present claims and counter-claims only in the embodied form of characters interacting, speaking, thinking, and feeling, as in this book, is this a weakness or a strength? *Elizabeth Costello* is good evidence of the value of this kind of fiction: we are left with an awareness of the power of certain ways of experiencing the world – dismay at factory farming, Christian religious conviction, horror at certain novelistic representations, creative openness to voices of otherness – without having been forced to make rational judgements on these issues. Any external knowledge we may have of John Coetzee's own views on these matters inevitably colours our reading, but need not determine it.

What are we to make of the book's subtitle, followed up by the naming of the chapters as 'lessons'? There is undoubtedly some irony in the use of a term suggestive of didacticism to label pieces of writing that question the authority of genres which rely exclusively on rationality. Nevertheless, the word does imply that there are issues of importance at stake. Coetzee himself, after a reading of a new Costello story in Buenos Aires in September 2017, said of the earlier collection: 'The subtitle of the book, "eight lessons", already suggested a certain moral didactic purpose'.[7] The new story appears in a collection of Costello pieces translated into Spanish under the title *Siete cuentos morales* (*Seven Moral Stories*), and returns to the elderly author's horror at the treatment of animals – seen once more through the lens of her son's mild but loving scepticism.[8]

We may suppose that the book *Elizabeth Costello* was not in Coetzee's mind when he first gave a lecture in the form of a story about a famous Australian author; rather, it seems likely that he found himself re-deploying his character as a way of responding to lecture invitations, and at some point the idea of a book emerged. Something similar appears to have happened in the case of *Diary of a Bad Year*. One piece of evidence is a reading Coetzee gave at the University of York in June 2006. The reading included a number of short pieces written over the previous nine months, texts which drew on a variety of different genres, from philosophical arguments to personal anecdotes. They were not fictions, although there was a certain amount of self-distancing, notably in the use of the phrase 'he writes' at the start of each piece. For example, a short (and very amusing) meditation on a magpie began as follows:

> Before I bought this block of land, he writes, there were birds who scavenged in the creek and cracked open the pine cones. Now suddenly there are human beings who perambulate the block as though they had a right to it. The birds, for the most part, keep their distance. All but the magpies. All but the magpie in chief (that is how I think of him), the oldest (at least the slowest and most battered). He (that is how I think of him) walks in slow circles around me when I am out in the garden.[9]

There is no reason to think of this as anything other than an example of writing inspired by a real bird in Coetzee's garden, which has pines and a creek, on the outskirts of Adelaide.

In *Diary of a Bad Year*, published in 2007, there is also a piece about a magpie. It is a longer text, and it begins as follows:

> Once upon a time the little strip of land across from the Towers belonged to the birds, who scavenged in the creek bed and cracked open pine cones for the kernels. Now it has become a green space, a public park for two-legged animals: the creek has been straightened, concreted over, and absorbed into the runoff network.
>
> From these new arrivals the birds keep a cautious distance. All save the magpies. All save the magpie-in-chief (that is how I think of him), the oldest – at least the stateliest and most battered looking. He (that is how I think of him, male to the core) walks in slow circles around me where I sit.   (*DBY*, 207)

As well as expanding the diary entry, Coetzee has transferred the location from his own house and garden to a tower block adjoining a public park. The slight distancing of 'he writes' has become a much stronger divorce between author and narrator, and we can no longer read the piece as autobiography, with an autobiographer's commitment to accuracy, but, it seems, must take it as the fictional experience of an equally fictional writer.

Diary of a Bad Year collects fifty-five such short pieces – thirty-one 'Strong Opinions' and twenty-four entries in a 'Second Diary' (including the expanded magpie piece) – on a variety of topics from avian influenza to Zeno. The distancing we saw in the magpie piece doesn't occur in the 'Strong Opinions'; had the book consisted only of these pieces it would have clearly belonged to the ostensible genre that their title proclaims: J. M. Coetzee's thoughts on a number of topics, written, as the title page of this section informs us, between 12 September and 31 May 2006 (shortly before his visit to York). When the author, who has published 'a collection of essays on censorship' in the 1990s (*DBY*, 22),[10] begins a comment about crime with the words 'During the years when Cape Town was my home' (*DBY*, 104) we have no reason not to think of Coetzee's time in that city. The pieces in 'Second Diary' are more personal, and now there are indications that the writer is *not* John Coetzee, such as references to 'the park' (as in the magpie piece) (*DBY*, 213, 215), to a 'flat down the corridor' (*DBY*, 211), and to the author's age ('By the time I reached my seventieth year' (*DBY*, 220); 'Though I have entered upon my eighth decade' (*DBY*, 169)) – older than John Coetzee at the time of the book's publication. However, those pieces that express opinions – on the authors and composers the writer most admires, for instance – are hard not to read as Coetzee's own. What is more, there are even stronger factual indications in the 'Second Diary' that the voice *is* Coetzee's: we learn that the writer's father's initials were, like Coetzee's father's, Z. C. (*DBY*, 165), and the clincher, one might think, that he is the author of *Waiting for the Barbarians* (*DBY*, 171). Once again, we are reading texts that both do and do not express the views of John Coetzee.

The most blatant challenge to the genre of the philosophical meditation, however, starts at the foot of the first page of the 'Strong Opinions'. Under a thin black line across the page, we find 'My first glimpse of her was in the laundry room', and we soon realize that the essayistic pieces are readable as part of a fiction, in which an imagined elderly writer (we only have his initials, JC) is responding to a commission from a German publisher while pursuing an unconsummated sexual relationship with a much younger fellow tenant, Anya. Each of the opinion pieces is part of a novel, just as Elizabeth Costello's lectures are; but, as with those lectures, the invitation to take their arguments and points of view seriously is no less strong than if they were uttered *in propria persona* – and all the stronger if we choose to read horizontally, completing the opinions before turning to the story beneath them.

The fiction that unrolls in the lower part of the page – JC's first-person recounting is soon joined, below another thin black line, by Anya's first-person recounting – is engaging but too skimpy to allow of any extensive narrative development. Its function is in part to round out the image of the writer that emerges from the upper part of the page: a man who is relying on the privilege of old age to express opinions without concern for conventional pieties, but who is out of touch with the realities of the world he finds himself in. There is further evidence in the fiction that this man is not John Coetzee: he lives not in Adelaide but in a ground-floor flat in Sydenham Towers, Darling Harbour, Sydney (hence the public park and the concreted creek), and he was born not in 1940 but 1934. Against these, he shares much with John Coetzee, from his initials (*DBY*, 123, 157) (and probably his first name, since Anya's partner calls him 'Juan' (*DBY*, 165)) to his South African origin (*DBY*, 50), the framed scroll on his wall which sounds like a Nobel Prize certificate (though the language would be Swedish, not, as Anya thinks, Latin) (*DBY*, 47), the long list of his publications as novelist and critic (*DBY*, 50), and his vegetarianism (*DBY*, 165). Hence the fictional context of the opinions, provided at the foot of the page, does nothing to settle their generic status.

This fictional context not only establishes a frame around the opinions, leaving open the question of the degree of authorial endorsement they have, but, through Anya's lively responses, offers a critique of them – functioning like the disagreements expressed by Abraham Stern and Norma in 'The Lives of Animals'. In particular, Anya, who has been employed by JC to transcribe his recorded discourses (though with a privately confessed ulterior motive), complains about their dullness and their irrelevance to the interests and commitments of her generation. The 'Second Diary' (which Anya christens his 'Soft Opinions') is, in part, a reaction to these complaints: the magpie piece, for instance, is removed even further from its origin in John Coetzee's Adelaide garden when seen as a response to Anya's earlier advice: 'Write about the birds. There are always a mob of magpies strutting around the park as if they own it, he could write about them' (*DBY*, 35).

Distanced by their fictional context though they may be, JC's opinions are thought-provoking contributions to a number of debates – on terrorism, paedophilia, the university, Australian politics, and many others. We catch an echo of Elizabeth Costello's denunciation of reason:

We assume that, as long as it is applied with enough tenacity, human reason must triumph (is fated to triumph) over other forms of purposive activity because human reason is the only form of reason there is ... But what if there are equally powerful modes of 'thinking', that is, equally effective biochemical processes for getting to where your drives or desires incline you?

(DBY, 70–1)

JC's scepticism about the choosing of governments by democratic vote – 'who would dare to claim that the world would be in a worse state than it is if rulers had from the beginning of time been chosen by the method of the coin?' (DBY, 14) – seems less outrageous in the age of Donald Trump than at the time of publication. But the full affective power of *Diary* really only emerges in the closing pages, when JC writes his pieces in praise of Bach, Dostoevsky, and Tolstoy, and Anya occupies both of the lower sections, the first in a long, moving letter (DBY, 191–227) and the second in an even more moving monologue expressing her acceptance of his love and her willingness to be with him at his death (DBY, 221–7). Here, for instance, in prose that one might not recognize as Coetzee's if encountered out of context, the magpie returns for the last time in a paragraph that captures both the humour and the poignancy of the relationship:

> I was the one he was in love with, in his old man's way, which I never minded as long as it did not go too far. I was his secret aria secretary, I used to say to him (just joking), and he never denied it. If I had cared to listen in on a warm spring night, I am sure I would have heard him crooning his love song up the lift shaft. Him and the magpie. Mr Melancholy and Mr Magpie, the amoro-dolorous duo.
> (DBY, 225)

Although *Diary of a Bad Year* is far from being a memoir, it does at times read as an attempt on the part of Coetzee to see himself, unflatteringly but amusedly, from the outside: the elderly writer, finding novels more and more difficult to write, letting off steam in opinion pieces, and, perhaps, liable to inappropriate and unfulfillable passions. This was not the first time Coetzee had treated himself with this kind of unforgiving scrutiny: whereas the genre of autobiography often impels writers towards self-exculpation, the accounts in *Boyhood* and *Youth* emphasize the failings and failures in Coetzee's early life (though in the former work the boy is young enough not to incur the reader's blame). The years which *Youth* deals with – 1962–5 – were, if the memoir is to be believed, years of unhappiness and thwarted ambition, but the period immediately after that, when Coetzee was a PhD student at the University of Texas at Austin, and then an assistant professor at the State University of New York at Buffalo (1965–71), may have been years of relative contentment: he moved from an outstanding degree programme to a post in an excellent department, and, with his wife, was raising their two children. The prospect of a comfortable, intellectually stimulating, life in the USA abruptly disappeared, however, when he lost the possibility of renewing his visa after an arrest for taking part in a demonstration against the police presence on the campus during anti-Vietnam War protests. His return to South Africa in May 1971 without a job and with an uncertain future must therefore have been devastating. But the memory of unhappiness and dissatisfaction seems to be what spurs Coetzee into autobiographical writing: those early years back in South Africa are the subject of *Summertime*.

If *Boyhood* and *Youth* challenge some of the generic expectations of the memoir – they are written in the third person and the present tense; they omit some of the most significant occurrences in the author's life – their departures are slight compared to those of *Summertime*. An unsuspecting reader familiar with the first two books, or having read them as the first two parts of the omnibus *Scenes from Provincial Life*, would expect a third volume to be in the same format, but, judging from the title, to have a more upbeat flavour. Such a reader would be quickly disabused on both counts. The opening presents a series of notebook entries dated 1972–5, which read more like JC's 'Soft Opinions' than the earlier memoirs, though, like the earlier memoirs, they are in the third person and present tense. The author of the notes is only retrospectively identified, but there are references that readers familiar with Coetzee's biography will recognize – attendance at St Joseph's College, for instance, and a house in Tokai Road, Cape Town. The second entry, dated 1 September 1972, however, begins, 'The house that he shares with his father' (*Sum*, 6), and such readers will know that this is a counterfactual statement. In 1972 Coetzee was living with his wife and children, and his mother was still alive. This erasure of mother, wife, and children serves an important purpose: it announces a major narrative strand of the book, the relation between son and father, both struggling to keep their heads above water. Autobiographical accuracy gives way to thematic and narrative demands.

The sixteen pages of notebook entries move between condemnation of the apartheid state and self-deprecating accounts of life on Tokai Road, and are accompanied by suggestions for further narrative development (later explained as notes toward a book). They are followed by something even more distanced from the genre of the memoir: the transcription of an interview between an unnamed interviewer (later identified as 'Mr Vincent') and a woman by the name of Julia Frankl. She is questioned about her relationship with 'John Coetzee', who, we learn – the revelation is a shock on first reading – is dead.[11] Vincent is writing a biography, for which he is conducting interviews (they are dated 2007 and 2008) with some of those who knew the author. *Summertime* is not that biography: it is a collection of transcripts (apparently unedited, since we are allowed to read material that Vincent promises to delete), bookended by notes left by Coetzee on his death. The period Vincent is interested in is 1972 to 1977, when Coetzee 'was still finding his feet as a writer' (*Sum*, 225) – though in fact his interviewees have very little to say about Coetzee as a writer. The bulk of the book is taken up by three interviews with women: Julia, with whom he had a brief liaison, Margot, his cousin, with whom he fell in love as a child, and Adriana, a Brazilian dance teacher for whom he conceived a passion. Two shorter interviews follow, one with Martin, who recalls being the successful candidate for a job at the University of Cape Town when Coetzee was a fellow interviewee, and the other with Sophie, a colleague in the same department – now joined by Coetzee – with whom he co-taught a course and had a brief sexual affair. The interview with Martin includes some passages Coetzee is said to have written in preparation for a third memoir in the same format as *Boyhood* and *Youth* (*Sum*, 205).

This approach would be enough to mark *Summertime* as an extremely unusual exercise in autobiography. But two other features add to its extraordinariness. First, the departures from the truth already evident in the second notebook entry extend, and are magnified, throughout the book. Although it is full of verifiable details about John Coetzee's life – interviewees mention his small pickup, his writing of *Dusklands*, his contributions to the UCT English Department, and so on – the departures from fact, starting with his death and the absence of his mother, wife, and children in the 1970s, are so great that unless we have independent information we can't rely on any statement being true. (A weakness of John Kannemeyer's enormous biography is its tendency to treat statements in the memoirs as factually true without any independent evidence.)[12] Second, the representation of the author that emerges from the interviews, and to a certain extent from the notebook entries, is even more unflattering than the one to be found in his earlier works. In particular, the three women whose accounts take up the major part of the book all reflect on his existence as a sexual being – all, in their different ways, pronouncing him unfitted for romantic relationships, uncomprehending of the ways of the body, callow, awkward, unrealistic. Time and again, his reported behaviour suggests a man woefully out of touch with the real world, comically inept at practical matters, doggedly following a personal philosophy that to outsiders looks absurd and often pathetic. Of the real John Coetzee's successes very little is made: he did in fact get the UCT job for which he was interviewed in 1971 and did not have to teach 'extra English' to schoolgirls. Even more significantly, although *Dusklands* and *In the Heart of the Country* are mentioned, the considerable achievement they represent is nowhere hinted at.

A redeeming aspect in the portrayal is his relationship with his father, one of the work's most original and touching strands. Where in *Boyhood* the boy was consumed with rage at his father, the older Coetzee has a much more complicated response: compassion for this lonely, disappointed man, admiration for his dogged perseverance, guilt at his younger self's anger towards him. When his father develops cancer of the larynx – this much is factually true – the Coetzee of *Summertime* experiences a moment of uncertainty about his feelings: 'He could stretch out and take his father's hand and hold it, to comfort him, to convey to him that he is not alone, that he is loved and cherished. But he does no such thing ... Is his father truly loved and cherished? Is his father truly not alone?' (*Sum*, 262–3). The work ends soon after this, with the prospect of an even more cribbed existence as his father's full-time nurse.

What genre, then, does this book belong to? Can we read it as autobiography, or is it better to classify it as fiction? As we have seen, although the subject of Vincent's biography is called John Coetzee and is the author of *Dusklands* and *In the Heart of the Country*, he is far from identical with the John Coetzee who is, thankfully, still alive. Mr Vincent and his biographical project are pure fictions.[13] In this respect, the work fails to function as autobiography. Yet if autobiography is a project of exploring, and perhaps coming to terms with, one's own past self, and particularly with those aspects of the self of which one is least proud, it could be said that *Summertime* does, in some degree, belong to this genre. Had the name on the title page differed from the name of the central character, there would be little of the autobiographical about it. But the coinciding of the names invites us to take the book as a droll self-examination, an attempt on Coetzee's part to imagine what kind of a figure he himself cut in this period, a comic representation of the sorriest aspects of his existence. In this respect, the book is a true successor to *Youth*, where the comedy depends on the reader's awareness of the smiling adult writer behind the immature, self-deceiving figure encapsulated in the prose.

Because of its generic ambiguity, *Summertime*, like *Elizabeth Costello* and *Diary of a Bad Year*, requires a degree of mental agility on the part of the reader: at the same time as we allow ourselves to become engrossed in the stories of Julia's failing marriage to a sexist husband, Margot's struggles to live morally in a corrupt society and her despair at the 'Çoetzee men', and Adriana's fierce protectiveness of her daughters in an estranging city, we are building up a picture of 'John Coetzee', but we are also – if we keep our wits about us – remaining aware that this is the real J. M. Coetzee's sardonic picture of himself that is being refracted through these fictional characters. For instance, we have to ask ourselves what Coetzee, the writer of these words, is saying about his own sense of his achievement when he has Sophie, at the end of the final interview, comment:

> [H]e had no special sensitivity that I could detect, no original insight into the human condition ... In general I would say that his work lacks ambition. The control of the elements is too tight. Nowhere do you get a feeling of a writer deforming his medium in order to say what has never been said before, which is to me the mark of great writing. Too cool, too neat, I would say. Too easy. Too lacking in passion. *(Sum,* 242)

The work in which these words appear, with its remarkable exploitation of generic expectations in the creation of a funny, painful, searching enquiry into the whole question of human self-understanding, seems to me sufficient evidence that Sophie, and perhaps Coetzee himself in certain moods, has got it badly wrong.

Notes

1. When writing in the genre of the critical essay, Coetzee is usually content to follow the established norms, as will be apparent from the collections *White Writing, Giving Offense, Stranger Shores, Inner Workings,* and *Late Essays.* His own interest in genre is most evident in *White Writing,* whose central topic is the fate of pastoral in South Africa, with particular attention given in two chapters to the narrower genre of the *plaasroman* or farm novel.
2. Some of the numerous studies of genre are given in the Further Reading at the end of this volume.
3. Coetzee's awareness of the role of readerly expectation surfaced very clearly when he indicated that he would have preferred *The Childhood of Jesus* to have appeared with no title (Jason Farago, 'J. M. Coetzee's Stunning New Novel Shows What Happens When a Nobel Winner Gets Really Weird', *New Republic,* 14 September 2013; https://newrepublic.com/article/114658/jm-coetzees-childhood-jesus-reviewed-jason-farago).
4. J. M. Coetzee, *The Lives of Animals,* ed. Amy Guttman (Princeton: Princeton University Press, 1999).
5. See, for example, 'Exposing the Beast: Factory Farming Must Be Called to the Slaughterhouse', *Sydney Morning Herald,* 22 February 2007.
6. These attributes are strongly in evidence in Eileen Atkins's portrayal of Costello in the BBC film of *The Lives of Animals,* directed by Alex Harvey (2002).
7. https://johannesburgreviewofbooks.com/2017/09/25/the-jrb-daily-jm-coetzee-reads-a-new-story-the-glass-abattoir-and-announces-a-new-book-to-feature-elizabeth-costello/
8. A further short fiction involving the relationship between John and his mother draws on the genre of the epistolary novel: 'Lies', *New York Review of Books,* 21 December 2017.

9. Personal communication. My thanks to John Coetzee for permission to quote from this unpublished work.
10. Coetzee published *Giving Offense* in 1996.
11. Given this stark difference between John Coetzee in the real world and the 'John Coetzee' of *Summertime*, it would be appropriate for the latter's name to be placed consistently between quotation marks, were it not intrusive. Invisible quotation marks should therefore be assumed from now on.
12. J. C. Kannemeyer, *J. M. Coetzee: A Life in Writing*, trans. Michiel Heyns (Melbourne and London: Scribe, 2013).
13. Coetzee was already working on *Summertime* when Kannemeyer wrote to him to ask permission to write a biography. Alison Flood, 'JM Coetzee's Official Biography to Hit Shelves This Summer', www.theguardian.com/books/2013/mar/21/jm-coetzee-biography-jc-kannemeyer.

PART II

Relations

6

JAN STEYN

Translations

Introduction

J. M. Coetzee has translated works from Dutch and Afrikaans; his own works have been translated into dozens of languages; he has engaged in re-translation; he has edited works in translation; he has critiqued the translations of others; he has taught books in translation and a translation workshop to university students; he has written about the theory of translation (or the impossibility of such theory); he has produced fictions using the technique of pseudo-translation; and he has regularly figured translation in his literary work. His is therefore a remarkably holistic view of translation, combining insights gleaned from the varying positions of its participants. This chapter will discuss Coetzee's practice as a translator of others' works, his relationship with the translators of his own works, and the views on translation that he has expressed either directly in his essays or indirectly in his fiction. From this broad view emerges a portrait of an author who has closely engaged over the course of several decades with the processes of translation, and who is deeply aware of the relationship between languages and cultures upon which these processes depend and which they lay bare. Seen in this light, far from its familiar caricature as marginal intellectual concern or mere writerly apprenticeship, translation is revealed as central to Coetzee's literary project.

Coetzee's Languages

There is no way to talk effectively about translation without talking about languages. Coetzee grew up speaking both Afrikaans (his father's first language) and English (his mother's mother tongue). He has also, at various times, studied Dutch, French, German, Latin, and Russian. To this must be added his persistent interest in other languages, notably Spanish in both its European and South American guises, his early work on Nama, as well as his training and original research in Linguistics. Coetzee has tended to downplay his language-learning efforts and abilities in his fiction, correspondence, and interviews. We see this, for example, in a conversation with David Attwell:

> I would like to be a polyglot but am not. My relationship with languages is an intimate but frustrated one. I have a poor ear and a distaste for memorizing. I pick up the principles of a new language quickly enough, perhaps even get a feel for it, then start looking for shortcuts, then get bored. So the pattern has been that I work on a language intensively for a period, usually for an immediate reason, then put it aside and do something else, and as a result never retain anything like a command. (DP, 57)

There is probably more to this account than false modesty, but if we lower the bar from 'a command' to an ability to communicate in or to have an aesthetic sense of languages, then Coetzee is far more accomplished than he lets on. In *Summertime* (2009), for example, John Coetzee's French-speaking colleague Sophie reports that she decided to be present whenever John was interviewed by French journalists – 'in case there were language problems, John's French was not good' (*Sum*, 236). In contrast, Coetzee's real-life former colleague and regular translator from French, the late Catherine Lauga du Plessis, was impressed with Coetzee's knowledge of French (a language I have myself heard him use with slow precision), remarking: 'J. M. Coetzee is an attentive reader, a punctilious re-reader, a demanding analyst of translations, and a scrupulous as well as inspired translator as is evident from his own translations'.[1] Coetzee's language skills may not always be up to his own demanding standards – he reports, for instance, that his Dutch in the 1970s was strong enough for him to 'reasonably think of [himself] as a translator of professional standard' but that it has subsequently waned (*DP*, 57) – but they are substantial. Moreover, regardless of his actual linguistic talents, it is clear that languages and the study of languages are *important* to him, a recurring concern in his life, and an ongoing preoccupation in his work.

When Coetzee taught a workshop in literary translation at the State University of New York at Buffalo, he asked his students to produce verse translated from Dutch, French, German, Latin, Russian, or Spanish only, and warned them in the course introduction, 'I do not recommend this course for students who have done no original writing. Note, too, that my Russian and Spanish are weak.'[2] In structuring this course, Coetzee responds to the divergent imperatives faced by translators of poetry: that of creativity and that of fidelity. The former relies on a mastery of the target language (not just, in Coetzee's case, English, but the specifically literary version of English practised by those who do 'creative writing'); the latter relies on a mastery of the source language (hence the warning about Coetzee's 'weak' Russian and Spanish – he would be of limited help to a student hoping to avoid translation 'errors'). These concerns are divergent insofar as true originality, originary creativity, seeks to bring about something new, while the extreme goal of the 'faithful' translator is merely to replicate. I will discuss below how Coetzee as translator takes the now-unpopular notion of 'fidelity' as his guiding star. Presently I would simply like to note the importance he places on language learning and his fine-grained sense of his own different levels of linguistic mastery.

Among the languages of Coetzee's ken, Afrikaans and Dutch stand out as those from which he has published translations. These two languages are, of course, closely related, with Afrikaans diverging from Dutch over four centuries through adaptation, creolization, and top-down national standardization, but also intermittently returning to Dutch through university exchanges, scholarly cross-pollination, the teaching of basic Dutch in Afrikaans-medium schools, and the literary affiliations of Afrikaans authors. Access to Afrikaans would have given the young Coetzee a significant start in learning Dutch. The protagonist of *Youth* (2002) refers to this as an 'insider's knowledge of Dutch', but when he contemplates leveraging his linguistic advantage for social and professional ends (by gaining entry into something like a Dutch poetry circle of London, if such a circle even exists) he disdainfully rejects the idea:

> Dutch poetry has always struck him as rather boring, but the name Simon Vinkenoog keeps cropping up in poetry magazines. Vinkenoog is the one Dutch poet who seems to have broken on to the international stage. He reads everything there is by Vinkenoog in the British Museum, and is not encouraged. Vinkenoog's writings are raucous, crass, lacking any dimension of mystery. If Vinkenoog is all that Holland can offer, then his worst suspicion is confirmed: that of all nations the Dutch are the dullest, the most antipoetic. So much for his Netherlandic heritage. He might as well be monolingual.   (*Y*, 76–7)

By 2002, when *Youth* first appeared, Coetzee had already published translations of a novel and several poems from Dutch; unlike his young double, he clearly believed neither that 'Vinkenoog is all that Holland can offer', nor that 'of all nations the Dutch are the dullest, the most antipoetic'. And yet in 2004, with the publication of *Landscape with Rowers*, a collection of Coetzee's translations of twentieth-century Dutch poets, Coetzee remains lukewarm in his praise of the language and its literary riches, describing it as a 'minor language' with a 'minor literature' suffering from 'paralyzing deference to fashions from abroad' and weighed down by 'a national way of life strongly imbued with such Calvinist virtues as propriety, dutifulness, and moral vigilance [that] has not conduced to boldness of thought'.[3] The dismissal of Dutch in *Youth* certainly has more to do with the protagonist's literary ambition and purely instrumental relationship to languages – it is because Afrikaans and Dutch have done so little *for him* that he 'might as well be monolingual' – than it does with the literary merit of Dutch writers. Nevertheless, it may also contain a kernel of truth about Coetzee's true assessment of this language (and its literature) that he has spent years studying, reading, and even translating: he may not truly believe it to be the very 'dullest', but he steadfastly refuses to overvalue the language simply because of his own 'Netherlandic heritage'.

Even more so than Dutch, Afrikaans stands out for its significance to Coetzee, who speaks and writes it fluently (we see evidence of the latter in the South African Ravan Press edition of Coetzee's second novel, *In the Heart of the Country* (1978), which contains significant sections of idiomatic dialogue in Afrikaans). But this language is also inextricably tied to the Afrikaner identity that, in *Boyhood* (1997), Coetzee portrays his younger self as alternately loving and fearing, approaching and refusing. In this first novel of Coetzee's quasi-autobiographical (or, as he would have it, *autre*biographical) *Scenes from Provincial Life* trilogy, part of the problem with Afrikaans is that as a language and a culture it is simultaneously too close to completely dissociate himself from and too far away to be attainable or inhabitable:

> Though his surname is Afrikaans, though his father is more Afrikaans than English, though he himself speaks Afrikaans without any English accent, he could not pass for a moment as an Afrikaner. The range of Afrikaans he commands is thin and bodiless; there is a whole dense world of slang and allusion commanded by real Afrikaans boys – of which obscenity is only a part – to which he has no access. (B, 124)

There is an interesting echo of this idea of not being able to 'pass' in a culture despite possessing a precise, if bookish, command of the language in a letter Coetzee addresses to Paul Auster dated 11 May 2009. Here he explains that, when he moved to England as a young man (the period corresponding to the one described in *Youth*), despite knowing that 'by textbook standards' his command of the English language was superior to that of most people he met there, he nevertheless found that whenever he spoke he betrayed himself 'as a foreigner, that is to say, someone who by definition could not know the language as well as the natives', the difference being that while he knew the language 'out of books', the English knew the language 'in their bones' (HN, 66–7). This experience of lacking a 'mother tongue' has little to do with linguistic competence or even the languages he grew up speaking. Inspired by Jacques Derrida's *Monolingualism of the Other* (1996), Coetzee evokes a sense of mastering a language without possessing it, since that language belongs to the (politically or geopolitically dominant, colonizing) other. Coetzee's disavowal of Afrikaans (and Afrikanerdom) is not, therefore, the counterpart of an avowal of and full identification with English (and 'being'

English). Rather, it pertains at least in part to the fact that, as human beings, we only ever learn language that pre-exists us, language over which we have no control, and which we can never fully claim or master: language that is always the language of the other.

There is, however, in the specific scenario described by Coetzee, a counter-vailing sense of limited choice or election: in the milieu of *Boyhood* one is either country *or* town, for the Russians *or* for the Americans, 'a Christian *or* a Roman Catholic *or* a Jew', Afrikaans *or* English (*B*, 18–19. Italics mine). In England, as a native of a settler colony, Coetzee feels he cannot fully lay claim to any language, even the English that was his mother tongue. But as a white schoolboy in a bilingual environment in South Africa he can opt to *be* 'English' in strict contradistinction to *being* 'Afrikaans'. Coetzee's transla-tions from this language are perhaps ways for him to revisit the path not travelled, 'a subject position' Rita Barnard characterizes as 'con-sciously refused', namely that of the 'Afrikaans boy and thus the Afrikaans man that [Coetzee] never became, but who nevertheless once presented himself as a shadowy alternative'.[4] For this reason, the translations from Afrikaans must be read alongside Coetzee's *autre*biographical fictions as linguistic counterparts to his fictional personas.

Two Translations from Afrikaans

As a translator, Coetzee is principally known for three works: an English version of the Dutch classic by Marcellus Emants, *A Posthumous Confession* (1975); a translation out of Afrikaans of Wilma Stockenström's strange novel *The Expedition to the Baobab Tree* (1983); and a selection of poems translated from the Dutch, *Landscape with Rowers* (2004). For illustrative purposes I would like, in this section, also to consider a less well-known example.

For a 2007 special issue of the journal *Poetry* dedicated to the topic of translation, Coetzee contributed his translation from the Afrikaans of Ina Rousseau's 'Eden' together with a substantial translator's note. 'Eden' is taken from Rousseau's 1954 volume of poetry, *Die verlate tuin* (the aban-doned/neglected garden); the same poem appeared in D. J. Opperman's authoritative statement of the Afrikaans poetry canon, *Groot Verseboek* (1951), removed from the sequence of which it forms a part, as it is in Coetzee's rendering. Going by Coetzee's note, context is the key to determin-ing the poem's meaning. But the context that he has in mind is the geogra-phical and historical context of South Africa in the 1950s, not the textual context of *Die verlate tuin*. There is, Coetzee admits, no internal evidence binding this poem to a South African context other than the fact of its composition in Afrikaans. Nevertheless, he suggests that 'once the key phrase "South Africa" is breathed, the poem opens like a flower'.[5] The mere fact of its South African author and Afrikaans medium may seem like scant evidence for reading Rousseau's elusive parabolic poem as being *about* South Africa, though the insightful reading that Coetzee delivers rewards our faith. Coetzee's insistence on the importance of the poet's political and cultural milieu – '1954, when white Afrikaner nationalists were riding the crest of a wave' – despite the absence of any explicit internal reference – 'it bears no trace of South Africa' – is especially interesting in the light of the critical reception of Coetzee's own works, especially those which lack a South African setting (think, for example, of *Waiting for the Barbarians* (1980), or *The Master of Petersburg* (1994)). Is Coetzee's contextual reading a tacit endorsement of critics who place his work, especially the work before *Elizabeth Costello* (2003), solidly in a South African frame? Perhaps. More apposite to the present chapter is what this privileging of context says about Coetzee's take on translation.

It is striking that the determinant of context, the element which whispers 'South Africa' in Coetzee's account, is Afrikaans. The language itself carries with it a frame of reference and a set of assumptions that are historically, geographically, and culturally bound. While these unstated concerns are not exactly untranslatable – Coetzee here translates them into his English version and into his translator's note – they are untranslatable in their unstated-ness; the assumptions and referents of Afrikaans can be explained and they can be imported into English, but this happens at the cost of easy expression. What comes naturally in Afrikaans becomes heavy going in English: an effect that is amplified by Coetzee's choice not to replicate Rousseau's free-flowing rhyme scheme. Taking the opening stanza as representative, it is easy to see, even for readers with no prior knowledge of Afrikaans, how the neat end rhymes and regular line lengths of the original are absent from the more ponderous English rendering.

Staan daar nog in Eden êrens,   Somewhere in Eden, after all this time,
verlate soos 'n stad in puin,   does there still stand, abandoned, like
met poorte grusaam toegespyker, a ruined city, gates sealed with grisly nails,
deur eeue die mislukte tuin?   the luckless garden?

Were the original read aloud, non-Afrikaans-speakers would also be able to hear the clear drum of iambs, occasionally varied for emphasis, an aural aspect that the English version makes no effort to match.

Dismissing the poem as 'traditional in its form and imagery', Coetzee chooses to focus on its 'cryptic' dimension (what is meant and what is hidden). Translation theorists have observed that all translation is an act of interpretation;[6] this translation is no different. According to his authorized biographer, the scholar of Afrikaans literature J. C. Kannemeyer, Coetzee too believes in the continuum between translation and other interpretative acts: 'Regarding translation, Coetzee makes the provocative comment that reading a text is in essence a translation, just as all translation is in the last instance literary criticism.'[7] This emphasis on the hermeneutic work of a translation is one that Coetzee has spoken of in his writing and interviews not only as a guide for translation but also as its purpose or originating impulse. In the case of his translation of Gerrit Achterberg's sonnet sequence 'Ballade van de gasfitter' (1953), for instance, he reports: 'I began to translate it into English sonnets in 1969 *in an effort to understand it*, then found that I couldn't translate it till I had understood it. Something any hermeneuticist could have told me' (*DP*, 58. Italics mine). For this particular interpretation of 'Eden', and consequently for the translation, the fact of South Africa is more important than any of the formal features.

It is unusual for poems to have long translator's notes: something occasioned in the case of 'Eden' by its appearance in the special issue of *Poetry* rather than by Coetzee's ideal of how poetry is to appear in translation. The presence of this extended translator's note makes the interpretation that shapes the translation especially visible. The relation of text to interpretation is one-to-many: there are always several competing interpretations possible for any given text, just as there are several possible translations. It is important in this context to see translations as embodiments of interpretative choices rather than as in some way 'right' or 'wrong'. Semantic errors, of course, do occur, but far more prevalent are deliberate choices made by the translator whose aims or interpretations are different to those of the critic. In this sense, it is useful to follow Coetzee in thinking of translation as a series of 'partial solutions' (*DP*, 88), in accordance with what he calls elsewhere 'the necessary imperfection of translation'.[8] The following brief comments on Coetzee's version of Rousseau's 'Eden' are to be taken in that spirit: as attempts to reveal the underlying interpretation informing the translator's choices rather than attempts at pointing out so-called translation 'errors'.

Coetzee chooses to forgo the repetition of the line that ends the first and last stanzas – 'deur eeue die mislukte tuin?' – instead giving first 'the luckless garden?' and then 'the failed garden?' The Afrikaans word 'mislukte' corresponds far more closely to 'failed' than it does to 'luckless', but 'misluk' (failure) does share an etymology with 'geluk' (luck). Coetzee probably didn't want to lose the theological echo of this allusion to luck or fortune at the scene of man's *felix culpa*, or fortunate fall from grace (fortunate because redeemed). There is in Coetzee's English a slight tendency toward personification absent from the Afrikaans. He chooses 'sultry' for 'swoele' (hot/humid/sweltering); in the Afrikaans the fruit are 'purper en donkergeel' (purple/royal purple and dark yellow) while in the English it is unclear whether it is the branches or the fruit that are, like a human bruise, 'sallow and purple'; the lodes (or veins) of onyx and gold are in the original 'onontgonne' (unexplored), in the English they are 'unexploited'. These are minor points of emphasis, but such slight moments of quasi-personification perhaps shift us toward an interpretation of the garden as representing both the biblical Eden *and* the Company Gardens in Cape Town, both the mythical origins of mankind *and* the origins of colonialism in South Africa. Here, as always, the translation embodies the interpretation.

The focus on the semantic rather than phonic dimension of 'Eden' might be contrasted with Coetzee's choices in his previous Afrikaans translation, the Englishing of Wilma Stockenström's *Die kremetartekspidisie* (1981) as *The Expedition to the Baobab Tree*, where Coetzee's priorities seem to be precisely reversed: sound first, meaning second. The fact that the translation of a novel privileges sound and the translation of a poem privileges meaning reveals something of Coetzee's hermeneutic method. Rather than conform with the putative demands of genres, Coetzee's translations follow from and embody his interpretations. Each work needs to be read afresh with the translator each time asking, what is the most important aspect of *this* text? What do I need to retain *this* time? While the paratexts to Coetzee's other translations clarify his answers to these questions, and thus help to explain his translatorly choices in these instances, *The Expedition to the Baobab Tree* is offered without commentary or translator's note. Critics must therefore undertake to recover Coetzee's interpretations from the translated text itself, viewed alongside the original. This is what Lily Saint attempts in a canny review that makes the unusual and, from the perspective of translation studies, very welcome gesture of discussing the translator's choices at length:

> Much like Coetzee's own apartheid-era writing, [*The Expedition to the Baobab Tree*] avoids overt mention of South Africa, yet there are plenty of references to the names of flora, fauna, and agricultural paraphernalia, which, even in translation, directly indicate the book's South African setting. From the *sanga* cattle herded by the indigenous Khoisan when the Dutch settled in 1652, the same cows that were also central in The Great Trek, to the diverse species of antelope – the steenbuck, the redbuck, the oribi, and the kudu – Coetzee takes considerable pains to translate Stockenström's precise zoological and botanical terminology into English prose that retains a certain loyalty to Afrikaans. Thus

safsafwilgers, in Coetzee's rendering, becomes saf-saf willows and the shrub *noemnoembos* becomes the num-num bush. In these instances and elsewhere, the sound of the language takes priority over any meaning translation might provide for non–South African Anglophone readers. This emphasis is made particularly apparent when Coetzee chooses to translate a word like *rooibok* as 'red buck,' instead of using the more colloquial 'impala,' which is derived from Zulu.[9]

In South African English, 'Saf-saf willow' and 'num-num bush' are in fact correct and commonly used names for the plants in question. But Saint is right to imply that their adoption in Coetzee's rendering is a deliberate choice. Other, non-onomatopoeic alternatives are available; Coetzee could have re-written Stockenström's '*safsafwilgers*' as 'Cape silver willows' and '*noem-noem-bos*' (with hyphens) as 'Natal plum'. By staying close to the Afrikaans terms, Coetzee also stays close to the other African languages that have influenced the Afrikaans botanical lexicon. In the case of the 'num-num bush', the passage where it appears in Stockenström's novel illustrates its origin:

> The hem of his clothes caught on a num-num bush and held him back; jerking and pulling desperately, beating the bush flat with his cane, he tried angrily to rid himself of the thorns' grip, but only got further entangled, and eventually had to tear his clothes free. All the while he hoarsely commanded us and the slaves to fall flat, to hide, to creep away, to make ourselves scarce.
>
> Instead of making ourselves scarce we all stood up straight and gazed dumbstruck at the spectacle. With a muffled curse he freed himself from the num-num thorns and stamped over to us and explained that there was an army on the way, on the river.[10]

The repetition, or stutter, in the name of the num-num bush derives from the double-take it inspires in those caught by its thorns. In the context of the (ultimately ineffectual) would-be colonizer getting caught while his slaves and servants refuse to look away, the indigenous name aligns with the resistance of the indigenous peoples and landscape to the foreign settler. As a local translation decision, 'num-num' rather than 'Natal plum' is doubly justified. As a global decision, given the continuous theme of local resistance to colonization in the novel, a systematic cleavage to indigenous terms seems warranted. Coetzee makes other notable choices here that confirm the interpretation inherent in his choice of 'num-num'. He divides a single paragraph into two, emphasizing the human echo of nature's resistance by giving it its own space. He also substitutes the idiomatic for the unidiomatic in translating '*ons klein te maak*' (make ourselves small) as 'make ourselves scarce'. This repeated phrase, conjoining Coetzee's two paragraphs, acts as a similar stutter to '*noem-noem*' in the Afrikaans. In opting for scarcity over small-ness, Coetzee is perhaps underlining the genocidal potential of colonization; in opting for a familiar idiom in the English over a strange expression in the Afrikaans, he is perhaps compensating for the excess strangeness that 'num-num' might have for a non-South-African Anglophone reader.

Coetzee's Theory of Translation

Coetzee has written and spoken about translation in a number of different venues, but never as extensively as in 'Roads to Translation' (2005), republished as 'Working with Translators' (2008), wherein he reflects on the efforts of those who have undertaken to translate his English into no fewer than twenty-five languages, as well as on translation more generally. As expressed in this piece, Coetzee's views on translation, while always interesting and grounded in enga-ging examples, are rarely unconventional: a text's meaning is independent of an author's intentions; translation aims for a 'best possible' solution rather than precise or 'perfect' equivalence; it is not always possible in the target language to reproduce every implication of a word in the source text; languages come in related clusters – a reference to a Latin phrase in English is not easily evoked in Korean.[11] In addition to these direct affirmations of common wisdom about the craft of translation, Coetzee has much to say that is relevant to the conceptual limits of translation and the limits to concepts that translation marks, as well as the competitive world of literature in translation, though for these views, one is best advised to turn to less direct sources. Two cases in point: the explicit discussion of translation in *Diary of a Bad Year* (2007) and Coetzee's writings and public talks on Samuel Beckett.

In *Diary of a Bad Year*, the Coetzee persona, JC, writes brief essays about the state of the world that are to be published alongside similar essays by other '*éminences grises* who have clawed [their] way up to the highest peak' of literary fame (*DYB*, 22). JC writes in English, but he knows that the volume will first appear in German: he writes, in other words, with his eventual translation firmly in mind. The volume's English translation will be called *Strong Opinions*, but the title for the German 'original' publication remains undetermined. This kind of reversal, whereby the translation comes before the original, is exactly what makes *Diary of a Bad Year* seem to fit Rebecca Walkowitz's paradigm of a 'born-translated' text, a paradigm to which I shall return below. But upon closer inspection, what Coetzee does with the multilingual matrix of *Strong Opinions* comes much closer to Barbara Cassin's exploration of philoso-phical translation – and especially the resistance of concepts to transla-tion, their so-called 'untranslatability' – expounded in her influential *Le*

Vocabulaire européen des philosophies: Dictionaire des intraduisibles (2004). JC's comparative linguistic and philological work could well have been expanded and adapted to serve as an entry in Cassin's *Dictionary*:

> *Opiniâtre*, say the French: obdurate, stony, mulish. Bruno [the editor of the volume], in his German, is more diplomatic. He is still wavering between calling these little excursions *Meinungen* or *Ansichten*. *Meinungen* are opinions, he says, but opinions subject to fluctuations of mood. The *Meinungen* I held yesterday are not necessarily the *Meinungen* I hold today. *Ansichten*, by contrast, are firmer, more thought out. In our last communication he was tending to prefer *Meinungen*. Six different writers, six different personalities, he says: how can we be sure how firmly wedded each writer is to his opinions? Best to leave the question open. What interests the reader more, anyhow, is the quality of the opinions themselves – their variety, their power to startle, the ways in which they match or do not match the reputations of their authors. I disagree. *Ansichten* is the word I want, I say, *Harte Ansichten*, if you can say that in German. *Feste Ansichten*, says Bruno. Let me give it further thought. Let me consult with the other contributors.   (*DYB*, 126–35)

Meinungen are allied to the diary format, they are time-stamped, perhaps valid only for the moment of their enunciation. *Ansichten* on the contrary are allied to the atemporal or extra-temporal pronouncements employed in the discourse of the 'classic' (see below). In advocating for *Meinungen*, the editor gives two arguments. The first is an argument from uncertainty: we do not know how dedicated each of the six contributors is to the opinions expressed in the volume. Given the uncertainty, it is better to use *Meinungen*, the broader of the two categories. This is what Bruno has in mind when he resolves to 'consult with the other contributors' – if as a matter of *fact* they are all determined to stick to their opinions at whatever cost, then *Ansichten* becomes the more appropriate word. The second, subtler, argument is presented 'anyhow', as an aside, as not an argument at all. It claims that the reader is more likely to be engaged by 'the opinions themselves', though not in and of themselves but rather in their difference from each other ('their variety'), their ability to be originary ('their power to startle'), and from 'the ways in which they match or do not match the reputation of their authors'. It is exactly in their difference, in the context of their presentation – placed among the opinions of five other writers, co-contributors whose opinions about their opinions must be consulted – and in the context of their reception, measured against the reputation of the author, that these opinions must be *Meinungen*, which allow for contradiction and negotiation, and cannot be *Ansichten*, which are fixed and tyrannical. The entire section rests on the small differences between languages, on the resistance to translation inherent in terms like *Ansichten, Meinungen,* opinions, and *opiniâtre,* a resistance that can be exploited in order to achieve philosophical precision and conceptual elaboration.

The difficulties and rewards of this everyday translator's activity – lingering with terms that are resistant to easy translation – are multiplied when this passage itself appears in translation. Catherine Lauga du Plessis, one of Coetzee's two regular translators into French, resorts to adding an asterisk after all the book's French terms, including '*Opiniâtre*'; the *foreignness* of the target language within the source text is something that either requires the translator's intervention or that must be lost. Translating '*Opiniâtre,* say the French: obdurate, stony, mulish', she writes, '*Opiniâtre*,* disent les Français: obstiné, buté, têtu comme une mule'.[12] Now, taking the *Oxford-Hachette French Dictionary* as a representative bilingual reference work, the primary definition for 'obstiné' is 'stubborn'; the primary definition for 'buté' is 'stubborn'; the primary definition for 'têtu' also is 'stubborn' with a note that it also occurs in the idiom 'être têtu comme un âne *or* une mule *or* une bourrique' which signifies 'stubborn as a mule'. So, an admittedly poor, but accurate, back-translation might read: '*Opiniâtre,* say the French: stubborn, stubborn, stubborn as a mule'. For '*Opiniâtre*' the *Oxford-Hachette* has, in order, 'dogged', 'relentless', 'tenacious', and 'persistent', each of which has a stronger emphasis on the temporal duration of being stubbornly *opiniâtre,* and none of which is exactly captured by 'obstiné, buté, têtu comme une mule'. However, the one thing Lauga du Plessis's translation doesn't have to do is explain the meaning of *opiniâtre* to a French readership – the connotations of the word are already present in the French reader's mind; instead she can look ahead in the passage to make sure that the French word appears in contradistinction to the German *Meinungen* and as loosely synonymous with *Ansichten.* Where Coetzee puts pressure, as he does here, on the differences between languages, it is an invitation for his translators to do the same, and reading their versions of his outward-looking Anglo-centered prose is bound to be conceptually fruitful.

A second example of an implicit theorization of translation can be found in an unexpected place in Coetzee's work: his recent writings on Samuel Beckett. In 2006, contributing to an edited volume celebrating the centenary of Beckett's birth, Coetzee wrote a rather odd piece entitled 'Samuel Beckett in Cape Town – An Imaginary History'. Beckett had, in 1937, at the urging of one of his professors at Trinity College, Dublin, applied for a position in the Italian department of the University of Cape Town where Coetzee would in 1956 commence his studies as an undergraduate and where he would, eventually, become a professor of English Literature. Part essay, part speculative fiction, Coetzee's very short text ponders what might have arisen had

Beckett's application been successful. Assuming that Beckett, stranded in South Africa during World War II, found 'easy colonial life' to his liking, his work might have had a very different local inflection. This consideration of the transversion of language and geographic location in literature is, of course, also a consideration of translation, albeit indirectly. And, as we've seen, it is Coetzee's practice when discussing matters of translation dutifully to note (and somewhat overstate) his own linguistic shortcomings:

> Knowing no Italian and only a few words of French, I would not have been able to study in Professor Beckett's department, but I would certainly have heard of him as the author of *Waiting for Godot*, and perhaps even attended a performance of the play written in an English scandalously inflected with the argot of the Cape Flats.[13]

With Beckett in Cape Town, so the claim goes, Coetzee would have been resistant to adopting the older writer as a 'spiritual father', and would 'certainly not have spent [his] time at the University of Texas labouring over a doctoral dissertation on Professor Beckett's prose style'.[14] According to this speculative account, had the two writers met in Cape Town, neither of them would have produced the work for which they were respectively awarded the Nobel Prize in Literature.

What is not clear from Coetzee's short piece is exactly why he thinks he would not have been drawn to Beckett's prose style as a dissertation topic. Is it that he would have found Beckett's proximity off-putting – that he considers material presence antithetical to 'spiritual fatherhood'? Is it that the young Coetzee's desire to study, and perhaps emulate, Beckett's prose had to do with it being produced in Europe, or Paris, the capital of the World Republic of Letters? Or is it rather – and this is the possibility that best fits the text – that there is a geographical contingency to literary 'greatness', that Beckett's prose, if issued from South Africa, would not have merited study (at least according to the values of the academic institutions of the day, the very values that Coetzee regularly, and most recently in his Argentinian pedagogical and publishing endeavours, seeks to upturn)?

It is easy to hear in Coetzee's imagining of a *Waiting for Godot* 'scandalously inflected with the argot of the Cape Flats' a parallel to an English-language *Waiting for Godot* (1954) inflected with the rhythms and idiom of Irish English. In a public discussion of his book of essays and interviews, *Doubling the Point*, reissued in a Spanish translation as *Cartas de navegación* in 2015, Coetzee dilates on his trajectory as a Beckett scholar:

> I wrote a fair amount on Beckett in the 1960s and 70s, always trying to discover the secret of the attraction that his prose held for me. I found his prose quite

mesmeric and I tried, you know, various forms of linguistic analysis to crack the secret of Beckett's prose ... What I have discovered more recently, from other critics of Beckett, is that – you know, this was staring me in the face but I just didn't recognize it – that Beckett is Irish. [Laughter]. And that in fact if you want to know the secret of Beckett's appeal, you have only to go to Ireland, because there are lots of people who talk and write like Beckett in Ireland.[15]

That Beckett's style can be reduced to his Irishness is perhaps an overstatement, but that the time and place of one's birth and upbringing have an impact on one's language is not a controversial claim at all. The South African *Godot* would presumably resemble the Anglo-Irish *Godot* in its excess of local idiom. But the language of Beckett's French original is stranger, harder to locate, more idiolect than dialect, bearing the trace of an individual rather than a region. There is a tension in Beckett studies between those who would see him first and foremost as an Irish writer, positioning him within or in relation to a national and inter-national literary history, and those who see his work, especially in French, as an abstraction from and denial of such categories. In Coetzee's counterfactual investigation, Beckett would use a South African version of English for the original. Both South African and Irish varieties of English reflect a colonial history, both stand in a relation of subjugation to the dominant form, and both are 'scandalous', in its quasi-religious, etymological sense. But to introduce the vernacular of the Cape Flats circa 1954 into *Waiting for Godot* is to give the play a racial and political dimension different (though not necessarily incomparable) to that of the original. Despite the stipulation that this play would carry the status of (an alternative) original, we, the implied readers of Coetzee's text who live in a world that already has an *En attendant Godot* (1952) and a *Waiting for Godot*, cannot but imagine it as a translation (or perhaps a translation of the translation) of the work we already know. Could this play by Professor Beckett of the University of Cape Town's Italian Department be translated back into a continental European language? Could it become a classic, if a classic is defined by its capacity to survive de-contextualization? Or are translatability and the potential to become a 'classic' attributes of the European *Godot*s alone?[16]

In an interview given shortly after receiving the Nobel Prize in Literature in 2003, Coetzee talks about a South African staging of Beckett.

Beckett was an Irishman and a European with no African connections at all. Yet in the hands of a dramatist of the sensitivity and skill of Athol Fugard, Beckett can be transplanted into South African surroundings in such a way that he seems almost native there. What does this show? That the history of the arts is a history of unceasing cross-fertilization across fences and boundaries.[17]

The success of Fugard's adaptation may have spurred the idea of a *Godot* originally composed in a South African setting. But unless we can imagine the transplantation moving in the opposite direction, with Beckett choosing to adapt one of Fugard's plays, say *Boesman and Lena* (1969) or *'Master Harold' and the Boys* (1982), into Parisian surroundings, *and* getting the funding and cultural support to do so, the claim about an 'unceasing cross-fertilization across fences and boundaries' is misleading. There is no technical or aesthetic reason why such an adaptation could not take place, but the prestige-gap between European and African cultural products, then and now, makes it hard to imagine the adaptation moving the other way. Paris sees plays from all over the world staged locally, especially during its annual *Festival d'Automne*, but the value of these plays is almost always framed in terms of 'windows on the world'; to adapt these plays to a French setting would work entirely counter to this market logic. Or, to put it differently, the 'unceasing cross-fertilization' across literary cultures occurs unevenly when the traffic is between global north and global south, or between vehicular and dominated languages or dialects, and it is this unevenness that makes the older Coetzee uncertain whether he, as a young writer and scholar just starting out, would have elected a South African Samuel Beckett as his guiding literary influence the way he did the French-Irish Beckett.

When asked about his relationship to South Africa in the same post-Nobel interview, Coetzee admits that his 'intellectual allegiances are clearly European, not African'. These allegiances make him a 'late representative' of European colonial expansion, together with its 'history of oppression', responding to the people of 'the part of the world' where this 'failed or failing colonial movement ... sought and failed to establish itself'. The hesitation between tenses – 'failed or failing' – suggests a temporal ambivalence, an uncertainty about the past-ness of the past regarding the future-less colonial project. Coetzee's response to this present/history comes in the form of his fiction and he has rigorously refused to reduce that response into 'abstract terms'. While his books are not simple *depictions* of (post)colonialism, few readers of works like *Waiting for the Barbarians*, *Life & Times of Michael K* (1983), *Foe* (1986), or *Disgrace* (1999) would dispute their responsiveness to various colonialisms and their legacies. There is, however, a tension between the sensitivity to historical oppression (and its legacy, which is ongoing, even in failure and without future) in Coetzee's work and his 'intellectual allegiances' to the canons and classics of European art. And never are these tensions more pronounced than when he thinks about translation or works in a translatorly mode. Ever scrupulous, Coetzee (or his persona) won't let us forget his own provincial origins. In the inter-lingual philosophizing aimed at understanding the epistemological possibilities for knowing the present, especially if one is already an '*éminence grise*', Coetzee gives us an implicit theorization of translation that emphasizes its world-expanding potential. And in his writings about Beckett and about the classic, Coetzee gives us a view of translation theory that acknowledges that the world, however much we expand it through contact with other languages and cultures, is fundamentally postcolonial. Here we can see Coetzee conceptualize the inequalities that condition and limit the transnational and translational exchanges of the literary sphere. Future scholars would do well to tease out this (indirect) aspect of Coetzee's relationship to translation.

Translation and the Style of Coetzee's Prose

In one of the most revealing passages in 'Working with Translators', Coetzee reflects not on the general problems of translation but on the translatability of his own novels:

> Are my books easy or hard to translate: Sentence by sentence, my prose is generally lucid, in the sense that within the sentence syntactic constructions are unambiguous and logical relations between components as clear as I can make them. Where ambiguity occurs, there is usually a reason for it.[18]

Coetzee's conscious quest for clarity in his prose may well stem from his early work in linguistics, and this clarity persists through whatever metafictional or self-reflexive aspects of his fiction tie him to the tradition of postmodernism. While Coetzee's prose is frequently difficult, it is rarely if ever opaque. In his book on Coetzee's style, Jarad Zimbler argues that such clarity, found in Coetzee since *Dusklands* (1974), his earliest work, can be attributed to concrete strategies including '(a) use of clauses that are short, and more often coordinated than embedded or subordinated; (b) careful handling of adverbials of place, time and manner; (c) preference for straightforward diction; and (d) avoidance of obscure constructions and analogies'.[19] Zimbler's list not only seems like a university professor's (rarely met) ideals for student prose, it also reads like a literary translator's wish list. Prose that is clear in this precise, ever-disambiguating sense is of course easier to translate than prose that fails to make what Coetzee calls the 'relations between components' obvious.

This does not mean that Coetzee's translators never face knotty problems. Coetzee is especially aware, or has been made aware through his interactions with his translators, of the difficulty of translating words used with 'the full freight of history behind them', which is how he uses certain words in his prose, and of literary allusion, which he frequently employs.[20] There are, of course, strategies by which translators can compensate for the use of words with literary or historical significance in the source text by finding (something as close as possible to) equivalents in the target language. Coetzee discusses several of these in 'Working with Translators'. More interesting are the other grounds, beyond 'clarity', for what Coetzee considers his works' easy translatability: dialogue and sociolinguistic specificity.

Coetzee recognizes that dialogue can be difficult for translators, but he doesn't believe his own use of dialogue ought to be:

> Dialogue comes with its own set of problems, particularly when it is very informal and incorporates regional usages, contemporary catch-phrases and allusions, or slang. My dialogue is rarely of this kind. For the most part its character remains formal, even if its rhythms are somewhat more abrupt than the rhythms of narrative prose. So hitting the right register is not difficult for the translator.[21]

Rumena Bužarovska, who has translated *Life & Times of Michael K* and *Disgrace* into Macedonian, claims that one of the most striking stylistic aspects of Coetzee's prose is its relentless formality. She is especially struck by the stiffness of David Lurie's speech when conversing with his daughter, the formal register of which she has attempted to retain in her version.[22] Indeed, I would argue that Coetzee's eschewal of informality, regionalisms, or contemporary slang extends beyond his use of dialogue to his deployment of *style indirect libre*. The language of his characters' interiority matches the formality of their speech.

Following this strategy of linguistic neutrality and a refusal to mark cultural, linguistic, class, or racial difference through word choice or syntax, Coetzee manages to avoid the pitfalls into which he believes previous South African writers have stumbled. In a chapter in *White Writing* (1988) entitled 'Simple Language, Simple People: Smith, Paton, Mikro' Coetzee laments that 'South African fiction is full of examples of people (and peoples) to whom a language limited and simplified in various ways is attributed, and whose range of intellection and feeling is by implication correspondingly limited and simplified' (WW, 116). Pauline Smith renders the interiority, as well as the dialogue, of her Afrikaans-speaking characters in a deliberately foreignizing manner; Alan Paton transposes the speech and thoughts of his Zulu characters into an archaic English that cannot but imply 'an archaic quality to the Zulu behind it, as if the Zulu language, Zulu culture, the Zulu frame of mind, belonged to a bygone and heroic age' (WW, 128); and C. H. Kühn, writing as 'Mikro', chooses to have his Coloured servants *internalize* the language that marks and reinforces their inferior status with respect to their White masters. Coetzee, in contrast, spends a career evading such problematic practices. As a byproduct, his prose is all the more translatable. By his own assessment, 'it is not prose one can translate while listening to the radio, and now and again one has to rack one's brains a bit, but the challenges it proposes are rarely insuperable'.[23] Bužarovska attests to this easy translatability in general, but points out that even a few scant references to race and to the official racial terms of apartheid can be difficult to translate into a language where all racial terminology has been imported from the United States, where the equivalent of 'coloured' and 'black' are consequently used synonymously, and all racial terms have a foreign feel to them.[24] This particular difficulty is, of course, somewhat exacerbated by Coetzee's general avoidance of racial terms and racialized dialect, since these, appearing with greater frequency, would at least give foreign readers a sense of the racial (and racist) norms of the source culture.

Faced with the combination of two postulates – (1) the relative accessibility or translatability of Coetzee's prose, and (2) the global circulation of Coetzee's works with the translations, especially those into Dutch, appearing simultaneously with, or even before, the English – Rebecca Walkowitz makes the claim that Coetzee's writing is not only easily translated, it is, in a sense, *written to be translated*: written in full awareness of its eventual translation and stylistically adapted to make this translation easier. The claim is certainly provocative and the idea that literary form is impacted by literary circulation is a useful one. But here, for me, the explanatory power of translation reaches its limit, even in the case of J. M. Coetzee, a translator/novelist deeply concerned with linguistic and cultural difference and with the craft and history of translation. Coetzee's translatability, where it in fact holds up to scrutiny, is an incidental effect of his style, not its cause.

Notes

1. 'J. M. Coetzee est un lecteur attentif, un relecteur pointilleux, un analyste de traductions exigeant et un traducteur scrupuleux et inspiré comme le montrent ses propres traductions.' Catherine Lauga du Plessis, 'Traduire J. M. Coetzee', *IFAS Working Paper Series / Les Cahiers de l' IFAS*, 6 (2005), 69–74 (p. 69).
2. Qtd in J. C. Kannemeyer, *J. M. Coetzee: A Life in Writing*, trans. Michiel Heyns (London: Scribe Press, 2012), p. 175.
3. J. M. Coetzee, *Landscape with Rowers: Poetry from the Netherlands* (Princeton: Princeton University Press, 2004), p. vii.
4. Rita Barnard, 'Coetzee in/and Afrikaans', *Journal of Literary Studies*, 25.4 (2009), 84–105 (p. 87).
5. Ina Rousseau, 'Eden', trans. J. M. Coetzee, *Poetry* 190.1 (2007), 10–11 (p. 11).

6. For examples, see the works by Steiner, Ricoeur, and Venuti included under Further Reading.
7. Kannemeyer, *A Life in Writing*, p. 180.
8. J. M. Coetzee, 'Working with Translators' in Alexandra Lianeri and Vanda Zajko (eds.), *Translation and the Classic* (Oxford: Oxford University Press, 2008), pp. 407–20 (p. 410).
9. Lily Saint, 'Traces of Glory: On Wilma Stockenström's *Expedition to the Baobab Tree*', *Los Angeles Review of Books*, 18 July 2017. https://lareviewofbooks.org /article/traces-of-glory-on-wilma-stockenstroms-the-expedition-to-the-baobab-tree/#!
10. Wilma Stockenström, *The Expedition to the Baobab Tree*, trans. J. M. Coetzee (Brooklyn: Archipelago Books, 2014), p. 85.
11. Coetzee, 'Working with Translators', pp. 409, 410, 412.
12. J. M. Coetzee, *Journal d'une année noire*, trans. Catherine Lauga du Plessis (Paris: Seuil, 2008), pp. 155–6.
13. J. M. Coetzee, 'Samuel Beckett in Cape Town – An Imaginary History' in James Knowlson and Elizabeth Knowlson (eds.), *Beckett Remembering, Remembering Beckett: A Centenary Celebration* (New York: Arcade, 2006), pp. 74–7 (p. 75).
14. Ibid., pp. 75–6.
15. J. M. Coetzee, 'John M. Coetzee: Cartas de Navigacion'. YouTube video, 1:03:45, lecture in 'Literaturas del Sur' series, Buenos Aires, on 15 April 2015, posted by Museo MALBA, 8 May 2015. www.youtube.com/watch? v=wnfjHQ48EMc
16. See Michelle Kelly's essay in this volume (Chapter 11) for a discussion of Coetzee's landmark essay 'What is a Classic?' and the sense that 'the aesthetic might be experienced as transcendent *and* demand reflection on individual material interests' in Coetzee's work. Clearly the fantasy of a *Godot* written in Cape Town, with its implications for Coetzee's career as a scholar and writer, is another instance of his continuous rumination on this theme.
17. 'An Exclusive Interview with J. M. Coetzee', by David Atwell, *Dagens Nyheter*, 12 August 2003, www.dn.se/kultur-noje/an-exclusive-interview-with -j-m-coetzee/
18. Coetzee, 'Working with Translators', pp. 408–9.
19. Jarad Zimbler, *J. M. Coetzee and the Politics of Style* (Cambridge: Cambridge University Press, 2014), p. 31.
20. Coetzee, 'Working with Translators', p. 409.
21. Ibid.
22. Interview with Rumena Bužarovska, 29 October 2018.
23. Coetzee, 'Working with Translators', p. 409.
24. Interview with Rumena Bužarovska.

7

RACHEL BOWER

Collaboration and Correspondence

J. M. Coetzee is often thought a solitary, reclusive figure, but he has long collaborated with other writers and artists, as well as with literary critics, philosophers, anthropologists, and psychologists. Indeed, two of his latest works, *Here and Now* (2013) and *The Good Story* (2015), are collections of correspondence: the first with the novelist Paul Auster, and the second with the psychotherapist Arabella Kurtz. Coetzee is no newcomer to collaborative work, however. He edited *A Land Apart: A South African Reader* with André Brink in 1986, and his hugely influential *Doubling the Point* (1992) – a volume of essays and interviews – was a shared enterprise with his former student, David Attwell. Many of the interviews in *Doubling the Point* were conducted by Attwell through a series of detailed letters between 1989 and 1991 and reflect the sustained dialogue that went into this book. In all of these collaborations Coetzee has worked with and against his interlocutors, questioning, returning, asking again.

Correspondence has also played an important role in Coetzee's fictional works. Perhaps the most obvious examples are *Foe* (1986), which relies heavily on epistolary conventions, and *Age of Iron* (1990), which is made up of a single long letter. If we look closer, however, we begin to see that epistolary conventions and techniques appear in many of Coetzee's narratives, from Eugene Dawn's unsent letter in *Dusklands* (1974) to the pivotal letter exchange between David and Lucy Lurie at the heart of *Disgrace* (1999); from the examination of interviewing and letter-writing conventions in *Summertime* (2009) to the lost letter of *The Childhood of Jesus* (2013). In each instance, the conditions for dialogue and working together come under scrutiny.

The claim that correspondence and collaboration are central to Coetzee's oeuvre, however, becomes more complicated when we ask how this fits with Coetzee's notorious resistance, even hostility, to being interviewed. In *Doubling the Point*, for example, Coetzee declares: 'If I had had any foresight, I would have had nothing to do with journalists from the start';

lamenting 'the violation of propriety, to say nothing of the violation of private space' in the 'journalistic' interview (*DP*, 65). We need only think of Coetzee's failed interview with Jayne Poyner to see this resistance in practice.[1] Coetzee repeatedly closes down Poyner's questions, giving curt, and sometimes even single-word answers. Coetzee seems to use this exchange to undermine the interview and the interviewer herself, responding with his own questions or evasions. He claims, for instance, that he does not 'know the range of current South African writing well enough to comment' on its 'strengths and weaknesses'.[2]

More recently, Coetzee has written to Kurtz about the extremely 'constrained and constraining' form of the 'so-called free-form interview common in the media';[3] and to Auster about avoiding the 'rounds of public questioning' at the Jaipur Literary Festival in 2011 (*HN*, 211). It is certainly the case that Coetzee has long refused interviews in public as well as the exposure associated with celebrity authorship. There seems then, at first glance, to be a contradiction, even a paradox here: the 'solitary', reluctant, deeply private Coetzee who avoids or stymies certain conversations, is also the Coetzee who, over his career, has pursued extensive collaborations, many of which have offered insights into his thoughts, feelings, and experiences. This is particularly the case in *Here and Now*, where the friendship with Auster deepens over the course of the correspondence, as we shall see.

However, this apparent paradox is resolved once we begin to look closer at the type of dialogue in which Coetzee is willing to participate, for we then begin to see that his hostility to the 'journalistic interview' actually plays a central role in the critical dialogue that he hopes to pursue with his chosen interlocutors; that his rejection of the immediate, unplanned response is aligned with the principles of his collaborative work. To put this differently, we might say that Coetzee's commitment to meaningful dialogue and correspondence is also a resistance to producing a single repeatable life story, a superficial interaction, or extractable facts and quotations. Just as Coetzee finds it necessary to turn epistolary conventions against themselves in the pursuit of a meaningful correspondence in his novel *Age of Iron*, so mediation, reflection, and criticism – even conflict – are necessary, Coetzee believes, if one is to pursue genuine exchange with other people. As such, this chapter will show that the apparently 'contradictory' aspects of Coetzee's work are in fact part of the same project of dialectical collaboration and dialogue. In seeking to understand this project better, the first half of the chapter focuses on interviews and the works of correspondence, particularly *The Good Story*, and the second on the use of epistolary conventions and techniques in his fictional works, especially *Summertime* and *Age of Iron*.

'I Hope You Will Help Me Get Further'

Doubling the Point puts on display some of the principles that have since underpinned Coetzee's collaborative work. In the series of detailed interviews which, in Attwell's words, 'tie this collection together', he and Coetzee explore different genres of correspondence and the kind of exchange that is made possible by refusing the veneer of superficial interaction (*DP*, 2). Coetzee describes a number of differences between the sustained, reflective exchange and the typical media interview. He writes:

> There is a true sense in which writing is dialogic: a matter of awakening the countervoices in oneself and embarking upon speech with them ... Whereas interviewers want speech, a flow of speech. That speech they record, take away, edit, censor, cutting out all its waywardness, till what is left conforms to a monologic ideal. (*DP*, 65)

The centrality of writing to Coetzee's experiments in correspondence cannot be overstated. Although there is a lot packed into these lines, let us focus on the perceived distinction between the unmediated, monologic speech which, in Coetzee's view, the typical interviewer requires, and the dialogue that writing, and written correspondence, seems to enable. Coetzee identifies the journalistic interview with the demand for an easily digestible, consumable story, which will be made to seem as if it tumbled spontaneously from the teller.

Coetzee later echoes this point in an email to Kurtz, replying to her request for his thoughts on their correspondence:

> The dialogue via email has been a great deal easier for me than a face-to-face or voice-to-voice exchange would have been. It releases me to go back over what I have said, revising and improving it. I have never believed that the first words that slip out, unchecked, unrevised, constitute the truth, 'what one wants to say'. Which is another way of saying that I am, by constitution, a writer.[4]

Coetzee again stresses the space for revision and mediation in the written exchange, as opposed to the supposed truth of the 'first words that slip out', echoing one of the early interviews with Attwell, in which he claims that 'Writing reveals to you what you wanted to say in the first place' (*DP*, 18).

There are no simple conclusions to be drawn from Coetzee's comments on the complex relations between writing and speech, which are not only accompanied by a long history of philosophical debate, but also become particularly acute in colonial and postcolonial contexts.[5] If we provisionally accept this distinction, however, two quite different forms of exchange begin to emerge: the first, and perhaps the simpler, is the public or face-to-face interview: spoken, seemingly spontaneous, and unmediated. The second is trickier, reflecting the kind of exchange Coetzee seeks through his collaborations, involving revision, interrogation, trust, and intimacy. Distinct principles appear to underpin these two forms, where spontaneous speech contrasts with reflective writing; monologue with dialogue; patter with meaningful exchange; the superficial with the intimate; surface with depth; stasis with motion; immediacy with mediation; authenticity with scepticism; and the single story with the multiple.

Coetzee develops these ideas further in his correspondence with Kurtz, describing how interviewers often demand *the* story: an authentic, repeatable narrative that is always susceptible to calcification and repetition, and which comes at the expense of all the other memories and versions of the story. To illustrate this, Coetzee describes an article in which Jonathan Franzen writes that 'after submitting to one promotional interview after another for his new book, he felt he had to break free or else he would begin to believe in the life-narrative that he had been spouting in the interviews' (*GS*, 13). Coetzee understands Franzen not to be saying that he has 'been telling untruths in the interviews' but instead 'that the repetitions of a single account of his own life were scouring so deep a trace that he would soon lose his freedom to interpret (remember) his life otherwise' (*GS*, 13). By contrast, engaging as an 'outsider' to Kurtz's discipline, Coetzee hopes to deepen his understanding of 'therapeutic dialogue', and to examine the various stories and kinds of truth that might emerge in such an exchange (*GS*, v–vi). *The Good Story* might well be understood, then, as a meditation on the value of dialogue and on the openings which emerge through it, offering alternatives to calcification and repetition.

It should be clear, however, that this is not a wholesale rejection of repetition per se, for there are clear continuities between the practice of 'doubling back' in *Doubling the Point* and Coetzee's later collaborative works, which all loop round to previous 'markers' in the hope that, in Attwell's words, this continual return and reflection 'will involve more than mere repetition' (*DP*, 3). This principle continues to shape Coetzee's later correspondence and fiction, where he frequently returns to, or circles around, a point in the hope of finding an opening or a slip: a fresh way of thinking or writing about the world. Coetzee and Kurtz are explicit about this process, suggesting that their exchanges, which are 'offered in an interdisciplinary spirit', do 'not always follow a linear train of thought. They sometimes repeat and contradict themselves, they return to insistent preoccupations, they pursue lines of thinking without always knowing where they will lead – all of this in the hope that they may here and there open a new or unusual perspective' (*GS*, vi). This is no mere academic exercise, as we shall see in the later discussion of *Age of Iron*, a novel concerned with the 'question of whether performative conditions for messengerhood are met' (*DP*, 340). *Age of Iron* rejects the 'stupidly unchanging' repetitive message and messengers of the apartheid regime: 'The message: that the message never changes. A message that turns people to stone' (*AI*, 29). Instead, this narrative is committed *only* to a changed and changing message, a message that can be created only through allegiance to a singular messenger, as well as by pursuing different ways of thinking and writing.

The challenge of developing modes of writing which can say something true of a specific time and place has long preoccupied Coetzee. In a review of Alice Walker's *The Temple of My Familiar* (1989), published the year before *Age of Iron*, Coetzee described the 'cliche-ridden prose' [*sic*] of parts of the narrative, and asked, '[h]ow deep can one's liberation run when its very language is secondhand?'[6] A year earlier, Coetzee had published *White Writing* (1988), a collection of essays that asked whether there is 'a language in which people of European identity, or if not of European identity then of a highly problematical South African–colonial identity, can speak to Africa and be spoken to by Africa?' (*WW*, 7–8). Two years earlier still, when work on *Age of Iron* had commenced, Coetzee remarked: 'The true challenge is: how not to play the game by the rules of the state, how to establish one's own authority, how to imagine torture and death on one's own terms' (*DP*, 364). In his review of Yvonne Burgess's *The Strike* (1975), Coetzee speaks of the '*automization*' of writing which 'explains how it comes about that sometimes a book can be conceived of without an author' (*DP*, 93). The challenge, of finding a language that is not 'second hand' or 'automized'; a language in which one can establish 'one's own authority' and speak 'on one's own terms', is central to understanding Coetzee's commitment to dialogue and correspondence, in his fiction and non-fiction.

It is through dialogue in writing, either with oneself or another, that openings are glimpsed; that possibilities for new perspectives emerge. This might be understood as a commitment to correspondence in the broadest sense: to changing one's ideas in light of another's, rather than doggedly adhering to a calcified monologue; to using differences to put pressure on previous thoughts or received opinion; to travelling further together than one could alone. This is captured nicely in a phrase that is passed back and forth in Kurtz and Coetzee's correspondence, where Kurtz writes, 'That is as far as I can get for now but I hope you will help me get further.'[7] Coetzee replies with an appeal to Kurtz: '[h]elp me to get beyond this point' (*GS*, 15). Both correspondents ask again and again for help when they are 'stuck', appealing for assistance to move beyond their own positions: seeking openings, seeking slips.

The Good Story

The clearest 'opening' in the Kurtz–Coetzee correspondence appears in a 'slip' in the email exchange dated May–December 2008, which was published prior to *The Good Story* in the journal *Salmagundi*, and which provides an insight into the processes through which the correspondence was initiated and developed. We must proceed with caution, as with any collection of letters or emails (fictional or not), because of the ever-present, often invisible hand of the epistolary editor who selects and orders the exchange. Nevertheless, to the best of our knowledge, the *Salmagundi* article opens with Kurtz's initial email to Coetzee, which asks whether he will 'consider being interviewed in front of an audience about what can be learned from your work from a psychological point of view'. Coetzee's reply is predictable: 'I am not a fluent speaker and don't easily see the point of questions. I am also dubious of the worth of opinions that are expressed by my public persona.' Coetzee does, however, embrace Kurtz's alternative suggestion of corresponding by email, remarking that he would prefer this more dialogic mode of exchange to 'something in one go'.[8]

After several emails, Coetzee slips up, accidentally calling Kurtz 'Amanda' rather than Arabella, and she then inadvertently sends him an unfinished email. Kurtz addresses this frankly: 'Dear John, I am Arabella not Amanda, though this makes me feel a little better about sending you an unfinished email by mistake.'[9] These errors, however, seem to provide the grounds for a different kind of dialogue. Until this point, the exchange is fairly formal, guarded, and, on Coetzee's part, curtailed (his early emails are only half a page in length). By contrast, the email in which he apologizes for 'the slip' is almost two pages long, and the correspondence thereafter becomes more detailed and probing. Coetzee's response to the error also includes a description of the kind of slip that is required when creating a fictional character. He refers to Kurtz's inadvertent email (which we do not see) in which she had (apparently) described the 'invention of fictional characters', and suggests that for him it is not invention, but

> a matter of putting together a pattern of clichés (the already-written) and patiently waiting for the slip when the 'character' puts in his/her own word; and then allowing that original word to grow and grow; and ultimately erasing all the earlier clichés, which you no longer need.[10]

One cannot avoid the feeling that something akin to this process occurs in the correspondence: both Coetzee and Kurtz initially rely heavily upon the conventions of letter-writing, the 'already-written', until it becomes possible, through their errors, to say something different. As in *Doubling the Point*, the correspondents interrogate dialogue and correspondence by *using* them, and by allowing the inevitable hurdles to get in the way. It seems that something is freed up in the 'slip' which enables Kurtz and Coetzee to establish a connection and acknowledge points of tension openly.

This difference, between the smooth exchange of conventions and the messier business of overcoming difficulties, has a parallel with the distinction between what we might call 'epistolary exchange' and 'clear communication'. The latter flows freely, quickly, and without error, but it cannot produce the kinds of opening that Coetzee, as a correspondent, is seeking. Although I will return to the epistolary narrative when I consider the fictional works in more detail, two of its characteristics are worth noting here, in light of this distinction. The first is its 'I-you' grammar: the basic syntactical structure that has historically underpinned the epistolary narrative, and which continues to define the form.[11] Kurtz and Coetzee begin by establishing the common ground between the psychotherapist and the novelist, suggesting that '[h]uman nature and human experience concern them both deeply, as do possibilities of growth and development' (GS, v). They are dependent, in other words, on a connection. They are also dependent, however, on the differences between their perspectives: they hope that by engaging as 'outsiders' to each other's work, the possibility of dialogue will be created (GS, v). The successful correspondence therefore relies on both connection and distance between writer and addressee. Even if we are rightly sceptical of the attribution of intrinsic meaning to particular literary forms, it remains the case that a letter is usually written by one (or more) persons, to one (or more) recipients. As epistolary theorist Janet Gurkin Altman argues, it is the addressee 'whose presence alone distinguishes the letter from other first-person forms', including diary and memoir.[12] The 'I-you' relationship is therefore at the heart of epistolary exchange, requiring connection and distance, and calling for a response from a specific addressee.

The second, and related, characteristic feature of the epistolary narrative, for the purposes of better understanding Coetzee's collaboration and correspondence, pertains more directly to the distinction between epistolary exchange and communication. The epistle is recorded and therefore re-readable. Its capacity to be edited and re-read is central to its composition and reception, and this becomes even more crucial in fictional works, where this makes possible the symbolic function of the letter in the text, and time lags between acts of narration. What is perhaps most significant here is the parallel that begins to emerge between the reflective collaboration that Coetzee seeks in his correspondences and interviews, and epistolary exchange, with its mediations, critical distance, and stress on the addressee, or other.

Here and Now

Let us turn briefly to *Here and Now*, the product of a three-year correspondence between Coetzee and Auster, which, unlike the Coetzee-Kurtz exchange, begins mid-correspondence, without any kind of prefatory framing. This is not dissimilar to the opening of *Age of Iron*, where we are dropped mid-stream into Mrs Curren's long letter to her daughter: in both books the reader is required to fill in the gaps to make sense of the bigger picture. This should not come as a great surprise: as Altman explains, readers of epistolary texts are often called upon to act as 'detective-collators': given responsibility for overcoming the discontinuity of epistolary narratives, for perceiving 'continuity from one letter to the next'.[13] *Here and Now* contains several letters that are out of sequence, lost, or opened belatedly.[14] The ghostly presence of the editor is apparent in the occasional annotations and in the ordering of the letters, but otherwise we are largely presented with the 'here' and 'now' of Coetzee and Auster's correspondence. The collection thereby reflects the common structure of epistolary temporality, and conforms with Samuel Richardson's famous description of the epistolary narrative as a 'way of writing, to the moment', as both Coetzee and Auster pivot from the present to recall the past or imagine the future for each other.[15]

Curiously, although both writers carefully craft their letters in response to their specific correspondent, and although their relationship seems closer by the end of the book, they reveal little about themselves or the history of their friendship. The correspondence covers a range of issues, from sport, the financial crisis, and literary events to the situation in Palestine but, as Attwell observes, the letters 'are written in a spirit of intelligent bonhomie, which sometimes makes it difficult to gauge their seriousness'.[16] There is a tendency to avoid the domestic in favour of intellectual discussion but, unlike in *The Good Story*, the central aim of the correspondence remains unclear, as does the question of whether Coetzee and Auster intended to publish their letters from the outset. In one letter, Auster reassures Coetzee that he is not asking about his birthday as a 'personal question' and the exclusion of the personal, except in the cover-notes which occasionally accompany the letters, is even more intriguing in light of Auster's later criticism of the 'distinction between "work" and "life"' in the first volume of Beckett's letters, from which Auster claims that 'too much is missing' (*HN*, 125, 48–9).

Coetzee and Auster seem to agree on many things, and *Here and Now* has been criticized for this by some reviewers. Martin Riker comments that 'the sheer amount of agreement in the pages of *Here and Now* eventually becomes a problem for the book, as their dialogical back-and-forth starts to read more like a monologue'.[17] Others have suggested that Coetzee bends Auster to his will. David Sexton, for instance, argues that they are 'plainly not equals' and that the letters consist 'mainly of Coetzee announcing what he has on his mind and Auster attempting to respond satisfactorily'.[18] If, as I have been suggesting, Coetzee's process of correspondence and collaboration depends crucially on friction or disagreement, and working against interlocutors, as well as with them, then the features targeted by these accusations present an obvious problem for the ideal of dialogue as I have characterized it so far.

Nevertheless, it also remains true that there is no single mould into which an epistolary exchange must fit, and even while the ideas in *Here and Now* develop through a less abrasive process than those in *The Good Story*, the entire book is still scaffolded around epistolary exchange and dialogue: the letters continue to depend on the I-you relationship, on reflection and mediation as well as connection, and they conform to common patterns of epistolary temporality. The letters even offer an insight into the importance of materiality and the traces of the writing body in a letter exchange: they are frequently written on paper and posted or faxed, and in one letter Auster asks Coetzee to '[e]xcuse the funny stationery' from the hotel room and the 'crappy ballpoint pen' (*HN*, 35). Although *Here and Now* therefore offers a gentler kind of correspondence, in which the aim seems to be to converse, share, and even commiserate, the differences between Coetzee's and Auster's positions and their seeming desire to engage in dialogue remain crucial to understanding this book and its epistolary techniques.

Epistolarity: The Fiction

Most of Coetzee's fictions reflect on exchange in some way, from the sustained consideration of interviews in *Summertime* to the many letters across the novels, variously sent, unsent, reciprocated, or unrequited. Eugene Dawn's inability to engage in dialogue, for instance, is expressed in the 'remarkably balanced and temperate letter' that he writes but never sends (*Dusk*, 44). This contrasts with the way that David and Lucy Lurie seem able to have a dialogue *only* by pushing notes under each other's doors, after failing to find common ground face-to-face. In order to write his letter, David Lurie must step into his daughter's shoes: 'The question is, does he have it in him to be the woman? From the solitude of his room he writes his daughter a letter' (*Dis*, 160). Lucy's reply offers no explicit agreement, but contains an echo of David's letter, so that we hear, in these notes, perhaps for the first time, a chime of connection:

But the road you are following is the wrong one.

...

Yes, the road I am following may be the wrong one. (*Dis*, 160–1)

An echo, of course, is not the same as shared understanding. Nevertheless, *Disgrace* offers an insight into the acts of empathy that letter-writing often demands. In contrast, *Foe* explores messages in bottles: unaddressed, unopened, scattered, and unsent letters; as well as exposing some of the cracks that appear in the attempt to use eighteenth-century anglophone epistolary conventions to say something true of colonial violence. *Age of Iron* presses epistolary conventions even harder, interrogating the adequacy of the epistolary first-person perspective in the face of systemic violence and suffering, especially since the epistolary 'I' in question is Mrs Curren, an educated, aged, middle-class woman, and above all 'a white' (*AI*, 79). Focusing on *Summertime* and *Age of Iron*, the remainder of this chapter examines Coetzee's exploration of the possibilities and constraints of epistolary conventions in the pursuit of meaningful dialogue.

Summertime, the third of Coetzee's memoir-fictions, appears to consist largely of dialogue and correspondence. The book opens and closes with a series of short third-person 'notebook' entries by 'John', and otherwise contains interviews conducted after John's death, presented in a variety of forms, including interview transcripts, edited testimonies, reported speech, and letters. Although the book initially seems to be woven from threads of connection and exchange, it frequently exposes acts of betrayal, miscommunication, self-interestedness, and superficiality. In the second section, for instance, the interviewer reads a transcript supposedly based on an interview with Margot Jonker, John's cousin. The interviewer transforms and translates the transcript into a third-person English narrative (from Margot's Afrikaans) and thoroughly embellishes (and even invents) the story that is relayed back to her.

Margot frequently protests or interjects during the reading of the transcript, and she is obviously bewildered about how this particular story has been spun as *hers*. The first letter in *Summertime* is a long, heartfelt missive from Margot to John, in which she talks about their shared childhood experiences and about the future (*Sum*, 135–6). Although the status of this letter is somewhat uncertain (being presented by the same interviewer who has freely embellished Margot's story), Margot's letter and John's reply show how the success of a 'dialogue' cannot simply be quantified by the number of letters exchanged, reminding us of Coetzee's earlier critique of patter.

Margot's letter, full of parentheses, changes in direction, allusions, and metaphors, brims with longing and 'tenderness' (*Sum*, 136). She discusses their childhood vows to marry and asks John to forgive her earlier crossness when they broke down on the Merweville road. Although the correspondence is superficially consummated when John sends a short reply ten days later, the 'cold formality of his response' brings 'an angry flush to her cheeks' (*Sum*, 139). There is nothing concrete in the letter that Margot can point to as problematic, so she simply tells her husband that it is 'just the tone' that has upset her (*Sum*, 139). And yet there is something more that blocks dialogue between the cousins. John's clipped sentences, rhetorical questions, brief references, and dependence on generic conventions constitute only a superficial response to Margot's words, deliberately avoiding her implicit questions. John relies heavily upon stock phrases, opening with thanks for her letter, closing by sending his father's love, and writing, for example, 'I trust that all is well on the farm' (*Sum*, 139). But, as Margot says, it 'was never just a question of Merweville, of John and his father, of who was going to be living where, in the city or in the country. *What are we doing here?*: that had been the unspoken question all the time. He had known it and she had known it' (*Sum*, 140). John deliberately ignores this 'unspoken question', designed by Margot for him alone, and as a consequence the letter might just as well have been returned to sender.

This is literally the case with the letters in the following section of the book, in which Senhora Adriana Nascimento, a Brazilian dancer with whom John becomes infatuated, ignores his correspondence. Although John sends many long, formal, typed letters through the post, she simply puts them 'away in the bureau', many of them unread (*Sum*, 172), and writes 'RETURN TO SENDER' on the unopened envelope of the final letter (*Sum*, 190). From Adriana's perspective, John's letters are not crafted around an addressee or 'you' who bears any resemblance to herself; rather, John is 'in love with some idea of me, some fantasy of a Latin mistress that he made up in his own mind' (*Sum*, 193–4). This experience recalls Coetzee's description of the long letters he receives from a woman in France. Coetzee tells Auster that the woman is 'well aware that the *vous* to whom she writes is a construct and may bear little relation to my own construct of myself' (*HN*, 186). By contrast, the letter from Margot to John is written solely for the unique 'you' that is John, her 'favourite cousin', her childhood friend, but John blocks the I-you appeal that this letter makes.

Margot's letter, however, is not without its own untruths and betrayals, raising the question of how far it is ever possible for written correspondence to capture truth. She also resorts to conventions, writing '*Am thinking of you*' at the foot of her letter, even though 'she has not given John a thought all day' (*Sum*, 138). This is not to suggest that such a correspondence is wholly dishonest, but that we must, as readers of these letters, scrutinize what is said (and not said) in order to distinguish between the 'already-said' and possible openings. Near the end of *Summertime*, the interviewer reports that he is pursuing interviews because Coetzee's diaries and letters cannot be trusted: '*In his letters he is making up a fiction of himself for his correspondents; in his diaries he is doing much the same for his own eyes, or perhaps for posterity*' (*Sum*, 225). The book therefore makes explicit the many ways in which authority might be mocked, made light of, or betrayed, and insists, over and again, that we read between the lines, that we return to stories, that we read harder to create threads of meaning. The correspondence between Margot and John therefore provides a glimpse of the intangible ways in which possibilities for dialogue can be opened, and also abruptly truncated or closed down.

If *Summertime* is centrally concerned with what is unspoken, betrayed, and lost in correspondence, even in seemingly intact exchanges, Coetzee's sixth novel, *Age of Iron*, asks how one might forge genuine dialogue in contexts in which this seems almost impossible. Written and set in the 1980s, during the nationwide State of Emergency in South Africa, the novel asks in particular whether an epistolary narrative, thoroughly reworked, can hope to offer any meaningful concept of connection or correspondence in a political context structured by systematized inequality, and incommensurability.

Made up of a single letter to Mrs Curren's daughter, who had left South Africa in 1976, *Age of Iron* seems, on the surface, to be less concerned with dialogue than *Summertime*, with its cover-to-cover interviews, letters, and edited journal entries. Mrs Curren's missive is certainly unconventional: from the outset we are dropped, mid-stream, into a letter without address, salutation, preliminaries, or date. Initially, in its opening pages, the writing itself also suggests monologue rather than dialogue:

> When I *write* about *him* I *write* about *myself*. When I *write* about his *dog* I *write* about *myself*; when I *write* about the *house* I *write* about *myself*.
> (*AI*, 9. My emphasis to denote rhythmic stress.)

In these lines Mrs Curren writes to her daughter about Vercueil, a homeless man who visits 'himself on' her, the day she is diagnosed with terminal cancer (*AI*, 4). However, the language revolves relentlessly around the 'I' (rather than being structured by the addressee, or 'you'), even though it refers constantly to the act of writing a letter. The phrasal repetition and strong beat of the lines bear down on the essential elements of the writing process: Mrs Curren 'writes' Vercueil to 'write' herself. The writing continually directs us back to the letter writer, partly through the regular march of the 'I' through this passage and partly through the way that the temporal structure of the language continually loops back on itself. This is an embodiment, at the level of syntax, of the way in which Mrs Curren constantly views herself through the eyes of others.

Mrs Curren addresses this self-serving function of her letter head-on, however, asking: 'To whom this writing then? The answer: to you but not to you; to me; to you in me' (*AI*, 6). Instead of inviting a response and embodying the 'reciprocality' of epistolary exchange, 'whereby the original *you* becomes the *I* of a new utterance',[19] Mrs Curren's answer to her own question directs the reader straight back to the writing 'I'. This is not to say that Mrs Curren's writing is a thinly disguised monologue or journal, but it does leave us in a curious situation. On the one hand, the narrative of *Age of Iron* is obviously determined by epistolarity: the grammar and language are shaped around the addressee and the I-you relationship, and the narration appears future-oriented. On the other hand, the narrative strains against these traits: in places, the I-you grammar is contorted through a relentless stress on the self or 'I'; the narration loops back on a present moment to continually replay the present time of narration; there is only a single act of writing and a bare hope that this will be received; and the ending of the novel, where the narrator narrates her own death, makes the letter itself seem implausible, if not impossible.

Why, then, does this novel refuse to abandon epistolary conventions, even while it puts so much pressure on them? Perhaps because by pressing these conventions so hard that they almost crack, *Age of Iron* works towards different ways of speaking and writing, towards slips and openings, reconfiguring the epistolary I-you grammar as demanded by the situation of late apartheid. Mrs Curren reflects on this task, writing that 'If Vercueil does not send these writings on, you will never read them. You will never even know they existed. A certain body of truth will never take on flesh: my truth: how I lived in these times, in this place' (*AI*, 130). The question of whether this 'body of truth' can be delivered, and the related, weightier question of whether it is possible to forge a literary material that can say something true about 'these times, in this place', lie at the heart of *Age of Iron*. The unique account and addressee therefore remain indispensable, at the same time as they are exposed as thoroughly inadequate to the situation.

An example would perhaps make this clearer. Mrs Curren knows that, in order to say anything true of 'these times, in this place', she cannot use anonymized or clichéd language (reminding us of Coetzee's letters to Kurtz about the need for a slip or opening). Halfway through the book, Mrs Curren writes to her daughter about driving her housekeeper, Florence, to Guguletu in the early hours of the morning in search of Florence's son, Bheki. Mrs Curren joins a crowd 'looking down upon a scene of devastation: shanties burnt and smoldering, shanties still burning, pouring forth black smoke' (*AI*, 95). Amongst the 'mess of rubble and charred beams' of a gutted hall Mrs Curren sees 'five bodies neatly laid out. The body in the middle was that of Florence's Bheki' (*AI*, 102). Mrs Curren relates this scene in detail: her physical shaking, her conversation with Florence's brother (*AI*, 102–3). She then pauses to remind her reader that, as letter writer, these events and perspectives are only available through her account:

> I tell you the story of this morning mindful that the story-teller, from her office, claims the place of right. It is through my eyes that you see; the voice that speaks in your head is mine. Through me alone do you find yourself here on these desolate flats, smell the smoke in the air, see the bodies of the dead, hear the weeping, shiver in the rain. It is my thoughts that you think, my despair that you feel, and also the first stirrings of welcome for whatever will put an end to thought: sleep, death. To me your sympathies flow; your heart beats with mine.
>
> (*AI*, 103)

For the story to be told at all, it must be told in the first person, by an intimate relation; it must be a direct address to a specific addressee, rather than the anonymous international reports that her daughter receives in America, or the accounts of a third-person omniscient narrator from whom the reader might more easily distance herself. She writes, 'It would be easier for you, I know, if the story came from someone else, if it were a stranger's voice sounding in your ear' (*AI*, 103). Painful though it is for the recipient, the narrative must therefore be an intimate first-person epistle if it is to contain any truth, and, as Mrs Curren tells us, 'there is no one else. I am the only one. I am the one writing: I, I' (*AI*, 103–4).

However, this sentence begins to reveal how inadequate the first-person narrative is to this situation. Although the use of this intimate 'I' is the only way to communicate something true about the situation, its repetition self-consciously directs the reader not to 'truth' but back to the letter writer herself. Yet sympathy with the individual is not at all what the situation calls for, and is particularly inappropriate when that individual is Mrs Curren, or someone like her:

> I, a white. When I think of the whites, what do I see? I see a herd of sheep (not a flock: a herd) milling around on a dusty plain under the baking sun. I hear a drumming of hooves, a confusion of sound that resolves itself, when the ear grows attuned, into the same bleating call in a thousand different inflections. 'I!' 'I!' 'I!'
>
> (*AI*, 79–80)

The I-you grammar is distorted again by the emphatic repetition of the 'I'. Mrs Curren is therefore required to create a response to her own words;

a rejection of the effects that her narrative has created: 'Now, my child, flesh of my flesh, my best self, I ask you to draw back. I tell you this story not so that you will feel for me but so that you will learn how things are' (*AI*, 103). The narrative is compelled constantly to undermine the conventions on which it is based in order to avoid the trap it sets itself: its necessary evocation of empathy with the writing 'I' is, under the circumstances, a betrayal of the place and times in which Mrs Curren is living. She instructs her addressee: 'Do not read in sympathy with me. Let your heart not beat with mine' (*AI*, 104). This novel therefore requires the narrator and narratee both to embrace and reject the 'I' and the 'you'. The complexity of this requirement is perhaps best captured in a single sentence: 'So I ask you: attend to the writing, not to me' (*AI*, 104). Here, it is necessary for the 'I' to ask 'you', in order for the letter to mean anything at all, but the 'you' is instructed to be vigilant about the distractions of the writing 'I'. Central to the composition of this narrative then, is the turning of the I-you epistolary convention against itself.

In its use of epistolary conventions, *Age of Iron* implicitly prescribes the way in which the various readers (we, the daughter, Vercueil) must read: at one and the same time, our hearts must beat with, and not with, that of the letter writer. As this chapter has shown, this kind of reading occurs across Coetzee's oeuvre, where it means scrutinizing, as well as connecting with, the language of one's correspondent or interlocutor, since it is never enough to rely optimistically upon a straightforward address to a future recipient.

This has implications for us, as readers of Coetzee's works, for, if we are to fulfil our responsibility as interlocutors, we must read both with and against them. Indeed, Coetzee continually calls upon correspondents to scrutinize, question, and return again to his words, in order to push, with him, towards new openings and slips; new ways of thinking and writing about the world. If we are to appreciate the importance of correspondence in Coetzee's work, then, we must look beyond the apparent contradiction between the private, reserved, and sometimes confrontational Coetzee, and the collaborative, communicative, and sometimes congenial Coetzee, and understand these as indispensable aspects of the same project of pursuing dialectical dialogue. Just as mediation and distance are necessary for moving beyond the stock phrases of epistolary exchange, so errors and conflicts are essential in creating meaningful exchanges with other people. We would therefore do well, as Mrs Curren suggests, to 'attend to the writing'.

Notes

1. 'J. M. Coetzee in Conversation with Jane Poyner' in Jane Poyner (ed.), *J. M. Coetzee and the Idea of the Public Intellectual* (Ohio: Ohio University Press, 2006), pp. 21–4.
2. Ibid., p. 24.
3. J. M. Coetzee and Arabella Kurtz, 'Nevertheless, My Sympathies are with the Karamazovs', *Salmagundi*, 166/167 (2010), 39–72 (p. 59).
4. Coetzee and Kurtz, 'Nevertheless', p. 64.
5. See *WW*, pp. 7–8. Jacques Derrida is a key figure in these debates about writing and speech, and Coetzee has read and quoted his work extensively.
6. J. M. Coetzee, 'Rev. of *The Temple of My Familiar* by Alice Walker' (1989), reprinted in Henry Louis Gates, Jr., and K. A. Appiah, (eds.), *Alice Walker: Critical Perspectives Past and Present* (New York: Amistad, 1993), p. 25.
7. Coetzee and Kurtz, 'Nevertheless', p. 54.
8. Ibid., pp. 39, 40, 43.
9. Ibid., p. 44.
10. Ibid., pp. 46–7.
11. See my book, *Epistolarity and World Literature, 1980–2010* (Basingstoke: Palgrave Macmillan, 2017) for a more comprehensive account of epistolary conventions. Some of the arguments in this chapter appeared there first.
12. Janet Gurkin Altman, *Epistolarity: Approaches to a Form* (Columbus: Ohio State University Press, 1982), p. 87.
13. Ibid., p. 173.
14. See, for example, the letter that belatedly 'surfaced' in the computer (*HN*, 25) or the footnote that describes a letter which 'went astray' (*HN*, 74).
15. John Carroll (ed.), *Selected Letters of Samuel Richardson* (Oxford: Clarendon Press, 1964), pp. 282–94.
16. David Attwell, *J. M. Coetzee and the Life of Writing* (Oxford: Oxford University Press, 2015), p. 233.
17. Martin Riker, 'Pen Pals: Rev. of *Here and Now* by J. M. Coetzee', *New York Times*, 15 March 2013.
18. David Sexton, 'Rev. of *Here and Now*', *Spectator*, 18 May 2013.
19. Altman, *Epistolarity*, p. 117 (original emphasis).

8

SUE KOSSEW

Criticism and Scholarship

Alongside J. M. Coetzee's remarkable body of fictional works are his works of criticism and scholarship, including a substantial number of literary reviews. These, like his novels, chart not just a life of writing, but also a life of reading. Dating from 1969 to the present, they attest to Coetzee's continued intellectual curiosity and the expanding reach of his critical activity. Some of the earliest scholarly articles arose from research conducted for his doctoral dissertation on Samuel Beckett, and appeared in a range of American, South African, and British academic journals. Others, such as the early essays on Alex La Guma, signalled an engagement with South African literary culture that culminated in his groundbreaking monograph *White Writing* (1988). Many of the early essays and reviews (though by no means all) were included in *Doubling the Point* (1992). Since the appearance of that important volume, Coetzee has published *Giving Offense* (1996), which gathers his writings on censorship, as well as three collections of literary essays and reviews: *Stranger Shores: Essays 1986–1999* (2001), *Inner Workings: Literary Essays 2000–2005* (2007), and, most recently, *Late Essays: 2006–2017* (2017). Unlike his novels, the essays and reviews are more direct and unambiguous, offering not only one writer's evaluation of other writers but also the astute assessments of a lifelong teacher of literature.

So, why read essays written by an author who has consistently refused to comment on his own works, even whilst these have been the subject of so much literary criticism? As Derek Attridge suggests in his Introduction to *Inner Workings*, the two obvious reasons include the hope that these essays will 'throw light on the often oblique novels', and the belief that a writer of such note will have 'much to offer' on the work of other writers: an inside view, as it were.[1] Additionally, whereas each essay, review, or lecture was previously available to be read only in isolation, the collections of such essays afford readers more concentrated exposure to Coetzee's literary judgements, encouraging us to consider them in relation to one another, and enabling comparisons across time periods. It is not surprising, then, that critics, scholars, and students of Coetzee's fictions so often turn to his critical writings not only as compelling instances of 'literary-critical-philosophical thinking', but also for clues and insights into his literary oeuvre.[2]

There is no doubt that Coetzee is an incisive and wide-ranging reader of literary works and literary scholarship. It is clear, too, that this reading informs his fictions: the Coetzee Papers at the University of Texas's Harry Ransom Center reveal that, like most novelists, he undertakes careful research before and during the composition of his fictions. In this chapter, I will consider Coetzee's scholarly essays and reviews in the contexts of the volumes in which they were collected, examining a number of themes or threads that run through them, and suggesting various ways in which they may throw light on the novelist as reader, and thus, in turn, on some of his writerly concerns. Coetzee has himself contrasted what he terms the 'rather tight discourse' of criticism with the relative freedom ('irresponsibility' is his word) of writing fiction (*DP*, 246). In another remark on the 'medium of prose commentary', he suggests that criticism can never quite capture or be equal to the passion of the creative writer whose work is being examined, so that it is always either 'a betrayal (the usual case) or an overpowering (the rare case) of its object' of study, the literary text (*DP*, 61). Whereas his concern in his novels is to push the boundaries of genre through formal inventiveness, his critical writings are less experimental. This does not mean that they are not of great interest and value. On the contrary, the essays and reviews have provided students of Coetzee's work with fertile ground both for reading his novels and for enabling insights into a scholarly mind wrestling with philosophical and literary-theoretical questions, most often as they arise in the work of other novelists.

Despite this, surprisingly little critical commentary focuses specifically on Coetzee as critic. An exception is Carrol Clarkson's chapter, 'Coetzee's Criticism'. Using a little-known Afrikaans-language conference paper, 'Die Skrywer en die Teorie' (1980, 'The Writer and Theory'), as a jumping-off point, Clarkson contends that, contra Coetzee's qualms about his own efficacy as a critic, he has often been able to liberate the discourse of criticism, making it 'less monological' and proving himself to be the 'truly creative critic' he envisaged as an ideal.[3] On the surface, this creativity may not always be immediately obvious. Indeed, one of the noteworthy aspects of Coetzee's book reviews (rather than his scholarly essays) is that they tend to follow a fairly similar pattern: an outline of the writer's life (often including the personal circumstances surrounding the writing of a particular work), the historical and literary contexts, concise summary of the plot, and investigation of the text's narrative and linguistic strategies. Nevertheless, they are carefully researched and are always alert to the cracks, ironies, and disconti-nuities in the texts; to the circumstances surrounding the work; and to the thought processes that led to writerly choices as these pertain to form, style, and theme.

Both reviews and essays attest to the global reach of Coetzee's critical mind and reading. With his training in linguistics, he is interested in non-Anglophone literatures as much as in English-language literature, although the non-Anglophone texts he reviews are usually English translations.[4] He writes about books from (among other places) South America, Europe, the United States, South Africa, and Australia, always taking care to situate these within their writers' personal and national contexts. As Derek Attridge suggests, 'Coetzee is an ideal reviewer' because he 'seems to have read every-thing relevant to his subject ... [and] writes with easy familiarity of the historical, cultural, and political background, whether it be the Austro-Hungarian Empire or the American South'.[5] His facility with Dutch and German gives him access to a number of important writers in these languages as well as the ability to reflect on the nature of translations of their works into English. He has, indeed, published three volumes of translation of his own. His much-quoted comment that 'all reading is translation, just as all transla-tion is criticism' is useful in illustrating his approach to his own reading and critical practice (DP, 90). For Coetzee, critical activity, like academic and literary work, places a value on scepticism and an ethics of interpretation in which 'nothing is taken for granted' and 'everything is capable of being questioned'.[6]

White Writing: On the Culture of Letters in South Africa (1988)

In his scholarly essays, Coetzee reveals both a situated (initially South African) and a comparative, even world-systemic approach that has been described as 'cosmo-local'.[7] White Writing, for example, was a groundbreaking study of South African literary history that, even at this relatively early stage of his academic and literary careers, displayed Coetzee's wide-angled critical perspective and his ability to position South African 'white writing' (that is, writing that is 'no longer European [and] not yet African') both as characteristic of a mindset peculiar to South Africa and as relevant to the problematic of other colonial and semi-peripheral writers (WW, 11). In its Introduction, he coins the memorable phrase 'unsettled settlers', which neatly captures the sense of insecurity that, in his opinion, attracted South African writers to the reassuring past-ness of the pastoral genre. Characteristically, too, his emphasis is on language and 'the question [for the settler writer] of finding a language to fit Africa, a language that will be authentically African', and that will therefore offer the settler writer 'an identity better than that of a visitor, stranger, transient' (WW, 6–10). While Coetzee's analysis in these essays echoes the postcolonial criticism that was then emerging, and draws for its insights on theorists of decolonization, it also depends on his own encounters with 'the great intellectual schemas through which South Africa has been thought by Europe' (WW, 10). In part, perhaps, because of his experience of living abroad, in England and the United States, Coetzee brings to his early South African criticism a broad theoretical perspective that differentiates it from many of the local critical responses of that time.

Amongst the most widely discussed chapters in White Writing is the one entitled 'Farm Novel and Plaasroman'. This essay provides historical context for the English- and Afrikaans-language versions of the farm novel. It shows Coetzee's familiarity and facility with Afrikaans writers (such as C. M. van den Heever, to whom he devotes an entire chapter) as well as with the canonical English-language farm novels of Olive Schreiner and Pauline Smith. Schreiner's The Story of an African Farm (1883) is described as a 'critique of colonial culture' and Pauline Smith's idylls, in The Beadle (1926), as 'nostalgic' and 'wishful' (WW, 66, 76, 78). However – and here we see again the tendency to avoid a too-narrow frame – Coetzee places his discussion of such works within the context of English, American, and German versions of the pastoral. South African genres of writing are, in this way, measured and discussed in terms of other national literatures, as well as their own local histories.

'Farm Novel and Plaasroman' has been especially useful in critical readings of Coetzee's own farm novels, or 'Karoo novels', as David Attwell more accurately describes them: In the Heart of the Country (1977), Life & Times of Michael K (1983), and Disgrace (1999).[8] It has also been put to work in discussions of his fictionalized memoirs, particularly Boyhood (1997) and Summertime (2009), where descriptions of the family farm, Voëlfontein, engender an affective yet doomed sense of place and belonging. In particular, the essay's emphasis on the struggle of colonial writers to find a language suitable for engagement with an alien and alienating African landscape, and on the inappropriateness of a European pastoral mode, has led some critics (including Teresa Dovey, Susan VanZanten Gallagher, and Elizabeth Lowry) to identify novels such as In the Heart of the Country and Disgrace as anti-pastoral, highlighting the ways in which this ambiguous settler identity affects interpersonal relations.

Coetzee's identification of the 'silence about the place of the black man in the pastoral idyll' has likewise provided a useful starting-point for approaching his own very different and deliberate fictional deployments of silence

(*WW*, 81), which might be understood as grounded in an ethical refusal to speak on behalf of others, and which might thus be distinguished from the 'erasure' of black life and labour in the farm novel, which, Coetzee argues, is engendered by paranoia. On the other hand, this refusal to give voice to figures of otherness might also be read as re-enacting the processes of authority Coetzee's works seek to dismantle, an interpretation pursued by Benita Parry, which prompted an early and intense debate about speech and silence in Coetzee's oeuvre.[9] In both cases, whichever particular argument critics have developed, Coetzee's essay about the rival incarnations of the South African pastoral mode has been taken not only as a scholarly analysis of the genre, but also as a text that hints at patterns of mythmaking and a sense of settler unbelonging applicable to his own writerly practices of place-making.

Doubling the Point: Essays and Interviews (1992)

Doubling the Point is unarguably the most influential of Coetzee's volumes of essays, not least because it includes interviews with David Attwell in which Coetzee reflects retrospectively on his career both as novelist and critic. This 'intellectual autobiography' has been the focus of much attention and there are few Coetzee scholars who have not mined its resources to throw light on Coetzee's philosophical, socio-political, and literary concerns. It collects in one volume a number of his most important articles and reviews (from 1970 to 1990) while its dialogical critical structure (with both Attwell and Coetzee commenting on the essays' motivations and contexts) expresses the constantly self-vigilant and not infrequently self-critical nature of Coetzee's scholarly prose. Until the writer's notebooks and other materials became available for study in the archive, it also provided insights into Coetzee's compositional practices and writerly preoccupations that were otherwise wholly unavailable, since he had elsewhere assiduously avoided commenting on his own works. In this respect, the interviews that accompany the essays are of major significance, although caution is required, since there is no simple equivalence between the critical and the creative works: Coetzee is too scrupulous a commentator (and reader) for any easy transfer of ideas from his observations to his fictions.

In its title, *Doubling the Point* alludes to the opportunity presented by the book for Coetzee retrospectively to investigate the writerly 'desire' in his own essays, enabling him to enter into a dialogue not just with David Attwell but with himself as critic, and to situate his own readings and judgements in their biographical, socio-political, and historical contexts. This phrase is taken – appropriately, given the influence of this book on

Coetzee's work – from Daniel Defoe's *Robinson Crusoe* ('at length, doubling the Point at about two Leagues from the Land, I saw plainly Land on the other Side to Seaward') and is a nautical term meaning 'to sail or pass round or to the other side of (a cape or point), so that the ship's course is, as it were, doubled or bent upon itself' (*OED*).[10] Its meaning in the context of the volume is, of course, that Coetzee is doubling back to look again at his critical essays, and, indeed, his entire oeuvre.

Across the volume, the inbuilt self-reflexivity of the novels is set against the more monologic (and perhaps necessarily more authoritative) mode of the essays and reviews, genres that, in his words, are not usually afforded 'room to reflect on themselves' (*DP*, 18). The self-curating nature of the choice and arrangement of the essays is also worth noting, framing Coetzee's scholarly concerns under headings that relate them to certain influences ('Kafka', 'Beckett') and interests ('The Poetics of Reciprocity', 'Popular Culture', 'Autobiography and Confession', 'Obscenity and Censorship'), to a single linguistic category ('Syntax'), and to a single literary culture ('South African Writers'). The essays are not, in other words, arranged chronologically or systematically, and nor is the volume comprehensive. Indeed, one of the most surprising omissions is 'The Novel Today' (1988), a text in which Coetzee had differentiated between the discourses of history and fiction, and which has been very widely cited.[11] Yet this piece – originally a speech – responded to a very particular historical-political moment, and, perhaps for this reason, was deemed too idiosyncratic for the kind of project undertaken by Coetzee and Attwell.

Of all the essays in *Doubling the Point*, perhaps the most significant for Coetzee's critics has been 'Confession and Double Thoughts: Tolstoy, Rousseau, Dostoevsky'. Published for the first time in 1985, the essay emerged from Coetzee's re-reading of the two Russian authors, and incorporated his 1984 inaugural professorial lecture at the University of Cape Town, entitled 'Truth in Autobiography'. Both in the interview that precedes the essay and in the essay itself – which he describes as 'the most ambitious piece of criticism' he had ventured on at that time – Coetzee muses on philosophical notions of shame, confession, and absolution (*DP*, 243). In writing of the kind of self-conscious confession that is infinitely regressive, he describes the complex desire for shame and simultaneous awareness of bad faith that itself 'fuels a sense of shame', applying this concept of 'double thoughts' to representations of secular confessions in fictional and autobiographical works (*DP*, 251). Contrasting Tolstoy's, Rousseau's, and Dostoevsky's confessants, he concludes that 'the self cannot tell the truth of itself to itself and come to rest without the possibility of self-deception' (*DP*, 291). It is not surprising that critics have found that the ideas in this essay resonate with David Lurie's refusal of public repentance in *Disgrace*, where he draws a distinction between a 'secular plea' of guilty, and the more religious notion of confession, which he believes belongs to 'another universe of discourse', that of the soul (*Dis*, 58). The idea of the impossibility of a sincere apology, too, emerges strongly in Lurie's prostration before Melanie Isaacs's father, even while he is conscious of his desire for her sister, Desiree. The 'strong opinion' entitled 'On Apology' in *Diary of a Bad Year* (2007) similarly draws attention to the blurring of the difference 'between sincerity and the performance of sincerity' in personal and national apologies (*DBY*, 109).

Coetzee himself suggests that 'Confession and Double Thoughts' is 'best read ... side by side with *Waiting for the Barbarians* (1980)'. This novel, he writes, 'asks the question: Why does one choose the side of justice when it is not in one's material interest to do so?' The essay, he continues, asks the same (Platonic) question of truth (*DP*, 394–5). It could be argued, too, that the essay's central thesis – that the confessant's self-interest (like that of the autobiographical writer) is always located at his or her 'blind spot', making it impossible to tell the 'truth' – is pivotal to all of Coetzee's novels, and to his fictionalized autobiographies in particular. The prevalence of metaphors of blindness in *Waiting for the Barbarians* is another noteworthy link between this essay and the novel, though the latter's concern with bodily pain and torture has also very often been read in relation to 'the authority of suffering and therefore of the body' in South Africa, which Coetzee discusses at several points across *Doubling the Point*, including 'Retrospect', the final interview in the volume, and 'Into the Dark Chamber: The Writer and the South African State', an essay that draws attention to the dangers for South African writers of spectacularizing 'the dark, forbidden [torture] chamber' (*DP*, 248, 364).[12]

Giving Offense: Essays on Censorship (1996)

Giving Offense: Essays on Censorship considers the ways in which censorship operates from the perspective, as the cover notes suggest, of a writer 'who has lived and worked in its shadow'. And yet, as Coetzee points out in *Doubling the Point*, his own books never achieved the 'badge of honour' of being banned by the South African censors. 'Besides coming too late in the era [of harsh censorship], my books have been too indirect in their approach, too rarefied, to be considered a threat to the order', he explains further (*DP*, 298). What interested Coetzee in the process of censorship was, perhaps predictably, not so much the convoluted and often contradictory political workings of the system itself, but rather the effect it had on authors, both within and beyond South Africa. In his words, he is concerned with the ways in which writers have 'responded to the attentions of the censor'. He finds this response mostly 'sterile': the 'game of slipping Aesopian messages past the censor' is one that diverts writers 'from their proper task' (GO, viii). Writing, he suggests, 'does not flourish under censorship' (GO, 11). He describes this response in terms of illness metaphors: it is a kind of contagion that 'infects' writers who begin to read their own work through the eyes of the censors, and who thereby 'internalize a contaminating reading' (GO, 36). In his essay on fellow South African author and sometime University of Cape Town colleague André Brink, who wrote fairly extensively on censorship and on the writer as 'diagnostician of society's sickness/ madness', Coetzee suggests that Brink's very language in making these claims has itself 'been infected with the violence of the state' (GO, 211). David Attwell, in his account of Coetzee's engagement with the South African censors, uses materials from the Coetzee Papers to suggest that the essays in *Giving Offense* were written in a spirit of 'impatience' with the 'stupidity' of censorship but also in the light of Coetzee's own 'self-reproach'. This self-criticism emerges from Coetzee's complex interactions with the 'literature police' (to use Peter McDonald's term), including 'the extraordinary step' he took 'of applying to be a censor himself', apparently in an attempt to 'call the censors' bluff'.[13] His application was not accepted but he had numerous other dealings, direct and indirect, with the South African censors.[14]

But this collection of essays is by no means restricted to an analysis of the South African system of censorship. Its range is transnational and remarkably varied. What is striking about a number of these essays is the depth of scholarship and the extensive reading that is evident, not least in the volume's bibliography. The reactions of Eastern bloc writers such as Osip Mandelstam, Aleksandr Solzhenitsyn, and Zbigniew Herbert to Stalinist state repression are analysed alongside the ways in which pornography is policed in Britain and the United States, in the essays on D. H. Lawrence and Catharine MacKinnon. The essay entitled 'Apartheid Thinking' provides an account of the 'madness' of apartheid propagandist Geoffrey Cronjé's writings and their warnings against racial 'blood-mixing'. Notable in this essay is the linguistic analysis Coetzee provides to illustrate Cronjé's linking of taint, infection, and miscegenation. This is clearly an extension of his earlier discussion of scientific discourses of race and racism in the essay 'Blood, Flaw, Taint, Degeneration: The Case of Sarah Gertrude Millin' (1980), which was included in *White Writing*.

And yet *Giving Offense* has received comparatively little attention from Coetzee scholars over the years, although it includes some important insights, not only into the working of censorship, but also into Coetzee's own ethical and writerly concerns. Particularly interesting in this regard is the self-analysis in the essay entitled 'Emerging from Censorship', where Coetzee detects even in his own account the 'taint' of the censor that he perceives in the work of others. This self-awareness is a crucial element of Coetzee's critical essays generally, and of this essay in particular, which thus illuminates his novelistic practice and explains his own attitudes to writing. There are two strands to this: first, his awareness that he detects in his own language the 'very pathology' he is discussing, the 'more secret and shameful effects' of censorship that have, despite his own finely attuned consciousness, 'infected' him also. In his words: 'this very writing may be a specimen of the kind of paranoid discourse it seeks to describe' (*GO*, 37). This excoriating self-criticism is apparent, too, in *Youth*, where the third-person autobiographical mode is deployed as a way of critiquing his younger self's actions, responses, and emotions, mitigated in part by ironic humour. The second strand to this critique of the censors' effects on writing is his insight into the very private and vulnerable nature of composition. Here, he remarks the delicate balance of creativity, the process of 'Managing the inner selves' that emerges in the activity of writing. Memorably, he describes writing under censorship as 'like being intimate with someone who does not love you, with whom you want no intimacy, but who presses in himself upon you', the censor personified as 'an intrusive reader ... who forces his way into the intimacy of the writing transaction' (*GO*, 38). The male-gendered language associated with the censor's 'gaze' provides a metaphor of bodily violation, described elsewhere as 'not unlike being stripped and searched' (*DP*, 299). In both cases, this physical intrusion is 'undesired to the core', as David Lurie's sexual assault on Melanie Isaacs is described in *Disgrace* (*Dis*, 25). On the other hand, as Coetzee points out, despite the violent paranoia that this subjection to the censor induces in the writer, a positive effect is the 'sign that one's writing is being taken seriously' (*DP*, 299).

Ultimately, though, in Coetzee's evaluation, the main point of the book is 'that the unintended or not-fully-intended consequences of censorship tend to be more significant than the intended consequences'. Among the former are the potentially impoverishing and stultifying effects on what is written and how it is written. Here, as elsewhere across the volume, Coetzee refuses to treat censorship as being simply either 'good' or 'bad', liberal or conservative, terms he views as belonging to the 'structures of opposition, of Either-Or', which he takes it as his 'task to evade'. Instead, he probes the often-contradictory positions of power and disempowerment in which writers, including himself, are placed by regimes of censorship.[15] In taking this perspective, he is clearly aided by Michel Foucault's ideas about 'forms of writing' and their 'bearing on, or use by, *power*', a debt he had already explicitly acknowledged in *Doubling the Point* (*DP*, 247).[16]

Stranger Shores: Essays 1986–1999 (2001), *Inner Working: Literary Essays 2000–2005* (2007), and *Late Essays: 2006–2017* (2017)

In all three of the volumes discussed thus far, Coetzee's focus, even in the more expansive texts, is predominantly on specific writers and their works. This tendency is all the clearer in the critical essays and reviews collected in *Stranger Shores*, *Inner Workings*, and *Late Essays*, many of which first appeared either in the *New York Review of Books*, to which Coetzee has been a regular contributor, or as introductions to newly published versions of 'classic' novels.

There are a number of writers with whom Coetzee engages several times across these volumes and whom he acknowledges, in an uncollected essay 'Homage', as his 'literary paternity'.[17] The word 'paternity', as Coetzee is aware, emphasizes the 'strongly male … literary tradition' on which he draws, and which is made manifest across the collections, where only Nadine Gordimer features prominently in more than one piece, and other women authors are far outnumbered by their male counterparts. This tendency, however, might be set against the prominence across Coetzee's oeuvre of women narrators and focalizers (Magda, Susan Barton, Mrs Curren, Elizabeth Costello) who are themselves frequently writers or scholars. In fact, Coetzee addresses the often vexed issue of male writers writing women characters directly in *Late Essays*, in 'Gustave Flaubert, *Madame Bovary*', where he refers to Baudelaire's suggestion that 'in order to write Emma, Flaubert must have inhabited her so thoroughly that in some sense he must have become her, become a woman' even though, 'driven by an essential masculine mode of desiring', Emma's 'female form' becomes 'somewhat "bizarre and androgynous"' (*LE*, 107). This reflection echoes David Lurie's question to himself in *Disgrace*: '[D]oes he have it in him to be the woman?', and is perhaps attuned to the critical debates that have surrounded Coetzee's own rendering of women's voices in his novels (*Dis*, 160).

Of those father figures identified in 'Homage', several have been the focus of the pieces collected in *Stranger Shores*, *Inner Workings*, and *Late Essays*. These include Samuel Beckett, of course, but also Franz Kafka,

Daniel Defoe, Fyodor Dostoevsky, Zbigniew Herbert, Rainer Maria Rilke, and Robert Musil. An intriguing omission is Miguel de Cervantes, whose influence on Coetzee's work is obvious (particularly in *The Childhood of Jesus*) but about whom Coetzee has written only briefly, and most strikingly in his essay on Gabriel García Márquez, where he traces the ways in which Márquez was influenced by Dostoevsky, William Faulkner, Vladimir Nabokov, and Cervantes, and in particular by their tales about the 'seduction' of young girls by older men (*IW*, 257–71).[18] An essay on another Latin American writer (and literary predecessor), Jorge Luis Borges, appears in *Stranger Shores*, where Coetzee offers the brilliant insight that the technical innovation of Borges's fictions lies in their being modelled on the 'anatomy or critical essay, rather than the tale' so that 'narrative exposition' is reduced to 'a bare minimum' and 'the action can be condensed to an exploration of the implications of a hypothetical situation' (*SS*, 169).

Most recently, in *Late Essays*, Coetzee has turned his critical attention to fellow Australian writers, among them Nobel Laureate Patrick White, who is mentioned in 'Homage' and whose novel *Voss* is taken as a model by Eugene Dawn in *Dusklands*. Also included in *Late Essays* is a piece on Heinrich von Kleist who, we now know from the Harry Ransom Center archive, provided Coetzee with a model for *Life & Times of Michael K*, the name of whose eponymous protagonist is derived not only from Kakfa's K (as critics had originally posited) but also from Kleist's Michael Kohlhaas.[19] This essay constitutes a belated acknowledgement of Kleist's influence, and offers remarkable insights into the paradox of the mature Kleist's scepticism 'of all systems, indeed of the systematizing spirit' existing alongside his 'youthful enthusiasm for reason, clarity, and order'. This, together with Kleist's Kantian acceptance of the unattainability of 'final knowledge', renders him and his work 'too elusive (or too inconsistent) to be stuffed into any particular ideological box' (*LE*, 90–1). There are echoes here of critical assessments of Coetzee and of his work.

Indications of the influence of Ezra Pound, T. S. Eliot, and Zbigniew Herbert, and reflections on the purpose of criticism, are to be found in the important essay 'What is a Classic?', which shares its title with Eliot's essay of 1944. Here, Coetzee discusses and critiques Eliot's disavowal of his provincial American roots in favour of European culture, echoing his earlier suggestion – made in spite of his own clear investment in European literary forms – that South African writers embrace their provinciality;[20] he also addresses the relationship between impersonality and self-revelation (recalling his reflections on truth and autobiography). Using his own first exposure to Bach's music as an autobiographical example, Coetzee argues that works considered classics need not be protected even against 'hostile' criticism but that, rather, 'criticism of the most sceptical kind' can and should be used to confront the classic and 'ensure its survival'. By enduring 'the assault of barbarism' the classic ensures its longevity and criticism plays its part in this process by asking hard questions (*SS*, 19).

Considering together these three volumes of scholarly writings and literary reviews enables one to pose the question of whether Coetzee's opinions have changed between the early and the 'late' essays. Here, the reader may, for example, compare the four 'late essays' on Beckett (published between 2009 and 2015) with the three 'early essays' in *Doubling the Point* (dated from 1970 to 1973). One clear difference is the more experimental style of the recently published 'Eight Ways of Looking at Samuel Beckett'. Part-parody, part-homage, it is written in an impressionistic way that is quite different from the other essays and reviews, incorporating echoes of Beckett's work and including a somewhat startling comparison with Herman Melville's *Moby-Dick* (1851). It includes the intriguing thought experiment in which Coetzee ruminates on how history may have been changed if Beckett had been successful in his 1937 application for a lectureship in Italian at the University of Cape Town, the university at which Coetzee himself was a student, and was then appointed as a lecturer in English thirty-five years later. The possibility that a Professor Samuel Beckett might have encountered a young John Coetzee is an enticing one.[21]

Since Coetzee's migration to Australia in 2001, his essays have been regularly included in the annual volume *The Best Australian Essays*. Introducing the 2016 edition, Geordie Williamson remarks that 'the essay creates a place for slow thought on hectic subjects'.[22] Coetzee's essays are certainly examples of this and of his own 'slow reading'.[23] They offer readers insight into what Coetzee has described as the 'hard thought' of writing criticism,[24] involving 'scholarly homework' and 'raids' into 'strange' and often 'foreign linguistic territory' (*DP*, 243). He does not resile in his essays from commenting on the success or failure of the works he writes about, often with dry humour, whilst always appreciating the difficult tasks that the writer faces. In his *Late Essays*, a noticeable stylistic change that may indicate a more intimate sense of his readership is that he sometimes writes in the role of the reader as well as the critic, using the pronouns 'we' and 'us' to intimate a community of readers reading alongside him. When Stephen Watson commented that '[a]lmost all the initial difficulties of his [Coetzee's] novels vanish when one happens to have read the same books that he has', he highlighted the inestimable value of the experience of reading over Coetzee's shoulder that can be gleaned from his critical essays and reviews, as well as the necessity of understanding the contexts out of which he writes.[25]

Notes

1. Derek Attridge, 'Introduction', *IW*, p. ix.
2. I am grateful to Carrol Clarkson for this phrase.
3. Carrol Clarkson, 'Coetzee's Criticism' in Tim Mehigan (ed.), *A Companion to the Works of J. M. Coetzee* (Rochester, NY: Camden House, 2011). See under Further Reading for Kenneth Parker's rather polemical analysis of *White Writing*.
4. See *European Journal of English Studies*, 20.2 (2016) for discussion of Coetzee, intertextuality and non-English literary influences, especially M. J. López and K. Wiegandt, 'Introduction', pp. 113–26.
5. Attridge, 'Introduction', *IW*, p. xiii.
6. Jean Sévry, 'An Interview with J. M. Coetzee,' *Commonwealth Essays and Studies*, 9.1 (1986), 1–7 (p. 6).
7. López and Wiegandt, 'Introduction', p. 121.
8. David Attwell, *J. M. Coetzee and the Life of Writing* (Melbourne: Text, 2014), p. 72.
9. See under Further Readings for Parry's critique, and also for Derek Attridge's and Gayatri Chakravorty Spivak's interventions.
10. Daniel Defoe, *Robinson Crusoe*, ed. and intro. Thomas Keymer, notes by Thomas Keymer and James Kelly (Oxford: Oxford University Press, 2007), p. 29. Thanks to Carrol Clarkson for reminding me of the significance of this allusion.
11. J. M. Coetzee, 'The Novel Today', *Upstream*, 6.1 (1988), 2–5.
12. This essay was first published in the *New York Times*, 12 January 1986.
13. See Attwell's chapter 'The Burning of the Books' in *J. M. Coetzee and the Life of Writing*.
14. Hermann Wittenberg's 'The Taint of the Censor: J. M. Coetzee and the Making of *In the Heart of the Country*', *English in Africa*, 35.2, (2008), 133–50, provides an absorbing account of the publication history of the novel including its reception by the censors. See also Peter D. McDonald's work on Coetzee and censorship, included in Further Reading.
15. J. M. Coetzee, 'An Interview with J. M. Coetzee', *World Literature Today*, 70.1 (1996), 107–10 (p. 108).
16. Italics in original. In the same answer, he draws attention to the fact that 'Foucault's shadow' also 'lies quite heavily over my essays about colonial South Africa' in *White Writing*.
17. J. M. Coetzee, 'Homage,' *Threepenny Review*, 53 (1993), 5–7 (p. 5).
18. He also briefly discusses the character Don Quixote in his 'Jerusalem Prize Acceptance Speech' in *DP*, pp. 98–9; and in his exchanges with Arabella Kurtz in *GS*, p. 74, p. 77.
19. See David Attwell's discussion in *J. M. Coetzee and the Life of Writing*, pp. 129–47.
20. J. M. Coetzee, 'SA Authors Must Learn Modesty', *Die Vaderland*, 1 May 1981, p. 16.
21. Chris Ackerley imagines this scenario in more detail in 'Style: Coetzee and Beckett' in Tim Mehigan (ed.), *A Companion to the Works of J. M. Coetzee* (Rochester, NY: Camden House, 2011), pp. 23–38 (p. 23).

22. Geordie Williamson (ed.), *The Best Australian Essays 2016* (Carlton: Black Inc, 2016), p. 3.

23. In his gray casebound notebook for *Life & Times of Michael K* (CP 33.5), Coetzee has written under the date 25 August 1982: '"Teacher of slow reading" (Nietzsche)'. The full quotation is from Nietzsche's 1881 *Daybreak: Thoughts on the Prejudices of Morality*: 'It is not for nothing that one has been a philologist, perhaps one is a philologist still, that is to say, a teacher of slow reading.' Coetzee references this in 'Homage,' in relation to Ezra Pound: 'In this sense, Pound is, as Nietzsche said of himself, a teacher of slow reading' (p. 6).

24. Coetzee uses this phrase in a podcast entitled 'J. M. Coetzee on Writing, followed by Reading in Dutch (subtitled) from *IJzertijd* (*Age of Iron*)', 200. Available at www/youtube.com/watch?v=LbL2BxyXQUE

25. Stephen Watson, 'Colonialism and the Novels of J. M. Coetzee', *Research in African Literatures*, 17.3 (1986), pp. 370–92 (p. 380).

9

PATRICK HAYES

Influence and Intertextuality

It is normally possible to consider questions about influence separately from questions about intertextuality: these concepts lead in different directions, to different kinds of literary discussion. But in the case of Coetzee, it is for a number of reasons very useful to bring them together. As a writer situated in the academy during what Patrick Ffrench has called the 'time of theory', it is important to understand that the literary-critical theory of intertextuality, as it was developed by such figures as Mikhail Bakhtin, Roland Barthes, and Julia Kristeva, was itself an influence upon Coetzee, though not a straightforward one. To make matters still more complicated, Coetzee has used some of his most important literary influences – especially Samuel Beckett and Fyodor Dostoevsky – to reflect upon the nature and value of intertextuality in his own writing. So while influence and intertextuality can be told apart, with Coetzee it is helpful to bring them together.

When we speak of 'influence', we usually mean those other writers who have done most to shape the imagination of the writer who interests us – perhaps especially, as Harold Bloom has argued in *The Anxiety of Influence* (1973), when those influences are contested or disavowed. Nowadays authors are expected to name their influences as part of the culture of interviews and public lectures that surrounds the marketing of literary texts. As a result, they often develop stories about key moments of their formation, and in a lecture given in Graz, Austria, in 1991, Coetzee offered his audience a highly self-conscious rendition of the 'influence story' (*SS*, 9). 'One Sunday afternoon in the summer of 1955, when I was fifteen years old', he tells us:

> I was mooning around our back garden in the suburbs of Cape Town, wondering what to do, boredom being the main problem of existence in those days, when from the house next door I heard music. As long as the music lasted, I was frozen, I dared not breathe. I was being spoken to by the music as music had never spoken to me before. (*SS*, 9)

It was a moment, Coetzee declares, in which 'everything changed', which was 'of the greatest significance in my life', and 'a key event in my formation'. What influenced him, he explains, was not precisely the individual piece of music being performed (Bach's *Well-Tempered Clavier*), but instead a wider encounter with 'ideas of exposition, complication and resolution that are more general than music' (*SS*, 10). It was a realization of something fundamental and powerful in aesthetic experience that Bach, in this moment, happened to instantiate for the young John Coetzee.

It would require several books to explore the wide range of writers and other artists who have influenced Coetzee at this level. However, as a starting point, the second volume of his fictionalized memoirs, *Youth* (2002), pursues this notion of the 'influence story' in relation to literary traditions. While he acknowledges that D. H. Lawrence is one of the 'great figures of the present age', the 'John' character finds Lawrence's virile idiom of a 'dark' and 'imperious' male self to be, in his own case, sadly unachievable; he admires Henry James, but 'try though he may, he cannot feel the ghostly hand of James extended to touch his brow in blessing' (*Y*, 67–8). It is not until he reads Samuel Beckett's novel *Watt* (1953) that he finds a true affinity:

> From the first page he knows he has hit on something. Propped up in bed with light pouring through the window, he reads and reads.
> *Watt* is quite unlike Beckett's plays. There is no clash, no conflict, just the flow of a voice telling a story, a flow continually checked by doubts and scruples, its pace fitted exactly to the pace of his own mind. *Watt* is also funny, so funny that he rolls about laughing. When he comes to the end he starts again at the beginning.
>
> (*Y*, 155)

The most immediate outcome of Coetzee's discovery of Beckett was his decision to write a doctoral thesis on Beckett's English fiction. As he explained later, the aim of his research was to uncover what he felt to be most primary in the experience of reading Beckett, what most resonated with that earlier experience of listening to Bach. 'Beckett's prose, up to and including *The Unnamable*', he told David Attwell in *Doubling the Point*, 'has given me a sensuous delight that hasn't dimmed over the years. The critical work I did on Beckett originated in that sensuous response, and was a grasping after ways in which to talk about it: to talk about delight' (*DP*, 20).

While Beckett is therefore a central influence, Coetzee discusses a wide range of other novelists in appreciative depth in his many scholarly essays and reviews. In even the briefest list of these writers it would be impossible not to include the following names: Miguel de Cervantes, Fyodor Dostoevsky, Leo Tolstoy, Franz Kafka, William Faulkner, and James

Joyce. And yet to confine the question of influence to the history of the novel, or even to the wider history of literature in general, would be to limit Coetzee's writing in a way it does not choose. His fiction is peppered with allusions to a range of philosophers, from Hegel, Nietzsche, and Sartre in *In the Heart of the Country* (1977), through to Plato and Wittgenstein in *The Childhood of Jesus* (2016). One of the directions recent scholarship on Coetzee has taken is the exploration of his relationship with traditions of Western philosophy, both in terms of influence but also – and more subtly – through questions about the broader continuities and divergences between literary experience and philosophical reasoning.[1] Coetzee's critical essays and his working notebooks allude to a number of theologians and religious thinkers, ranging from Augustine and St Paul through to Rudolf Bultmann, Martin Buber, and René Girard. This important area of influence is only just beginning to be explored by literary scholars, not least because of the prompting given by the inclusion of the name 'Jesus' in the title of Coetzee's three most recent fictions.[2] Complicating the influence of European and American novelists, philosophers, and theologians is Coetzee's relationship with South African writers and literary traditions. *White Writing: On the Culture of Letters in South Africa* (1988) is devoted to an exploration of this complex legacy, which Coetzee has frequently criticized, but which he cannot disavow. It ranges from William Burchell's nineteenth-century travel narratives, and later engagement with South Africa by such figures as Thomas Pringle, W. E. G. Louw, Roy Campbell, and Olive Schreiner, through to the ideas about race developed by Sarah Gertrude Millin, Pauline Smith, and Alan Paton. Other more contemporary South African writers, particularly Nadine Gordimer, André Brink, and Etienne Leroux have also been important sources of provocation and intellectual exchange.[3]

Turning now to intertextuality, it is important to understand that this concept is used in two very different ways. On the one hand, the term 'intertextuality' is often used to describe something similar to influence: not in the strong sense, defined above, of being captivated by something essential in aesthetic experience, but instead in the much looser sense of a self-conscious practice of literary allusion. In this definition, intertextuality refers to techniques of literary parody and pastiche, which we encounter, for example, in James Joyce's rewriting of *The Odyssey* (among many other texts) in *Ulysses* (1922). In *The Politics of Postmodernism* (1989), Linda Hutcheon has shown that in the post-war period this enterprise of parodic rewriting became unusually prominent: it became linked to various kinds of cultural politics, from feminism through to postcolonialism, which place importance on recovering hitherto marginalized voices. We see this kind of intertextuality – 'historiographic metafiction' is Hutcheon's name for it – in Jean Rhys's *Wide Sargasso Sea* (1966), which recovers Bertha Mason's voice from *Jane Eyre* (1847); or in Peter Carey's *Jack Maggs* (1997), which revisits *Great Expectations* (1860–1) from an Australian perspective. In some ways the concept of historiographic metafiction offers a useful frame for understanding the moral and political dimensions of Coetzee's *Foe* (1986), which returns to the fiction of Daniel Defoe, revising the place that Susan Barton and Friday were given in the novels *Roxana: The Fortunate Mistress* (1724) and *Robinson Crusoe* (1719) respectively. But to understand the more enigmatic aspects of this text, and to get anywhere at all with *The Master of Petersburg* (1994), which revisits Dostoevsky's *The Devils* (1872) and *The Brothers Karamazov* (1880) without any obvious moral project in view, we need to address the more philosophical register in which intertextuality has also been discussed in the post-war period.

In 'From Work to Text' (1971), Roland Barthes defined intertextuality as an attempt to describe the impact of the major new modern disciplines, including 'linguistics, anthropology, Marxism and psychoanalysis', on the nature of literary expression.[4] Marx and Freud (to deal with only those two) had each, in different ways, sought to show that the human subject is never in full possession of the meaning of his or her words and actions. In the Marxist account, the bourgeois subject's image as a self-reliant individual is produced by ideology that deflects from the reality of social relations, particularly from the manifold forms of dependency that make up the international economic system. In the Freudian account, the subject is split between conscious and unconscious selves, and never ultimately able to understand fully the drives and traumas that lead him or her to repeat certain compulsions, or have certain desires, or use some forms of expression over others. For Barthes, what follows from the decentring of the subject accomplished by these intellectual disciplines is the decentring of the author (the 'death of the author', as an earlier and less subtle essay put it), and a shift in the way we ought to think about the meaning of a literary text. 'The intertextual in which every text is held,' he argued, 'is not to be confused with some origin of the text: to try to find the "sources", the "influences" of a work, is to fall in with the myth of filiation; the citations which go to make up a text are anonymous, untraceable, and yet *already read*: they are quotations without inverted commas'.[5]

As Barthes thereby insists, intertextuality in this sense has nothing to do with influence or literary allusion, but is instead a general condition of writing which derives from the fact that an author is a split subject, creating a text that will in some sense speak against itself, be permeated by an alterity it cannot master. In Marxist terms, it might be intertextual with economic or political relationships upon which it depends for the values it asserts; in Freudian terms, it might bespeak forms of desire, or at least certain kinds of ambivalence, that cannot be openly acknowledged. The 'intertexts', in this sense, are the conflicting echoes, resonances, and meanings that are 'already read', as Barthes puts it – meaning that they are always already readable in the text. As an example, return to Coetzee's lecture on his youthful enthusiasm for Bach. Rather than accepting his love of 'the classic' at face value, as the lecture continues Coetzee instead treats himself as an intertextual subject, potentially blind to the nature of his desires. 'Is there some non-vacuous sense', he asks himself, 'in which I can say that the spirit of Bach was speaking to me across the ages, across the seas, putting before me certain ideals; or was what was really going on at that moment that I was symbolically electing high European culture, and command of the codes of that culture, as a route that would take me out of my class position in white South African society?' (SS, 11). Can the call of Bach to this *ephebe* be understood as a disinterested summons to a vocation as an artist, or 'was it really the masked expression of a material interest?' (SS, 11). As Coetzee points out, this is 'a question of a kind which one would be deluded to think one could answer about oneself', though in no sense can the unanswerability of the question, he insists, be taken to imply that it should not be asked (SS, 11).

However, it is important to understand that the theory of intertextuality, as pursued in this more philosophical register, is not simply an attempt to describe writing in a way that takes into account modern understandings of the subject. In several of the leading accounts there is a movement away from merely defining intertextuality, towards an advocacy of it as a specific literary practice, and a celebration of those texts that decentre the subject in the most radical ways. In his essay, Barthes distinguishes between the 'work' and the 'text', and while he protests otherwise, it is hard not to see this distinction as the valorization of avant-garde experimental writing against a more conventionally representational handling of language. Taking his lead from Nietzsche, for Barthes the text – as opposed to the work – is a space where the experimental author can transgress against the domesticating routines of what he calls 'doxa'. Doxa is that body of 'general opinion – constitutive of our democratic societies and powerfully aided by mass communications – defined by its limits, the energy with which it excludes, its *censorship*'. In defiance of doxa, 'it may be said that the Text is always *paradoxical*', a protest against the moral ordering of the self into an ego-bound subject.[6] A comparable movement away from description towards valuation can be seen in the writing of Julia Kristeva, who studied under Barthes's supervision in Paris in the 1960s. In *Revolution in Poetic Language* (1974), Kristeva defined intertextuality in specifically post-Freudian terms, as a condition of language that exceeds the unilluminating practice of communicative rationality, and which places us in touch with affective dimensions of the self that our very formation as subjects in language excludes – energies and drives that she names 'the semiotic'. As with Barthes, Kristeva maintains that all writing necessarily contains a tension between the communicative and the antirational, or 'the symbolic' and 'the semiotic', to use her terms. But she goes further than Barthes in specifically naming modernist writing as the moment when literature began self-consciously to exploit this tension. In Joyce, Proust, and Kafka, she argues, we encounter a textual experience that penetrates the banality of communicative language, making unconscious desire speak in a way that is both profound and imaginatively compelling.

There is no doubt that Coetzee was influenced by these theorists, but he engages with intertextuality in a circumspect and critical way. No small part of what makes him distinctive as a writer is that he is much more attuned than theorists such as Barthes and Kristeva to certain registers of moral concern that arise when the most impressive and appealing kinds of imaginative experience are connected with the decentring of the subject.

Coetzee first started to question the nature and value of intertextuality through his response to the fiction of Samuel Beckett. In an early literary essay, 'The Comedy of Point of View in Beckett's *Murphy*' (1970), Coetzee drew attention to what he called Beckett's 'attitude of reserve' towards the novel's expressive powers. What interested him was Beckett's play with the illusion of objectivity, or what he rather ironically calls 'the principle of the separation of the three estates of author, narrator and character' (*DP*, 36). As Coetzee goes on to suggest, this 'attitude of reserve' towards the novel, and the disturbance of the communicative rationality assumed by the form in its most conventional modes, gained ever more importance to Beckett, such that 'by the time of *The Unnamable* (1953) [it] has become, in a fundamental sense, the subject of Beckett's work'. '"The Unnamable" as a name', Coetzee continued, 'is a token of an inability to attain the separation of creator and creature, namer and named, with which the act of creating, naming, begins ("To be an artist is to fail", wrote Beckett in 1949). "I seem to speak", says The Unnamable, "it is not I, about me, it is not about me"' (*DP*, 37).

Coetzee's attitude to Beckett's negation of novelistic representation is complex. While he clearly admires the logic of what Beckett is doing to the novel's illusion of objectivity, he is at the same time concerned that Beckett is nonetheless driving fiction into an imprisoning solipsistic impasse. Citing the endlessly self-undoing sentences of *The Unnamable*, in which statements about reality are relativized or contradicted as soon as they are announced, he points out that the endgame of Beckett's writing is that 'consciousness of self can only be consciousness of consciousness. Fiction is the only subject of fiction. Therefore, fictions are closed systems, prisons' (*DP*, 38). *In the Heart of the Country* is the Coetzee text that most closely resembles a Beckett narrative, featuring as it does the fragmentary and self-ironizing monologue of a solitary fictional voice, known only as 'Magda'. But even here, in a moment that is dizzyingly metafictional, Magda asks herself whether she is in fact imprisoned in her own intertextuality. 'Is it possible', she asks, 'that I am prisoner not of the lonely farmhouse and the stone desert but of my stony monologue?' (*IHC*, 13). She is both delighted and appalled by her own power to undo the reality claims that make up herself and her world. 'There is finally only I', she muses, 'drifting into sleep, beyond the reach of pain. Acting on myself I change the world. Where does this power end? Perhaps that is what I am trying to find out' (*IHC*, 39).

It is what Coetzee was trying to find out too. His 1985 essay 'Confession and Double Thoughts' pursued these questions about intertextuality by considering how Rousseau, Tolstoy, and Dostoevsky had explored the nature of the subject and the possibility of self-knowledge. In a series of close analyses, Coetzee showed how, for each writer, the pursuit of the truth of the self was troubled by the ultimate inability of the conscious subject to understand his or her own desires. Rousseau and Tolstoy, he argued, tended either to conceal or evade the ways in which human consciousness fails to grasp the possibility of an unconscious truth that 'slips out', as he puts it, 'in strange associations, false rationalisations, gaps, contradictions' (*DP*, 257). In Dostoevsky, though, Coetzee encounters a writer acutely aware of the infinite regress of self-doubt to which the modern subject is vulnerable, and both able and willing to explore that regress to its furthest horizon. He alludes to a range of Dostoevsky novels, but gives particular attention to *Notes from Underground* (1864), describing how the protagonist moves through a bewildering – but increasingly fascinating – array of explanations and counter-explanations of his desires and actions, always falling short of a final truth. In this way, Coetzee concluded, Dostoevsky points to 'the malaise that renders confession powerless to tell the truth and come to an end' (*DP*, 282), and he exposes 'the helplessness of confession before the desire of the self to construct its own truth' (*DP*, 279).

As this register of moral concern and pathos suggests, Coetzee does not embrace the celebratory tone which Barthes and Kristeva apply to intertextuality. 'Not all of us', Coetzee rather stoically noted in an interview that accompanies the essay in *Doubling the Point*, 'have the power to accept, pessimistically (Freud) or with equanimity (Derrida, it seems), the prospect of endlessness' (*DP*, 249). And yet despite these downbeat conclusions, it remains impossible to ignore the sheer energy and imaginative reach of the

'Confession' essay. It is the longest critical essay that Coetzee has written, and in it he is clearly fascinated by the unruly imaginative life, the enigmatic and counterintuitive movement of writing, which is awakened when an author of Dostoevsky's powers pursues the winding intertextual logic of 'double thoughts'.

This mix of moral concern and imaginative appeal is equally palpable in *Foe*, a text in which Coetzee avows the influence of the tradition of the English novel, even as he seeks to complicate and disrupt the terms upon which he belongs to it. The first section of the book is a narrative, represented throughout in quotation marks, by Susan Barton, the character who winds up as the female lead in Defoe's novel *Roxana*. In this narrative Susan attempts to define herself as a 'female castaway', a strong-willed individualist who – much like the Robinson Crusoe described in Defoe's novel – has confronted adversity and, with the help of Divine Providence, survived the ordeal. Saying little about her former life or her marital status, other than that her story should be understood as a heroic search for her abducted daughter, she tells of how she washed up on a desert island, where she lived with a morose and unimpressive man called Cruso and his servant Friday. Susan's attempt at self-presentation reads very flat, and the second section of the book is made of up her increasingly plaintive letters to the author Daniel Foe, asking that he write her story in a more imaginatively compelling way, so that she might win recognition from the general public for the identity she wants to claim, and (hopefully) make some money as well. She ends up living in Foe's house in Stoke Newington, and the house of Foe (which resonates with Henry James's House of Fiction) turns out to be an uncanny place, in which Susan's ego-ideal as the female individualist hero starts to give way to other voices – possibly from inside her, possibly through Foe's invention. A mysterious woman arrives claiming to be her abandoned daughter, thereby undercutting her rescue-mission narrative; and as she revisits the story of the island she is struck by the manifold meanings it might have ('Alas', she complains, 'my stories always seem to have more applications than I intend' (*F*, 81)) and by the stories within it that remain enigmatic. In particular, there is the untold story of Friday's severed tongue, and the mystery of his desire. As she spends more time in the disturbing atmosphere of the house of Foe, she starts to acquire a strange sense of her own otherness. Following a trance-like dance that imitates Friday, she feels a 'glow of after-memory', as she obscurely puts it, that acts as a 'message (but from whom?) to tell me there were other lives open to me than this one' (*F*, 104).

As this brief account must already suggest, the experience of reading *Foe* is morally complex in a more pointed way than either Coetzee's 'Confession' essay or his response to Beckett. On the one hand, when we enter the house of Foe the writing itself becomes increasingly compelling on an imaginative level, not least because we move from a rather bland voice asserting its identity into an uncanny space where strange desires and repressed, half-articulate voices start to emerge in ways that fascinate. But the pleasure of the text – its *jouissance*, Barthes would say, of self-loss – is accompanied by a queasy sense of moral dubiousness and pathos. Susan might in a certain sense be read as an early feminist, determined not to be defined by others but to tell her own story in her own way – but what we as readers at some level take pleasure in involves the bewildering of this ambition by a male author. 'Nothing is left to me but doubt', she complains to Foe towards the end of the text: 'I am doubt itself. Who is speaking me?' (F, 133).

In defining its concerns about the self-undermining process of intertextuality from the specific viewpoint of the female subject, Foe resonates with – and might even be said to allude to – debates taking place in the academy during its composition. In 'Changing the Subject: Authorship, Writing, and the Reader', a widely discussed paper that was first delivered at the Pembroke Center at Brown University in Spring 1985, Nancy K. Miller argued that the version of intertextuality that had been popularized by Barthes and Kristeva was, at best, unhelpful to the ways feminists need to use literature:

> The postmodernist decision that the Author is Dead and the subject along with him does not, I will argue, necessarily hold for women, and prematurely forecloses the question of agency for them. Because women have not had the same historical relation of identity to origin, institution, production that men have had, they have not, I think, (collectively) felt burdened by *too much* Self, Ego, Cogito, etc.[7]

Attacking what she calls 'death of the author' theory as merely another false universal, Miller juxtaposed Barthes's celebration of self-fragmentation with the attempts made by the feminist poet Adrienne Rich to construct a new and reimagined identity for women. She quoted from Rich's famous essay 'When We Dead Awaken' (1972), which emphasizes the importance of creating female traditions and models for emulation. 'I write for the still-fragmented parts in me, trying to bring them together', Rich had claimed. 'Whoever can read and use any of this, I write for them as well.'[8]

Coetzee's Foe also sets up a Barthesian textuality against a more subject-centred feminist project, but it does so with greater complexity than Miller allows for in her essay. If we were to read Miller's essay in an intertextual way, we might observe that one of the stories it represses in its insistence on the priority of gender is the story of race, and the extent to which both male and female Western identities have a shared history in the production of silence about other kinds of difference. In an equally widely discussed essay of the year before, 'Three Womens' Texts and a Critique of Imperialism' (1985), Gayatri Chakravorty Spivak had written about the tendency of contemporary feminism to identify naïvely with an individualistic, self-determination model of feminist identity. This kind of subject-centred feminism, she argued, is complicit with the imperialist form of the bourgeois ego, which relied for its sense of identity on creating an opposition with a muted, or even irrational, colonial 'other' – an unquoted and invisible intertext, which is nonetheless ever present in this kind of subject, as its political unconscious. In *Foe*, as we have seen, part of the uncanniness of the house of Foe resided in Susan increasingly coming to regard Friday as – mysteriously, in ways she cannot articulate – the hole in her story, believing that he is in some way her intertext, and that without his story hers is untellable too. In the third section of the book, Susan and Foe agree that somehow Friday is the key to her story, but neither can make him speak in a way that does not simply subject him to their desires. This part of the book slows down almost to a halt, in a series of torturous and inconclusive discussions about what it means to give voice to Friday, thereby powerfully evoking the limits of the ego-bound consciousness to understand itself. But in the final section of *Foe* all discussion ends, and we abandon the discursive realm of the human subject entirely. Here, an unnamed author figure in an unnamed time mysteriously descends through the ocean and encounters Friday, alongside Susan and Foe, in the sunken slaving vessel that must have brought him to the island:

> His mouth opens. From inside him comes a slow stream, without breath, without interruption. It flows up through his body and out upon me; it passes through the cabin, through the wreck; washing the cliffs and shores of the island, it runs northward and southward to the ends of the earth. Soft and cold, dark and unending, it beats against my eyelids, against the skin of my face.
>
> (*F*, 157)

In this extraordinary passage, through a language in which 'bodies are their own signs', Friday's voice comes to us from an unnamed source, and takes flight as a pre-symbolic language of the body – a 'semiotic' utterance, as Kristeva would call it – which signifies powerfully without being reducible to communicative rationality.

Imaginatively rich though it may be, this semiotic undoing of the subject in language is in fact complicated by an awkward literary allusion. Recalling Nancy Miller's juxtaposition of 'death of the author' theory and a more subject-centred feminism, the allusion is to an Adrienne Rich poem, 'Diving into the Wreck', from her 1972 collection of the same name. Rich's poem is about the feminist subject figuratively diving into the wreck of history to undertake purposeful inquiry into 'the book of myths / in which / our names do not appear'.[9] The start of the poem describes the poet putting on her diving gear ('the body armour of black rubber') and learning the rudiments of diving on her own. As she descends into the deep, she encounters a disturbing realm that cannot be prepared for fully: she finds herself 'blacking out' in the deep; then, in adapting to this very different space, her own identity starts to shift ('I am she: I am he'), even as she uncovers 'purposes' and 'maps' to the creation of a self that has taken on – as the title of her previous collection put it – 'the will to change'. Given this allusion, it is very notable – and morally disturbing – that in the final section of *Foe*, Susan, the feminist subject, is not the diver into the wreck, but part of the wreckage, and not purposeful but silent: indeed we encounter her locked in an embrace with Foe, the very writer whose house of fiction has evacuated her voice of its attempts at self-formation. In this way the ending of Coetzee's complex book encloses a difficult thought that intensifies, rather than resolves, the moral concerns it raises throughout. It allows for the possibility that the radically venturesome and imaginatively fascinating kind of self-displacement that might disclose Friday's voice may well come at the cost of other moral projects that are premised upon more subject-centred models of acting and being; moreover, it suggests that there may be no final language for adjudicating between these different and incommensurate ideals. The value of the book lies not least in the affective power and intellectual acuity with which it articulates this problem, and its refusal to oversimplify this complex intersection between ethics, politics, and aesthetics.

   The Master of Petersburg takes the questions that 'Confession and Double Thoughts' and *Foe* both explore, and escalates the stakes still further. Whereas Defoe was a shadowy character in *Foe*, here Coetzee places the 'master' artist Dostoevsky at the centre of the text, and uses his example to explore the kinds of risk that are most at stake in the intertextual literary imagination.

   The book tells the story of Dostoevsky arriving in Petersburg in October 1869 to pay his respects to his stepson, Pavel Isaev, who has died in mysterious circumstances. (While some aspects of the book draw on fact, Coetzee improvises with the particulars of Dostoevsky's life.) Dostoevsky lingers for several weeks in and around his dead son's rented apartment, for reasons that are hard to define. 'His excuse for staying on', Dostoevsky notes to himself, is 'as obscure to others as to himself' (*MP*, 66). The main 'excuse' he has is couched in ethical terms. He tells Pavel's landlady, Anna Sergeyevna, that he is trying in some way to find a link to his dead son's voice, and to reawaken some buried connection to the young man. He thereby figures Pavel as a missing intertext in his own life in much the way Friday was for Susan, as a silent presence that needs to be articulated. As with Susan, the attempt to access what remains of Pavel – the boy he may not have served well as a father – requires him to decentre and destabilize his ego-bound subjectivity. But as an experienced writer, this is something Dostoevsky does in a self-conscious way, and is even something that he has developed theories about. Almost directly echoing Barthes, in one passage he attempts to think of his writer's consciousness as an intertext that is fired by a process of substitution. Knowing, on the logic of double thoughts that his fiction so powerfully articulates, that any intentional act will serve only as a screen to deflect him from truths that his ego finds shameful or self-destructive, he explains to himself that he must expect to find Pavel where he does not expect him to be found. Perhaps he will hear him if he allows the howling of a dog into his mind, to do its estranging work there; or perhaps Pavel will come if he enters into dialogue with the derelict man who oddly arrives at his apartment building: such unlikely means might provide him with 'an opportunity for leaving himself as he is behind and becoming what he might yet be' (*MP*, 82).

But while this ethical way of understanding Dostoevsky's interest in lingering around Pavel's apartment for weeks on end can never be discarded, and in fact is held open as a possibility until the very end of the text, *The Master of Petersburg* also explores the possibility that an ethical self-description might in a writer only ever be a mask, or an 'excuse', to use Dostoevsky's word, that enables something that is both stranger and more imaginatively powerful to emerge in the writing. In one early scene Dostoevsky starts to encounter in himself violent and even sadistic feelings towards Matryosha, the landlady's young daughter, with whom Pavel appears to have had a sibling-like connection. As he 'stares at her with what can only be nakedness', and watches the child flinch beneath his gaze, and then flee 'the room', he becomes aware of other motives for staying in Petersburg:

> He is aware, even as it unfolds, that this is a passage he will not forget and may even one day rework into his writing. A certain shame passes over him, but it is superficial and transitory. First in his writing and now in his life, shame seems to have lost its power, its place taken by a blank and amoral passivity that shrinks from no extreme. It is as if, out of the corner of an eye, he can see clouds advancing on him with terrific speed, stormclouds. Whatever stands in their path will be swept away. With dread, but with excitement too, he waits for the storm to break. (*MP*, 24)

Perhaps what is enticing him to linger in Petersburg is a growing discovery that he can exploit Pavel's 'erotic surround', as he calls it – the rooms he slept in, the women he knew – to access an amoral imaginative power, one that draws upon regressive impulses involving sadism and sexual aggression, and which 'shrinks from no extreme'. The excitement at his realization of the power to be won from these sources is equally laden with dread, because of the shameful nature of the sadistic sexual energy it draws upon, and the various kinds of betrayal – both of himself, and of the child – that it requires. 'I write perversions of the truth', Dostoevsky tells himself late in the text: 'I choose the crooked road and take children into dark places. I follow the dance of the pen' (*MP*, 236).

Strong writing, Dostoevsky comes to understand, might only emerge from a displacement of the regulatory ego-bound consciousness, a capacity to follow the dance of the pen even as it starts to make articulate the potent drive energies that moral consciousness needs to either sublimate or repress. He puts this in the strongest possible terms: his own life, he tells himself, is 'a price or a currency. It is something I pay with in order to write ... A life without honour; treachery without limit; confession without end' (*MP*, 222). What is most troubling about this book is therefore not only the way it follows Dostoevsky by insinuating that the most compelling imaginative energies – those which make for a master writer – may derive from obscure and perverse sources of the self, but its suggestion that the semiotic movement of desire has a certain autonomy, a wayward logic of its own. In a later passage involving Matryosha, Dostoevsky suddenly realizes that, while he is ostensibly comforting her about Pavel's death, he is at the same time 'imagining this child in her ecstasy'. This thought leads him on, and he follows the dance of his imagination as it swells into a paedophilic fantasy:

> He thinks of child-prostitutes he has known ... he thinks of men who search out such girls because beneath the garish paint and provocative clothes they detect something that outrages them, a certain inviolability, a certain maidenliness. *She is prostituting the Virgin*, such a man says, recognizing the flavour of innocence in the gesture with which the girl cups her breasts for him, in the movement with which she spreads her thighs. In the tiny room with its stale odours, she gives off a faint, desperate smell of spring, of flowers, that he cannot bear. Deliberately, with teeth clenched, he hurts her, and then hurts her again and again, watching her face all the time for something that goes beyond mere wincing, mere bearing of pain: for the sudden wide-eyed look of a creature that begins to understand its life is in danger.   (*MP*, 76–7)

This is what Dostoevsky, recovering, names 'the vision, the fit, the rictus of the imagination' (*MP*, 77). In 'The Cruel Practice of Art' (1949), Georges Bataille suggested that part of the appeal of art, especially tragic art, lies in its power to evoke the affective range that primitive societies encountered more directly through sacrifice rituals: the sadistic fascination of watching death happen, of being able to gain entry to psychological states that normally remain closed. The moment when the girl takes on that sudden, wide-eyed look speaks to this kind of imaginative excitement – an excitement laced with dread.

However, what is even more disturbing than this kind of transgressiveness is the way *The Master of Petersburg* also explores how not only the most crudely potent, but also the most fascinating and subtle kinds of imaginative complexity, might emerge in and through, rather than in spite of, a threateningly amoral semiotics of self-loss. One of the most memorable passages of the book comes when Dostoevsky is having dinner with Anna and Matryosha, and is suddenly, out of nowhere, possessed by a crudely pornographic vision of Anna. Fuelling this vision, he dimly acknowledges, is a desire to humiliate Anna's daughter by dominating and depraving her mother; but then Dostoevsky realizes that the vision has as its source a piece of paedophile pornography he purchased many years earlier in Paris – a photograph entitled 'Gypsy Love', involving a 'girl with long dark hair lying underneath a moustachioed man'. And yet here in his fantasy, transposed over the girl of the photo, is the mature adult body of Anna:

> The thighs of Anna Sergeyevna, of the Anna Sergeyevna of his memory, are leaner, stronger; there is something purposeful in their grip which he links with the fact that she is not a child but a fullgrown, avid woman. Fullgrown and therefore open (that is the word that insists itself) to death. A body ready for experience because it knows it will not live forever. The thought is arousing but disturbing too. To those thighs it does not matter who is gripped between them; beheld from somewhere above and to the side of the bed, the man in the picture both is and is not himself.
>
> (MP, 131)

Notice that the word 'open' comes to him unbidden, from a movement through language – a 'dance of the pen' – that is not wholly authored by the conscious subject. What is initially most remarkable here is the way a certain kind of human profundity emerges out of the pornography, for Dostoevsky's fantasy cascades towards an unforgettable insight into what it is to live fully in a body: 'A body ready for experience because it knows it will not live forever'. To think of this insight as profound is to suggest something of the beauty and pathos it expresses within the lust, as well as the empathetic connection with Anna herself that the phrase sustains. But it clearly cannot be elevated into a moral sententia, for Dostoevsky's capacity to reach this insight is both repulsively arousing, in that it derives from an erotic channel sparked by child pornography, and disturbing, in that it then gives rise, in the final sentence, to a sudden apprehension of the inhuman anonymity of bodies: 'to those thighs it does not matter who is gripped between them'. It is an empathy born out of sadistic lust, which turns into a vivid apprehension of the relationship between desire and mortality, and then turns again into an inhuman apprehension of the body as sheer desiring force, the one inside the other, like a series of Russian dolls. This is truly a 'rictus of the imagination', an ecstatic dancing of the pen that carries the author as it carries the reader into an unnameable form of human insight, shamelessly uncensored. 'Every word double', as Dostoevsky puts it later in the text: 'Split writing from a split heart' (*MP*, 219). The writing is as disturbing as it is fascinating, as threatening to any morally normative sense of our humanity as it is imaginatively compelling.

If *Foe* explored the pathos of intertextuality, the kinds of self-realization it excludes, *The Master of Petersburg* explores its unruliness, and the elements of risk involved in taking literary writing seriously. As Coetzee pointed out in his contemporaneous essay 'The Harms of Pornography', there is little to protect the kind of writing found in Dostoevsky's oeuvre, a writing which venturesomely follows the dance of the pen, from falling under the same strictures that moralists use to condemn sadistic pornography – 'except', he added, 'perhaps its *seriousness* (if that were recognized) as a philosophical project' (*GO*, 73. Italics original). Immediately Coetzee qualified himself, noting that seriousness is itself 'deconstructible as a feature of the ideology of so-called high art and the drive to power of the high artist' (*GO*, 73). There is of course no way to measure seriousness at the level of the intention of the artist, on the very logic that his own essay 'Confession and Double Thoughts' had already exposed. Unless, that is, seriousness is in some way measurable as an approach that is able to scrutinize the commitments as well as the imaginative possibilities at stake in its own influences and writerly allegiances – which is, as I have argued, precisely what Coetzee's writing does.

Notes

1. See under Further Readings the volumes edited by Leist and Singer, and by Hayes and Wilm.
2. See, for example, Alicia Broggi's 'J. M. Coetzee and the Religious Tradition: Navigating Religious Legacies in the Novel' (unpublished D.Phil thesis, Oxford, 2017); and, under Further Reading, Broggi's article.
3. Gordimer reviewed *Life & Times of Michael K* ('The Idea of Gardening', *New York Review of Books*, 2 February 1984, 3–6), and it is possible to read Coetzee's 'The Novel Today' (1988) and 'Erasmus: Madness and Rivalry' (1996) as an extended response to her appraisal. For more on Coetzee's relations with South African contemporaries, see his interview with Jean Sévry (1986), his review

of Michael Wade's study of Gordimer (1980), and his article 'The Great South African Novel' (1983).

4. Roland Barthes, 'From Work to Text' in *Image, Music, Text*, trans. Stephen Heath (London: Fontana Press, 1977), p. 155.
5. Ibid., p. 160.
6. Ibid., p. 158.
7. Nancy K. Miller, 'Changing the Subject: Authorship, Writing, and the Reader' in her *Subject to Change: Reading Feminist Writing* (New York: Columbia University Press, 1988), p. 106.
8. Ibid., p. 109.
9. Adrienne Rich, *Diving into the Wreck: Poems 1971–72* (New York: W. W. Norton, 1973), p. 55.

10

BEN ETHERINGTON*

Worlds, World-Making, and Southern Horizons

The question of the location and horizon of J. M. Coetzee's fictions is a matter of intense debate. Some insist that he is a writer of South Africa and that his work ought to be read in relation to the history and culture of that country. For others, he is an exemplary figure of 'world literature'. His works are widely translated and celebrated, and so properly belong to a global field of literary endeavour. If these accounts at first appear to pull in different directions, they might nevertheless share a common horizon. It may well be that the South African location and locatedness of Coetzee's early and middle fictions were precisely what allowed them to resonate with readers across the world. After all, the struggle against apartheid was considered by many to be of world-historical significance. Like Nelson Mandela's march to freedom, Coetzee's fictional explorations of the South African situation come to stand for the general struggle of literature in the face of oppression. That he writes in the 'hypercentral' language of English, and in a syntax and diction that seem to facilitate ready translation, only smooths the way for his colonial parables to be read and appreciated across the literary world. His decision to relocate to Australia in 2002 appeared to confirm a universalizing trajectory. Australia, that immense landmass popularly regarded as being mostly empty of humans, is an appropriately blank canvas on which to elaborate works increasingly concerned with general philosophical and ethical problems.

In any case, both localists and universalists implicitly agree that the question of the horizon of Coetzee's fiction is one that hinges on reception. Even the most possessive of South African specialists concede that other interpretative approaches are valid; and even the most universalizing of world literature critics can see that his works have meanings and significances that speak to local conditions. In this chapter I will be approaching the

* Research for this chapter was supported by the Australian Research Council Discovery Project *Other Worlds: Forms of World Literature*.

question of location and horizon from a different angle. I will focus not on the competing claims of Coetzee's various interpreters but on the locations and latent horizons of Coetzee's literary practice. Particularly, I want to think about the worlds that he makes in his fictions and the ('real') world that gives rise to this making. To adapt terms used by Eric Hayot, I am interested in exploring the relation between his work's world-making and world-relating dimensions.[1] What worlds do his fictions create? And to what world(s) are they oriented? Addressing these questions takes us away from a local/universal dichotomy and prompts us to think about the relations between literary localities that his writing brings into play.

The following exploration of these questions will proceed in three stages. First, I scrutinize the now widely held view that Coetzee is an exemplary 'world' writer by considering the way in which his character Elizabeth Costello handles this same moniker. I next discuss the distinctive repertoire of world-making techniques that he employs across his fictional corpus, and the way in which this repertoire was forged as a response to the conditions of apartheid and the South African literary field in the 1970s and 1980s. I conclude by considering the way in which his recent interest in the literary relations between South Africa, Australia, and Argentina points to a Southern horizon that is latent across his corpus. What we discover is a practice that has been situating itself in what I will call a *literary meridian* of the 'South'. It is from within this southern sensibility that Coetzee's work escapes the traps of nationalism and encounters an indifferent 'world literary space' with inner certitude.

World Literature and World-Making in *Elizabeth Costello*

In the opening chapter, or 'lesson', of *Elizabeth Costello: Eight Lessons* (2003) the eponymous Australian novelist travels with her son John to Altona College in the north-east of the USA to receive the Stowe Award, a biennial prize that acknowledges the achievement of 'a major world writer' (*EC*, 2). It is not at first clear what is meant by 'world writer', but there are indications as the chapter unfolds. In a conversation with the chair of the jury, John learns that it had been determined that in 1995 the prize would go to someone from Australasia. This suggests a conception of the literary world as being the sum of its various regions. This usage is reflected in the organization of many anthologies of world literature from the 1960s to the period of the narrative.[2] For instance, *The Oxford Guide to Contemporary World Literature* (1997), which was published during the period of *Elizabeth Costello*'s composition, covers twenty-eight regional entities. Some of these entities are countries, like those that make up Great Britain, some are nation-states, like Australia and Hungary, some are regions, like Scandinavia and the West Indies, some are continents, like 'African countries' and 'Spanish America', and some are linguistic and/or cultural groupings like 'German-speaking countries' and 'Arab countries'. All the regions of the world deserve attention but, it would seem, they are not equally endowed with resources and talent. Some areas will contain a greater density of writers worthy of interest, and others will be more sparse.[3]

'World' thus becomes a means by which implicit regional and ethno-linguistic hierarchies are both reinforced and overcome. We can assume that if the Stowe Award were simply for a 'major writer' a disproportionate number of writers from those regions with a greater concentration of talent would win. The criterion of 'world' ensures that the net is more evenly cast and thus prestige distributed more widely. Behind the qualification there might even be a kind of affirmative action, one that hopes to produce a more inclusive literary universe.

Costello's son tells the chairman of the jury that his mother would be disappointed if she knew that a regional criterion had been applied. She would hope to be deemed 'not the best Australian, not the best Australian woman, just the best' (*EC*, 8). The chairman responds with an oblique analogy with mathematics that suggests that applying parameters is a necessary condition for making judgements about what is best. In a metafictional aside that follows this brief dialogue, the narrator explains that such interactions in novels usually take place in scenarios that have been contrived to debate ideas. Characters are compelled to 'embody' certain ideas, which then become tied to the 'matrix of individual interests out of which their speakers act in the world – for instance the son's concern that his mother not be treated as a Mickey Mouse post-colonial writer, or Wheatley's concern not to seem an old-fashioned absolutist' (*EC*, 9). This begs the question: if these are the 'embodied' versions of the ideas, what are the, as it were, disembodied versions of the ideas being debated? One gloss might be that they are debating the problem of making absolute judgements about literary value in view of the world's regional diversity. Another, shorter gloss might be that they are debating world literature.

That world literature could be up for debate points to a more unstable usage of 'world' than that implied in the title of the Stowe Award. 'World' becomes the terrain within which the problematic of the *totality* of the literary world is considered. And, indeed, theoretical debates about the constitution and scope of literary totality have been taken up in earnest over the two decades since *Elizabeth Costello* was written. One position in this debate views world literature as the totality of national and regional literatures, as per the Stowe Award. But there are several other accounts. For some, world literature is simply literature writ large in the period encompassing the global expansion of capitalism. For others, world literature is a universal canon of masterpieces that have established their presence across literary cultures via the agency of translation. Some world literary theorists focus on the ways in which literary genres and practices travel and mutate in the world; others prefer to look at the different linguistic ecologies in which literary cultures thrive. Reacting against the tendency to think of world literature as an interconnected global network, some posit world literature as entailing resistance to literature's integration into global capitalism. To call Elizabeth Costello a 'world' writer today would likely provoke the question: in what sense?

If the pragmatic usage of 'world' in the title of the Stowe Award recalls a moment when understandings concerning the 'world' of literature were more stable, its transfiguration into a problem to be debated by the novel's characters anticipates the theoretical disputes that were then getting started. Just as the fictional studies of colonial violence in Coetzee's early novels anticipated postcolonialism, and the intertextuality and metafiction of his middle fictions chimed with the surge of poststructuralist ideas, so *Elizabeth Costello* appears to resonate, even in its themes and events, with the upswing of theorizing around 'transnationalism' and 'world literature'. As Rebecca Walkowitz summarizes, over the course of the novel we are exposed to the 'exigencies of book publishing, classifying, reviewing, interviewing, prize-reviewing, and lecture-giving' in venues that include 'the lecture hall, the banquet room, the seminar table, the academic conference, the cruise ship, and the radio station' in geographic locations spread across the Earth's continents. Finally, there are discussions of 'world' classics by Joyce, Kafka, Poe, Stowe, and others.[4] Insofar as Costello negotiates this 'world literary space' as a female Australian novelist, she appears to be contending with the global hierarchy of national literary fields described by Pascale Casanova in her influential 1999 study.[5] One of Costello's youthful academic minders lets her know that A. S. Byatt had visited Altona College the previous year and then asks for her thoughts on Doris Lessing. This situates Costello in a global cohort of eminent female novelists. It also reminds her of her competitors. Costello wryly acknowledges this when she refers to 'all the effort I put into not writing like anyone else' (*EC*, 8).

These internal themes appear to align with the novel's external positioning within national and international fields of evaluation. It was shortlisted for the Miles Franklin, Australia's most prestigious prize for fiction, and long-listed for the Man Booker Prize, which at the time was the signal prize for writers in the British Commonwealth. And, of course, by the time of *Elizabeth Costello*'s appearance in 2003, Coetzee's publishers could boast that their author had just received the Nobel Prize in Literature. He could now be proclaimed one of the best, full stop. Accordingly, Coetzee is routinely treated in world literary debates as an exemplary figure of contemporary world literature. His work can be made to fit just about any theoretical model of world literature one cares to name. Stefan Helgesson writes: 'In the contemporary system of world-literary exchange, Coetzee scores highly on every chart: he writes in the hyper-central language of English, he is widely translated, and his works are recognized globally for their aesthetic qualities.'[6] It is as though he had masterminded the timing of his ultimate consecration to give charge to *Elizabeth Costello*'s thematic concerns.

Returning to the metafictional aside that follows the exchange between Costello's son and the chair of the prize committee, it is worth reminding ourselves that when the narrator points to the 'matrix of individual interests' out of which fictional characters 'act in the world', the 'world' in question is not ours but that which the narrator is manufacturing before us. The creation of fictional realities is the declared theme of the novel's opening 'lesson', whose title is 'On Realism'. If we would like to believe that the scene and theme of this opening chapter is 'world literature', the 'world' in question is one that has been made. To be sure, some of its elements are recognizable from the real world, but such interpolations stand against conspicuously fictionalized elements and the narrator's heightened self-consciousness in constructing them.

And so we find that Costello's interviewers and audiences interact with her in her capacity as a master world-maker. When asked whether she finds it easy to write from the position of man, as she has done in her most recent novel about an Australian painter, she responds that the challenge is what makes the exercise worthwhile: 'Making up someone other than yourself. Making up a world for him to move in. Making up an Australia' (*EC*, 12). Whatever eminence she has as a 'world' writer she has attained by dint of her abilities as a world-maker. Is there an implied interdependence between the two? To use Hayot's terms, do the 'world-relating' aspects of reputation and prestige supply the horizon for her 'world-creating'? Are we to infer that an overriding motive throughout her career has been to capture a prominent position in the world literary system?

The subsequent chapter, 'The Novel in Africa', is explicitly concerned with the relationship between literary regionalism and transnational prestige. A friend engineers an invitation for Costello to lecture on a cruise ship. A fellow lecturer is Emmanuel Egudu, an African writer who delivers the talk that supplies the chapter's title. In a conversation that takes place after they have delivered their respective lectures, Costello tells Egudu that the African novel continues to suffer from exoticism. 'How can you explore a world in all its depth if at the same time you are having to explain it to outsiders?', she asks (*EC*, 51). She compares this to the healthier situation of

Australian novelists who, she explains, 'got out of the habit of writing for strangers when a proper Australian readership grew to maturity' (EC, 51). The decisive factor, she goes on, was 'our Australian market', which 'decided that it could afford to support a home-grown literature' (EC, 52). According to the logic that the novel is setting out, the basis for Costello's reputation as a 'major world writer' lies in her reputation as a world-maker, and this has a precondition in national circumstances of production and reception.

If the relation between Costello's world-making and world-relating were complementary, one might expect that she would accept her international recognition as the vindication of a strategic victory in the contest for prestige. What the novel in fact chronicles is her highly uneasy relationship with sites of global literary consecration and her resolve that these sites not determine the content of her creative work and thought. This points to a dialectical situation in which literature conspires with only to push against the terms by which its value is externalized.

Drawing attention to the novel's reflexive concern with world literature and world-making has served two purposes. First, it warns against treating the external markers of participation in an international cosmopolitan literary domain as grounds for proclaiming this space as the most essential for understanding the horizon of meaning in Coetzee's fiction. Such manoeuvres of context lead to the kinds of interpretation that the novel mocks at; a literary world in which writers, works, and audiences float freely in global space to be picked over for their 'issues'. Second, it prompts us to think more concertedly about the relationship between the world-making and world-relating aspects of Coetzee's practice. If Coetzee is drawing on his canonical status and experiences of literary celebrity to fabricate the transnational scenes of *Elizabeth Costello*, he is also sending strong signals that this world may not only be inessential for the task of world-making, but inimical to it. Like multinational banks, the actors in this world literary space hope to capture and remediate value that first has been forged in local conditions. It is with these local conditions, and with the worlds that they make possible, that the remainder of this chapter will be concerned.

Coetzee World

Let us entertain, for a moment, a theme park called Coetzee World. It might have a haunted castle in each of whose dusty, rock-strewn rooms we witness a different death of Klawer from *Dusklands* (1974). There might be a Michael K game in which contestants attempt to bring water up from a disused mine shaft using a teaspoon, with prizes of raw cauliflower, carrot, or potato. We might stand next to a wax Elizabeth Costello on a rock in the middle of a confected ocean and watch an animatronic albatross shield its young. Children might don a pair of golden dance shoes and have a go at 'dancing down the numbers' as per the *Schooldays of Jesus* (2016) or visit a petting zoo of rescued, wounded animals. The main auditorium might host daily re-enactments of scenes of heightened drama from Cruso's island, Magda's farm, or Señor C's flat.

It could not be said that the rides and attractions of Coetzee World belong to a single, encompassing fictional reality. Yet the park would have a distinct and largely consistent character. One would repeatedly encounter isolated figures in bare landscapes or claustrophobic interiors. The scenes in the auditorium would have casts of two or three. It would be a quiet park, pervaded perhaps by the sound of dogs barking and Señor Arroyo's organ fantasias interrupted by muffled outbursts of violence. The foreground would have clear outlines, but the background would be indistinct, with broad and empty horizons. One would leave depressed, but the experiences would nevertheless lodge in the mind.

Coetzee's fictional worlds have much in common, but they are not co-extensive like those of Jane Austen, Henry James, J. K. Rowling, Sergio Leonie, and Roberto Bolaño. One could not bring David Lurie, Susan Barton, and Michael K to interact with each other without undermining the peculiar logic of the worlds in which they exist. This is not only because the realities that each novel constructs are incommensurate with each other. It is also because these novels depart from the reality effect in work-specific ways. If one attempted to synthesize Coetzee's worlds in the manner of 'fan fiction', say by confecting a scene involving the two colonized subjects, Klawer and Friday, it would compromise the world-making logic that allows Klawer repeatedly to die in one novel and that keeps ambiguous the nature of Friday's muteness in the other.

If Coetzee's fictional worlds are neither co-extensive nor consistent in their anti-realist or irrealist procedures, what gives the attractions of our notional theme park their consistent character? The answer, I believe, is that they share a common *repertoire* of world-making. This includes matters of content – common themes and types of character – but extends to all aspects of composition including style and form. The forging of certain world-making techniques and their reuse and adaptation cumulatively create the sense of a corpus in more than just the technical sense of having been authored by a single author. One can navigate this corpus in any number of ways and a focus on any given element typically will enable one to see lines of connection between conceptual themes, generic forms, and literary techniques. To take an obvious example, a focus on animals allows us to connect their role as characters in plots, as the source or target of metaphors and other conceptual mappings, as construed through intertextual interpolation, as stylistic cues, as allegorical figures, and as the subject of reflexive discourse.

To cover all aspects of this world-making system would be a major undertaking. The best I can do is to outline three aspects that strike me as central: (1) the *shallow amplitude* of Coetzee's fictional worlds, (2) the use of *temporal elision* and the *present tense*, and (3) the stylistic predominance of *simple and coordinated clauses*. Starting with amplitude, it is frequently remarked that the social and physical backgrounds of Coetzee's novels are spare. One is given only the most perfunctory indications of the broader social reality and physical locations of his characters. The town at which Simón, Inés, and Davíd arrive on the first page of *The Schooldays of Jesus* is rendered simply: 'Estrella is no more than a sprawling provincial town set in a countryside of hills and fields and orchards, with a sluggish river meandering through it' (*SJ*, 1). In saying 'no more than', the narrator makes it clear that further details will not be necessary. Where Coetzee uses place names, it is often only to create the stylistic effect of locality. The 'Dulgannon River' about whose existence Costello is so adamant at the end of *Elizabeth Costello* sounds vaguely like an Australian Aboriginal name, but, as Melinda Harvey has noticed, no such place exists. (There is a Dandenong Creek in Melbourne.)[7]

Similarly, Coetzee's novels largely dispense with calendrical markers and elide the connectors between scenes. Rather than being embedded in an enveloping temporal context, the plotting is produced by the paratactical juxtaposition of narrative events. The most pronounced instance of this is *In the Heart of the Country*, which is arranged into numbered sections. Sections 59, 60, and 61 begin, respectively, 'It rained this morning', 'Today I darned six pairs of socks for my father', and 'Today's leg of mutton was excellent' (*IHC*, 33). These todays could be the same day, they could be months apart. The impression created is that all events are integral to the particular *sequence* that yields the novel's story. One exception comes in the second part of *Foe*, where each section is marked with a date, starting '*April 15th*' (*F*, 47). These ostensibly are letters to Foe from Susan Barton. After '*June 1st*'(*F*, 71), though, the dates disappear, and sections acquire that same sense of time passing without a calendrical referent as *In the Heart of the Country* (1977).

This quality of sequentiality is strengthened by the narrative tense. All Coetzee's fictions are anchored to the present tense, from which they only occasionally deviate. The implications of this for world-making should be obvious enough: there is no retrospective narratorial vantage from which events can be joined together and so the perspective cleaves to them as the narrative unfolds. It is worth emphasizing, though, that the present tense does not necessarily produce temporal immediacy and simultaneity. As Carrol

Clarkson has shown, the use of the present tense in conjunction with the third person allows Coetzee 'to disaggregate the narrated consciousness from the time of the utterance, and hence from the narrating consciousness'.[8] This only strengthens our sense of the narrator's power. In the opening passages of *Elizabeth Costello*, for instance, the narrator comments: 'We skip to the evening, to the main event, the presentation of the award' (*EC*, 15). The collective pronoun is apophatic, further emphasizing the narrator's singular prerogative in sequencing and orchestrating scenes.

Finally, to Coetzee's syntax, about which much has been written. From the earliest reviews, Coetzee's readers have been struck by his short and clinical sentences. The following two descriptive passages are typical, if pronounced: 'The girl re-emerges bearing a plate and a pitcher. The pitcher holds water. The plate holds four slices of bread spread with margarine' (*CJ*, 7); 'The schoolhouse is empty. The ashes in the grate are cold. The rack above the stove is bare. The bed is stripped. The shutter flaps' (*IHC*, 49). Each detail has its own sentence which, to make an analogy with cinema, produces the effect of rapid jump-cuts. We might oppose this to the panning shot in which the spatial relations between objects can clearly be made out. This stripped-down syntax also has a peculiar effect on the representation of thought and speech. In the following pivotal moment in *Diary of a Bad Year* (2007), Anya starts to perceive her boyfriend's malignancy: 'I nod. But it is not true. I only half believe him. I believe him only half. The other half is darkness. The other half is a dark hole into which one of us is falling, I hope not me' (*DBY*, 151). The intuition that something is wrong goes through a series of phases with each apportioned a separate sentence. We might oppose this to the clause that sets up a summary account ('Only then did she realize ... '). Consciousness in Coetzee World is not a 'stream' but a series of segments.

These world-making strategies combine to produce fictional worlds that share distinct qualities. Coetzee's worlds lack, or at least de-emphasize, what usually gets called 'context', but which might more usefully be called narrative background. The shallow amplitude, paratactical temporality, and pared-down syntax ensure that we are exposed only to the narrative foreground. This produces one of the most distinctive qualities of reading Coetzee's fiction: the need to construe his worlds from only foreground elements. Each element thereby acquires the sense of necessity: if any is removed, the sequence is altered and the world otherwise construed.[9] This helps to account for why each element of Coetzee's worlds seems to have essential relations to all other elements. It also helps to explain why the use of metafictional devices does not diffuse his novels' world-making logic. Where each narratorial act is conducted with heightened deliberation, we accept interjection and inconsistency as the narrator's prerogative.

In claiming all this, we must be careful not to assume that the experience of Coetzee's worlds consists in the naïve reception of his novels' foregrounded-ness. If the secular experience of the modern world is one in which we habitually perceive ourselves to be interacting with the complex web of human totality, then the conspicuous absence of that web calls for us either to infer it from the available data or to rationalize its absence. In *Ways of Worldmaking*, Nelson Goodman calls this cognitive process *supplementation*.[10] According to Goodman, the greater the elision when representing a world, the greater the supplementation required to make it cohere. This calls for us to attend to the ways in which Coetzee's elisions condition our processes of supplementation rather than treating them as sheer absence. For it is supplementation that makes a world.

It is worth citing Erich Auerbach's comment in *Mimesis* on the mytholo-gizing function of the absence of narrative background in the book of Genesis: '[the Biblical narrative] seeks to overcome our reality: we are to fit our life into its world, feel ourselves to be elements in its structure of universal history'.[11] We are called into its world because its coherence relies on a high degree of supplementation. In so doing, we are drawn into provid-ing rationales for the peculiar logic which prevails in that world. If this is true also of Coetzee's worlds, does it mean that his overriding purpose is the same as that which Auerbach imputes to the Bible? To 'overcome our reality' so that we 'fit our life into its world'? To answer this, we need to turn now from the world-making to the world-relating aspects of his fiction.

An Orientation to the World

Jarad Zimbler begins his study of Coetzee's prose style by observing the 'remarkably uniform characterization' of Coetzee's use of language among the reviewers of his early novels. Critics continually reached for the same words to convey the force of his work, especially 'vivid', 'taut', 'stark', 'hard', 'bitter', 'sharp', 'intense', 'brooding', and 'oppressive'.[12] Zimbler goes on to anatomize the ways in which Coetzee pares down his syntax and limits description to only the most clear and precise terms. This 'bare prose', Zimbler argues, renders a 'world … laid bare, reduced to its brute constitu-ent parts' (45). A world laid bare is one that lacks the fullness achieved when the elements of fiction are interwoven with a rich background of people, places, and things.

According to Zimbler, we should not regard the emergence of Coetzee's bare prose as a free-standing 'signature' style, but as a highly self-aware aesthetic positioning within the South African literary field in the apartheid era. Zimbler shows that Coetzee was peculiarly attentive to the ways in which other South African writers responded to the conditions of apartheid. This field did not lack for writers prepared to indict these conditions, but many did so by insisting on their creative autonomy from them. Where the apartheid regime thoughtlessly brutalized the world, Alex La Guma attentively catalogued each brutality; where it sought to restrict aesthetic styles, the Sestigers responded with conspicuously excessive experimentation; where it produced a thin, two-dimensional social reality, Nadine Gordimer constructed a rich and intricate fictional totality. Coetzee, by contrast, absorbed the evil he saw around him into the logic of his prose style. Zimbler shows that his 'bare prose' is at its most economical, spare, and brutal in scenes of Manichean violence. He cites as typical the following passage from *Waiting for the Barbarians* (1980): 'The Colonel steps forward. Stooping over each prisoner in turn he rubs a handful of dust into his naked back and writes a word with a stick of charcoal. I read the words upside down: *ENEMY ... ENEMY ... ENEMY ... ENEMY*. He steps back and folds his hands. At a distance of no more than twenty paces he and I contemplate each other. Then the beating begins' (*WB*, 115). Coetzee's purpose was not to win a contest, to assume the mantle of being the *most* anti-apartheid writer. It was to immerse his South African readers especially in the truth, and not merely the appearance, of their world and so to reorient them toward it.

This goes some way to answering the question posed at the end of the last section. At least in his early fictions, Coetzee devised world-making techniques that called on readers to undertake a high degree of supplementation in order that they be brought to *inhabit* the evil and violence of South African society. Among other things, this meant enduring the entanglement of rationalism in colonialism and the brutalizing relation humans had adopted toward their world. To be oriented to this world was not a matter of soapboxing about its self-evident evils or flicking on the switch of the enduring power of the human imagination. It was to know the damage wrought to the human soul by bad history and so to be open to its rehabilitation.

This puts a different spin on the relation between world-making and world-relating in Coetzee's fictions. His world-making strategies were forged in contradistinction to other local stylistic repertoires as the South African literary field collectively contended with the apartheid situation. His work was distinguished by its willingness to draw the evils of apartheid into the stylistic logic of his prose. Zimbler's is a persuasive account of the power of Coetzee's early South African novels. When considering Coetzee's middle fictions from *Foe* (1986) to *Disgrace* (1999), he argues that Coetzee increasingly became concerned with what it would take to rehabilitate the soul. Not all of these works have a tangible relation to South Africa, but, on Zimbler's account, they arise from the exigencies of the South African experience. In concluding, Zimbler suggests that Coetzee's later fictions irradiate outwards from these established preoccupations. From being quite a specific project embedded in the predicament of apartheid South Africa, his fictions come to be concerned more generally with questions 'about the formation and transformation of subjectivity, about the meaning of care in the face of age, illness and death, and about the consequences of treating others as if they were things' (200). Does this suggest an overall movement in his corpus from the particular to the general? The historical to the universal? Might it even signal a transition from being a South African writer to being a 'world' writer? One whose fiction 'in innumerable guises portrays the surprising involvement of the outsider', as the Nobel prize committee put it?[13]

The 'Real South'

It is often remarked that Coetzee is indifferent if not allergic to national sentiment and belonging. For some, this makes him a natural cosmopolitan. Just as his novels typically lack cultural, geographical, and historical markers, so his disposition toward the world at large is that of a stateless writer in a world in which the state itself is supposed to be withering. Yet it is wrong to assume that the only meaningful bonds of belonging beyond the nation-state are those of a de-territorialized cosmopolitanism. As we observed earlier, much of the intellectual power of Elizabeth Costello's various public talks arises from her evident frustration with the codes and expectations of that sphere. We also observed that she is conscious of the local circumstances of literary production that enabled her to forge her distinctive literary approach. This seems to parallel the deliberate way in which Coetzee went about responding to the South African literary tradition and positioning himself within its literary field. Insofar as we read Elizabeth Costello as an alter ego, she too confronts 'world literary space' from the vantage of a particular literary environment. Does Australia thus come to serve an allegorical function? One provincial white settler literary culture standing in for another? Could Costello just as well be Canadian?

The question of place and allegory arises in the final of the novel's 'lessons'. Costello arrives in a border town somewhere in Europe seeking passage through a large guarded gate. To pass through it she must give an account of her beliefs to a panel of judges. The whole business, she sees clearly, is 'straight out of Kafka' (*EC*, 209), and she wonders whether she hasn't in fact been installed 'in a kind of literary theme park' (*EC*, 208). At her first hearing, Costello is adamant that her writerly vocation prevents her from holding fixed beliefs. At her second, she changes tack and, in a lyrical monologue, professes to believe in the frogs of the 'Dulgannon' mud flats to whose chorus she raptly had listened as a girl. She states: 'the Australian continent, where I was born into the world, kicking and squalling, is real (if far away), the Dulgannon and its mudflats are real, the frogs are real' (*EC*, 217). She goes on to explain that she believes in the frogs because their existence is independent of her belief in them. The judges deem Costello's frogs to symbolize 'the spirit of life' and pronounce that she has contradicted herself: at first she denied that a writer could hold beliefs, now she professes to believe in the principle of life (*EC*, 219). Reaching this judgement, though, involves an allegorical sleight of hand. They do not consider the possibility that she might believe in the frogs themselves rather than that which they purportedly symbolize.

Following her second failure, Costello remains under the spell of the frogs – the thoughts of them 'ring true' (*EC*, 219). The same, it would seem, applies to the Australian continent and the Dulgannon mudflats. They too 'ring true' as irreducibly specific objects to consciousness. That there is no such place as 'Dulgannon' is no more important than whether the memory of the frogs is accurate. Irreducible specificity can be experienced in fiction as much as it can in the world.

If the impulse to orient readers to the world identified by Zimbler persists in *Elizabeth Costello*, its *raison d'être* can hardly be to orient them to the spiritual ruination of apartheid and its aftermath. Yet nor do the novel's lessons encourage us to adopt an indifferent relation to place. If we believe in Elizabeth Costello we also believe in the Australia that has formed her and which she remakes in her fiction. We perceive that she approaches the ethical and philosophical conundrums posed to her by her hosts in the Northern Hemisphere as a world-maker who stands within yet also at a certain distance from their traditions. All the while, we should bear in mind, the world-making strategies that we touched on earlier persist through Coetzee's post-South African novels. This all tends to suggest that the world or, perhaps, *earthly habitat* of Coetzee World is greater than South Africa but less than the globe. It leads away from a dichotomy of national/world literature and towards conceptualizing the *relations* between the literary worlds of his corpus and the broader domain to which these relations orient us.

This brings us, finally, to Coetzee's declared interest in the 'South'. In the period 2014–18, Coetzee travelled each year to the Universidad Nacional de San

Martín in Argentina to convene a seminar on the 'Literatures of South'. These aimed, as James Halford has summarized, 'to develop comparative perspectives on the literatures of the three countries [South Africa, Australia, and Argentina], to establish new intellectual networks, and to build a corpus of translated works from across the South through collaborative publishing ventures'.[14] On each occasion Coetzee invited fellow Southern African and Australian writers and publishers to accompany him, including Antjie Krog, Mia Couto, Zoë Wicomb, Ivan Vladislavić, Nicholas Jose, Gail Jones, and Ivor Indyk. In 2016, he delivered some opening remarks in which he mused on the idea of the South. He began by introducing the ideas of 'North' and 'South' as they appear in the economic and sociological literature on globalization. He noted that these are not so much cartographical designations as terms that speak to global relations of wealth and power. Like other 'specialist terms of the social sciences', he expects that they will lapse as social relations evolve. 'What will be left', he continued:

> will be the real South, the South of this real world, where most of us present here today were born and most of us will die. It is a unique world – there is only one South – with its unique skies and its unique heavenly constellations. In this South the winds blow in a certain way and the leaves fall in a certain way and the sun beats down in a certain way that is instantly recognizable from one part of the South to another. In the South, as in the North, there are cities, but the cities of the South all have a somewhat phantasmatic quality. The peoples of the South are all, in one way or another, rough and a bit lazy. We have troubled histories behind us, which sometimes haunt us. It is nothing like this in the North. I can go on endlessly with my list. And the literatures of the South do indeed go on endlessly as they try to pin down in words their intuitions of what a life in the South consists in.[15]

In the light of *Elizabeth Costello*'s lessons, we should be careful around the word 'real'. It need not signal the sheer existence of the South as a cartographical fact. Coetzee's South is one whose realness must be made to ring true as an irreducibly specific object to consciousness. This appears to be role of the literatures of the South: to 'pin down in words' the substance of life in the Southern world.

Coetzee's worlds are not confined to a nation, but nor is their habitat the world at large. The 'South' has given the later Coetzee a way of pointing to affinities that have long been latent in his work. I want to conclude by suggesting that his South is not so much a latitudinal alignment, as a *literary meridian*. I adapt the term from the German-French poet Paul Celan's well-known speech 'Der Meridian', delivered in 1960 on the occasion of being awarded the Büchner prize. This speech is crafted in such a way as to be unparaphrasable, though many have provided glosses. The following comments are only what I take away from it, not any underlying discursive meaning that I believe can be rescued from its delicately pitched obscurity. The notion of the meridian gives Celan a way of thinking the lines of connection between the place of departure and the point of arrival of poetic experience. Entering poetry is a movement beyond what is human, into a realm that is nevertheless turned back toward the human. He asks repeatedly how he can locate this realm which speaks 'on behalf of the *strange . . . on behalf of the other*'. To get to this region one needs to undertake 'topological research', suggesting, Celan hints in a series of puns, the study of tropes and of topography as well as topology.

It seems important to Celan that the meridian is neither given over entirely to the ideal world of the poem nor to the material world of reality; it is 'immaterial . . . yet earthly'. Saying the word 'meridian' cannot but call up the sense of an arc that passes around the earth, objectively aligning all those places that simultaneously experience a particular position of the sun. For Celan, though, the light shed by the poem does not come from the sun. It is a 'U-topian light'. The arc must therefore run through those points the poem's light simultaneously connects. The key idea for thinking about Coetzee's South is that the literary works themselves constitute and produce relations; or, as Celan puts it, encounters.

Reading across Coetzee's corpus in the (U-topian) light of Celan's meridian, one can start to pick out the points of a literary meridian of the South. I would like to identify just three.

(i) Towards the end of *In the Heart of the Country* Magda starts forming giant messages with stones. The first is 'POEMAS CREPUSCULARIAS' (twilight poems), though she runs out of stones so ends up rendering it 'Poemas Crepusclrs'. This is followed by 'SOMNOS DE LIBERTAD' (dreams of liberty) and 'AMOR SIN TERROR' (love without terror) (*IHC*, 145). She believes she is addressing 'skygods'. The Chilean poet Pablo Neruda's first published collection of poetry was titled *Crepusculario*.[16] Crepuscular poems: poems reaching across a twilight meridian.

(ii) One of the Sydney-based writer Señor C's short essays in *Diary of a Bad Year* is on Zeno's paradox (*DBY*, 87–96). After going over two ways in which counting is conventionally conceived – as either discovery or invention – he comes to discuss Borges's fable 'Funes the Memorius', in which the character of the title has created a sequence in which numbers are replaced by things – 'sulphur, the reins, the whale, gas, the cauldron, Napoleon'.[17] In the meantime, the banker boyfriend of Señor C's typist concocts a scheme to filch money from Señor C's bank account in order to make its numbers multiply upwards endlessly on the stock market.

(iii) *The Schooldays of Jesus* is set in a town called 'Estrella', a word that approximates the pronunciation of 'Australia' in Broad Australian English ('straya'). The Spanish word means 'stars'. In the novel, the boy David enters the town's Academy of Dance. To this point he has always resisted or been unable to follow the process of counting as pure sequencing of n+1. At the academy he learns to 'dance down the numbers', a dance for which numbers are palpable things with specific identities. By the novel's conclusion, Simón has stopped insisting that the boy conform to an education centred on maths and himself starts to learn to dance.

To be sure these intertextual relations are readily identifiable. This is not deep t(r)opological research. Their significance lies not in being 'Easter eggs', as though Coetzee has carefully hidden clues as to the true location and horizon of his life's work. It lies in thinking about how the alignment of these points of literary reference orients us to the South. What these moments do not share in any obvious way is the 'real' experience of a particular latitude or constellation. There is only space left for the speculative claim that the characteristic homelessness and yearning of Coetzee's characters evident in these passages is a characteristic of his South. They cue different ways of appealing to the literary imagination against realities formed by brutality and the indifferent calculi of finance and dogmatic reason; appeals that are nevertheless strangely detached from historical self-awareness. The characters along this meridian share a quality of being stranded with a worldview that is not adequate to the world in which they live. The South is a literary meridian that passes through them as they strive to become Southern.

Notes

1. Eric Hayot, 'On Literary Worlds', *Modern Language Quarterly*, 72.2 (2011), 129–61.
2. See Sarah Lawall, 'Anthologizing "World Literature"' in Jeffrey R. Di Leo (ed.), *On Anthologies: Politics and Pedagogy* (Lincoln: University of Nebraska Press, 2004), pp. 47–89.
3. John Sturrock (ed.), *The Oxford Guide to Contemporary World Literature* (Oxford: Oxford University Press, 1997), pp. v–vi, viii.
4. Rebecca L. Walkowitz, *Born Translated: The Contemporary Novel in an Age of World Literature* (New York: Columbia University Press, 2015), p. 58.
5. Pascale Casanova, *The World Republic of Letters*, trans. M. B. DeBevoise (Cambridge, MA: Harvard University Press, 2004).

6. Stefan Helgesson, 'Translation and the Circuits of World Literature' in Ben Etherington and Jarad Zimbler (eds.), *The Cambridge Companion to World Literature* (Cambridge: Cambridge University Press, 2018), pp. 85–9 (p. 89).
7. Melinda Harvey, '"In Australia You Start from Zero": The Escape from Place in J. M. Coetzee's Late Novels' in Chris Danta, Sue Kossew, and Julian Murphet (eds.), *Strong Opinions: J. M. Coetzee and the Authority of Contemporary Fiction* (London: Continuum, 2011), pp. 19–34 (pp. 21–2).
8. Carrol Clarkson, *J. M. Coetzee: Countervoices* (Basingstoke: Palgrave Macmillan, 2009), p. 27.
9. Clarkson has analysed Coetzee's practice of sequencing active and passive constructions when his 'human characters experience some kind of ethical tie to other creatures' (p. 117). This underscores my earlier point that to focus on animals in Coetzee's corpus allows us to move from theme to syntax. *J. M. Coetzee*, pp. 117–20.
10. Nelson Goodman, *Ways of Worldmaking* (Indianapolis: Hackett, 1978), pp. 14–16.
11. Erich Auerbach, *Mimesis: The Representation of Reality in Western Literature*, trans. Willard R. Trask (Princeton: Princeton University Press, 2003), p. 15. This passage is also cited in Hayot's 'On Literary Worlds', p. 143.
12. Jarad Zimbler, *J. M. Coetzee and the Politics of Style* (Cambridge: Cambridge University Press, 2014), p. 4. Further page references are in the text.
13. Nobel Media AB, 'The Nobel Prize in Literature 2003', Nobelprize.org (2014), www.nobelprize.org/nobel_prizes/literature/laureates/2003/ [3 September 2018]
14. James Halford, 'Southern Conversations: J. M. Coetzee in Buenos Aires', *Sydney Review of Books* (28 February 2017), <https://sydneyreviewofbooks.com/southern-conversations-j-m-coetzee-in-buenos-aires/> [3 September 2018].
15. Halford, 'Southern Conversations'.
16. The connection with Neruda's first collection was pointed out to me by Peter D. McDonald.
17. Jorge Luis Borges, *Labyrinths: Selected Stories & Other Writings*, ed. Donald A. Yates and James E. Irby (New York: New Directions, 1962), pp. 65–6.

PART III
Mediations

11

MICHELLE KELLY

Other Arts and Adaptations

References to and descriptions of visual and performing arts have been a consistent feature of J. M. Coetzee's fiction, from the photographic prints pored over by Eugene Dawn in 'The Vietnam Project' section of *Dusklands* (1974) to the mystical dancing of David in his very recent novel, *The Schooldays of Jesus* (2016). Aesthetic experiences of film, dance, and photography enjoy prominence across the fictional autobiographies of *Scenes from Provincial Life* (2011) and in essays and interviews. Music, especially, is a recurring source of aesthetic pleasure across the Coetzee corpus, particularly the music of Johann Sebastian Bach. In *Diary of a Bad Year* (2007) the protagonist JC singles out the work of the German composer as 'The best proof we have that life is good' (*DBY*, 221). More recent biographical and archive-based accounts of Coetzee's life and work reveal an author whose first artistic medium was photography and who has expended much creative energy in translating his prose fiction into other art forms: producing screenplays of his early novels and opera libretti of his later ones, pursuing possible adaptations with enthusiasm, and collaborating in some cases with artists, composers, and film-makers.[1]

What then does this evidence of Coetzee's interest in 'other arts' contribute to our understanding of his work? While Coetzee scholarship has been attentive to the vast range of literary intertexts invoked across an almost fifty-year writing career, few have concentrated on other art forms or questions of medium. Yet the prominence of visual and performing arts in Coetzee's work and their framing within and against exclusively written forms suggests that much is to be gained from more sustained analysis. Across the entire corpus there is a consistent alertness to the distinct aesthetic power of particular art forms and media, and a succession of characters susceptible to them. Descriptions of particular art *works*, therefore, occur alongside, and are often superseded by, descriptions of the aesthetic, emotional, and ethical responses that they elicit. We also find a rigorous attention to the materiality of different aesthetic media: prints of film stills in *Dusklands*, musical recordings in *Summertime* (2009), the Everyman cinema in Hampstead where John first saw Monica Vitti in Michelangelo Antonioni's *Eclipse* (1962).

Visual and performing arts in Coetzee's work are repeatedly endowed with expressive powers that seem to distinguish them from prose fiction. Film and photography, for example, tend to be invested with a privileged access to the real, while music possesses the power to transcend difference and speak directly to the heart. These capacities are tied both implicitly and explicitly to the non-verbal forms of signification involved, and are frequently placed in opposition to the mediated nature of linguistic expression. The *otherness* of other arts in Coetzee's work owes much to this apparent opposition. But what authority should we attribute to these ideas about the distinctive aesthetic experience of visual and performing arts, and how do they relate to Coetzee's own chosen artistic medium of *writing*? W. J. T. Mitchell suggests that ekphrasis, the verbal description of visual art, is distinguished less by a disturbance at the level of sign or medium and more by the thematizing of such dissonance, which in Mitchell's account is related to various forms of difference or otherness in a text.[2] In Coetzee's work references to other arts similarly gesture towards the limits of prose fiction and the possibilities of other forms and media, and often intersect with a given text's concern with particular varieties of difference or otherness. While ideas that circulate about the difference of other arts might be traced back to Roland Barthes's writings on photography, or to Romantic thinking on music, accounts of aesthetic experience and the distinctive powers of particular art forms are spoken in a range of voices in Coetzee's work, in both the fiction and the non-fiction, and are frequently identified with a particular character or worldview. They therefore provoke questions about narration, point of view, authorial voice, autobiography, and self-reflexivity that feature centrally in considerations of other aspects of his work.

Moreover, to the extent that music, dance, film, and photography all proceed at least in part through non-verbal forms of signification, they also intensify our attention to the *written* texts in which they appear; their otherness is poised between their presumed difference from writing and, in the context of Coetzee's fiction, their reliance on writing. In other words, if references to visual and performing arts in Coetzee's work frequently gesture towards the availability of forms of expression, meaning, aesthetic experience, and connection *beyond* the printed text, they are all the while encoded within it. A focus on other arts is therefore closely tied to what Peter McDonald has termed Coetzee's 'critique of language' and the desire or fantasy to transcend one's own language, or indeed, language as such.[3] In this context, we must see Coetzee's interest in other art forms as continuous with his interest in non-verbal, albeit aestheticized modes of expression and physical embodiment. As a result, among the 'other arts' that I include are the patently literary – or semi-literary – forms of theatre, opera, and film, in which the balance between embodied performance and text is constantly in question.

In what follows I will explore a selection of references to visual and performing arts from across the Coetzee corpus, focusing in particular on the representation of aesthetic experience, claims about the distinctive capacities of what I am loosely terming 'other arts', and their relationship to writing, self-reflexivity, and the body. I will conclude with a brief account of adaptations of the fiction. If visual and performing arts are constructed as other to and encoded within writing in Coetzee's work, how do artists committed to the aesthetic conventions and histories of their own forms negotiate the expectations of *fidelity* that so often overshadow literary adaptations?

Aesthetic Experience

The encounter with Beckett's *Watt* (1953) described in *Youth* (2002) marks a turning point in John's engagement with literature, but in an autobiographical anecdote in the 1993 essay 'What is a Classic?' Coetzee narrates an even earlier transformative aesthetic experience: hearing the music of Bach as it drifted from a record player at a neighbouring house in suburban Cape Town. He is fifteen years old, bored, in 'an historical dead end', 'And then the afternoon in the garden, and the music of Bach, after which everything changed': 'As long as the music lasted, I was frozen, I dared not breathe. I was being spoken to by the music as music had never spoken to me before' (*SS*, 9–11). The encounters with Bach and Beckett differ greatly insofar as the would-be writer of *Youth*, a graduate in English and mathematics, is drawn to the 'chunky little book with a violet cover' based on his reading of other works by Beckett and his contemporaries and the reputation of Olympia Press for avant-garde publishing (*Y*, 155). 'What is a Classic?' on the other hand describes an encounter with music that the young Coetzee – and even the older Coetzee, retrospectively – experiences as transcending his relative ignorance of classical music and his historical circumstances. For all the essay's elaborate scene-setting, the description of the young Coetzee, 'frozen', not daring to 'breathe', 'spoken to by the music', suggests an unmediated encounter with art, and a model of the aesthetic close to its Greek etymology as the *sensible*. His relative inexperience in part explains the dramatic nature of the encounter with Bach. For the young provincial or colonial, the adult Coetzee speculates, 'the high culture of the metropolis may arrive in the form of powerful experiences which cannot, however, be embedded in their lives in any obvious way, and which seem therefore to have their existence in some transcendent realm' (SS, 7). The essay's framing around T. S. Eliot offers a more clear-headed explanation: just as Eliot's idiosyncratic construction of the classic shows 'a writer attempting to *make a new identity*', he too has engaged in an act of self-making through the *classical*, selecting European high culture as a gateway out of colonial Cape Town (SS, 7. Italics original). The essay, however, refuses to privilege the materialist explanation over the experience of transcendence prompted by that first encounter with Bach.

The essay format of 'What is a Classic?' makes explicit the seeming paradox that music (and aesthetic experience in general) is both transcendent and a means through which culturally specific or material interests are expressed. This paradox pervades Coetzee's work, but in the fiction, including the fictionalized autobiographies, varieties of aesthetic experience are refracted through narrative point of view, irony, tone, and the broader context of the work. Reflections on other art forms therefore frequently follow the same logic as other representations in Coetzee's work, identifiable with a particular narrating consciousness and worldview, thus both allowing for a transcendent encounter with art and also situating it within a particular material context.

The kind of self-making through aesthetic experience that we find in 'What is a Classic?' is a prominent theme of the *Scenes from Provincial Life* trilogy, notably in *Youth* where the earnest John's determination to become an artist is treated with considerable irony and humour. A student in Cape Town and a lover of music frustrated by his slow progress with the piano, John develops a technique to enable him to play, one day, a work by Beethoven and Bach. His method involves playing only these two pieces 'unremittingly', learning the notes slowly, then gradually increasing the pace until he masters them. The halting pace of his playing leads him to fly 'into a rage' as he 'hammers his fists on the keys, and storms off in despair' (Y, 16). Here John's commitment to music and pretentious investment in a narrow definition of the classical is the stuff of comedy, generating frustration and rage rather than transcendence.

John's plodding, mechanical approach to the piano is echoed in Adriana's description of John Coetzee's dancing in *Summertime* ('*he could not dance to save his life*'), which prompts her to call him '*The Wooden Man*', and gives rise to an explicitly Bergsonian comedy grounded in the mechanical rigidity of the marionette (*Sum*, 198, 200).[4] A similar comedy informs Julia's account of her relationship with John Coetzee and his suggestion that they should coordinate their love-making to a cassette-recording of Schubert's string quintet. The trilogy's comedy is largely self-directed as the older Coetzee gently mocks an earnest younger self, but it also often emerges in the context of lessons or practice in a particular art, including poetry, in which the mechanical repetition of the beginner or amateur falls far short of the fluency required for mastery. If we read *Youth* as a *Künstlerroman*, a fictional account of the emergence of an artist, we find an additional irony in John's apparent amateurism. But the irony and the comedy never fully eclipse the commitment to aesthetic education across a range of art forms, the seriousness of which, especially in the face of technical inadequacy, shows an unflinching determination and enormous privileging of art and its mysteries.

In contrast to provincial Cape Town, metropolitan London is a gateway to world culture in *Youth*. John's 'eyes are opened' at the Everyman cinema in Hampstead (*Y*, 48). He is transfixed by the distinctively European anguish of Monica Vitti in Antonioni's *Eclipse* and later, wearing his new spectacles, is moved to tears by the joyous resurrection of Pasolini's *Gospel according to Matthew* (1964): 'his own heart wants to burst; tears of an exultation he does not understand stream down his cheeks, tears that he has surreptitiously to wipe away before he can emerge into the world again' (*Y*, 154). While he sympathizes with the realist 'pale, bony' Jesus of Pasolini's film, his intensely emotional response is prompted by its soundtrack, the *Missa Luba* Gloria sung by Congolese choir *Les Troubadours du Roi Baudouin*, a setting of the Latin mass sung in the style of traditional Congolese song. Similarly, it is the soundtrack of Satyajit Ray's *Apu* trilogy (1955–9) that makes the biggest impression on him: 'he encounters something that is not in Bach, though there are intimations of it: a joyous yielding of the reasoning, comprehending mind to the dance of the fingers' (*Y*, 93). He is inspired to buy an LP of Ustad Vilayat Khan: 'It is all there: the hovering exploration of tone-sequences, the quivering emotion, the ecstatic rushes. He cannot believe his good fortune. A new continent, and all for a mere nine shillings!' (*Y*, 93–4).

Coetzee's immersion in avant-garde cinema in this period would have a far-reaching influence, but music is the emotional connection to different worlds, a vehicle for a specific emotional range that transcends time and cultural difference. A belief in music's capacity to enable feelings to 'speak across the ages', which is already evident in 'What is a Classic?', re-emerges later in *Diary of a Bad Year*, as JC speculates that the history of music is the history of the 'feeling soul', allowing the twenty-first-century listener access to the same modes of feeling elicited by the music's earliest performances (*DBY*, 131). The prevalence of these ideas suggests that they are treated with some seriousness, but they are also frequently undermined by the framing or tone of the passage in which they appear. JC's unusually affirmative comments on the swell of pride stirred by early performances of Sibelius in Finland, that '*one of us* could put together such sounds', are framed within a piece on the US-led war on terror titled 'On National Shame', reinforcing the connection between nineteenth-century Romanticism and toxic forms of nationalism (*DBY*, 45. Italics in the original). Shared aesthetic and emotional experience also marks the limits of reciprocity and mutual understanding between characters in *Summertime*. As we have seen, John's injunction to Julia to 'feel through the music' as they attempt to have sex is met with her irritation and bemusement. The failure of mutual understanding is evident too in the tense relationship between John and his father, which is reinforced through their different appreciation of music, notably John's strong identification with Bach in opposition to his father's taste for opera. It is this fault line that John attempts to repair with his ageing father in the closing pages of the book, only to discover that his father no longer shows any interest in music. Channelled through John's diary entries, the significance of music to their relationship – within the logic of the text – is now apparent to John alone.

The limits of music's ability to transcend difference are traced also in *Age of Iron* (1990), as Mrs Curren imagines Verceuil listening to her halting recital of Bach:

> So I played Bach for him, as well as I could. When the last bar was played I closed the music and sat with my hands in my lap contemplating the oval portrait on the cover with its heavy jowls, its sleek smile, its puffy eyes. Pure spirit, I thought, yet in how unlikely a temple! Where does that spirit find itself now? In the echoes of my fumbling performance receding through the ether? In my heart, where the music still dances? Has it made its way into the heart too of the man in the sagging trousers eavesdropping at the window? Have our two hearts, our organs of love, been tied for this brief while by a cord of sound? (*AI*, 24)

Mrs Curren and Verceuil are joined as performer and listener in their shared experience of the music, the 'cord of sound' that binds them. This is complicated by narrative point of view, however. The scene is focalized through Mrs Curren's consciousness: we know nothing of Verceuil's experience of Bach, nor indeed whether he hears the music at all. Based in an understanding of music as transcending difference (Bach's 'pure spirit'), her fantasy of the 'two hearts ... tied ... by a cord of sound' is a wishful projection onto Verceuil. An interest in Bach, and even an understanding of music as transcendent, is therefore part of her characterization, her commitment to the classical. Like other aspects of the novel, it communicates her desire for a connection with Verceuil, but cannot offer insight into his experience.

The terms in which Mrs Curren describes – or fails to describe – the music are also significant. Her physical description of the portrait of Bach contrasts with the figurative language associated with the music – 'pure spirit', the music that 'dances' in her 'heart', the 'organ' of love, the 'cord of sound' – which refers to the effect rather than to the sound of the music. The description of the portrait might be understood as ekphrastic, but it serves less to enhance our understanding of Bach than to draw attention to the challenge of representing music itself within prose narrative. Coetzee's use of the word *cord* is also significant; it has a Greek etymology meaning the string of an instrument made from the gut. It is also the term used by Coetzee to figure the relationship between Michael K and the land on which he grows pumpkins, 'a cord of tenderness' (*LT*, 66). In *Age of Iron* the 'cord of sound' joins the hearts, the 'organs of love', of Mrs Curren and Verceuil. Kathryn Lachman notes the relationship of cord to the Latin *cor*, heart, in her reading of music in Coetzee.[5] As with John's response to Pasolini in *Youth* ('his own heart wants to burst'), other art forms, and especially music, are figured as speaking directly to the heart in Coetzee's work.

This idea is expressed too by David Lurie in *Disgrace* (1999), in opposition to the instrumental view of language employed by his institution's Department of Communications: 'His own opinion, which he does not air, is that the origins of speech lie in song, and the origins of song in the need to fill out with sound the overlarge and rather empty human soul' (*Dis*, 4). Both Lachman and McDonald note the Romantic genesis of David's statement, which Lachman identifies with Rousseau and McDonald relates to Coetzee's interest in von Humboldt and the linguistic relativity thesis.[6] For Lachman this fits with David's romantic assumptions about music and his conviction that writing an opera will be an easy endeavour for an untrained literary scholar, something she contrasts with the 'surprisingly mute quality' of his *Byron in Italy* opera. She aligns the opera with the novel's emphasis on non-verbal signification, gesture, and animals, as opera's 'otherness' to novelistic discourse opens 'a space of opacity and unreadability in the narrative'.[7]

The emphasis on non-verbal signification takes more and less explicitly aestheticized forms in *Disgrace*, among them its preoccupation with performance. If *Byron in Italy* is the other art form of the novel's second part, Melanie Isaacs's performance in *Sunset at the Globe Salon* dominates its first. Michael Holland describes them as the novel's twin *mise en abymes*, the term used to describe an art form repeated in miniature within itself (the play within a play, or a picture within a picture), which acts both as a commentary on the themes of the work itself and as a meta-reflection on its aesthetic procedures.[8] In the case of *Disgrace*, the use of a play and an opera in an ostensibly realist novel offers an interesting twist on the usual repetition of the *mise en abyme*, however, fracturing the potentially endless metafictional reflection that the device typically enables. Rather than limiting the self-

193

MICHELLE KELLY

reflexivity prompted by the *mise en abyme*, the shift in form re-directs our attention to the shared and differing modes of expression available across prose fiction, theatre, and opera (and opera libretto): linguistic, musical, non-verbal gesture, and embodied performance.

A similar logic is evident when David shows Melanie a Norman McLaren film as part of his seduction.

> Sitting side by side they watch. Two dancers on a bare stage move through their steps. Recorded by a stroboscopic camera, their images, ghosts of their movements, fan out behind them like wingbeats. It is a film he first saw a quarter of a century ago but is still captivated by: the instant of the present and the past of that instant, evanescent, caught in the same space.
> He wills the girl to be captivated too. But he senses she is not.   (*Dis*, 14–15)

Here the failure of shared aesthetic experience interrupts, temporarily, David's seduction of his student. It is a symptom of his inability to read her desires and further evidence of the generational and cultural differences between them. Although it is not named in the novel, David and Melanie are watching McLaren's *Pas de deux* (1968), a short film featuring first one and then two dancers, a woman and a man, whose real-life performance is given an animated and stroboscopic effect through McLaren's use of back lighting and animation, creating the 'evanescent' and ghostly effect that David describes.[9] The *pas de deux* historically formed the opening act of an opera or ballet, but is now a fundamental component of ballet, taking more and less structured forms. In McLaren's film the arrival of first the female and then the male dancer creates the effect of an elaborate seduction, as he coaxes her into the partnering that forms the core of the *pas de deux*. The dance film, in the novel's opening act, therefore echoes the seduction taking place in Lurie's living room – another *mise en abyme* that proceeds through a shift in medium.

Introducing the film to Melanie, David heavy-handedly distinguishes the 'dance' of McLaren's film from 'dancing' (*Dis*, 14). But another, later example of dancing in the novel echoes the structure of McLaren's film without being explicitly framed as an aesthetic object. When David and Lucy attend a party to celebrate the transfer of land from Lucy to Petrus, the guests are dancing to 'old-fashioned African jazz' (*Dis*, 128). Extracting herself from an awkward conversation with Petrus, Lucy goes to dance. In David's account of his daughter's movements 'she dances by herself in the solipsistic way that now seems to be the mode' and is soon joined by a 'tall, loose-limbed, nattily dressed' young man, who 'dances opposite her, snapping his fingers, flashing her smiles, courting her' (*Dis*, 130). Lucy's dancing and the young man's 'courting' echo the *pas de deux* of McLaren's film, as the woman is interrupted by the attentions of the male dancer. But Lucy's dancing comes to an abrupt end when she sees Pollux, the youngest of her rapists, and insists on leaving, at which point the party is interrupted by David's confrontation with the young man.

The novel's two instances of dance, in other words, are stalked by the shadow of rape: David's seduction and rape of Melanie and the gang rape of Lucy at her farm. Both dance scenes act out seemingly innocuous forms of courtship or seduction. In *Youth*, John is dismissive of dancing as a mere substitute for 'the real thing', the real thing being sex. David intends McLaren's *Pas de deux* to be a prelude to 'the real thing', whereas the public courtship of Lucy by the young man at the party stands in stark contrast to the preceding rape, which remains unrepresented in the novel. We might contrast this with the work of Royal Ballet choreographer Kenneth Macmillan who notoriously staged detailed and realistic representations of rape onstage, including the rape of an adolescent girl by an older man in *The Invitation* (1960) and a gang rape in *The Judas Tree* (1992). The form of Coetzee's novel, strictly focalized through Lurie, allows no scope for the spectacle of rape that haunts it. This absence is sharpened by the scenes of dance that act as aesthetic doubles of the novel's dark events. The pattern is reinforced by the light comedy of *Sunset at the Globe Salon* and *Byron in Italy*, whose generic conventions likewise demand the exclusion of acts of violence.

Dance may be a substitute for 'the real thing' that takes place in the realist novel, but the photographic or filmic image is frequently associated with a privileged access to the real in Coetzee's work. In an essay on John Huston's film *The Misfits* (1961), first published in 2000 and therefore more or less contemporaneous with *Disgrace*, Coetzee argues that 'there remains something irreducibly different about the photographic image, namely that it bears in or with itself the trace of a real historical past' (*IW*, 226). Coetzee's focus in the essay is on the wild horses who are being rounded up by the film's main characters: 'The horses used in the filming of *The Misfits* were wild horses; the exhaustion and pain and terror one sees on the screen are real exhaustion and pain and terror. The horses are not acting' (*IW*, 225). For Coetzee, the aesthetic and ethical challenge posed by the presence of the horses brings us to 'the heart of film as a representational medium', that is, its status as 'the visual record of something that once really happened'. Writing, in contrast, is more abstract; it relies not on 'a real hand' but 'the idea of a hand' (*IW*, 225–6). Coetzee's account of film is closely tied to its relationship to the photographic image, and his reading of the photographic image is deeply informed by Barthes's assertion in *Camera Lucida* that the essence of the photograph lies in the fact that 'I can never deny that *the thing has been there*', which Barthes too contrasts with writing, which cannot 'authenticate itself'.[10]

But Coetzee's investment in the real of film in the case of *The Misfits* is also particularly motivated by the injury suffered by the film's real horses, and the medium's ability to replay and therefore repeat the injury, which seems to cause genuine distress to Coetzee as a viewer: 'Who would dare to say it is just a story?' (*IW*, 227). Coetzee links the status of the photograph as 'something that once really happened' with debates about visual pornography. This is the territory that he elaborates in his essay on Catherine MacKinnon in *Giving Offense* (1996), published four years earlier, in which he disagrees with MacKinnon's stance on censorship but comes surprisingly close to endorsing what he terms the 'special ontological status' that she claims for pornographic films: 'the status not of the realistic (that is, the successfully illusionistic) but of the real', which in Coetzee's account is tied to what he imagines as the 'numinous' and 'emotionally complex' experience of bodily penetration (*GO*, 77–9). Coetzee's reflections on pornographic films come noticeably closer to engaging with a woman's experience of sex and sexual assault than anything available through David's consciousness in *Disgrace*. We therefore find Coetzee testing the ethics of representing the body and especially violence against the female body across the technologies and ontologies of multiple performative and embodied art forms. This occurs alongside and within the ostensibly realist fiction of *Disgrace*, whose 'idea' of the body is implicitly contrasted with the 'real' bodies of photography, film, and dance.

So far it is clear that Coetzee's representation of the aesthetic experience of visual and performing arts in his work is shaped to a significant extent by narrative point of view, and acts therefore to amplify our understanding of the narrative's focalizing consciousness. This is also the context in which we must read the apparent *otherness* of other arts in Coetzee's work. While there is ample archival evidence of Coetzee's deep knowledge of, for example, the music of Bach, the techniques and history of photography, and avant-garde cinema of the 1960s, music, photography, and film appear for the most part in his work not through the lens of the creator but through that of the listener or viewer. The aesthetic experiences that are recounted are frequently those of the student, the amateur, the novice, or the enthusiast, and not those of the expert or master. This might partly explain the consistent framing of aesthetic experience in terms of its emotional and physical effects. It is also a notable contrast with explicit references to the literary in Coetzee's works, which are often focalized through writers or scholars.

The possibility of and limits to shared aesthetic experience between characters, or across time or cultures, are closely related to ideas about music especially, but also visual and performing arts, as transcending the mediation and abstraction of language in their emotional immediacy and access to a historic real. Notwithstanding their prominence across the Coetzee corpus, these ideas are frequently exposed as fantasies, identified with the amateur's wonder at mastery of a particular art form, or revealing the ideological investments and worldview of the characters who hold them. The presumed otherness to language of visual and performing arts also tests and revises the limits of novelistic discourse. McDonald argues that Coetzee's early work was concerned with the 'philosophical question' deriving from the Humboldtian linguistic relativity thesis – 'is it possible to transcend the language you take to be your own?' – and suggests, via the writings of Fritz Mauthner, that this might go as far as the fantasy of transcending language as such.[11] McDonald ties this to the emphasis on non-linguistic forms of expression in *Disgrace*, specifically the idea of the look. As I have shown, this also takes more explicitly aestheticized forms in the novel's preoccupation with theatre, opera, film, and dance. Indeed, I would suggest that the fantasy of transcending language frequently manifests itself through other art forms in Coetzee's work, even as these fantasies are undermined. I have also shown how the ethics of representing the body and bodily violence, so central to Coetzee's work, are tested in relation to the technologies and ontologies of such art forms. All of this helps to explain why the metafictional *mise en abyme* that has been ever present in Coetzee's work increasingly pushes at the limits of the printed text. The shift in form has the effect of disrupting the potentially recursive logic of such self-reflexivity, opening up questions about the limits of the novel and its shared and differing representational modes vis à vis other arts.

Many of these issues have been keenly debated in relation to *Foe* (1986), as Susan Barton's fascination with the apparently silent Friday marks the limits of her ability to tell the full story of 'Cruso's island'. In a novel that relentlessly probes the constraints and possibilities of linguistic expression in speech and writing, it is through Friday's mysterious dancing that she claims his truth is revealed to her: 'What had been hidden from me was revealed. I saw; or, I should say, my eyes were open to what was present to them' (*F*, 119). Friday's dancing bears comparison with the representation of other art forms in Coetzee's work insofar as it is focalized through Barton, and therefore shaped to an extent by her fantasies and desires. In engaging questions around the history of slavery, colonialism, and race, the novel also foregrounds the extent to which fantasies of transcendent non-linguistic art forms run the risk of a certain kind of exoticism or primitivism. And as an expressive mode of the silent Friday, the dancing anticipates the novel's closing section in which 'bodies are their own signs' and the solid stream emanating from Friday is experienced by the unidentified narrator as a rhythmic physical sensation (*F*, 157).

Friday's dancing is both implicitly and explicitly aligned with writing. Not only does it fuel Barton's narrative ('there is never a lack of things to write of' (*F*, 93)), she also repeatedly insists on the link between Friday's dancing and his adoption of the robes and wig of Foe, suggesting that Friday is performing the role of author through the expressive mode of dance. The archive too encourages us to look beyond the dance as exotic content for Susan's narrative. The *Foe* notebooks from late 1984 to March 1985 suggest that Coetzee was inspired by dance and reflections on the aesthetics of movement, and was also exploring the distinctive challenge of translating physical movement into narrative prose. Meditations on Friday's dance and its relationship to language occur alongside references to Heinrich von Kleist's 'Essay on the Marionette Theatre' (1810), Nietzsche's *The Birth of Tragedy* (1872), and the poet Charles Olson, all of whom share an interest in dance. The notebook suggests that Coetzee initially sees Friday's dance as an alternative to language and a means of communication. The entry for 16 January 1985, the day before he mentions Kleist, reads: 'The answer to the question of how you talk with Friday is of course that you and he dance.'[12] But it is also clear from the *Foe* notebook that writing about dance presented a formal and ontological challenge for Coetzee. An entry on 20 March 1985 in which Coetzee writes 'End of the project in sight – project becomes possible', is followed immediately by a reference to another dance film by Norman McLaren, this time his 1983 film *Narcissus*: 'Saw Norman Maclaren's [*sic*] Narcissus last night. Flurries of motion on the canvas. Can it ever be written? How is it done (technically)?'[13] Similar concerns are evident in the notebooks to *Life & Times of Michael K*. He imagines a kind of unselfconscious dance for Michael K, suggesting that he 'dances when alone (e.g. in the flat)', but this is immediately qualified by the challenge of writing about dance: 'though I shouldn't make the mistake of trying to describe it too fully'.[14]

Adaptation

Dance features in *Slow Man* as one of the many therapies thrust on Paul Rayment after he has lost a leg in a bicycle accident. He attends a dance workshop that aims to 're-program the body's memories' (*SM*, 60). The movements of his fellow participants with prostheses recall Kleist's marionettes, whereas Paul 'sways in time with the music', hypnotized (*SM*, 60–1). References to dance in the novel persist through the figure of the puppet. In the immediate aftermath of his accident Paul describes himself as '*unstrung*': 'that is the word that comes back to him from Homer. The spear shatters the breastbone, blood spurts, the limbs are unstrung, the body topples like a wooden puppet. Well, his limbs have been unstrung and now his spirit is unstrung too. His spirit is ready to topple' (*SM*, 27). But as the novel develops, Paul's identification with the puppet acquires new force directly related to the metafictional world opened up by the arrival of Elizabeth Costello. He complains about being manipulated by Costello: 'You treat me like a puppet ... You treat everyone like a puppet. You make up stories and bully us into playing them out for you. You should open a puppet theatre, or a zoo' (*SM*, 117).

Slow Man was adapted for opera by composer Nicholas Lens with Coetzee writing the libretto, and first performed in Poznan, Poland, in 2012. The opera focuses on a single episode from the novel: the encounter between Paul Rayment and the blind Marianna contrived by Elizabeth Costello, and which provokes Paul's complaints about being treated like a puppet. In its translation to the stage, the role of dance becomes ever more central. The cast of the opera features not only the characters of Paul, Marianna, and Elizabeth Costello, but doubles the characters of Paul and Marianna so that they appear both as singers and dancers.[15] Puppet master Elizabeth Costello, on the other hand, is simply a sung part, reinforcing the metafictional role of dance in the opera. As in the novel, Paul berates Elizabeth Costello for treating him like a puppet, but in Coetzee's libretto his words are betrayed by the movement of his dancer alter ego Rayment, who, we are told in the stage directions, listens, and moves his arms in gestures that might be those of a puppet. The doubling of the characters as dancers and singers introduces a kind of Cartesian split between mind and body, or voice and body.

Although the staging by Opera Poznan incorporates vivid screen images by Wojciech Puś which also act as doubles of the singers, the centrality of photography to the plot of the novel is sidelined in the adaptation. Instead the novel's few references to dance and puppetry are amplified by the opera's staging, and its metafictional concerns, channelled through the writing of Costello and the deviant creative activities of Drago, are reframed in the adaptation around dance and theatre. In this regard, the selection of this particular episode for the opera adaptation is significant. The encounter between Paul and the blind Marianna already sits uneasily within the novel, the most contrived of Costello's efforts as author and creator. The episode is difficult to accommodate within an account of the novel as a realist fiction in part because it is explicitly framed as a piece of theatre or opera being performed by Paul and Marianna. This explains some of the more extravagant details of the episode: the emphasis on costume, masks, and performance. Paul invites Marianna to sing, aware of the staginess of the encounter, but also conscious of being observed:

'If you would sing, that would be best of all', he says. 'We are on stage, in a certain sense, even if we are not being watched.'

Even if we are not being watched. But in a certain sense they are being watched, he is sure of that, on the back of his neck he can feel it.

(*SM*, 103. Italics original)

The metafictional dimensions of the novel are here figured as a literal staging of the action of Costello's fiction, while she is the ghostly observer of the scene. Paul insists that they are not reading from a script: 'There is no need', he begins again, 'for us to adhere to any script. No need to do anything we do not wish. We are free agents' (*SM*, 105). His assertion that they are 'free agents' flies in the face of Costello's apparent control of the entire encounter. The references to theatre, singing, and ornate costume point to an operatic interlude within the novel. Elizabeth Costello, in other words, like David Lurie in *Disgrace*, is writing an opera or a libretto, or at least briefly experimenting with the opera form. Indeed, Marianna's articulation of desire in the *Slow Man* libretto has echoes of the passion and longing of David Lurie's Teresa Guiccioli.

The opera adaptation and libretto expand on the concerns of Coetzee's novel in a manner specific to the form of contemporary opera and the expressive modes available to it. But the adaptation also alerts us to the theatricality of Coetzee's novel. In an interview Nicholas Lens describes a long-standing correspondence with Coetzee about the possibility of working together on an opera that pre-dates the writing of *Slow Man*, and raises interesting questions about the extent of their collaborative endeavours. Lens heard from Coetzee in 2005 'that he was busy writing a book [*Slow Man*] and one of the scenes [the meeting of Paul and Marianna] could be our starting point'.[16] Lens's account, together with the operatic nature of the episode from the novel, raises the possibility that the theatricality of Coetzee's novel in part emerges from the collaborative dialogue with Lens. This adds an additional layer to the relationship between an original art work and a copy or a forgery which drives the plot surrounding Drago Jokić's playful reworking of Rayment's Fauchery photograph in the novel, complicating the presumed single direction of influence between original and copy – or adaption. It adds a new dimension too to the expectations of fidelity owed by the adaptation to the original.

The *Slow Man* libretto is not Coetzee's first attempt to adapt his work for another medium, but it is undoubtedly the most successful and the result of a fruitful and ongoing collaboration with Lens that extends at least to another adaptation, this time of *Elizabeth Costello* under the title

Costello: This Body That I Am, which is written but yet to be produced. There have been numerous adaptations of Coetzee's work for stage and film over the years, and his involvement has ranged from the full collaboration with another artist, as with Lens, to granting permission for his work to be adapted. One of the most high-profile examples of the latter was Philip Glass's adaptation of *Waiting for the Barbarians*, produced in 2006 by Theater Erfurt and staged in Amsterdam, which set a libretto by Christopher Hampton to a typically minimalist Glass score. The production was notable for a staging that evoked the contemporary concerns about torture and detention in the war on terror through illuminated orange figures suspended above the action, occasionally descending to occupy the full stage. The earliest attempt to adapt Coetzee's work for opera, however, emerges from the archive and remains unheard. Among the documents relating to *In the Heart of the Country* (1977) at the Harry Ransom Center is a short, undated libretto titled 'Lament from the Heart of the Country: for Soprano and Chamber Ensemble', written by Coetzee.[17] It is not difficult to imagine Magda's passion, like that of Teresa Guiccioli or Marianna, expressed through the opera form.

There have also been numerous adaptations of Coetzee's work for the stage, but so far none that has attracted his direct involvement.[18] He has, however, especially encouraged and collaborated with film-makers interested in adapting his work, and for a range of reasons. His immersion in avant-garde cinema in London in the early 1960s and the impact of film on the *nouveau roman* clearly left him with a strong sense of the creative and narrative possibilities of the medium. In an interview in *Doubling the Point* (1992) he describes being drawn to the use of montage, stills, and voice-over in avant-garde cinema of the 1960s and suggests that this style 'imprints' itself on *In the Heart of the Country* through the numbered sections and pace of narration (*DP*, 60). These observations have shaped critical commentary on the novel and on adaptations of his work for film, frequently focusing on the reciprocal influence between fiction and film. Forthcoming work by Iona Gilburt takes us beyond Coetzee's own self-commentary to show the influence of photographic and cinematographic techniques on the novels including and beyond *In the Heart of the Country*.[19] An essay by Teresa Dovey and Lindiwe Dovey and a series of essays by Hermann Wittenberg emphasize the influence of film on Coetzee's fiction, against which adaptions, completed and imagined, are measured.[20]

Wittenberg's archival and editorial work offers the fullest picture of Coetzee's efforts to balance the potential for creative experimentation, exposure to new audiences, and commercial gain that film as a medium makes available.²¹ Coetzee completed screenplay adaptations of *In the Heart of the Country* (1981) and *Waiting for the Barbarians* (1995), which have yet to be produced but have been edited for publication by Wittenberg (2014), as well as an incomplete and undated screenplay of *Life & Times of Michael K*.²² As Wittenberg documents, this creative activity occurred in the context of extensive communication with film-makers, some of which produced completed films but more of which resulted in various dead ends and creative impasses. To date there have been four adaptations for the screen: Marion Hänsel's adaptation of *In the Heart of the Country*, *Dust* (1985), Alex Harvey's *The Lives of Animals* (2002), which was produced for television by the BBC, Steve Jacobs's *Disgrace* (2008), and Ben van Lieshout's *The Muse* (2009), with the promise of a forthcoming adaptation of *Waiting for the Barbarians* by Ciro Aguerre starring Mark Rylance, as well as a feature documentary by South African film-maker Francois Verster titled *The Last Days of Elizabeth Costello: A Film About J. M. Coetzee*. So far, Coetzee's closest involvement has been with Marion Hänsel's *Dust*, but notwithstanding this, she eschewed Coetzee's own screenplay and guidance on the significance of the novel's Karoo setting, as well as his taste for stills and voiceover, and ignored the novel's section breaks. The film 'loses a lot of vitality thereby', according to Coetzee (*DP*, 60). In keeping with this reading, the Doveys offer a devastating account of the myriad ways in which Hänsel's film was 'wrong' – culturally, geographically, and formally. They describe a profound 'ambivalence' at the heart of Coetzee's interactions with film-makers: a deep interest in film and a willingness to have his work adapted by other artists, but equally a desire to retain some control over the screenplay.²³

Wittenberg's work details this ambivalence in accounts of numerous failed collaborations, sensitive to the various factors shaping the optioning and adaptation of novels for cinema. He draws on extensive archival sources to document Coetzee's enthusiasm for the potential of film and his awareness of and resistance to the priorities of commercial cinema, and argues persuasively that the interest in film grows with Coetzee's reputation, and that the author saw the potential for a major film adaptation of *Barbarians* in particular to transform his writing career. But the protracted efforts to adapt *Barbarians* also capture the clear conflict between the requirements of commercial cinema and Coetzee's desire to protect the creative vision of the novel (which ultimately is *his* vision). In a letter to British television producer Eric Paice, he writes 'I must make it clear from the start that the main responsibility I feel is towards the book. I don't want to conclude a deal which results one day in a film that leaves me feeling sick.'²⁴ Some sources of conflict are also particularly telling: while Coetzee went to great lengths to encourage Hänsel to be faithful to *In the Heart of the Country*'s South African location, he insisted that a clause be inserted in the contract to option *Waiting for the Barbarians* preventing it from being filmed in a South African location.

In the case of Steve Jacobs and Anna Maria Monticelli's adaptation of *Disgrace*, the problem of fidelity to the location of the novel presents different challenges. An Australian production to all intents and purposes, *Disgrace* was nonetheless filmed on location in South Africa, with international actors in two of the main roles, John Malkovich as David Lurie and Eriq Ebouaney as Petrus. The Cape Town scenes are largely filmed at the University of Cape Town, where Coetzee studied and worked for most of his career. Lucy's farm, however, is relocated to the dramatic natural environment of the Cederberg, north of Cape Town, thus forgoing the precision of the novel's depiction of the politics of land and language in the Eastern Cape. The film also controversially reverses the order of the novel's closing scenes, concluding not with Lurie's sacrifice of his favourite dog, but with the pregnant Lucy located in the landscape of the Cederberg mountains, therefore associating her seemingly intractable commitment to remaining on the farm with the beauty of the landscape. The film thus loses the irony of Lurie's almost instinctive positioning of his daughter within his anachronistic romantic worldview as '*das ewig Weibliche*', figured in the novel in relation to the paintings of Sargent and Bonnard, instead framing her within just such a romantic aesthetic (*Dis*, 218. Italics original).

Coetzee's wide-ranging engagement with other art forms opens up a set of questions about intertextuality, medium, writing, and language. These are related to the existing terms in which his work is read, but also offer new ways of thinking about aestheticized forms of embodiment and non-verbal expression that test and revise our understanding of the limits of prose fiction and its relationship to other art forms. Adaptations might not liberate Coetzee's characters from the languages in which they frequently feel imprisoned, but the best may at least offer them the grammars of new media in which to express themselves. Within the framework of adaptation, Coetzee's engagement with other art forms has the potential to generate collaborative works that complicate and exceed the conventional terms of fidelity against which adaptations are frequently measured. This can be seen in the opera adaptation of *Slow Man*. But his willingness to incorporate and test the conventions of other arts in his fiction also presents challenges to artists whose commitment is to their own media, who must therefore move beyond the terms determined by the original, and whose adaptations should be untethered from the understandable ambivalence of Coetzee himself.

Notes

1. *Photographs from Boyhood*, a recent exhibition of Coetzee's own photographs at the Irma Stern Gallery in Cape Town curated by Hermann Wittenberg and Farzanah Badsha, shows the young Coetzee's technical mastery of photography.
2. W. J. T. Mitchell, *Picture Theory: Essays on Verbal and Visual Representation* (Chicago: University of Chicago Press, 1995), p. 158.
3. Peter D. McDonald, *Artefacts of Writing: Ideas of the State and Communities of Letters from Matthew Arnold to Xu Bing* (Oxford: Oxford University Press, 2017), p. 196. See also his discussion of Coetzee's relationship to the linguistic relativity thesis in 'Coetzee's Critique of Language' in Patrick Hayes and Jan Wilm, (eds.), *Beyond the Ancient Quarrel: Coetzee and Philosophy*, (Oxford: Oxford University Press, 2018), pp. 161–80.
4. See Henri Bergson, *Laughter: An Essay on the Meaning of the Comic*, trans. Cloudesley Brereton and Fred Rothwell (New York: Macmillan, 1914), p. 35.
5. Kathryn Lachman, *Borrowed Forms: The Music and Ethics of Transnational Fiction* (Liverpool: Liverpool University Press, 2014), p. 122.
6. Lachman, *Borrowed Forms*, p. 116; and McDonald, 'Coetzee's Critique of Language', p. 170.
7. Lachman, *Borrowed Forms*, p. 132.
8. Michael Holland, '"Plink-Plunk": Unforgetting the Present in Coetzee's *Disgrace*', *Interventions: International Journal of Postcolonial Studies*, 4.3 (2002), 400–3.
9. Norman McLaren, *Pas de deux* (National Film Board of Canada, 1968): www .nfb.ca/film/pas_de_deux_en/
10. Roland Barthes, *Camera Lucida: Reflections on Photography*, trans. Richard Howard (London: Vintage, 2000), pp. 76, 85.
11. McDonald, *Artefacts of Writing*, p. 196. For Coetzee and Mauthner, see McDonald, 'Coetzee's Critique of Language'.
12. J. M. Coetzee, *Foe*, green casebound notebook with gilt edges (1982–5), CP 33.6, 16 January 1985.
13. Ibid., 20 March 1985.
14. J. M. Coetzee, *Life & Times of Michael K*, gray casebound notebook (1972–82), CP 33.5.
15. Coetzee's early draft of the libretto, from which I quote here, identifies the character as Marianna. Although the later score identifies her as Marijana, and her dancer double as Maria, I use the earlier form for the sake both of clarity and of consistency with the novel.
16. Nicholas Lens and Dorota Semenowicz, 'An Ordinary Man: An Interview with Nicholas Lens by Dorota Semenowicz', *Werkwinkel*, 7.2 (2012), 49.
17. J. M. Coetzee, 'Lament from the Heart of the Country: for Soprano and Chamber Ensemble', CP 59.6.
18. The more high-profile stage adaptations include: two of *Foe*, one by Complicité (West Yorkshire Playhouse, 1996), adapted by Mark Wheatley and directed by Annie Castledine and Marcello Magni, and the other adapted and directed by Peter Glazer (Zellerbach Playhouse, University of California, Berkeley, 2003); *Waiting for the Barbarians*, directed by Alexander Marine (Baxter Theatre, Cape Town, 2012); the 'Eros' section of *Elizabeth Costello*, by Krzysztof Warlikowski

as part of his *Phaedre(s)* (The Barbican, London, 2016), with Isabelle Huppert as Elizabeth Costello.

19. See Iona Gilburt, 'Cinematographic and Photographic Aesthetics in the Work of J. M. Coetzee', unpublished PhD thesis, University of the Western Cape (2017).

20. Teresa Dovey and Lindiwe Dovey, 'Coetzee on Film' in Graham Bradshaw and Michael Neill (eds.), *J. M. Coetzee's Austerities* (Farnham: Ashgate, 2010), pp. 57–78.

21. See Hermann Wittenberg, 'Coetzee in California: Adaptation, Authorship, and the Filming of *Waiting for the Barbarians*', *Safundi: The Journal of South African and American Studies*, 16.2 (2015), 115–35 and Hermann Wittenberg, 'Film and Photography in J. M. Coetzee's *Life & Times of Michael K*', *Texas Studies in Literature and Language*, 58.4 (2016), 473–92.

22. J. M. Coetzee, *Two Screenplays: 'Waiting for the Barbarians' and 'In the Heart of the Country'*, ed. Hermann Wittenberg (Cape Town: University of Cape Town Press, 2014). See Wittenberg 'Film and Photography' for an account of the latter screenplay.

23. Dovey and Dovey, 'Coetzee on Film', pp. 61, 77–8.

24. Wittenberg, 'Coetzee in California', p. 121.

12

ANTHONY UHLMANN

Philosophies

A number of prominent philosophers have recently been drawn to J. M. Coetzee's works. They have focused in particular on the problems of human relations to animals, and, more generally, on questions of ethics. However, the interest of philosophers in Coetzee's oeuvre is only one dimension of his encounter with philosophy. This chapter will consider some of Coetzee's own philosophical engagements, in terms of his formation and institutional affiliations. It will then consider how his fictions confront and offer provocations to philosophy. Finally, it will consider how and why philosophers and literary theorists have responded to these confrontations and provocations.

Encounters with Philosophy

In *Youth* (2002), the narrator underlines the protagonist's interest in pure ideas, and how this led him towards mathematics:

> What draws him to mathematics, besides the arcane symbols it uses, is its purity. If there were a department of Pure Thought at the university he would probably enrol in pure thought too; but pure mathematics appears to be the closest approach the academy affords to the realm of the forms.   (Y, 22)

Youth is by no means a straightforward autobiographical record – 'he' is not identical with the author J. M. Coetzee, and is often the focus of an excoriating humour – but this passage does reflect two significant features of Coetzee's undergraduate education at the University of Cape Town (UCT) in the late 1950s. First, in referring to 'the realm of forms', and, therefore, to Plato, it alludes to an interest which, as we will see, informed Coetzee's thinking and writing from the very beginning. Second, it gestures to the fact that, though Coetzee enrolled in a variety of courses whilst at UCT, none of these was in the Department of Philosophy.

A tension, then, is projected onto the very beginnings of Coetzee's career: an attraction to 'pure' or systematic thought and to philosophical concerns, but no particular interest in the formal methods or schools of philosophy. In fact, the work describes a progressive disenchantment with such methods. Late on in *Youth*, the narrator affirms:

> He is reading in the history of logic, pursuing an intuition that logic is a human invention, not part of the fabric of being, and therefore (there are many intermediate steps, but he can fill them in later) that computers are simply toys invented by boys (led by Charles Babbage) for the amusement of other boys. There are many alternative logics, he is convinced (but how many?), each just as good as the logic of *either-or*. (*Y*, 159–60)

For Coetzee, then, an interest in thought (whether pure or otherwise) may entail an interest not in a single logic, but in a variety of logics, which might be drawn into dialogue, and which might at times contradict one another. Indeed, if Coetzee is attracted to Plato, this is in part because of his concern with the dialogic, that is, with forms of discourse involving the clash of perspectives.

The interests in mathematics, poetry, and pure thought which are described in *Youth*, as well as the mistrust of binary logic, can be seen coalescing in Coetzee's PhD dissertation, 'The English Fiction of Samuel Beckett: An Essay in Stylistic Analysis', which he completed at the University of Texas at Austin. Drawing on his experience as a computer programmer, Coetzee's analysis of Beckett's manuscripts relied on the branch of computer-based stylistics known as stylometrics. In *Doubling the Point* (1992), he disparages stylometrics as 'a false trail' (*DP*, 22). Yet a false trail need not be worthless. A worm leaves a trail or thread of silk, a trail is a kind of path or way, a way is a method. Even a false method can lead to meaningful outcomes. In this case, Coetzee's work in stylometrics prompted him to engage with important philosophical debates about language, and about the relationship between linguistic structure and meaning, which I will explore in greater detail in the next section.

Having completed his PhD, Coetzee's first academic job was at the State University of New York at Buffalo, which was teeming with intellectual life in the late 1960s and early 1970s. Bruce Jackson has written about this vibrant 'community of words and ideas', where novelists, poets, and critics worked in close proximity with philosophers and theorists, including three of the most important French thinkers of the period, René Girard, Michel Foucault, and Hélène Cixous.[1] 'Other universities had the best English departments for history or criticism or philology or whatever', Jackson writes, 'But UB was the only place where it all went on at once: hot-center and cutting-edge scholarship and creative writing, literary and film criticism, poem and play and novel writing, deep history and magazine journalism.'

Whilst at Buffalo, and as he began working on his first novel, *Dusklands* (1974), Coetzee was thus part of a dynamic intellectual community. It was a community, moreover, in which the boundaries between disciplines were blurred, in a way that foreshadowed developments in the intellectual cultures of France and the United States especially, where, during the 1970s and 1980s, literature and philosophy intermingled under the banner of what has come to be known as 'literary theory'. Both Foucault and Cixous are often identified with these developments, as are Jacques Derrida, Jacques Lacan, Roland Barthes, Julia Kristeva, and Gilles Deleuze – French philosophers and psychoanalysts united in the belief that literature, film, and the arts were themselves vehicles for powerful kinds of thinking, able to offer insights into profound questions that could not properly be understood through the clear, unambiguous logic of analytical philosophy.

Coetzee's archives include a remarkably detailed document, running to forty-one pages, listing his 'record of reading' in the 1970s and 1980s, most of which period he spent at UCT, having moved there from Buffalo in 1971.[2] The works on the list can be divided into three broad categories: those on linguistics and rhetoric (often in the Anglo-American tradition); those on literature and literary history; and those which might collectively be described as works of 'theory', whether originating in philosophy or psychoanalysis. Taken together, this list attests to the fact that, like many younger scholars in literature departments across the English-speaking world, Coetzee was alert to the intellectual currents of his moment, and drawn to formalism, structuralism, semiotics, and post-structuralist theory (the list includes numerous works by Mikhail Bakhtin, Émile Benveniste, Roman Jakobson, Pavel Medvedev, and Valentin Volosinov; by Barthes, Maurice Blanchot, Cixous, Jonathan Culler, Deleuze, Terry Eagleton, Umberto Eco, Foucault, Lacan, Girard, and Kristeva).

If anything, Coetzee is distinguished by the catholicity of his tastes. His list is full of works identified with deconstruction and the Yale School of literary theory, and includes multiple titles by Derrida, J. Hillis Miller, Harold Bloom, Paul de Man, and Geoffrey Hartman, along with other philosophically inspired American literary theorists such as Stanley Fish and Charles Altieri (another colleague at Buffalo). But it is also replete with works on Marx and materialism, by thinkers such as György Lukács and Theodor

Adorno, and by others in the German tradition of hermeneutics and critical theory, such as Wolfgang Iser, Hans Robert Jauss, and Jürgen Habermas. And alongside them one also finds philosophers of language, such as Ludwig Wittgenstein, George Lakoff, and J. L. Austin; as well as existentialist thinkers, such as Jean-Paul Sartre, Friedrich Nietzsche, and Søren Kierkegaard, and anti-colonialist theorists, such as Frantz Fanon and Aimé Césaire.

While far from being a comprehensive account of Coetzee's encounter with philosophy, the list suggests something of his efforts to engage with philosophical ideas, and to think through their relevance to literary criticism, and, indeed to literary creation. This engagement developed and shifted as Coetzee took up a visiting position as Professor in the University of Chicago's Committee on Social Thought in the 1990s. Others on the Committee included philosophers, such as Robert Pippin, and psychological and social theorists, such as Jonathan Lear. As a member of the Committee, Coetzee was able to engage with thinkers in other disciplines, and delivered a series of lectures, which were ultimately recast as *Elizabeth Costello: Eight Lessons* (2003).

This was also the period in which Coetzee began to receive a great many invitations to deliver lectures and participate in colloquia, which again allowed him to speak across disciplinary boundaries. The most famous of these were the Tanner Lectures at Princeton, later published as *The Lives of Animals* (1999), in which Coetzee directly engaged with philosophers, critics, and social theorists. Here, although he undertook a serious programme of reading into the philosophical arguments for and against animal rights, he responded not by dealing theoretically with the nature of relations between humans and animals, but, instead, provocatively, by offering two stories. In taking this approach, his implicit claim was that fiction is capable of thinking in ways that unsettle philosophical ideas, and of approaching questions along avenues that may be closed to the kind of rational argument associated with philosophy in its analytical tradition.

Thus, late in his career, and in spite of an enduring commitment to reading and responding to philosophers, Coetzee seems to remain as suspicious of philosophy's methods and disciplinary formations as he was whilst an undergraduate student at UCT. If anything has changed, it is that his scepticism about the capacity of philosophical discourse to uncover the truth has become increasingly wedded to a belief in the truth-telling powers inhering in literary expression. On the other hand, if we take the JC of *Diary of a Bad Year* (2007) to be a close approximation of John Coetzee, then it would seem that even this belief is of long standing. For, amongst other things, Strong Opinion 30, entitled 'On Authority in Fiction', describes an intuitive sense that the force of literary fiction could not be wholly captured or explained in the sceptical accounts of critics, theorists and philosophers:

> Announcements of the death of the author and of authorship made by Roland Barthes and Michel Foucault a quarter of a century ago came down to the claim that the authority of the author has never amounted to anything more than a bagful of rhetorical tricks. Barthes and Foucault took their cue from Diderot and Sterne, who long ago made a game of exposing the impostures of authorship. The Russian formalist critics of the 1920s, from whom Barthes in particular learned much, concentrated their efforts on exposing Tolstoy, above all other writers, as a rhetorician. Tolstoy became their exemplary target because Tolstoy's storytelling seemed so natural, that is to say, concealed its rhetorical artistry so well.
>
> As a child of my times, I read, admired, and imitated Diderot and Sterne. But I never gave up reading Tolstoy, nor could I ever persuade myself that his effect on me was just a consequence of his rhetorical skill.　　　(*DBY*, 149–50)

Fiction and Philosophy

The drafts of *Dusklands* demonstrate that, from the beginning of Coetzee's career as a novelist, he had an interest in incorporating conceptual or philosophical themes into his writing. Coetzee had begun, on the 1st of January 1970, with what would become the second part of *Dusklands*, 'The Narrative of Jacobus Coetzee'. Only later, after he had returned to Cape Town from Buffalo, did he start working on the novel's first part, 'The Vietnam Project'. The earliest draft – under the working title 'Lies' – is dated 11th June 1972, and begins as follows:

> I saw Coetzee today. He wants a philosophical introduction.
>
> HE: How do you place yourself philosophically?
> I: Post-Marx.
> HE: Meaning?
> I: I show why Marx is superseded.
>
> So now I am committed to writing it in.[3]

In developing readings of Coetzee, there are a number of ways of taking philosophy into account. One way is to attend to Coetzee's archive in the Harry Ransom Center, which provides extensive information – of the kind detailed above – about what Coetzee was reading when he wrote his fictions. However, this is only one approach, and critics certainly need not feel limited to working only with those philosophers or theorists explicitly mentioned in Coetzee's corpus. As I will explain in the third part of this chapter, Coetzee's work sometimes offers intellectual provocations to scholars in philosophy and other disciplines (history, politics, psychology), who are thereby called upon to respond. In this part, however, I will set out some of the lines of interpretation that the archives do open up.

Beginning with *Waiting for the Barbarians* (1980), evidence might be found, for example, of Coetzee's engagement with philosophical questions about justice. Considering the idea of justice towards the end of the novel, the Magistrate states:

> I had no doubt, myself, then, that at each moment each of us, man, woman, child, perhaps even the poor old horse turning the mill-wheel, knew what was just: all creatures come into the world bringing with them the memory of justice. 'But we live in a world of laws,' I said to my poor prisoner, 'a world of the second-best'. (*WB*, 152)

What we now know from the archives is that, after he had written this passage, with its seemingly purposeful allusion to Plato's conception of an innate knowledge of truth, Coetzee remarked in his notebook: 'I discover that the man is straight out of Plato. "memories of justice"'.[4] Here it seems that Coetzee is drawn to the notion of an ideal justice in the process of composition, and only realizes through this process that the Magistrate is making use of Platonic ideas.

The archives also provide evidence of a second kind of engagement with philosophical or theoretical texts. Whilst working on *Life & Times of Michael K* (1983), Coetzee cast about for ways to advance the narrative, and was drawn to J. Hillis Miller's essay 'The Critic as Host', which develops certain ideas of Derrida's in its reading of the relation between the 'parasite' and 'host'.[5] Hillis Miller underlines the fluid and reversible nature of these two entities, and, in a long paragraph in the novel which meditates on their relation, Coetzee takes up and develops these ideas (*LT*, 116).

A similar example can be found in the notebooks to *Age of Iron* (1990), where Coetzee draws upon Roland Barthes's reading of the story of Orpheus to come to terms with and move away from the temptation of turning to nostalgia in developing this novel. Coetzee juxtaposes Barthes's essay with his own reading of Dante's *Divine Comedy*. In the latter, Dante teaches us to return to life, to live well; in the former, Orpheus is frozen by nostalgia, and so loses everything. Coetzee writes: 'Barthes interprets the Orpheus myth as about nostalgia. By looking back on what you love, you kill it.'[6]

Many other such examples can be found across his corpus, and the archives will therefore prove an invaluable resource for leveraging Coetzee's engagement with other texts into readings of his own works. In this way, it should allow scholars to build on the work of predecessors who had relied on allusions to philosophical or theoretical texts in Coetzee's fictional and critical writings to develop their own interpretations of his oeuvre, from Teresa Dovey's use of Lacan in *The Novels of J. M. Coetzee: Lacanian Allegories* (1988) to Derek Attridge's engagement with Derrida and Levinas in *J. M. Coetzee and the Ethics of Reading* (2005).

Yet, as stated at the outset, there are other approaches to understanding Coetzee's engagement with philosophy. One crucial way is through form. Coetzee shifts the form, or the sets of relations that operate within his work, from novel to novel. For example, *Age of Iron* makes use of an epistolary form, with Mrs Curren, approaching death, writing from South Africa to her daughter in America, and depending on the medium of angels for her letter to be transmitted and understood. This is in contrast to Coetzee's use of cinematic forms in his earlier novel *In the Heart of the Country* (1977), whose debts to experimental film he discusses in *Doubling the Point* (*DP*, 60); and again much later in *Summertime* (2009), which adopts a structure similar to that used in Orson Welles's *Citizen Kane*, using interviews with associates to build up an idea of the dead 'John Coetzee'. In four other novels – *Elizabeth Costello: Eight Lessons*, *Diary of a Bad Year*, *The Childhood of Jesus* (2013), and *The Schooldays of Jesus* (2016) – there is a related attempt to stage an encounter between literary forms and philosophical forms. In the discussion which follows I discuss this group of novels and argue for correspondences and differences between these forms.

However, since 'form' might seem an imprecise term to some readers, I will first try to explain how I understand it, by examining the way Coetzee himself uses it in his PhD dissertation. Here, Coetzee draws a distinction between content and form and insists that these terms should not be collapsed into a single concept. In arguing this, he sets himself against both Russian Formalists and structural linguists, who saw content as a function of form. Coetzee summarizes his position in the final chapter of his dissertation under the subheading 'Forms of thought and language':

> The opposition of structural linguists to a dualism of idea and word is too well known to need exposition. 'Linguistic features do not reproduce ... meaning,' writes one of them, 'they produce it.' Recently, however, there has been something of a philosophic revolution in linguistics, led by Noam Chomsky, against logical empiricism and in favor of a revived Cartesianism in which the 'mental act' is distinct from the verbal act.[7]

Coetzee's own position is aligned with this Chomskyian revolution insofar as it maintains a dualistic distinction between content and form, whilst recognizing a nuanced and complex interaction between them.

The nature of this interaction is discussed in the first chapter of Coetzee's dissertation. After giving an account of the five ways in which Morris Weitz describes the relationship between form and content in *Philosophy of the Arts* (1950), Coetzee states that his own position is 'closest to ... but not identical with' Weitz's position (b), which is that 'Content is the aggregate of elements, form the relations among them'. Coetzee goes on to clarify this position:

> The form of a literary work is that conception of it which enables the reader to comprehend its entire structure of interrelationships and references. But not all elements of the work are parts of its content. The narrator of *Watt*, for example, is in the novel for formal reasons, and is thus a formal element.[8]

These remarks allow us to understand, in turn, what Coetzee means by 'style', since this is itself described, in the opening pages of his dissertation, as a function of relations between form and content:

> I therefore imply that there is in literary work a content which exists in some sense prior to its expression, that the expression can be adequate or inadequate to the content, and that in the latter case one can perceive disjunction between expression and pre-existent content. I imply that there is a general area of literary study which investigates the determination of each other by content and form – content by content, content by form, form by content, form by form – and that the investigation of the last three, but not the first, includes the study of *style*.[9]

What needs to be emphasized here is that Coetzee considers form and content distinct, though mutually determining rather than entirely separable. He also claims that different forms will enable different kinds of expression and thus meaning. Moreover, though it develops and shifts, Coetzee's dualistic conception of form and content persists from the beginning of his career all the way through to his engagement with Plato in his recent novels *The Childhood of Jesus* and *The Schooldays of Jesus*.

By 'form', then, in what follows, I understand the sets of relations (the modes, genres, techniques, and methods) used to express the content and to create meaning. I am contending that the forms (or sets of relations) used by philosophy sometimes differ from and sometimes converge with the forms used in literary works. To my mind Coetzee's term 'form' is superior to 'genre' because it encompasses cross-generic modes (like realism or satire), as well as instances of generic blending, such as occur, for example, in

ANTHONY UHLMANN

Coetzee's *Dusklands*, in which the genre of the story of exploration is juxtaposed with the genre of the analytical essay, and which, moreover, mixes realist and satirical modes. I therefore speak, for example, of 'epistolary form' rather than 'epistolary genre' because the former involves relations that are not purely generic.

Turning now to *Diary of a Bad Year*, although not all of the notebooks related to this novel are currently available, it seems apparent that it began as an actual diary in which Coetzee set out a range of opinions on various topics. He then worked these into a frame in which the character JC is asked by a German publisher to write a collection of essays which is to be called 'Strong Opinions'. The essay form offers a space in which literary tropes and speculative ideas might come together, with Michel de Montaigne's essays providing a template for this kind of writing and thinking (though one could just as well look to Seneca and any number of models drawn from other periods). So too, as Paul Patton has argued, the concept of the 'opinion' confronts and provokes philosophical thinking.[10] Just as Elizabeth Costello's lessons deliberately do not meet the expectations of philosophical form, the frames that Coetzee develops in *Diary of a Bad Year*, where the opinions are juxtaposed with comments offered by JC and his secretary Anya, render the novel enigmatic and unstable, provoking thought as well as philosophical and critical responses.

With *Elizabeth Costello: Eight Lessons*, it is possible to relate the work's engagement with philosophical form more clearly to the circumstances of its genesis. By the time Coetzee wrote the first Elizabeth Costello 'Lessons' – which began life as public addresses written for particular occasions – he had published works, such as *White Writing* (1988) and *Giving Offense* (1996), that engaged in more or less conventional ways with literary-critical, theoretical, and socio-political questions. Yet, from 1996, when invited to give lectures on specific topics he instead began to write stories about another, imagined writer confronted by the same task.

Nevertheless, the archives show that in preparing to write these lectures, or, rather, the stories about them, Coetzee read extensively in the relevant philosophical scholarship. Thus, when invited to address the question of animal rights in the Princeton Tanner Lectures on Human Values (which became 'The Lives of Animals', or Lessons 3 and 4 of *Elizabeth Costello*) he consulted works on the nature of animal/human relations – many of which appear in footnotes in Amy Gutman's edition of *The Lives of Animals* – and educated himself in the history of the debates played out within the discipline of philosophy. This involved engaging with a wide range of philosophers, such as Thomas Nagel, Peter Singer, Tom Regan, Carol J. Adams, Wolfgang Kohler, and Michael P. T. Leahy. Yet that engagement is ultimately framed

214

by dramatic form, with the position adopted by Elizabeth Costello rendered provisional and open to question. If readers tend to associate Elizabeth Costello's position with Coetzee's own, it is worth noting that something takes place within the narrative form which would not take place within a standard logical philosophical argument. This has to do with what Bakhtin describes as the polyvocality or dialogism of the novel – a notion with which Coetzee was familiar – which is different in kind from the form of the philosophical dialogue produced by Plato.

A number of philosophers and philosophically minded critics have drawn attention to Coetzee's interest in Plato in his most recent novels, *The Childhood of Jesus* and *The Schooldays of Jesus*. Here, not only are philosophical ideas explicitly discussed, in the manner of Plato, but the works, more so than Coetzee's previous fictions, are also largely constituted by discussions and debates, that is, by dialogues, in which particular positions are identified with particular characters. There is also evidence here of the kind of literary dialogism Coetzee discusses at length in relation to Dostoevsky, but it is the Platonic dialogue especially that resonates in these novels. Yet how does literary dialogue differ from Plato's dialogue? In *Problems of Dostoevsky's Poetics* (1963), *The Dialogic Imagination* (1975), and elsewhere, Bakhtin claims that the novel is able to allow the expression of a whole range of ideas, a whole range of ideological positions, without choosing between them: it can show us how ideas engage with one another and refract and bounce off one another, making us think about the problems at stake, without telling us what to think.

Writing on Dostoevsky in *Stranger Shores* (2001), Coetzee has offered a point of critique concerning the limits of Bakhtin's idea. It is not enough, Coetzee suggests, simply to recognize that Dostoevsky put ideas into play, that he, like the compulsive gambler he was, put them forward as stakes in a game. We need to realize that Dostoevsky's stakes were not just anything; rather, among the things he put on the table were his own most cherished beliefs. The very idea of his soul, in effect, was bet and perhaps lost along with the other trinkets of the age. In reviewing Joseph Frank's biography of Dostoevsky, Coetzee states:

> Frank loses an opportunity to supply what is missing in Bakhtin, namely, a clear statement that dialogism as exemplified in the novels of Dostoevsky is a matter not of ideological position, still less of novelistic technique, but of the most radical intellectual and even spiritual courage. (*SS*, 145)

Coetzee goes on to quote Frank, who underlines how Dostoevsky 'fearlessly submits his own most hallowed convictions to the same test that he had used for those of the Nihilists'.

Yet, for Coetzee, if Bakhtin demonstrates how dialogism might be developed within a work and act upon readers (carrying with it a power to generalize ideas and free them somewhat from the moorings of their beginnings), he in turn understates the importance of the disposition, place, and situations from which the work emerged:

> implicit in Frank's account is what Bakhtin leaves out: that to the degree that Dostoevskian dialogism grows out of Dostoevsky's own moral character, out of his ideals, and out of his being as a writer, it is only distantly imitable. (*SS*, 145–6)

In effect, Coetzee points out that dialogism is not simply a cold intellectual matter. It is tied to the specific, indeed personal contexts from which the work emerges and with which it engages. As such, the ideas and positions it puts into play are deeply felt, in a way that may even hurt. In short, Coetzee's inflection of Bakhtin's concept of dialogism entails that you *feel* dialogue, to the depths of your being, as much as you think through dialogue. We might read Plato, but do we stop to imagine the experience of Socrates's hapless interlocutors as the very fabric of their worlds is unravelled through what Mrs Curren calls 'ventriloquism' (*AI*, 98)? How does it feel for a belief to ebb from or collapse within the self under the sustained assault of unrelenting dialogue?

The 'lecture' which forms the heart of some of the lessons, then, becomes displaced and altered. Rather than directly setting out and defending a thesis in accordance with the conventions of academic forums, Coetzee offers provocations that carry paradoxes and contradictions with them. The challenge implicit in this method was immediately apparent to philosophers, and, in responding to the *Lives of Animals*, the philosopher and animal rights theorist Peter Singer took issue with Coetzee's approach, arguing, in a piece that tries unsuccessfully to mimic Coetzee's story-form, that it amounts to a kind of trick: 'Call me old-fashioned ... but I prefer to keep truth and fiction clearly separate.'[11]

Perhaps the earliest example of an argument over the nature of 'literary' and 'philosophical' form can be found in Plato's dialogues. In *Gorgias* and *The Sophist* Socrates opposes 'rhetoric', which we now associate with literary techniques which aim to convince by appealing to the emotions, to 'dialectic', which traces a line of argument step by step and convinces through reason. Nietzsche contends in *The Birth of Tragedy* (1872) that Socrates cannot properly maintain this distinction: that Socrates too is a rhetorician. Thus, Nietzsche argues, while Plato attacks art and artists in the *Republic*, seeking to cast them out, he provides them with a life raft in his dialogues.[12] That is, the dialogue form developed by Plato is already 'literary', a fictional mode through which to explore and test ideas and arguments. For his part, Coetzee underlines the value of techniques that allow ideas to be incorporated within realist novels. In *Elizabeth Costello*, he writes:

> Realism has never been comfortable with ideas. It could not be otherwise: realism is premised on the idea that ideas have no autonomous existence, can exist only in things. So when it needs to debate ideas, as here, realism is driven to invent situations – walks in the countryside, conversations – in which characters give voice to contending ideas and thereby in a certain sense embody them. The notion of *embodying* turns out to be pivotal. In such debates ideas do not and indeed cannot float free: they are tied to the speakers by whom they are enounced, and generated from the matrix of individual interests out of which their speakers act in the world. (EC, 9)

Provocations and Truth in Fiction

Literary critics working on Coetzee have long drawn upon philosophical paradigms in their readings of his fictions, but his work has more recently drawn responses from philosophers themselves, addressing a wide range of issues. For example, in *J. M. Coetzee and Ethics: Philosophical Perspectives on Literature*, edited by Anton Leist and Peter Singer, Robert Pippin considers the question of power in the early fiction; Jonathan Lear considers communication in *Diary of a Bad Year*; Leist considers social organization; and Martin Woessner considers the problem of reason itself.[13]

However, although recent articles and studies continue to explore a range of subjects, the principal line pursued in philosophical responses to Coetzee's work has to date concerned human relations to and responsibility towards animals. These issues have been the focus of several prominent publications. These include an edition of *The Lives of Animals* with essays by Gutmann, Singer, and a number of other philosophers and critics; the collection *Philosophy and Animal Life*, which offers readings by Cora Diamond and Stanley Cavell; *The Death of the Animal: A Dialogue*, a volume conceived by Paola Cavalieri, whose contributors include Coetzee as well as Matthew Calarco, Harman Miller, and Cary Wolfe; and Stephen Mulhall's *The Wounded Animal*, a book-length study of *Elizabeth Costello* and *The Lives of Animals*.[14] These interventions have led, in turn, to a good deal of debate and secondary literature on the topic.

It is important to note, however, that while human/animal relations are the focus or point of departure in these texts, their authors often aim or arrive at questions of a more foundational nature. Diamond, for example, explains that what is at issue in *Elizabeth Costello* is not so much how the problem of human/animal relations might be solvable by philosophy, but rather whether philosophy is even capable of coming to terms with this issue in all its complexity, or with the horror that is induced when one looks squarely at the human treatment of animals. Cavell's response to Diamond likewise addresses the limitations on philosophical thinking. Both, in other words, express an anxiety about trying (and possibly failing) to find effective ways of confronting seemingly intractable problems.

With regards to human/animal relations, then, Coetzee's work raises two key questions: how might one adequately conceive the nature of these relations, and especially the horror of industrial exploitation of animals? And what are the innate capacities and limitations of philosophy? As such, Coetzee's challenge to philosophy might be set alongside his critique of other disciplinary formations, such as history in 'The Narrative of Jacobus Coetzee' or the kind of academic 'critical analysis' parodied in 'The Vietnam Project'. For, as these examples from *Dusklands* suggest, Coetzee's works have from the outset raised important (philosophical) questions about the embedded procedures of different disciplines – history, politics, philosophy, literary criticism – and about the understandings their approved forms of discourse allow, and those they disallow, ignore, or efface.

These questions in turn indicate Coetzee's ongoing interest in the capacities of language per se, which on the one hand offers a means of thinking, but on the other is something that might limit our capacity to think; either in the Whorfian sense (what we are able to think is largely determined by the language we use), or in the Foucauldian sense (discourses order and determine what it is possible to say). It is an interest that Coetzee has pursued through intensive reading in linguistics, semiotics, philosophy of language, and the structuralist and deconstructive theories that followed the 'linguistic turn' in mid twentieth-century philosophy. But what is especially striking is that Coetzee has never simply followed the received opinion of any one discipline. Rather, he has responded to problems by developing provocations, whose aim is not to provide neat answers to questions (such as 'what might an ethical human/animal relationship look like?'), but to bring to light what is excluded by the form of the question being asked.

More than being merely a loose way of describing a feature of Coetzee's works, *provocation* might be understood to characterize their method or approach. In general terms, philosophical discourse is built either upon induction from experience or experiment (*a posteriori*), or upon deduction from first principles (*a priori*) in the manner of mathematics, metaphysics, or logic. Induction works from the particular to the general, while deduction works from the general to the particular. In contrast, Coetzee underlines the importance of the *provocation* as the point from which his fictions start and towards which they tend. If you are arguing a priori you necessarily begin with a postulate, which either establishes or claims the firm ground from which arguments might be built or against which they might be tested. If you are working inductively, from experience or experiment a posteriori, you are establishing facts that will allow you to predict how materials behave. The provocation, on the other hand, makes you think either by questioning the value or condition of an assumed truth (or facts), or by requiring the creation of new truths adequate to the provocation.

One of Coetzee's key provocations is that fiction is capable of generating truths. This can be understood in two ways. First, Coetzee points us towards the idea that we inhabit 'fictions of the truth'; that is, we surround ourselves with stories, and these stories in large part construct the realities we live among. He articulates this line of thinking in *The Good Story* (2015), where he states: 'I believe most exchanges between human beings to be exchanges between projected fictions' (*GS*, 50); and also in the earlier volume *Giving Offense*:

> Affronts to the innocence of our children or to the dignity of our persons are attacks not upon our essential being but upon constructs – constructs by which we live, but constructs nevertheless ... The infringements are real; what is infringed, however, is not our essence but a foundational fiction to which we more or less wholeheartedly subscribe. (*GO*, 14)

The second way of understanding Coetzee's assertion of the truth-telling capacity of fiction is with regards to his claim that there is 'truth in fiction'. This is perhaps made most clearly in *Doubling the Point*:

> we should distinguish two kinds of truth, the first truth to fact, the second something beyond that; and that, in the present context, we should take truth to fact for granted and concentrate on the more vexing question of a 'higher' truth ...
>
> As you write ... you have to feel whether you are getting closer to 'it' or not ... Writing reveals to you what you wanted to say in the first place ...
>
> Writing, then, involves an interplay between the push into the future that takes you to the blank page in the first place, and a resistance ... Out of that interplay there emerges, if you are lucky, what you recognize or hope to recognize as the true. (*DP*, 17–18)

This claim is itself a provocation, which I attempt to unpack in greater detail elsewhere.[15] Here, however, I wish simply to note that claims to a truth status for literature and, indeed, a status for literature as a kind of thinking which might provide necessary insights into, for example, ethical concerns, are claims that bring literature into relation with philosophy. For one can confront such claims only in theoretical terms.

Notes

1. Bruce Jackson, 'Buffalo English: Literary Glory Days at UB', *Buffalo Beat*, February 1999. www.acsu.buffalo.edu/~bjackson/englishdept.htm

2. J. M. Coetzee, 'Record of Reading' (1970s–80s), CP 99.4.

3. J. M. Coetzee, *Dusklands*, 'Lies' second sketch for 'The Vietnam Project', handwritten draft (11 June 1972–13 February 1973), CP 1.1, 11 June 1972. I develop a fuller reading of *Dusklands* in relation to the archives in Anthony Uhlmann, '*Dusklands* and the Meaning of Method', *Textual Practice*, 30. 3 (2016), 399–415.

4. J. M. Coetzee, *Waiting for the Barbarians*, small spiral notebook [2] (30 August 1978–29 June 1979), CP 33.3, 20 September 1978.

5. J. M. Coetzee, *Life & Times of Michael K*, grey casebound notebook (1972–82), CP 33.5, 19 September 1981; 1 August 1982; J. H. Miller, 'The Critic as Host' in H. Bloom, P. de Man, J. Derrida, G. Hartman and J. H. Miller (eds.), *Deconstruction and Criticism* (New York: Seabury, 1979), pp. 217–53.

6. J. M. Coetzee, *Age of Iron*, small red notebook (June 1986–June 1988), CP 33.6, 1 December 1987.

7. J. M. Coetzee, 'The English Fiction of Samuel Beckett: An Essay in Stylistic Analysis', unpublished PhD dissertation, University of Texas at Austin (1969), pp. 156–7.

8. Ibid., p. 15.

9. Ibid., p. 5.

10. Paul Patton, 'Coetzee's Opinions' in Chris Danta, Sue Kossew and Julien Murphet, (eds.), *Strong Opinions: J. M. Coetzee and the Authority of Contemporary Fiction*, (London: Bloomsbury, 2011), pp. 53–62.

11. Peter Singer, 'Reflections' in Amy Gutman (ed.), *The Lives of Animals* (Princeton: Princeton University Press, 1999), pp. 85–92 (p. 86).

12. Friedrich Nietzsche, *The Birth of Tragedy out of the Spirit of Music*, trans. Shaun Whiteside, ed. Michael Tanner (London: Penguin, 1993), p. 69.

13. Anton Leist and Peter Singer (eds. and introd.), *J. M. Coetzee and Ethics: Philosophical Perspectives on Literature* (New York: Columbia University Press, 2010). See under Further Reading for individual chapters.

14. Stephen Mulhall, *The Wounded Animal: J. M. Coetzee and the Difficulty of Reality in Literature and Philosophy* (Princeton: Princeton University Press, 2009). Details of the other volumes I mention here can be found in Further Reading

15. Anthony Uhlmann, 'Process and Method in *Waiting for the Barbarians*', *Texas Studies in Literature and Language*, 58.4 (2016), 435–50.

13

ANDREW DEAN

Lives and Archives

Since the opening in 2013 of the J. M. Coetzee Papers at the Harry Ransom Center (HRC), scholars have been coming to Austin, Texas, from far and wide, and critical engagements with Coetzee's archive have proliferated. The newly available materials at the HRC dramatically expand on the thirty-two containers that had been on deposit at the Houghton Library at Harvard since 1995. Those materials, scarcely known about even among Coetzee scholars, were available only under relatively tight restrictions. Kai Easton, who heard about the papers through an 'offhand remark at a seminar', writes that in her 1998 trip to the Houghton there were no online records of the papers, and that even gaining access to them required 'some detective work'.[1] Today the papers are fully catalogued and very much available to researchers, comprising 153 containers and one gallery file, along with material restricted until after the deaths of both Coetzee and his partner, Dorothy Driver. The holdings are comprehensive, including manuscripts for the majority of the novels, business correspondence, scrapbooks, and research and teaching notes of all kinds.

Of special interest are the writing notebooks, which Coetzee used to record his doubts, hesitations, and insights throughout the composition of his novels. David Attwell puts these notebooks at the centre of his story of Coetzee's creative process. He shows, for example, how *Waiting for the Barbarians* (1980) was profoundly affected by Steve Biko's death at the hands of the South African security services, since it was this event that allowed Coetzee to transform early sketches into the novel that he wanted them to become. 'The novel's emergence', Attwell writes, 'took the form of a simultaneous, seemingly contradictory, two-way process: both a distancing ... and a homecoming into the violence of apartheid.' Here we see how the novel, which readers have long connected with apartheid, was the result of a conscience that was stricken by what white was doing to black in South Africa, albeit treated through Coetzee's 'psychological drama of displacement'.[2]

As this new archivally focused critical work aims to transform our understanding of Coetzee's writing, the provenance and nature of the papers upon which such scholarship is based have become a central concern. In this chapter I situate the archive in relation to Coetzee's published autobiographical texts, critical work, and writings on the themes of secrets and lies. I argue that the nature of Coetzee's long-standing explorations of archival themes in his fiction, placed alongside particular passages I draw from material that is now at the HRC, encourage critics to confront methodological questions about their own practices. Rather than presuming that the materials have arrived to us in some unmediated and unselfconscious way, we are encouraged to develop approaches that are commensurate with the challenges presented both by this author and the literary situation in which he writes. I ask, how may the Coetzee archive be read? What kind of truth are we seeking when we read his work (both published and archival)? What ends do archives achieve for writers themselves?

Coetzee has drawn from auto/biographical resources throughout his career. On 1 January 1970, he wrote in his clear longhand the first lines of what became his debut novel, *Dusklands* (1974): 'Among ~~those~~ the heroes who first ventured into the interior of Southern Africa and brought us back ~~the~~ news of what we had inherited ~~won~~, Jacobus Janszoon Coetzee has hitherto occupied an honorable but if minor place.'[3] Writing here in a name that both is and is not his own – these lines turn out in *Dusklands* to be authored by one 'S. J. Coetzee' and translated by 'J. M. Coetzee' – his composition, for the first time, could proceed. In later fictions, such as *Elizabeth Costello* (2003) and *Diary of a Bad Year* (2007), figures of the author ('Elizabeth Costello' and 'JC' respectively) seem to be responding to the demand that the public makes upon Coetzee that he enter into political discourse as a political voice. Looking back across his career, David Attwell in *Life of Writing* suggests that 'Coetzee's writing is a huge existential enterprise, grounded in fictionalized autobiography. In this enterprise the texts marked as autobiography are continuous with those marked as fiction – only the degree of fictionalization varies.'[4]

One claim is worth dispensing with immediately: Coetzee's auto/biographical practices are not atypical in this period. On the contrary, the dispersal of the subject in post-war writing, linked to 'postmodern' understandings of identity and the self, did not put an end to life-writing, but saw it transformed and even expanded in its creative possibilities. It is telling that Attwell refers to the influence of Roland Barthes's autobiographical writing on Coetzee. As Paul Eakin has argued, Barthes's work, often taken to be the paradigmatic instance of postmodern autobiography, in fact undertakes a process of 'concealment and display', simultaneously affirming and denying a relationship with the 'world of reference'.[5] Max Saunders argues that interactions of forms of 'auto/biography' and forms of fiction are central to modern literature in general, including what has become known as postmodernism. Specifically, he suggests that auto/biographical work in the period in which Coetzee was writing developed a 'meta' relationship with itself. This is 'meta-auto/biografiction': writing that relies on identifications between fiction and the self's *auto/biography* (as opposed simply to the self), and which, in so doing, both lays claim to a particular genre and calls attention to its constructedness.[6]

What *is* distinctive about Coetzee's auto/biographical practice, though, is the extent to which it is preoccupied with the archive itself. As Jan Wilm writes, Coetzee's work was from the outset impelled by 'archival dynamics'. Eugene Dawn, in 'The Vietnam Project', works in a library, and the text is structured such that it 'mimics an archiving of another text'. 'The Narrative of Jacobus Coetzee' parodies the treatment of archival documents, and is itself an archive, one in which historical manuscripts have been tampered with. Indeed, once one begins to look, archives are everywhere in Coetzee's writing: Wilm points out more or less direct examples, such as William Burchell's volume in the British Museum in *Youth* (2002) and the author's notebooks in *Summertime* (2009).[7] Coetzee has written in an autobiographical mode about his own encounter with an archive too. While a doctoral student at the University of Texas at Austin in the late 1960s, he consulted manuscripts of Samuel Beckett's *Watt* (1953). He has recalled the weeks he spent 'perusing' the manuscripts, 'pondering the sketches and numbers and doodles in the margins'. He became 'disconcerted', he writes, 'to find that the well-attested agony of composing a masterpiece had left no other traces than these flippancies' (*DP*, 51).

Like many of Coetzee's characters, and indeed like Coetzee himself, critics are finding that their encounters with archival materials carry an affective charge. Martin Woessner writes of discovering an author suddenly personalized. There is 'a magic' that 'still seemed to cling to the various notebooks, drafts, and clippings I felt and held', he explains.[8] Attwell recalls that the materials cast a 'spell' over him; the archive shows 'the remarkable ways' in which Coetzee has transformed 'quite ordinary materials into unforgettable fiction'.[9] It is perhaps no surprise that the author himself has a sense of all of this. In one notebook fragment in *Summertime*, the John character compares his work with that of the labour of building 'roads, walls, pylons'. The 'secret authors' of our built world achieve '[i]mmortality of a kind, a limited immortality'. This leads him to wonder why 'he persist[s] in inscribing marks on paper' – is it 'in the faint hope that people not yet born will take the trouble to decipher them?' The archive in Texas makes this 'faint hope' much more distinct: it too is a 'well-laid slab whose well-laidness is plain for all to see' (*Sum*, 7).

Part of what is so extraordinary about the materials stored at the HRC is the order and neatness of what is available for researchers, especially in comparison with other author archives. Professional cataloguing alone does not account for this – it is rather a consequence of the fact that Coetzee was his own first archivist, cataloguer, printer, and binder. There may indeed be some truth in the memory of John offered by one of the characters in *Summertime*, that 'he had missed his calling, that he should have been a librarian' (*Sum*, 212). Coetzee, for example, bound the nine drafts of *Life & Times of Michael K* (1983) by hand, transforming them into five covered volumes;[10] he also bound many other manuscripts with string, including the first draft of 'The Vietnam Project' from *Dusklands*. Coetzee's self-archiving in fact pre-dates his first novel. He kept scrapbooks of cuttings of articles or items of interest, including a number from the 1950s, and six volumes of clippings from the *Times Literary Supplement* spanning 1969–77. Carefully recorded research notes, records of reading, and so on, speak of a mind dedicated to this kind of industry.

Critics have argued that the legibility and completeness of the papers 'would have served the creative process'. Having these materials accessible and at hand, Attwell argues, allowed the author to 'move blocks of text around and to recover discarded fragments'.[11] This is no doubt true. Late in the drafting of *Foe* (1986), for example, when Coetzee was at a creative impasse, he mined his notebook ideas, creating a 'salvage' list in which he looked for inspiration among his otherwise discarded or forgotten thoughts on the novel, dating back to 1982. In 1975, working on *In the Heart of the Country* (1977), Coetzee collected twenty-four previous notebook entries, with the comment, 'The following notes may be useful.'[12] There are many other examples of similar practices.

Yet the very excessiveness of Coetzee's self-archiving suggests that his papers are not a mere precursor to the published works. Rather, they serve some independent function for him. As in *Summertime*, it is tempting to see the bound pages of drafts, the carefully ordered notebooks, and the other material, as part of a bid for '[i]mmortality of a kind, a limited immortality'. Coetzee's papers are now housed in perpetuity at the HRC, after all, along-side those of many other major writers. They can be called up after reading some of Beckett's papers, for example, and the doodles and hesitations of the manuscripts of *Watt* compared with the moments of struggle and resolution in the manuscripts of *Foe*. Readers of the archive now inevitably participate in this bid: working through the materials, developing articles and mono-graphs based on the archives, contemporary critics guarantee Coetzee a certain kind of immortality (limited though it may be). As a salaried literary critic, Coetzee has long been aware both of the potential value of archival remains for scholars, and of the nature of work they would have to undertake. His career too has unfolded within one of the institutions – academia – principally responsible for preserving, sponsoring, and disseminating manuscripts and research. It is no surprise, then, that what he calls his 'marks on paper' have proven especially amenable to and generative of further cataloguing, preservation, and scholarly labour.

As we have already begun to observe, Coetzee is self-conscious in his published writing about the ways in which an author's supposedly hidden 'marks' may serve his own emotional needs. Yet it is another example, from *Youth*, which stands out for how it connects personal papers, an author's biographical life, and the conditions of possibility for writing itself. In one passage, John's diary is discovered by his girlfriend of the moment, Jacqueline. Reading his hostile comments about her, she decides to end their relationship. The narrator, inhabiting John's thoughts, wonders:

> Is he sorry? Certainly he is sorry Jacqueline read what she read. But the real question is, what was his motive for writing what he wrote? Did he perhaps write it in order that she should read it? Was leaving his true thoughts lying around where she was bound to find them his way of telling her what he was too cowardly to say to her face? (*Y*, 9)

Here, his apparently secret papers might have been created to serve an ignoble end – the suggestion is that they might always have been intended to be made public. This leads John to reflect that the 'question of what should be permitted to go into his diary and what kept forever shrouded goes to the heart of all his writing' (*Y*, 9). These reflections are given an extra piquancy in this work of *autre*biography, a work which establishes a distance between the protagonist ('he') and the autobiographer. The reflections have the feeling, that is, of a theoretical exploration of what we are reading: what 'he' is revealing in *Youth* is that which need *not* be forever shrouded, what is permitted to be revealed. Those looking for the private truth of an 'I', the suggestion goes, are going to be disappointed.

This episode in *Youth* further parallels an early draft of 'The Vietnam Project', dating from the beginning of Coetzee's writing career. The composition and use of this work show that the questions 'he' asks in the later *autre*biography had emerged in Coetzee's own writing and life. Labelled on the front of the manuscript as 'Discarded First sketch for The Vietnam Project', this early draft was composed between 11 and 25 May 1972. It comprises a dialogue in seven parts between a 'Mrs C.' and a counsellor. The dialogue centres on Mrs C.'s unhappy marriage to Mr C., who has recently told his wife of an extra-marital affair. At first, Mrs C. explains, her husband 'wanted us to be friends . . ., this other woman and me':

> He was always pushing for that. I was terribly jealous, I was quite sick with jealousy, I can see that now. I used to follow him when he went to see her, I wouldn't let him out of my sight. Then he stopped trying to shake me off and took me with him. So we all sat around in his girl-friend's apartment, all being very polite. Then he wanted to go to bed with us, both of us.[13]

In the final section of the draft, Mrs C. brings her husband's diary to her session with the counsellor. The counsellor asks whether he has Mr C.'s 'authorization to read this', to which she responds, '[n]ot officially'. This begins a conversation between them about privacy and reading diaries: the counsellor tells Mrs C. that what happens between her and her husband is her 'own affair', and that he does not wish to 'interfere in domestic affairs'. Mrs C. responds that the counsellor is already involved in such matters – 'you are a presence in the home and we're both very much aware of you all the time' – before asserting that she did not take the diary 'without his knowledge'. She explains:

> He knows that I read it. That is one of his ways of keeping control of me. The big lie is that his diary is private. But I read it and he knows that I read it. So if he wants to tell me a lie, all he does is to write it in his diary. Or if he wants to hurt me. For instance, there are all kinds of things there about him and his girlfriend. Officially I don't read it, so officially I don't know about it, so he needn't accept responsibility for hurting me.

Mrs C. compares reading the diary to 'reading pornography' – 'suddenly you're at the dirty bit, at the secret of the diary' – and she and the counsellor further discuss the ethics of reading such materials.[14] As in Youth, supposedly personal papers are used here both to tell and not to tell intimate partners hurtful things; in both the draft and the published autrebiography the diary form itself provides an alibi. And, reading now in the terms of what is housed at the HRC, insofar as it reveals the potentially hurtful elements of Coetzee's own writing, the archive too contains its own alibi: it is both what should not be seen and what inevitably will be seen, hidden from critics and readers, but also in plain sight.

For critics, the draft returns us to the status of the archive itself, and particularly to the nature of Coetzee's understandings and anticipations of its likely readers. This sense is developed by the draft's own transmission history. It was held back from the Houghton, where the material for Dusklands had otherwise been put on deposit; the bound manuscript is now located in container thirty-three, the first of the container series that is new to scholars at the HRC. One possible explanation for this delay is that Coetzee was using elements of it for the passage in *Youth* in which Jacqueline finds the diary. Another is that he was protecting reputations. Whatever the case, when reading it we are confronted with our situation as readers. What Mr C. has decided to hide and display will achieve particular ends. Wilm suggests that since 'the archive as a trope, as a figure, as a phenomenon, both narrated and reflected, is part of Coetzee's fictional world, readers and scholars working with the Coetzee Papers are asked to reflect on the status of his archive'.[15] This first sketch of 'The Vietnam Project' and its history of preservation and transmission certainly corroborate the need for this kind of reflection, but also suggest that it must involve at least some degree of wariness. The archival materials are always in some sense self-conscious, and there is no simple way for us to get past Coetzee to the truth of the archive. Ours is not a task of opening tombs and finding the bodies within (and even if it were, what kind of truth is a corpse?), but rather one of reading the signs of history and composition.

This example represents, albeit at a high pressure, the more general difficulty for critics handling the archives of living authors. In an era when the university is playing an ever-greater role in literary reception (not to mention production), we must now confront how academic critical labours participate in the literary field. John Bolin, in his review of *J. M. Coetzee and the Life of Writing*, finds that Attwell 'never truly confronts the methodological questions that are only becoming more pressing for archival scholars in an age when (famous) writers, at some stage, begin to consider that their papers will be read'. Bolin suggests that readers will eventually be 'forced to extend and invert the kinds of questions Attwell poses' if they are to come to grips with Coetzee's 'grey canon' (works that do not belong to the published oeuvre, but which are now becoming part of the recognized corpus of writing). Beginning this project would involve asking not how Coetzee's published writing is autobiographical, as Attwell does in *Life of Writing*, but rather, according to Bolin, 'how closely related are the voices in his notebooks to the selves who emerge from and disappear in the pages of his books'.[16]

Coetzee's own writings on secrets and lies in autobiographical discourse allow us to further develop Bolin's sense that Coetzee's archive challenges the usual methodologies, derived from biographical and genetic traditions, which critics use to approach such materials. In *Youth*, Coetzee makes two suggestions about the relationship between writing and life: the first is that what appears to be personal may have been created for other peoples' eyes, to achieve particular ends. The second is that there may be no such thing as truly personal or at least private writing anyway. Instead, writing is always in some way public. This second point is certainly true of the period in which Coetzee has been working: there are any number of institutions which will make 'private' writing public, including the research university with its staff of literary critics, the endowed archive, and publishers. Nevertheless, he suggests that there will always be secrets that such institutions cannot contain or transmit.

There are reflections on the nature of the *true* secret throughout Coetzee's published writing – beyond the episode of the diary, the topic of what is not being said or cannot be said emerges with notable frequency. In *Boyhood* (1997) 'he' holds his school life as a 'tight secret' from his mother (*B*, 5). His preference for the Russians over the Americans in the Cold War 'is a secret so dark that he can reveal it to no one'; he soon reflects that '[w]hatever he wants, whatever he likes, has sooner or later to be turned into a secret' (*B*, 26, 28). Even cricket is part of his hidden world, as 'the secret that he manages to cover up elsewhere is relentlessly probed and exposed' while he is batting (*B*, 54). In *Youth*, the young John tells bafflingly inconsequential lies. At the Poetry Society, he is asked his age: '"Twenty-one," he says. It is a lie: he is twenty-two.' His many difficult sexual liaisons cause him to wish that he could 'put the whole shameful business behind him, close the book on it' (*Y*, 73, 130). In *Summertime*, the right of John to be protected from 'academic newshound[s]' seeking to 'get some dirt on him' is a recurring concern, while Vincent's various interlocutors also have their own secrets to hide (*Sum*, 35). In the volume of exchanges with psychologist Arabella Kurtz, *The Good Story* (2015), Coetzee wonders whether the return of the repressed predisposes us to presume that secrets always come back. It may be, he says, that the 'true secret, the inadmissible secret, the secret about secrets, is that secrets can indeed be buried and we can indeed live happily ever after' (*GS*, 34). Of course, these suggestions about secrets are at odds with his practice of self-archiving: they imply that there is another order of secrets, one which can never be displayed.

Coetzee explores secrets more fully in his literary criticism, arguing that some may be impossible to tell in autobiography. In his inaugural professorial lecture at the University of Cape Town in 1984, published as *Truth in Autobiography*, he focuses on secrets and desire in Rousseau's *Confessions* (1782–9).[17] Shameful desires are valuable for Rousseau in the 'economy of confession', Coetzee argues, as 'every secret or shameful appetite' becomes 'confessable currency'. There is ultimately a convention of blindness in autobiography: by storing up shameful desires – the apparent truth of oneself – as assets in the economy of confession, Rousseau ensures that desires cannot be told (or 'spent'). This is not because these desires 'lie too close to the autobiographer's heart but because they lie too close to his art'. Holding onto his 'mysterious contradictions', Rousseau is free to write – but 'take away the last veil' and 'no further confession is necessary.' *Truth in Autobiography* suggests that truth for the autobiographer primarily serves a narrative function, helping him to 'get from point A to point B in the text'; the absolute truth, whatever that may be, cannot enter into the discourse, as it is not commensurate with writing.[18]

As truth becomes something *of* the narrative, rather than something existing prior to it, the task of the critic working with the materials of Coetzee's life is unsettled. It is not merely that questions of fidelity – 'is this true of the author's life?' – become irrelevant, pitched as they are at an order of truth that cannot enter writing, but also that criticism faces its own otherwise unacknowledged conditions of truth-making. In the conclusion of *Truth in Autobiography*, Coetzee asks: 'have I not, in unveiling what I seem to be claiming to be the secret of the economy of Rousseau's *Confessions*, broken the very pact I have been talking about?' In short, as the critic, Coetzee has been claiming to be able to see what Rousseau cannot, and he has been doing so under the aegis of the distinct enterprise, with its own registers and protocols, known as literary criticism. But does that not mean that criticism is 'the only mode in which final truths can be told'? Just as with Rousseau the autobiographer, Coetzee the critic decides that if he is to continue he must keep his answer in reserve. To 'tell the truth of literature' that literature does not know, he concludes, would be to 'tell a truth that criticism cannot afford to tell', namely 'why it needs literature'. Instead of speaking this impossible truth, he simply calls the whole enterprise to a halt. 'The present discourse has gone on', he says, 'now it stops'.[19]

In his various accounts of his own writing practice, Coetzee reflects that he is motivated by a *narrative* understanding of truth. This is the case not just of autobiographical writing, he proposes, but also of all writing properly considered – including all that is now contained in the archive. In *Doubling the Point* (1992), Coetzee argues that truth is discovered in the act of composition itself:

> This massive autobiographical writing-enterprise that fills a life, this enterprise of self-construction ... – does it yield only fictions? Or rather, among the fictions of the self, the versions of the self, that it yields, are there any that are truer than others? How do I know when I have the truth about myself? ...
>
> As you write – I am speaking of any kind of writing – you have a feel of whether you are getting close to 'it' or not. You have a sensing mechanism, a feedback loop of some kind; without that mechanism you could not write ... Writing reveals to you what you wanted to say in the first place ...
>
> I don't see that 'straight' autobiographical writing is any different *in kind* from what I have been describing. Truth is something that comes in the process of writing, or comes from the process of writing.
>
> (*DP*, 17–18. Italics in the original)

The central question of all writing, in this view, is one of truth. Specifically, it is the question of the particular truth of the writing's self, a truth that has been created in the gambit that is writing, the getting from A to B. Feeling one's way toward this truth is what makes enterprises of self-construction in writing something other than a series of groundless fictions. In this process of writing, he continues, the self is written – 'writing writes us' (DP, 18).

In these reflections on what kind of truth motivates and is produced by writing, and what kind of truth criticism can access, Coetzee is thinking about the very questions of critical method that are now emerging in the treatment of his archival materials. Yet he is also rendering strange such terms as 'personal' and 'impersonal', which become mere secondary functions of writing. Refusing both Attwell's and Bolin's approaches – ones centred on the composition and development of works, or on reading the notebooks against the novels and autrebiographies – he focuses on the experiences and subjects that are created in the texts themselves.

Such a desire to move away from predetermined critical paradigms certainly reflects a pressurized moment in the history of Coetzee's reception. In the 1980s, alongside celebrations of his fiction, there was also some criticism of Coetzee's apparent failure to write works that were committed in the right way to the struggle against apartheid. Nadine Gordimer famously claimed in her review of Life & Times of Michael K that Coetzee's 'heroes are those who ignore history, not make it'; which is a 'challengingly controversial position for a writer to take up in South Africa'.[20] This review, in particular, stung Coetzee. (In notebook entries from immediately afterward, he wrote with distaste, 'They want my books to be-about. Specifically, to be-about South Africa, about social relations in that country.'[21]) His public response in 'The Novel Today', an address given at the Cape Town Book Week in 1987, was to call into question a mode of reading in which 'the novelistic text becomes a kind of historical text, an historical text with a truth-value that requires a fairly sophisticated mode of interpretation'.[22]

At the same time, though, Coetzee's reservations also draw on his own enduring efforts to think about critical method. Simply put, he is not certain that the process by which the critic converts the author's words from one discourse into another gives access to truths intimate to the author. It is a function of rhetoric for truths to feel intimate, but there is ultimately an order of truth not containable within the discourse of criticism as it stands. In this view, criticism as the attempt to draw off the last veil is misguided: as he says in Doubling the Point, 'in the act of triumphantly tearing the clothes off its subject and displaying the nakedness beneath –"Behold the truth!" – [literary criticism] exposes a naïveté of its own' (DP, 106). The situation of biographical criticism – hunting out the diary entry, letter, or manuscript note that will reveal it all – is merely another version of the same problem, the pursuit of an impossible and inaccessible truth.

Faced with such scepticism toward the way literary criticism *in general* handles literary texts, Coetzee has attempted to develop alternatives. In his essay on Erasmus's *The Praise of Folly*, he advocates (if it makes sense to speak in such terms) reading from a position of 'weakness', an 'evasive (non)position inside/outside the play' (*GO*, 103). This is the logical end-point of Coetzee's thinking about truth in autobiography, truth in criticism, and even truth in writing: refusing to evaluate writing by standards that are determined in advance, by what he elsewhere calls the 'rather tight discourse of criticism itself', he instead imagines criticism that is simultaneous with reading, just as truth and the self are simultaneous with composition (*DP*, 246). The *experience* itself, the getting from A to B in a text, with all of its affective loading, is what matters for the critic. Wilm takes up such a challenge in the context of the archive. Rather than reading the published works as a 'surface that needs to be looked through so as to get a glimpse at the archival depths, the hidden truths', Wilm borrows from Hans Magnus Enzensberger to argue for the archive as a 'compost heap' – one that simultaneously contains 'decomposing rubbish' and 'productive humus'.[23]

Yet if we were to read both inside and outside the play would we be giving up the autonomy of the discipline – a discipline which privileges the language and tradition of reason – in which we are engaged? It is certainly the case that Coetzee limits the authority of criticism in favour of litera-ture. The archive as it is now used by critics functions in a remarkably similar way, as a source of authority that is not determined in advance by the critical enterprise, but rather by the author himself and the institutions which he allows to mediate his work. Coetzee (again) recognizes that reading in a non-critical way may be impossible. In a comic moment, the John character in *Summertime* asks to play a Schubert cassette while he and his lover have sex. The attempt to make the meaning of the music simultaneous with its experience, to circumvent the rather tight discourse of musical appreciation, perhaps, is ultimately a failure. His lover is not moved by the history of feelings John believes contained in the music, and the two of them remain in the grips of the rather tawdrier order of truth associated with this world (*Sum*, 68–70). The suggestion is that the version of the critical enterprise that 'John' has imagined – a version grounded in aesthetic experience – cannot be converted into a methodology in any positive sense.

As Coetzee's career has developed, the extent to which his writing is invigorated by questions of life and life-writing has only become clearer.

His papers at the HRC, the 2012 Kannemeyer biography, and the autobiographical trilogy have all focused attention on these elements. Critics have further emphasized that Coetzee is always, and has always been, an archival writer. The research emerging out of encounters with the archive is no doubt producing new insights – we can now see more clearly certain of the situations out which his writing has emerged. Yet, even as more materials become available, problems of critical method have only become more pressing. In light of Coetzee's own writing, and of what is in the archive, the traditions through which archives are generally handled, auto/biographical archives in particular, must now be brought into the debates about reading methods which have again returned to the centre of literary studies.

These debates have revolved especially around the value of critique. In particular, Rita Felski and others have argued that moving beyond critique, and away from a 'hermeneutics of suspicion', might allow us to make better account of our enduring attachments to literary texts. Yet I suggest that reading which is more clearly grounded in institutions, as well as sensitive to questions of form, would allow critics to evaluate Coetzee's archive with an eye toward both the particular literary and material situations out of which they have emerged and the nature of the texts themselves. This does not mean either suspicion or enchantment, but rather a critical practice grounded in particular literary environments, including our own, as critics whose future labours are inscribed in advance in the modern literary archive. To do otherwise is to risk insularity, especially in the context of an academy very much smitten with Coetzee's interventions into everything from social politics to the relationship between humans and animals.

In making these remarks, I am suggesting that interpretation, as opposed to historical description or excavation, must remain the primary focus of studies of Coetzee. The most compelling criticisms of his writing are still those that were published before the archive became available in its present form. While some of what is housed at the HRC may call into question elements of Derek Attridge's thinking, it is in fact by demoting historical and contextualist approaches to the novels that *J. M. Coetzee and the Ethics of Reading* (2004) is able to sustain its powerful and sensitive readings of Coetzee's fiction. The risk with the archive is that it will move critics away from such richly speculative responses to powerful writing, and draw scholars instead into a labyrinth of authorial motivation and biographical resonance. There may be certain intellectual satisfactions with such endeavours, but they ultimately do not respond to what has motivated the scholarship in the first place: the public and private significance of the fictions.

Notes

1. See Kai Easton, 'Coetzee, the Cape and the Question of History', *Scrutiny2*, 11.1 (2006), 5–21 (p. 10).
2. David Attwell, *J. M. Coetzee and the Life of Writing: Face to Face with Time* (Oxford: Oxford University Press, 2015), pp. 113–15.
3. Qtd. in Attwell, *Life of Writing*, p. 51.
4. Ibid., p. 26.
5. Paul John Eakin, *Touching the World: Reference in Autobiography* (Oxford: Princeton University Press, 1992), p. 23.
6. See Max Saunders, *Self Impression: Life-Writing, Autobiografiction, and the Forms of Modern Literature* (Oxford: Oxford University Press, 2010), pp. 484–99.
7. Jan Wilm, 'The J. M. Coetzee Archive and the Archive in J. M. Coetzee' in Jan Wilm and Patrick Hayes (eds.), *Beyond the Ancient Quarrel: Literature, Philosophy, and J. M. Coetzee* (Oxford: Oxford University Press, 2017), pp. 215–31, 225–7.
8. Martin Woessner, 'The Writing of Life', *Los Angeles Review of Books*, 17 April 2016 <https://lareviewofbooks.org/article/the-writing-of-life/>.
9. Attwell, *Life of Writing*, 18.
10. Molly Schwartzburg, 'A Glimpse into J. M. Coetzee's Bound Drafts: *Life & Times of Michael K*', *Cultural Compass*, 2011 <http://blog.hrc.utexas.edu/2011/10/10/a-glimpse-into-j-m-coetzees-bound-drafts-life-times-of-michael-k/>.
11. Attwell, *Life of Writing*, p. 20.
12. J. M. Coetzee, *In the Heart of the Country*, small notebook (16 March 1974 – 9 February 1976), CP 33.3, 8 October 1975.
13. J. M. Coetzee, *Dusklands*, 'Discarded First sketch of Vietnam Project', handwritten draft (11–27 May 1972), CP 33.2, 11 May 1972.
14. Ibid., 19 May 1972.
15. Wilm, 'The Coetzee Archive', p. 231.
16. John Bolin, Review of '*J.M. Coetzee and the Life of Writing: Face to Face with Time*', *Review of English Studies*, 67.281 (2016), 824–6 (p. 826).
17. *Truth in Autobiography* explores many of the points of the much longer essay, 'Confession and Double Thoughts: Tolstoy, Rousseau, Dostoevsky' (1985).
18. J. M. Coetzee, *Truth in Autobiography* (Cape Town: University of Cape Town, 1984), pp. 3–5.
19. Ibid., pp. 5–6.
20. Nadine Gordimer, 'The Idea of Gardening', *The New York Review of Books*, 2 February 1984, 3–6, (p. 3, p. 6).
21. J. M. Coetzee, *Foe*, green casebound notebook with gilt edges (1982–5), CP 33.6, 17 March 1984. For a more detailed analysis of this period and Coetzee's responses, see my chapter, 'Double Thoughts: Coetzee and the Philosophy of Literary Criticism' in Patrick Hayes and Jan Wilm (eds.), *Beyond the Ancient Quarrel: Literature, Philosophy, and J. M. Coetzee* (Oxford University Press, 2017), pp. 52–69.
22. J. M. Coetzee, 'The Novel Today', *Upstream*, 6.1 (1988), 2–5 (p. 2).
23. Wilm, 'The Coetzee Archive', p. 221.

14

ANDREW VAN DER VLIES

Publics and Personas

Few in attendance at the 2003 Nobel Prize banquet, held in Stockholm's City Hall on 10 December that year, could have expected Literature Laureate J. M. Coetzee to deliver the speech that he did. His Nobel Lecture, delivered three days earlier, had, as David Attwell comments, 'done little to mend a reputation for reserve and severity'.[1] On that occasion Coetzee had read not a lecture, but a story, 'He and His Man', in which 'He' appeared to be Robinson Crusoe and 'His Man' a version of Daniel Defoe. Dinner guests might have expected something similarly severe. What they heard instead, a moving reflection on what the prize might have meant to his mother, was indeed unusual, though for its disarmingly emotional tone:

> And for whom, anyway, do we do the things that lead to Nobel Prizes if not for our mothers?
>
> 'Mommy, mommy, I won a prize!'
>
> 'That's wonderful, my dear. Now eat your carrots before they get cold.'
>
> Why must our mothers be ninety-nine and long in the grave before we can come running home with the prize that will make up for all the trouble we have been to them?[2]

There was 'a conspicuous reaching for tissues' around the hall, Attwell reports.[3]

The exchange between mother and child staged imaginatively here is useful for understanding what we might call Coetzee's approach to the problem – if not the paradox – of cultural capital. This, in broad terms, and in relation to multiple publics and institutions of publication and reception, is the subject of this chapter. In Coetzee's speech, the parent encourages modesty (*don't rest on your laurels; pay attention to the everyday business of life*), but she also models circumspection about any external authority's power to adjudicate merit. Such healthy scepticism characterizes the manner in which Coetzee himself, with a few no less exemplary exceptions, has responded at occasions requiring him to perform in person – *in propria persona*, as it were – rather than through his fiction. His oft-remarked-upon reputation for reserve and severity arises in part from a refusal to behave as expected. Consider, for example, how those interviews in which lengthy questions about the meaning or political implications of the fiction meet with excruciatingly brief retorts attest to impatience with attempts to force writing to recognize structures of validation extrinsic to itself. In a June 1988 letter, preserved in the Coetzee Papers at the Harry Ransom Center in Texas, answering fan-mail from a reader in Cleveland, Ohio, Coetzee wrote: 'I appreciate your comments on my novels. I am tired of hearing them discussed as political statements dressed up as fiction; it is a relief to find that at least one reader reads them as they were written: as accounts of the possible lives of possible people.'[4]

We might say indeed that Coetzee has repeatedly and in sustained fashion sought to disrupt the terms under which cultural capital accrues, what James English, drawing on Pierre Bourdieu's elaboration of the idea of a 'field' in which relations of value are negotiated, calls its 'general economy of practices'. 'Every field (by virtue of its recognition *as* a field) is possessed of its own forms of capital', English explains; its 'boundaries and constraints' involve participants with vested interests, and with differential access to varied kinds of capital, in a 'struggle for power to produce value, which means power to confer value on that which does not intrinsically possess it'.[5] Coetzee's questioning of the rules by which the field operates has taken the form either of conscious foregrounding of the terms by which institutions presume to ascribe value according to extrinsic criteria (for instance, service to an idea of the state, human rights, or even merely taste), or of speaking in an unexpected register (as at the Nobel banquet). In 1978, for example, accepting South Africa's then-premier literary award, the CNA prize, for *In the Heart of the Country*, he reminded dinner guests that not all of the country's literary production could even be considered for such awards in the reigning climate of censorship. While the prize was an honour, another recent 'distinction' had, he noted, been 'no less important': 'a poem of mine, along with other poems in the journal *Staffrider*, has been found an undesirable publication, and banned'.[6] *You think this is the 'best' work published in English or Afrikaans this year*, we might understand him to be saying here, *but what do you mean by 'published'? What is it that you haven't even been* allowed *to read?*

Then there are those occasions on which Coetzee's response to invitations to appear in the role of public intellectual has been to read a story in which a proxy author-character negotiates similar occasions and pressures. *Elizabeth Costello* (2003) started life as a series of such fictions, in which the eponymous author-character delivers lectures on – or grapples privately with the difficulty of holding positions about – such sensitive issues as industrial farming, the value of art, even the capacity of language to communicate.[7] Explaining Costello's origins, Coetzee noted in preliminary remarks in Mexico City in 1998, before a reading of what was to become another of her 'lessons', 'The Novel in Africa', that while he initially complied with invitations 'to all corners of the globe to give lectures', he had grown to find them 'a waste of time, of my time and of my auditors' time', and had begun to 'tell stories' instead; 'it has been better ever since'.[8]

A more serious temperamental reason for Coetzee's unease at performing his own positions in public is intimated in comments made in explanation of the origins of another of *Elizabeth Costello*'s lessons, 'At the Gate', to an audience at the University of Oklahoma, in 2003. Some years previously, on the final day of a colloquium in Rome, he had, he explained, found himself unable to respond to a demand that participants 'speak about what they believed'. While the Italians, familiar with an ancient rhetorical tradition, had no difficulty complying,

> [f]or people like myself ... with our chilly north-European, Protestant inheritance, suspicious of rhetoric, suspicious of fluency in any guise, doubtful that it is possible to tell the truth without endless self-scrutiny, self-interrogation, revision after revision, the occasion was impossible. With as much grace as I could muster, I bowed out.
>
> But, being a conscientious Protestant, and therefore full of guilt about unfulfilled obligations, I continued to mull over the question: not the question of what I believed in but the question of how to act, what to say, when you are hauled before the bar, which you certainly will be, and told to present your case.[9]

In an essay first published in 1992 and later included in the collection *Giving Offense* (1996), Coetzee had written about a related desire to escape categorical positions, given expression by the Renaissance humanist Desiderius Erasmus, who attempted, in his 1509 work *In Praise of Folly*, to steer between the poles represented by the Papacy and Luther. Erasmus was in sympathy with the Protestant reformers, Coetzee explained, and yet remained 'disturbed' by their 'intolerance and inflexibility'. Finding rivalry uncongenial, he had instead explored 'the possibility of a position ... not simply impartial between the rivals but also, by self-definition, off the stage of rivalry altogether, a *non*position' (*GO*, 83–4. Italics original).

The attractions of a similar strategy in the cultural minefield of late-apartheid South Africa were strong, though their possibilities revealed themselves to Coetzee only after several bruising contests in the public sphere during the most polarized years of the middle and late 1980s, in which he sought to cast the literary as more directly opposed – as *other* – to the instrumentalist discourses of politics, or, as he put it, the narrative of history. We see this most clearly in a lecture, 'The Novel Today', delivered at a book festival sponsored by the anti-apartheid *Weekly Mail* newspaper in late 1987 and published in the small South African journal *Upstream* in 1988. Coetzee argued that the polarized politics of that moment – with apartheid ideologues on one side, the anti-apartheid movement (with its distaste for writing not overtly engaged with the repressive conditions in the country) on the other – invariably cast the literary only as 'supplementary' to other kinds of factual (or counterfactual) narrative, as evidence for or against ideologically inflected representations of then pertaining circumstances.[10] 'In the position I am calling into question, then, the novelistic text becomes a kind of historical text . . . with a truth-value', he wrote; in such an atmosphere, fiction was forced into a position either of 'supplementarity or rivalry'.[11]

A version of this construction is implicit, too, in Coetzee's denunciation of the withdrawal of an invitation to Salman Rushdie to appear at the same festival a year later. Both authors had been billed to appear at an event in Cape Town on 31 October 1988, barely a month after Rushdie's novel *The Satanic Verses* had been published; it was already eliciting condemnation from Muslim communities around the world, although the *fatwa* had not yet issued from the Iranian Ayatollah. When the scale of the objections to Rushdie's appearance raised by representatives of South African Muslim organizations (none of whom had read the novel) became clear, the Congress of South African Writers (COSAW) tried to broker an agreement that would recognize a religious community's right to protest the author's work but nonetheless allow him to attend the festival. It soon appeared, however, that Rushdie's safety could not be guaranteed, and his invitation was withdrawn. Coetzee delivered a stinging critique of this decision from the stage, accusing the organizers of complicity with religious fundamentalism.[12] Nadine Gordimer had acted as a representative for COSAW in the off-stage deliberations, and in consequence the press seized gleefully on what it cast as a bust-up between South Africa's most acclaimed novelists, a characterization that a trail of letters between Gordimer and Coetzee, preserved in the archive, suggests each regarded as deeply regrettable. Attempting to engage with the language of politics, with its absolute positions and strategic impatience with nuance, had produced little but misunderstanding and bad feeling. Coetzee's later elaboration of the possibilities of the non-position suggests a serious attempt to revisit and reconsider some of his earlier constructions. It is worth noting that he has never given permission for 'The Novel Today' to be republished. Similarly, while the text of his denunciation of the treatment of Rushdie is reproduced (in an endnote) in J. C. Kannemeyer's authorized biography, it has never appeared under Coetzee's own name.

A non-position, however, is always susceptible to becoming a position itself, even if its power lies precisely in what Coetzee calls 'its jocoserious abnegation of big-phallus status, its evasive (non)position inside/outside the play' (*GO*, 103). If the disruptive humour at the heart of these negotiations is not always clear, however, in Elizabeth Costello's sub-scription to the idea that '[u]nbelief is a belief' (*EC*, 201), it is certainly more in evidence in *Diary of a Bad Year* (2007). There we witness the bathetic misadventures of a novelist who, while writing a series of 'Strong Opinions' commissioned by his publisher, discovers the difficul-ties of attempting to maintain a distinction between a future public (textual) performance of those opinions and a private life, a non-position that is at odds with the public expectation that authors believe certain things strongly, and express themselves categorically. *Diary of a Bad Year*'s 'Soft Opinions' undercut the strong, and two other narra-tives unfolding simultaneously (in sections that have their own space on each page) cast the public position-takings as sometimes pompous, hubristic, or offered in bad faith.

Coetzee's Nobel Lecture stages a double reversal, so to speak, that attempts a comparable unsettling of public and private, figuring in fiction a 'real' character (from another author's fiction) who becomes 'author'; this is a different kind of (metafictional) non-position. In an anecdote framing the lecture's delivery, Coetzee recounted his own confusion on discovering, aged ten, that someone called Daniel Defoe had written *Robinson Crusoe*, that the information on the text's famous original frontispiece that Crusoe's 'life and surprising strange adventures' was 'written by himself' was, in fact, a fiction.[13] Coetzee's point was surely to indicate not the way in which a particular author produces a fiction, but rather how a fiction comes to author a persona of the author, the construct named by what is in essence a label, in this case 'J. M. Coetzee', and that is not quite the same as the flesh-and-blood human being (John Maxwell Coetzee). Such slippage is always at play in those instances in which some variant of the author's name features in the work: the numerous Coetzees in *Dusklands* (1974); JC in *Diary of a Bad Year*; 'John' in the part-fictionalized memoir-project *Scenes from Provincial Life* (2011), whose volumes, following 'J. M. Coetzee's' own claim that all autobiography is necessarily the writing of the other one can only speculate one might once have been, have come to be called the *autre*biographies (*DP*, 391–5). There is a 'John' in *Age of Iron* (1990), too, a *nom de guerre* for a young opponent of the apartheid regime, and another 'John', Elizabeth's son, embattled in a different sense, in several of the Costello fictions. There are also writer or author figures in others of the books, most notably *The Master of Petersburg* (1994) and *Foe* (1986). Thus the play on and with questions of authorship, the personas so instantiated, and the demands of their publics, is everywhere performed and at stake.

The body of work collected under the label 'J. M. Coetzee' indeed offers an uncommonly nuanced case study of the operation, though perhaps also the limits, of what Michel Foucault, in 'What is an Author?' (1969), called the 'author function'. The author's name, Foucault argued, has a 'classificatory function' that ascribes ownership to a defined body of work (an oeuvre), delimiting the proliferation of meanings intrinsic to writing as *écriture*.[14] Quoting Samuel Beckett, Foucault suggests that the author function is central to the question 'What does it matter who is speaking?'[15] In 1970, the year Foucault delivered the text of this essay as a lecture in the United States, Coetzee wrote, as if in echo (or answer), in 'The Comedy of Point of View in Beckett's *Murphy*':

> As author, Beckett (or 'Beckett') lends his authority to these sentences by printing them under his name; he also delegates this authority to his narrator, who on occasion delegates it in turn to various of the characters. He accomplishes this last by quoting their words (dialogue) or by retiring from the page and allowing them to take over his narrative authority . . .
>
> Sometimes, however, what poses as a problem for the reader of choosing rationally among authorities may be a false problem, a problem designed to yield no solution, or only arbitrary solutions. (*DP*, 31)

Choosing rationally among authorities, a choice that is crucial not only for meaning but also for the determination of value, is likewise a problem for writer- and reader-figures throughout Coetzee's work. Nearly every text restages such paradoxes and problems – for instance in the contest between the magistrate and the Empire in *Waiting for the Barbarians* (1980), in the framing of Mrs Curren's dilemma about the efficacy of the humanist tradition in *Age of Iron*, in Dostoevsky's encounters with the police and with Nechaev in *The Master of Petersburg*, in Paul Rayment's meditation on his and other characters in *Slow Man* (2005) being 'like tramps in Beckett' (*SM*, 141), and, perhaps most unsettlingly for the reader – and certainly for a species of institutional reader – in the case of the unreliably focalized *Disgrace* (1999).[16]

Just as Coetzee's writer-characters are often themselves embroiled in contests over the meaning and import of their own words, so too has the author found himself in struggles to manage the terms under which work gathered by the function of the proper name 'J. M. Coetzee' has entered the world. The story of how John Maxwell Coetzee has negotiated the process is clear in an account of his attempts to publish his first book, *Dusklands*. Coetzee's initial approach was to write from Buffalo to the London firm Calder & Boyars about what would become 'The Narrative of Jacobus Coetzee', the second of the book's two fictions. This he described as 'a fiction which sets itself out, with editorial introduction and so forth, as the autobiographical narrative of ... a remote ancestor of mine'. It was 'of no historical value, in the narrower sense', he noted, but did seek to 'trace a line between so-called autonomous fictions and the psychology of the conquistador'.[17] Coetzee's eagerness to present the work as engaging with the discontents of realism and of colonialism is clear, as is his aspiration to secure a publisher who would recognize affiliations with a post-war avant-garde and grant access to an international readership of a certain type. John Calder had, after all, made a name publishing Beckett, and Coetzee noted in his covering letter that he had contributed a chapter on Beckett to a forthcoming collection. Calder also published, amongst others, Henry Miller, William Burroughs, and, in translation, such leading writers of the *nouveau roman* as Marguerite Duras, Alain Robbe-Grillet, and Nathalie Sarraute. Calder's business partner, Marion Boyars, did not, however, accept Coetzee's manuscript, nor in due course would the firms Farrar Straus Giroux or Knopf. It would take a return to South Africa in May 1971 and unsuccessful submissions to a local journal, *Contrast*, as well as to at least two local publishers, Human & Rousseau and Macmillan (South Africa), before *Dusklands*, in which the 'Narrative' is augmented with 'The Vietnam Project', would be published, by Ravan Press, in 1974.[18]

By this stage, in late 1971, having approached a number of agents (presenting himself as 'by profession a mathematician and linguist, aged 31'), Coetzee had found representation in David Stewart Hull at James Brown Associates in New York, with Murray Pollinger as London co-agent.[19] He retained overseas rights to *Dusklands*, but his agents had no success submitting the full manuscript to US or British publishers and Coetzee had to be content with local readers for his first book – at least until after the success of *Waiting for the Barbarians* abroad secured a deal with Penguin to publish the backlist. Letters to Ravan's Peter Randall attest to his displeasure with the material inadequacies of local production (Coetzee thought the initial binding 'only about par for South Africa, i.e., rather poor'[20]) and to his frustration with attempts to situate his work entirely in relation to local cultural and ethnic markers. His response to Randall's request for personal information ('your school education, for example, or your family background') anticipates the tone of the curt interview answer:

I am in two minds about supplying the particular personal information you suggest, not because I am at all against idle curiosity, and not either because I think the facts of a writer's background irrelevant to his work (they are and they aren't), but because the information you suggest suggests that I settle for a particular identity I should feel most uneasy in. A few words about my schooling, for example, makes me a player in the English-South African game of social typing and can even be read as a compliment to those monsters of sadism who ruled over my life for eleven years. As for my family background, I am one of the 10, 000 Coetzees, and what is there to be said about them except that Jacobus Coetzee begat them all?[21]

Coetzee compromised by sending a photograph and the information that his 'non-professional' interests included 'crowd sports; other people's ailments; apes and humanoid machines; images, particularly photographs, and their power over the human heart; and the politics of assent'. The information is both banal and enlightening, but in a manner not easily indexed to any 'particular identity' familiar to local readers: for one, here was an author writing in English, whose name would have more readily suggested an Afrikaans speaker (Ravan would, tellingly, use the line about his being 'one of 10, 000 Coetzees' on the jacket).[22]

Randall had sought to make clear to Coetzee his admiration for the manuscript of *Dusklands* and his sense that Ravan might not be best equipped to publish it. He was keen, too, that Coetzee understand that it was 'not an ordinary commercial publishing house' and that royalties could only follow a recouping of costs. Coetzee told Peter McDonald that he had known little about the firm 'except that it had been in trouble with the government, which was a good sign, and that it had some kind of Christian background, which was not necessarily a good sign'.[23] Ravan – named for the first letters of the surnames of founders (Peter Randall, Danie *van* Zyl, Beyers Naudé) – began as a spin-off of the Study Project on Christianity in Apartheid Society, funded variously by northern European religious and human rights organizations, in late 1972. *Dusklands* was to be among the first titles published by the press in its newly independent phase, during which it would develop community programmes for black South Africans (co-run by anti-apartheid activist Stephen Biko until his banning and subsequent murder by the police). Although white-owned, Ravan was resolutely anti-apartheid, routinely targeted by the police, and its books were regularly banned by the censors.[24]

It was anxiety about the potential banning of his second novel, *In the Heart of the Country*, that occasioned complex negotiations amongst Coetzee, Ravan, and the British firm Secker & Warburg, Coetzee's first international publishers; these are revealing about the costs of a desire to balance aspirations for international exposure and the exigencies of the

South African context. Ravan agreed to publish the novel, which, in its original manuscript, included long passages of Afrikaans dialogue, in 1975. Coetzee worried that its representation of trans-racial sex and violence by black farmworkers might attract the unfavourable attention of the euphemistically named Publications Control Board, but Randall opposed pre-publication submission to the authorities (which Coetzee mooted), reaffirming Ravan's commitment to publication despite possible censorship. In the meantime, Coetzee's agents sought international publishers for an English version. Hermann Wittenberg, who first detailed *In the Heart of the Country*'s tortuous publication process, speculates that Coetzee might have been anxious that a ban would prevent distribution of the novel were it published only in South Africa, though his intention to reach a wider readership was certainly already in evidence.

Simon & Schuster, Knopf, Dutton, Morrow, Vanguard, Doubleday, and Putnam's all declined the novel, but Secker's Tom Rosenthal was interested, though he wished to publish nine months before a South African edition, which he also insisted could not undercut the price of the imported British edition.[25] These demands made Ravan's publication economically unfeasible and Randall withdrew, leaving the field to Secker. The British firm, however, unlike Ravan, then took the position that it could not lose the local market to a potential banning and would not attempt distribution there – sending Coetzee back to Randall to negotiate a local edition after all. Things were not yet settled, however: Secker subsequently decided that it *would* export its edition to South Africa, and it was a shipment of these books that was impounded at the Cape Town docks in July 1977, embargoed, and sent to the censors. This forced Coetzee and Randall to consider eliminating passages to which the censors might object; Coetzee even secured the advice of a former reader for the censors, Klaas Steytler, husband of the novelist Elsa Joubert. In the event, the censorship board found the novel, in the formulation then in use, 'not undesirable', and Ravan was free to publish a local edition (including the original Afrikaans dialogue), although it took some months (until February 1978) to bring this to press, giving Secker time to market its edition without competition.[26] The English text appeared in the United States, from Harper & Row in New York, under the slightly different title *From the Heart of the Country*.

Coetzee would remain with Ravan for another decade. In the words of Mike Kirkwood, who succeeded Randall when he was placed under severely restrictive banning orders by the government in late 1977, Coetzee's support amounted to the action of 'a committed opponent of the *apartheid* structure'. His growing success – Ravan could eventually expect to sell around 3,000 hardback copies of the titles locally – effectively cross-subsidized other publications. Kirkwood recalls that when, in 1982, Rosenthal tried to deny Ravan rights to publish a local edition of *Life & Times of Michael K,* Coetzee's fourth novel, on economic grounds, Coetzee offered to 'phone Tom and throw some of his moral rhetoric back at him', after which Rosenthal called with 'second thoughts' and Ravan continued as local publisher for another four years, up through *Foe.*[27] While it seems reasonable to suggest that this demonstrates a commitment to *local* publication, and that Coetzee was prepared to use his growing reputation to support his South African publisher and indeed its anti-apartheid activities, it is too easy to claim that he *chose* Ravan over alternatives, or indeed that his commitment to a local publisher was without price. 'At some moment or other', Coetzee wrote to Randall as early as 9 July 1976, confirming his deal with Secker to publish *In the Heart of the Country,* 'I have to break out of the local market and it appears that if one writes minority-taste novels one has to offer up the local market as the price for overseas publication'.[28] In 1978, he had observed that South Africa's literary culture was inherently colonial – its 'literary products' were routinely 'flown to the metropolitan centre and re-exported ... from there at a vastly increased price'.[29] But by the late 1980s, having briefly bucked this trend, Coetzee was to accept it as unavoidable. The nobility of the cause of supporting local oppositional presses did not outweigh the perils of not reaching beyond a market catering to only a few thousand regular purchasers of books. It is possible, too, that the models of Nadine Gordimer and André Brink, both published and widely read abroad during the period (both, incidentally, had novels banned in South Africa in the 1970s), provided confirmation of the wisdom of this position.

Another reason for the accommodation Coetzee was prepared to make was a growing sense that to regard himself first and foremost as a 'South African' author was to submit to a variety of expectations that his work would perform in particular ways, or should address certain themes and issues. Was it, he wondered elsewhere, indeed merely a 'vast and wholly ideological superstructure constituted by publishing, reviewing and criticism' that had unjustly forced upon him 'the fate of being a "South African novelist"'?[30] Coetzee's statements about the merits of 'provincial literature' – that it was 'not necessarily minor' – on accepting the CNA Prize for *Waiting for the Barbarians,* give pause to any attempt to oversimplify this complex negotiation he was attempting between local context and a recognition of the conditions of the field in which he was forced to navigate sometimes competing value-conferring operations. Indeed, in relation to this prize in particular, he is resisting the specifically (dual) 'national' terms of the prize itself (it was for writing in English or Afrikaans). It also confirms his sense of the inevitable tension between local subject matter and a temperamental and formal affinity with Euro-American literary forebears and peers, and its likely resolution in favour of aspirations to be read as supra-national.[31]

Wittenberg argues that that resolution resulted directly from the struggles over *In the Heart of the Country*; *Waiting for the Barbarians*, apart from abandoning a recognizable local setting, was edited and typeset in London, with Ravan forced to act simply as 'a distributor and re-seller under license'.[32] Indeed, having judged Secker & Warburg a suitable imprint, Coetzee would remain loyal to the firm, despite good offers from Collins, Faber, and Bantam in 1982, and from others in ensuing years.[33] Harvill Secker, Secker & Warburg's successor imprint, now owned by the conglomerate Penguin Random House (and in turn by the multinational publishing giant Bertelsmann), continues to publish Coetzee's books in Britain. Viking, owned by the same global firm, does so in the United States. Coetzee's books have, since *Diary of a Bad Year*, been published in Australia, by Text Publishing (Melbourne), for the Antipodean markets (*Three Stories*, 2014, is in fact only available as a Text book).

Indeed, as his publishing venues became more international and foreign awards accumulated (amongst others, two Booker and two Commonwealth Writers' prizes, the French Prix Femina Étranger, the Jerusalem Prize, awards from European and United States newspapers, and honorary doctorates from universities in Australia, France, Mexico, Poland, South Africa, the United Kingdom, and the United States), so Coetzee's work has come to appear amenable to international validation by readers *inside* the country, which is to say as proof that 'literary' writing that might reach beyond the country's borders was capable of being produced there. There is something of the complex combination of pride and cultural cringe too in the award of South Africa's national Order of Mapungubwe (gold class) to Coetzee by the country's ANC-led government for his 'exceptional contribution in the field of literature and for putting South Africa on the world stage'. The award came in 2005, only five years after the ANC had labelled *Disgrace* racist – but, crucially, after the award of the Nobel Prize. Another perhaps unexpected set of readers in this category include those – incidentally fellow writers and academics – tasked with considering *In the Heart of the Country*, *Waiting for the Barbarians*, and *Life & Times of Michael K* for potential censorship. None of these readers felt that Coetzee's books could be regarded as undesirable locally, but their reasoning had in view the books' aspirations to escape being read merely as 'South African'. Coetzee might have had a poem in *Staffrider* suppressed, but there the reason was the context of publication. Here what was effectively a validation of his work – as sufficiently literary to escape instrumental reading – put him in a tricky position, Peter McDonald comments. If the censors

passed him as 'A Great South African Writer', in the nationalistic sense Coetzee refused ..., they also believed him to be a 'Great Novelist' whose works displayed all the traditional qualities, verities, and canonical authority of the novel and, by extension, of Western art in general. This was perhaps the greatest paradox of their response.[34]

Amenability to canonization was driven abroad by slightly different investments, including by foreign readers seeking textual intermediaries for vicarious encounters with a country that, as a reviewer of novels by Coetzee and Brink in the *New York Review of Books* in 1982 suggested, had replaced the Gulag as 'the revealed outrage of the literary season'.[35] In an early assessment of Coetzee's global reputation, Clive Barnett suggested that these reviewers often read the novels as allegories with universal resonance, recasting what might otherwise have seemed politically engaged in relation to South Africa as instead broadly liberal humanist: South Africa is identified as 'context and referent', but simultaneously 'idealised as a stage for more general moral dramas of human suffering and violence', the realities of suffering in the country relegated to a safe distance.[36] For readers in this group, chiefly reviewers in international newspapers, agreement grew – as Jarad Zimbler has shown – about the qualities of Coetzee's prose, and that these elevated the writing above a level of interest dependent on subject matter. The novels were repeatedly described as '*gripping, compelling, forbidding, disturbing*', '*hard, bitter* and *sharp*', but also '*vivifying, exciting* and even *purifying*'.[37]

The citations of prize juries evidence similar operations. Consider the statement by Gerald Kaufman, the chair of the panel that awarded Coetzee's second Booker Prize, that *Disgrace* was an 'allegory about what is happening to the human race in the post-colonial era': here race is central, but not in the way that South Africa's ruling party averred; this is not expressly a book about South Africa, Kaufman's formulation insists.[38] It is clear, too, in the Swedish Academy's description of Coetzee's repeated portrayal of 'the surprising involvement of the outsider' 'in innumerable guises' such that the precise nature of the outsider remains deliberately undefined.[39] Of course, Coetzee is no more able to control *how* his books are read or positioned than any author is, even if he is more disinclined than most to offer guidance; any work is situated in a manner beyond the author's control through any number of readings and misreadings of paratextual devices or marketing ploys. Perhaps the strangest of the latter to date was the 1983 promotion of *Life & Times of Michael K* in British newspaper advertisements placed by Booker McConnell, sponsor of the Booker prize (which Coetzee's novel had recently won), alongside the firm's nutritional supplement 'Super Gev-e-tabs'. The 'perverse irony' of Coetzee's under-nourished protagonist K 'being linked to a health supplement' participates, too, Patrick Flanery notes, in the construction of certain kinds of difficult literary work as 'good' for the reader, a construction in which the Booker was deeply invested by the early 1980s.[40]

Coetzee has himself, of course, also participated in the dispersal of cultural capital, choosing to promote some writers by providing endorsements to appear on book covers, and lending an air of authority to academic confer-ences on his work at which he has offered readings and attended sessions.[41] In Australia in particular, where he has lived since 2002, Coetzee 'is fre-quently called upon to lend *gravitas* to official functions', Attwell comments, as well as being involved in advocacy on a number of social causes, environ-mental (for the rights of animals; against coal mining) and progressive (for marriage equality; against censorship).[42]

Ironically, or perhaps entirely understandably given how difficult Coetzee found navigating the pressures that late-apartheid politics placed on any desire for a private life (or for the literary to resist being too crudely ideolo-gically positioned), as he has grown more distant from South Africa, so he has, on occasion, spoken in more ostensibly political ways without the mask of a writer-character persona. An example is a speech at the Palestinian Festival of Literature, in Ramallah, in May 2016, in which he sketched broad similarities between apartheid-era South Africa and the conditions pertaining in parts of Jerusalem and the Palestinian territories. Even here, however, Coetzee left the final act of interpretation to his audience, offering the challenge: 'Draw your own conclusions.'[43]

Notes

1. David Attwell, *J. M. Coetzee and the Life of Writing: Face to Face with Time* (Oxford: Oxford University Press, 2015), p. 162.
2. J. M. Coetzee, 'The Acceptance Speech', *Lecture and Speech of Acceptance Upon the Award of the Nobel Prize in Literature, Delivered in Stockholm in December 2003* (New York: Penguin, 2004), pp. 21–2 (p. 22).
3. Ibid., p. 161.
4. J. M. Coetzee, Business Correspondence, J. M. Coetzee to Ms C. Coatoam, 4 June 1988, CP 73.4.
5. James F. English, *The Economy of Prestige: Prizes, Awards, and the Circulation of Cultural Value* (Cambridge, MA: Harvard University Press, 2005), p. 9.
6. Handwritten text on reverse of fourth page (of four) of typescript unpublished address, 'Writing in South Africa', delivered 18 April 1978, CP 63.6. The prize was sponsored by South Africa's leading newsagent, CNA (Central News Agency Ltd.).

7. For an account of what is at stake in the publication contexts of *Elizabeth Costello*'s constituent 'lessons', see Patrick Flanery, '(Re-)marking Coetzee and Costello: The (Textual) *Lives of Animals*', *English Studies in Africa*, 47.1 (2004), 31–46.

8. J. M. Coetzee, 'Preamble', 'Centro Historica Mexico, 1998', CP 61.1.

9. J. M. Coetzee, '"At the Gate": Introduction', CP 61.4. Coetzee was giving an address on receipt of the Neustadt International Prize.

10. See J. M. Coetzee, 'The Novel Today', *Upstream*, 6.1 (1988), 2–5 (p. 3).

11. Ibid., pp. 2, 3.

12. J. C. Kannemeyer, *J. M. Coetzee: A Life in Writing*, trans. Michiel Heyns (Johannesburg: Jonathan Ball, 2012), pp. 658–61.

13. Quoted in Attwell, *J. M. Coetzee and the Life of Writing*, p. 148.

14. Michel Foucault, 'What is an Author?' (1969), trans. Josué V. Harari, in James D. Faubion (ed.), *Aesthetics, Method, and Epistemology: Essential Works of Foucault 1954–1984* (New York:New Press, 1998), vol. 2, pp. 205–22 (pp. 211, 212).

15. Ibid., p. 205.

16. For the African National Congress's citation of *Disgrace* as evidence of racism 'in the media', see the party's submission to South Africa's Human Rights Commission hearing on 5 April 2000, www.anc.org.za/content/anc-submission-human-rights-commission-hearings-racism-media. For a debate about its implications for reading Coetzee's novel, see David Attwell, 'Race in *Disgrace*', *Interventions*, 4.3 (2002), 331–41, and Peter D. McDonald, '*Disgrace* Effects', *Interventions*, 4.3 (2002), 321–30.

17. J. M. Coetzee, Business Correspondence, Letter to Mssrs Calder & Boyars, Ltd, 3 December 1971, CP 69.1.

18. J. M. Coetzee, Business Correspondence, CP 69.1. Coetzee sent the 'Narrative' to Human & Rousseau in December 1972 and it was rejected the following March; he sent it to Jack Cope, editor of *Contrast*, in May 1973, and, on Cope's recommendation, in July to Macmillan, who rejected it in October.

19. J. M. Coetzee, Business Correspondence, Letter to the Joan Daves Agency, New York, 20 December 1971, CP 69.1. Coetzee's correspondence indicates that at least seventeen agents were approached, including Curtis Brown and William Morris.

20. J. M. Coetzee, Business Correspondence, Letter to Peter Randall, 23 April 1974, CP 69.1.

21. J. M. Coetzee, Business Correspondence, Letter to Peter Randall, 17 January 1974, CP 69.1.

22. Ibid.

23. See Peter D. McDonald, *The Literature Police: Apartheid Censorship and its Cultural Consequences* (Oxford: Oxford University Press, 2009), pp. 137, 374.

24. Ibid., pp. 132–5. See also Peter Randall, 'Introductory Remarks' in Susan Gardner (ed.), *Publisher/Writer/Reader: Sociology of Southern African Literature* (Johannesburg: Wits University Press, 1986), p. 14.

25. Hermann Wittenberg, 'The Taint of the Censor: J. M. Coetzee and the Making of *In the Heart of the Country*', *English in Africa*, 35.2 (2008), 133–50 (p. 138).

26. For full descriptions of the various stages in the negotiations, see ibid., pp. 144–5.

27. See Andrew van der Vlies, *South African Textual Cultures* (Manchester: Manchester University Press, 2007), p. 137.

28. Wittenberg, 'The Taint of the Censor', p. 138.

29. Stephen Watson, 'Speaking: J. M. Coetzee', *Speak*, 1.3 (1978), 23–4.

30. Tony Morphet, 'Two Interviews with J. M. Coetzee, 1983 and 1987', *From South Africa: New Writings, Photographs & Art, TriQuarterly*, 69 (1987), 454–64 (p. 460).

31. J. M. Coetzee, 'SA Authors Must Learn Modesty', *Die Vaderland*, 1 May 1981, 16. For a discussion of the implications of this revaluation of the marginal, see McDonald, *The Literature Police*, pp. 305–6.

32. Wittenberg, 'The Taint of the Censor', p. 147.

33. J. M. Coetzee, Business Correspondence, CP 70.4.

34. McDonald, *The Literature Police*, p. 316.

35. Jane Kramer, 'In the Garrison', *New York Review of Books*, 2 December 1982, 8–12 (p. 8). See further Andrew van der Vlies, 'South Africa in the Global Imaginary' in Derek Attridge and David Attwell (eds.), *The Cambridge History of South African Literature* (Cambridge: Cambridge University Press, 2012), pp. 697–716 (pp. 699–700).

36. Clive Barnett, 'Constructions of Apartheid in the International Reception of the Novels of J. M. Coetzee', *Journal of Southern African Studies*, 25.2 (1999), 287–301 (pp. 294, 290).

37. Jarad Zimbler, *J. M. Coetzee and the Politics of Style* (Cambridge: Cambridge University Press, 2014), p. 4.

38. Sarah Lyall, 'South African Writer Wins Top British Prize for Second Time', *New York Times* (26 October 1999), A.4c; see also McDonald, 'Disgrace Effects', p. 321.

39. The Nobel Prize in Literature 2003, www.nobelprize.org/nobel_prizes/literature/laureates/2003/.

40. Patrick Flanery, 'Becoming Global: J. M. Coetzee and 1980s International Literary Prize Culture', MLA Convention, San Francisco, December 2008, unpublished paper.

41. This has been true at least since 2016, with appearances at conferences on his work in Argentina, Australia, Italy, and the United Kingdom.

42. Attwell, *J. M. Coetzee and the Life of Writing*, p. 240. See J. M. Coetzee, 'Animals Can't Speak for Themselves – It's Up to Us to Do It', *Age* (22 February 2007), www.theage.com.au/news/opinion/animals-cant-speak-for-themselves–its-up-to-us/2007/02/21/1171733841769.html. Coetzee was a signatory to 'An open letter on same-sex marriage', encouraging a vote in its favour in the 2017 postal referendum, in the *Australian Review of Books* (September 2017), www.australianbookreview.com.au/commentary/yes-to-equality-open-letter.

43. 'JM Coetzee on Israeli Occupation and South African Apartheid: "Draw Your Own Conclusions"', *Daily Vox*, 4 February 2017, www.thedailyvox.co.za/jm-coetzee-israeli-occupation-south-african-apartheid-draw-conclusions/; the speech is available online here: www.youtube.com/watch?v=uDUnimxSAyk.

General

Attridge, Derek, *J. M. Coetzee and the Ethics of Reading: Literature in the Event* (Chicago: University of Chicago Press, 2004).

Attridge, Derek, (ed.), 'J. M. Coetzee's *Disgrace*', special issue of *Interventions*, 4.3 (2002).

Attwell, David, *J. M. Coetzee: South Africa and the Politics of Writing* (Berkeley: University of California Press, 1993).

J. M. Coetzee and the Life of Writing: Face-to-Face with Time (Oxford: Oxford University Press, 2015).

Boehmer, Elleke, Katy Iddiols, and Robert Eaglestone, (eds.), *J. M. Coetzee in Context and Theory* (London: Continuum, 2009).

Bradshaw, Graham, and Michael Neill, (eds.), *J. M. Coetzee's Austerities* (Farnham: Ashgate, 2010).

Clarkson, Carrol, *J. M. Coetzee: Countervoices* (Basingstoke: Palgrave Macmillan, 2009).

Crew, Jonathan, *In the Middle of Nowhere: J. M. Coetzee in South Africa* (Lanham, MD: University Press of America, 2015).

Danta, Chris, Sue Kossew, and Julian Murphet, (eds.), *Strong Opinions: J. M. Coetzee and the Authority of Contemporary Fiction* (London: Bloomsbury, 2011).

Hayes, Patrick, *J. M. Coetzee and the Novel: Writing and Politics after Beckett* (Oxford: Oxford University Press, 2010).

Hayes, Patrick, and Jan Wilm, (eds.), *Beyond the Ancient Quarrel: Literature, Philosophy, and J. M. Coetzee* (Oxford: Oxford University Press, 2017).

Head, Dominic, *The Cambridge Introduction to J. M. Coetzee* (Cambridge: Cambridge University Press, 2009).

Helgesson, Stefan, *Writing in Crisis: Ethics and History in Gordimer, Ndebele, and Coetzee* (Pietermaritzburg: UKZN Press, 2004).

Huggan, Graham, and Stephen Watson, (eds.), *Critical Perspectives on J. M. Coetzee* (Basingstoke: Macmillan, 1996).

Kannemeyer, J. C., *J. M. Coetzee: A Life in Writing*, trans. Michiel Heyns (Johannesburg: Jonathan Ball, 2012).

Kossew, Sue, (ed.), *Critical Essays on J. M. Coetzee* (New York: G. K. Hall, 1998).

Kossew, Sue, and Melinda Harvey, (eds.), *Reading Coetzee's Women* (London and New York: Palgrave Macmillan, 2019).

Kossew, Sue, Julieanne Lamond, and Melinda Harvey, (eds.), 'Thematising Women in the Work of J. M. Coetzee', special issue of *Australian Literary Studies*, 33.1 (2018).

Leist, Anton, and Peter Singer, (eds.), *J. M. Coetzee and Ethics: Philosophical Perspectives on Literature* (New York: Columbia University Press, 2010).

Lopez, María J., and Kai Wiegandt, (eds.), 'J. M. Coetzee and the Non-English Literary Traditions', special issue of *European Journal of English Studies*, 20.2 (2016).

Macaskill, Brian, (ed.), 'J. M. Coetzee: Contrapuntal Mediations', special issue of *Media Tropes*, 4.2 (2014).

Marais, Mike, *Secretary of the Invisible: The Idea of Hospitality in the Fiction of J. M. Coetzee* (Amsterdam: Rodopi, 2009).

Mehigan, Tim, (ed.), *A Companion to Works of J. M. Coetzee* (Rochester, NY: Camden House, 2011).

Mehigan, Tim, and Christian Moser, (eds.), *Intellectual Landscapes in the Works of J. M. Coetzee* (Rochester, NY: Camden House, 2017).

Mulhall, Stephen, *The Wounded Animal: J. M. Coetzee and the Difficulty of Reality in Literature and Philosophy* (Princeton: Princeton University Press, 2009).

Nashef, Hania A. M., *The Politics of Humiliation in the Novels of J. M. Coetzee* (New York: Routledge, 2009).

Poyner, Jane, (ed.), *J. M. Coetzee and the Idea of the Public Intellectual* (Athens: Ohio University Press, 2006).

Sanders, Mark and Nancy Ruttenburg, (eds.), 'J. M. Coetzee and his Doubles', special issue of *Journal of Literary Studies*, 25.4 (2009).

Uhlmann, Anthony, (ed.), 'J. M. Coetzee: Fictions of the Real', special issue of *Textual Practice*, 30.3 (2016).

Uhlmann, Anthony, and Jennifer Rutherford, (eds.), *J. M. Coetzee's 'The Childhood of Jesus': The Ethics and Ideas of Things* (London: Bloomsbury Academic, 2018).

Van der Vlies, Andrew, *J. M. Coetzee's 'Disgrace'* (London: Continuum, 2010).

Wilm, Jan, *The Slow Philosophy of J. M. Coetzee* (London: Bloomsbury Academic, 2016).

Wright, Laura, *Writing 'Out of All the Camps': J. M. Coetzee's Narratives of Displacement* (New York and London: Routledge, 2006).

Wright, Laura, Jane Poyner, and Elleke Boehmer, *Approaches to Teaching Coetzee's 'Disgrace' and Other Works* (New York: MLA, 2014).

Zimbler, Jarad, *J. M. Coetzee and the Politics of Style* (Cambridge: Cambridge University Press, 2014).

1. Composition and Craft

Barthes, Roland, *The Preparation of the Novel: Lecture Courses and Seminars at the Collège de France, 1978–1979 and 1979–1980*, trans. Kate Briggs, ed. and introd. Nathalie Léger (New York: Columbia University Press, 2011).

Bernaerts, Lars, and Dirk Van Hulle, 'Narratology Meets Genetic Criticism', *Poetics Today*, 34.3 (2013), 281–326.

de Biasi, Pierre-Marc, 'What is a Literary Draft? Toward a Functional Typology of Genetic Documentation', *Yale French Studies*, 89 (1996), 26–58.

Deppman, Jed, Daniel Ferrer, and Michael Groden, (eds.), *Genetic Criticism: Texts and Avant-Textes* (Philadelphia: University of Pennsylvania Press, 2004).

Moody, Alys, 'Starving across the Colour Line: J. M. Coetzee in Apartheid South Africa' in her *The Art of Hunger: Aesthetic Autonomy and the Afterlives of Modernism* (Oxford: Oxford University Press, 2018), pp. 156–98.

Robinson, Benjamin Lewis, 'Passions for Justice: Kleist's Michael Kohlhaas and Coetzee's Michael K', *Comparative Literature*, 70.4 (2018), 426–43.

Sullivan, Hannah, *The Work of Revision* (Cambridge, MA: Harvard University Press, 2013).

Uhlmann, Anthony, 'Process and Method in *Waiting for the Barbarians*', *Texas Studies in Literature and Language*, 58.4 (2016), 435–50.

Van Hulle, Dirk, *Modern Manuscripts: The Extended Mind and Creative Undoing from Darwin to Beckett and Beyond* (London: Bloomsbury Academic, 2014).

2. Scenes and Settings

Barnard, Rita, *Apartheid and Beyond: South African Writers and the Politics of Place* (Oxford: Oxford University Press, 2007).

Clarkson, Carrol, 'Names' in her *J. M. Coetzee: Countervoices* (Basingstoke: Palgrave Macmillan, 2009), pp. 133–52.

Darian-Smith, Kate, Liz Gunner, and Sarah Nuttall (eds.), *Text, Theory, Space: Land, Literature and History in South Africa and Australia* (London: Routledge, 1993).

Easton, Kai, 'Travels to the Metropolis: Cape Town, London, and J. M. Coetzee's *Youth*', *Moving Worlds*, 4.1 (2004), 72–84.

Kossew, Sue, 'Literary Migration: Shifting Borders in Coetzee's Australian Novels' in Chris Danta, Sue Kossew, and Julian Murphet (eds.), *Strong Opinions: J. M. Coetzee and the Authority of Contemporary Fiction* (London: Continuum, 2011), pp. 113–24.

López, María J., *Acts of Visitation: The Narrative of J. M. Coetzee* (Amsterdam: Rodopi, 2011).

Rutherford, Jennifer, '"Washed Clean": The Forgotten Journeys of "Irregular Maritime Arrivals" in J. M. Coetzee's *Estralia*' in Lynda Mannik (ed.), *Migration by Boat: Discourses of Trauma* (New York: Berghahn Books, 2016), pp. 101–15.

Wicomb, Zoë, 'Setting, Intertextuality and the Resurrection of the Postcolonial Author', *Journal of Postcolonial Writing*, 41.2 (2005), 144–55.

'*Slow Man* and the Real: A Lesson in Reading and Writing', *Journal of Literary Studies*, 25.4 (2009), 7–24.

Wittenberg, Herman, and Kate Highman, 'Sven Hedin's "Vanished Country": Setting and History in J. M. Coetzee's *Waiting for the Barbarians*', *Scrutiny2*, 20.1 (2015), 103–27.

Wenzel, Jennifer, 'The Pastoral Promise and the Political Imperative: The *Plaasroman* Tradition in an Era of Land Reform', *Modern Fiction Studies*, 46.1 (2000), 90–113.

3. Stories and Narration

Attridge, Derek, 'Confessing in the Third Person: *Boyhood and Youth*' in his *J. M. Coetzee and the Ethics of Reading: Literature in the Event* (Chicago: University of Chicago Press, 2004), pp. 138–61.

Barthes, Roland, 'An Introduction to the Structural Analysis of Narrative', trans. Lionel Duisit, *New Literary History*, 6.2 (1975), 237–72.

Coetzee, J. M., 'Fictional Beings', *Philosophy, Psychiatry, & Psychology*, 10.2 (2003), 133–4.

Fessenbecker, Patrick, 'In Defense of Paraphrase', *New Literary History*, 44.1 (2013), 117–39.

Genette, Gérard, *Narrative Discourse: An Essay in Method*, trans. Jane E. Lewin (Ithaca: Cornell University Press, 1980).

Huber, Irmtraud, *Present Tense Narration in Contemporary Fiction: A Narratological Overview* (London: Palgrave Macmillan, 2016).

Jacobs, J. U., 'A Bridging Fiction: The Migrant Subject in J. M. Coetzee's *The Childhood of Jesus*', *Journal of Literary Studies*, 33.1 (2017), 59–75.

Phelan, James, 'Present Tense Narration, Mimesis, the Narrative Norm, and the Positioning of the Reader in *Waiting for the Barbarians*' in James Phelan and Peter J. Rabinowitz (eds.), *Understanding Narrative* (Columbus: Ohio State University Press, 1994), pp. 222–45.

Propp, Vladimir, *Morphology of the Folktale*, trans. Svatava Pirkova-Jakobson and Louis A. Wagner, ed. Louise A. Wagner, and introd. Alan Dundes (Austin: University of Texas Press, 1968).

Scanlan, Margaret, 'Incriminating Documents: Nechaev and Dostoevsky in J. M. Coetzee's *The Master of St. Petersburg*', *Philological Quarterly*, 76.4 (1997), 463–77.

Shklovsky, Viktor, *Theory of Prose*, trans. Benjamin Sher and introd. Gerald L. Bruns (Normal: Dalkey Archive Press, 1991).

Seshagiri, Urmila, 'The Boy of La Mancha: J. M. Coetzee's *The Childhood of Jesus*', *Contemporary Literature*, 54.3 (2013), 643–53.

Thaventhiran, Helen, 'Empson and the Orthodoxy of Paraphrase', *Essays in Criticism*, 61.4 (2011), 382–404.

4. Styles

Ackerley, Chris, 'Style: Coetzee and Beckett' in Tim Mehigan (ed.), *A Companion to the Works of J. M. Coetzee* (New York: Camden House, 2011), pp. 23–38.

Attridge, Derek, 'Age of Bronze, State of Grace: *Disgrace*' in his *J. M. Coetzee and the Ethics of Reading: Literature in the Event* (Chicago: University of Chicago Press, 2004), pp. 162–91.

Boehmer, Elleke, 'J. M. Coetzee's Australian Realism' in Chris Danta, Sue Kossew, and Julien Murphet, (eds.), *Strong Opinions: J. M. Coetzee and the Authority of Contemporary Fiction* (London: Bloomsbury, 2013), pp. 202–18.

McDonald, Peter D. 'Coetzee's Critique of Language' in Patrick Hayes and Jan Wilm (eds.), *Beyond the Ancient Quarrel: Literature, Philosophy, and J. M. Coetzee* (Oxford: Oxford University Press, 2018), pp. 173–9.

Said, Edward, *On Late Style: Music and Literature Against the Grain*, with foreword by Mariam C. Said, introd. Michael Wood (New York: Pantheon, 2006).

Williams, Daniel, 'Coetzee's Stones: *Dusklands* and the Nonhuman Witness', *Safundi*, 19.4 (2018), 438–60.

Zimbler, Jarad, 'Neither Progress, nor Regress: *Dusklands* and the Emergence of a Literary Style' in his *J. M. Coetzee and the Politics of Style* (Cambridge: Cambridge University Press, 2014), pp. 25–55.

5. Genres

Derrida, Jacques, 'The Law of Genre' in *Acts of Literature*, ed. Derek Attridge (New York: Routledge, 1992), pp. 221–52.

Effe, Alexandra, *J. M. Coetzee and the Ethics of Narrative Transgression: A Reconsideration of Metalepsis* (London: Palgrave Macmillan, 2017).

Frow, John, *Genre* (London: Routledge, 2006).

Geertsema, Johan, '*Diary of a Bad Year*' in Tim Mehigan (ed.), *A Companion to Works of J. M. Coetzee* (Rochester, NY: Camden House, 2011), pp. 208–21.

Heath, Stephen, 'The Politics of Genre' in Christopher Prendergast, (ed.), *Debating World Literature* (London: Verso, 2004), pp. 163–74.

Kossew, Sue, '*Scenes from Provincial Life*' in Tim Mehigan (ed.), *A Companion to Works of J. M. Coetzee* (Rochester: Camden House, 2011), pp. 9–22.

Ogden, Benjamin H. 'The Coming into Being of Literature: How J. M. Coetzee's *Diary of a Bad Year* Thinks through the Novel', *Novel*, 43 (2010), 466–82.

Todorov, Tzvetan, *Genres in Discourse*, trans. Catherine Porter (Cambridge: Cambridge University Press, 1990).

6. Translations

Barnard, Rita, 'Coetzee in/and Afrikaans', *Journal of Literary Studies*, 25.4 (2009), 84–105.

Casanova, Pascale, *The World Republic of Letters*, trans. M. B. DeBevoise (Cambridge, MA: Harvard University Press, 2007).

Cavagnoli, Franca, '"In Every Story There is a Silence": Translating Coetzee's Female Narrators into Italian', *Australian Literary Studies*, 33.1 (2018).

Derrida, Jacques, *Monolingualism of the Other: Or, The Prosthesis of Origin*, trans. Patrick Mensah (Stanford: Stanford University Press, 1998).

Helgesson, Stefan, 'Clarice Lespector, J. M. Coetzee and the Seriality of Translation', *Translation Studies*, 3.3 (2010), 318–33.

'Translation and the Circuits of World Literature' in Ben Etherington and Jarad Zimbler (eds.), *The Cambridge Companion to World Literature* (Cambridge: Cambridge University Press, 2018), pp. 85–99.

Jacobs, J. U., '(N)either Afrikaner (n)or English: Cultural Crossover in J. M. Coetzee's *Summertime*', *English Academy Review*, 28.1 (2011), 39–52.

Mayoux, Sophie, 'J. M. Coetzee and Language: A Translator's View', *Commonwealth Essays and Studies*, 9.1 (1986), 8–10.

Mukherjee, Ankhi, *What is a Classic? Postcolonial Rewriting and the Invention of the Canon* (Stanford: Stanford University Press, 2014).

Ricoeur, Paul, *On Translation* (London: Routledge, 2006).

Steiner, George, *After Babel: Aspects of Language and Translation* (Oxford: Oxford University Press, 1998).

Venuti, Lawrence, *Translation Changes Everything: Theory and Practice* (London: Routledge, 2013).

Walkowitz, Rebecca, 'Comparison Literature', *New Literary History*, 40.3 (2009), 567–82.

Born Translated: The Contemporary Novel in an Age of World Literature (New York: Columbia University Press, 2015).

Zimbler, Jarad, 'New Dimensions: *In the Heart of the Country*'s Repetitions' in his *J. M. Coetzee and the Politics of Style* (Cambridge: Cambridge University Press, 2014), pp. 56–86.

7. Collaboration and Correspondence

Altman, Janet Gurkin, *Epistolarity: Approaches to a Form* (Columbus: Ohio State University Press, 1982).

Attridge, Derek, 'Trusting the Other: *Age of Iron*' in his *J. M. Coetzee and the Ethics of Reading: Literature in the Event* (Chicago: University of Chicago Press, 2004), pp. 90–112.

Attwell, David, '"Dialogue" and "Fulfilment" in J. M. Coetzee's *Age of Iron*' in Derek Attridge and Rosemary Jolly (eds.), *Writing South Africa: Literature, Apartheid and Democracy, 1970–1995* (Cambridge: Cambridge University Press, 1998), pp. 166–79.

Beebee, Thomas O., *Epistolary Fiction in Europe, 1500–1850* (Cambridge: Cambridge University Press, 1999).

Bower, Rachel, *Epistolarity and World Literature* (Cham, Switzerland: Palgrave Macmillan, 2017).

Coetzee, J. M., 'Review of The Letters of Samuel Beckett, Volume 1: 1929–1940', *New York Review of Books*, 30 April 2009.

'Rev. of *The Temple of My Familiar* by Alice Walker' (1989), reprinted in Henry Louis Gates, Jr., and K. A. Appiah (eds.), *Alice Walker: Critical Perspectives Past and Present* (New York: Amistad, 1993), p. 25.

'Speaking: J. M. Coetzee', with Stephen Watson, *Speak*, 1 (1978), 3, 21–4.

'Two Interviews with J. M. Coetzee, 1983 and 1987', with Tony Morphet, *Northwestern University Triquarterly*, 69 (1987), 454–64.

Derrida, Jacques 'Signature Event Context', trans. Alan Bass, in his *Margins of Philosophy* (Brighton: Harvester, 1982), pp. 307–30.

Further Reading

Favret, Mary A., *Romantic Correspondence: Women, Politics and the Fiction of Letters* (Cambridge: Cambridge University Press, 1993).
Gilroy, Amanda and W. M. Verhoeven, (eds.), *Epistolary Histories: Letters, Fiction, Culture* (Charlottesville: University Press of Virginia, 2000).
Goldsmith, Elizabeth C., (ed.), *Writing the Female Voice: Essays on Epistolary Literature* (Boston: Northeastern University Press, 1989).
Hayes, Patrick, 'Literature, History and Folly' in Elleke Boehmer, Robert Eaglestone, and Katy Iddiols (eds.), *J. M. Coetzee in Context and Theory* (London: Continuum, 2009), pp. 112–22.
Kauffman, Linda S., *Discourses of Desire: Gender, Genre, and Epistolary Fictions* (Ithaca: Cornell University Press, 1986).
Roach, Rebecca, *Literature and the Rise of the Interview* (Oxford: Oxford University Press, 2018).

8. Criticism and Scholarship

Attridge, Derek, 'Literary Experience and the Value of Criticism' in Rónán McDonald, (ed.), *The Values of Literary Studies: Critical Institutions, Scholarly Agendas* (Cambridge: Cambridge University Press, 2015), pp. 249–62.
'Oppressive Silence: J. M. Coetzee's *Foe* and the Politics of the Canon' in Karen R. Lawrence, (ed.), *Decolonizing Tradition: New Views of Twentieth-Century 'British' Literary Canons* (Urbana: University of Illinois Press, 1992), pp. 212–38.
Bethlehem, Louise, *Skin Tight: Apartheid Literary Culture and its Aftermath* (Pretoria: UNISA Press, 2006).
Clarkson, Carrol, 'Coetzee's Criticism' in Tim Mehigan (ed.), *A Companion to the Works of J. M. Coetzee* (Rochester, NY: Camden House, 2011), pp. 222–34.
Dean, Andrew, 'Double Thoughts: Coetzee and the Philosophy of Literary Criticism' in Patrick Hayes and Jan Wilm (eds.), *Beyond the Ancient Quarrel: Literature, Philosophy, and J. M. Coetzee* (Oxford: Oxford University Press, 2017), pp. 52–69.
Dovey, Teresa, *The Novels of J. M. Coetzee: Lacanian Allegories* (Craighall: A. D. Donker, 1988).
During, Simon, 'Coetzee as Academic Novelist' in Tim Mehigan and Christian Moser (eds.), *The Intellectual Landscape in the Works of J. M. Coetzee* (Rochester: Camden House, 2018), pp. 233–53.
Gallagher, Susan Van Zanten, *A Story of South Africa: J. M. Coetzee's Fiction in Context* (Cambridge, MA: Harvard University Press, 1991).
McDonald, Peter D., *The Literature Police: Apartheid Censorship and its Cultural Consequences* (Oxford: Oxford University Press, 2009).
Parker, Kenneth, 'J. M. Coetzee: The Postmodern and the Postcolonial' in Graham Huggan and Stephen Watson (eds.), *Critical Perspectives on J. M. Coetzee* (Basingstoke: Macmillan, 1996), pp. 82–104.
Parry, Benita, 'Speech and Silence in the Fictions of J. M. Coetzee', *New Formations*, 21 (1993), 1–20.
Spivak, Gayatri Chakravorty, 'Theory in the Margin: Coetzee's *Foe* Reading Defoe's *Crusoe/ Roxana*', *English in Africa*, 17.2 (1990), 1–23.

9. Influence and Intertextuality

Allen, Graham, *Intertextuality* (London: Routledge, 2000).

Attwell, David, 'J. M. Coetzee's South African Intellectual Landscapes' in Tim Mehigan and Christian Moser (eds.), *Intellectual Landscapes in the Works of J. M. Coetzee* (Rochester: Camden House, 2017), pp. 274–93.

Barthes, Roland, *Image, Music, Text*, trans. Stephen Heath (London: Fontana, 1977).

Bloom, Harold, *The Anxiety of Influence* (New York: Oxford University Press, 1973).

Broggi, Alicia, 'What Does it Mean to Speak of ——? Rudolf Bultmann, Biography, and J. M. Coetzee's *Life & Times of Michael K*', *Review of English Studies*, 69.289 (2017), 336–55.

Coetzee, J. M., 'The Great South African Novel', *Leadership SA*, 2.4 (1983), 74, 77, 79.

'An Interview with J. M. Coetzee', with Jean Sévry, *Commonwealth Essays and Studies*, 9.1 (1986), 1–17.

Etherington, Ben, and Jarad Zimbler, 'Field, Material, Technique: On Renewing Postcolonial Literary Criticism', *Journal of Commonwealth Literature*, 49.3 (2014), 279–97.

Ffrench, Patrick, *The Time of Theory: A History of 'Tel Quel' (1960–1983)* (Oxford: Clarendon Press, 1995).

Lopez, María J. and Kai Wiegandt, 'Introduction: J. M. Coetzee, Intertextuality, and the Non-English Literary Traditions', *European Journal of English Studies*, 20.2 (2016), 113–26.

Kristeva, Julia, *Revolution in Poetic Language*, trans. Margaret Waller (New York: Columbia University Press, 1984).

Van der Vlies, Andrew, 'Farming Stories (II): J. M. Coetzee and the (Heart of a) Country' in his *South African Textual Cultures: White, Black, Read All Over* (Manchester: Manchester University Press, 2007), pp. 134–54.

10. Worlds, World-Making, and Southern Horizons

Clarkson, Carrol, 'You' in her *J. M. Coetzee: Countervoices* (Basingstoke: Palgrave Macmillan, 2009), pp. 47–74.

Connell, Raewyn, *Southern Theory: The Global Dynamics of Knowledge in Social Science* (Sydney: Allen and Unwin, 2007).

Goodman, Nelson, *Ways of Worldmaking* (Indianapolis: Hackett, 1978)

Harvey, Melinda, '"In Australia You Start Zero": The Escape from Place in J. M. Coetzee's Late Novels' in Chris Danta, Sue Kossew, and Julian Murphet (eds.), *Strong Opinions: J. M. Coetzee and the Authority of Contemporary Fiction* (London: Continuum, 2011), pp. 19–34.

Hayot, Eric, *On Literary Worlds* (Oxford: Oxford University Press, 2012).

Helgesson, Stefan, *Transnationalism in Southern African Literature: Modernists, Realists, and the Inequality of Print Culture* (London: Routledge, 2009).

Hofmeyr, Isabel, 'Against the Global South' in Russel West-Pavlov (ed.), *The Global South and Literature* (Cambridge: Cambridge University Press, 2018), 307–14.

Lavery, Charne, and Meg Samuelson, 'The Oceanic South', *English Language Notes*, 57.1 (2019), 37–50.

Maine, Barry, 'Erich Auerbach's *Mimesis* and Nelson Goodman's *Ways of Worldmaking*: A Nominal(ist) Revision', *Poetics Today*, 20.1 (1999), 41–52.

Malmgren, Carl D., 'Worlds Apart: A Theory of Science Fiction' in Anne Heller et al. (eds.), *Utopian Thought in American Literature* (Tübingen: Gunter Narr, 1988), pp. 25–42.

11. Other Arts and Adaptations

De Bruyckere, Berlinde, J. M. Coetzee, Philippe van Cauteren, and Herman Parret, *Cripplewood/Kreupelhout* (Brussels: Mercatorfonds, 2013).

Dovey, Teresa, and Lindiwe Dovey, 'Coetzee on Film' in Graham Bradshaw and Michael Neill (eds.), *J. M. Coetzee's Austerities* (Farnham: Ashgate, 2010), pp. 57–78.

Coetzee, J. M., *Two Screenplays: 'Waiting for the Barbarians' and 'In the Heart of the Country'*, ed. Hermann Wittenberg (Cape Town: University of Cape Town Press, 2014).

Coetzee, J. M., *De Foto's van Jongensjaren (Photographs from Boyhood)*, comp. and introd. Hermann Wittenberg, trans. Peter Bergsma (Amsterdam: Cossee, 2018).

Englund, Axel, 'Intimate Practices: Music, Sex, and the Body in J. M. Coetzee's *Summertime*', *Mosaic: An Interdisciplinary Critical Journal*, 50.2 (2017), 99–115.

Lachman, Kathryn, *Borrowed Forms: The Music and Ethics of Transnational Fiction* (Liverpool: Liverpool University Press, 2014).

Macaskill, Brian, 'Translating and Transforming J. M. Coetzee's *Slow Man* from Novel to Opera: an Ambling, Doubling, and Trippling Pursuit of the Opera's Cinematographic Beginning', *Mise en Scene: The Journal of Film and Visual Narration*, 2.1 (2017), 1–21.

McDonald, Peter D., *Artefacts of Writing: Ideas of the State and Communities of Letters from Matthew Arnold to Xu Bing* (Oxford: Oxford University Press, 2017).

Wittenberg, Hermann, 'Coetzee in California: Adaptation, Authorship, and the Filming of *Waiting for the Barbarians*', *Safundi: The Journal of South African and American Studies*, 16.2 (2015), 115–35.

12. Philosophies

Attridge, Derek, 'Expecting the Unexpected in Coetzee's *Master of Petersburg* and Derrida's Recent Writings' in John Brannigan, Ruth Robbins, and Julian Wolfreys (eds.), *Applying: To Derrida* (London: Macmillan, 1996), pp. 21–40.

Cavalieri, Paula, et al., *The Death of the Animal: A Dialogue* (New York: Columbia University Press, 2009).

Cavell, Stanley, 'Companionable Thinking' in Stanley Cavell et al., *Philosophy and Animal Life* (New York: Columbia University Press, 2008), pp. 91–126.

De Gaynesford, Maximilian, 'Attuning Philosophy and Literary Criticism: A Response to *In the Heart of the Country*' in Jan Wilm and Patrick Hayes

Further Reading

(eds.), *Beyond the Ancient Quarrel: Literature, Philosophy, and J. M. Coetzee* (Oxford: Oxford University Press, 2017), pp. 35–51.

Diamond, Cora, 'The Difficulty of Reality and the Difficulty of Philosophy' in Stanley Cavell et al., *Philosophy and Animal Life* (New York: Columbia University Press, 2008), pp. 43–90.

Flynn, Jennifer, '*The Lives of Animals* and the Form-Content Connection' in Anton Leist and Peter Singer, (eds.), *J. M. Coetzee and Ethics: Philosophical Perspectives on Literature* (New York: Columbia University Press, 2010), pp. 317–35.

Hämäläinen, Nora, 'Sophie, Antigone, Elizabeth: Rethinking Ethics by Reading Literature' in Garry L. Hagberg, (ed.), *Fictional Characters, Real Problems: The Search for Ethical Content in Literature* (Oxford: Oxford University Press, 2016), pp. 15–30.

Lear, Jonathan, 'Ethical Thought and the Problem of Communication: A Strategy for Reading *Diary of a Bad Year*' in Anton Leist and Peter Singer, (eds.), *J. M. Coetzee and Ethics: Philosophical Perspectives on Literature* (New York: Columbia University Press, 2010), pp. 65–88.

Leist, Anton, 'Against Society, Against History, Against Reason: Coetzee's Archaic Postmodernism' in Anton Leist and Peter Singer, (eds.), *J. M. Coetzee and Ethics: Philosophical Perspectives on Literature* (New York: Columbia University Press, 2010), pp. 197–222.

Marais, Michael, '"Little Enough, Less than Little: Nothing": Ethics, Engagement, and Change in the Fiction of J. M. Coetzee', *MFS: Modern Fiction Studies*, 46.1 (2000), 159–82.

Pippin, Robert, 'The Paradoxes of Power in the Early Novels of J. M. Coetzee' in Anton Leist and Peter Singer, (eds.), *J. M. Coetzee and Ethics: Philosophical Perspectives on Literature* (New York: Columbia University Press, 2010), pp. 19–41.

'Philosophical Fiction? On J. M. Coetzee's *Elizabeth Costello*' in Tim Mehigan and Christian Moser, (eds.), *Intellectual Landscapes in the Works of J. M. Coetzee* (Rochester: Camden House, 2017), pp. 294–310.

Sellbach, Undine, '*The Lives of Animals*: Wittgenstein, Coetzee, and the Extent of the Sympathetic Imagination' in Aaron Gross and Anne Vallely (eds.), *Animals and the Human Imagination: A Companion to Animal Studies* (New York: Columbia University Press, 2012), pp. 307–30.

Woessner, Martin, 'Coetzee's Critique of Reason' in Anton Leist and Peter Singer, (eds.), *J. M. Coetzee and Ethics: Philosophical Perspectives on Literature* (New York: Columbia University Press, 2010), pp. 223–47.

Wright, Laura, 'Breaking the Laws in J. M. Coetzee's *The Childhood of Jesus*: Philosophy and the Notion of Justice', *African Literature Today*, 32 (2014), 77–90.

13. Lives and Archives

Anker, Elizabeth S., 'Why We Love Coetzee; or, *The Childhood of Jesus* and the Funhouse of Critique' in her *Critique and Postcritique* (London: Duke University Press, 2017), pp. 183–208.

Boehmer, Elleke, 'Reading Between Life and Work: Reflecting on "J. M. Coetzee"', *Textual Practice*, 30.3 (2016), 435–50.

Bolin, John, 'Modernism, Idiocy, and the Work of Culture: J. M. Coetzee's *Life & Times of Michael K*', *Modernism/Modernity*, 22 (2015), 343–64.

Easton, Kai, 'Coetzee, the Cape and the Question of History', *Scrutiny2*, 11.1 (2006), 5–21.

Saunders, Max, *Self Impression: Life-Writing, Autobiografiction, and the Forms of Modern Literature* (Oxford: Oxford University Press, 2010).

Sheehan, Paul, 'Coetzee & Co: Failure, Lies and Autobiography', *Textual Practice*, 30.3 (2016), 451–68.

Uhlmann, Anthony, '*Dusklands* and the Meaning of Method', *Textual Practice*, 30 (2016), 399–415.

Wilm, Jan, 'The J. M. Coetzee Archive and the Archive in J. M. Coetzee' in Jan Wilm and Patrick Hayes (eds.), *Beyond the Ancient Quarrel: Literature, Philosophy, and J. M. Coetzee* (Oxford: Oxford University Press, 2017), pp. 215–31.

14. Publics and Personas

Attwell, David, 'Mastering authority: J. M. Coetzee's *Diary of a Bad Year*,' *Social Dynamics*, 36.1 (2010), 214–21.

Barnard, Rita, 'On Public and Private in J. M. Coetzee', *Cultural Studies*, 27.3 (2013), 438–61.

Evans, Nicholas and Monica Seeber, (eds.), *The Politics of Publishing in South Africa* (London: Holger Ehling Publishing; Scottsville, South Africa: University of Natal Press, 2000).

Flanery, Patrick Denman, '(Re-)Marking Coetzee & Costello: *The* [Textual] *Lives of Animals*,' *English Studies in Africa*, 47.1 (2004), 61–84.

'Limber: The Flexibilities of Post-Nobel Coetzee' in Andrew van der Vlies (ed.), *Print, Text, and Book Cultures in South Africa* (Johannesburg: Wits University Press, 2012), pp. 208–24.

Geertsema, Johan, 'Coetzee's *Diary of a Bad Year*, Politics, and the Problem of Position,' *Twentieth-Century Literature*, 57.1 (2011), 70–85.

McDonald, Peter D., 'The Writer, the Critic and the Censor: J. M. Coetzee and the Question of Literature', *Book History*, 7 (2004), 285–302.

'Ideas of the Book and Histories of Literatures: After Theory?', *PMLA*, 12.1 (2006), 214–28.

Van der Vlies, Andrew, 'Bad Feelings in the Provinces of History' in his *Present Imperfect: Contemporary South African Writing* (Oxford: Oxford University Press, 2017), pp. 51–74.

'Print, Text, and Books in South Africa' in Andrew van der Vlies (ed.), *Print, Text, and Book Cultures in South Africa* (Johannesburg: Wits University Press, 2012), pp. 2–48.

Zimbler, Jarad, 'Under Local Eyes: The South African Publishing Context of J. M. Coetzee's *Foe*', *English Studies in Africa*, 47.1 (2004), 47–59.

INDEX

Abrahams, Peter, 37
Achterberg, Gerrit, 109
adaptation, 10, 117, 189, 200, 201, 203, *see also under* J. M. Coetzee
Adelaide, 38, 40, 91, 93
Adorno, Theodor, 209
affect, 5, 59–60, 65, 66, 69, 77, 157, 164–165, 196, 223, 231
Afrikaans, 7, 84, 103, 105, 106–107, 108, 109, 110, 111, 119, 131, 241, 242
literature, 7, 22, 85, 103, 107–112, 141, *see also* André Brink, Antjie Krog, Etienne Leroux, W. E. G. Louw, Mikro, D. J. Opperman, *plaasroman*, Ina Rousseau, Sestigers, Wilma Stockenström, C. M. van den Heever
animals, 68, 80, 91, 93, 94, 110, 174, 184, 193, 196, 241, *see also under* human
Antonioni, Michelangelo, 188, 191
apartheid, 1, 5, 9, 11, 15, 18–19, 21, 22, 24, 32, 35, 36–37, 38, 42, 61, 69, 70–72, 95, 108, 120, 126, 131, 133, 134, 145, 168, 169, 178–79, 180, 221, 230, 236–37, 238, 241–43, 245–46, *see also* Steve Biko, censorship, race, violence
archive, the, 10, 222, 223, 225, 226–28, 231–32, *see also* J. M. Coetzee: Coetzee Papers, Harry Ransom Center, manuscripts
Argentina, 115, 181, 248
literature of, 9, 140, 148, 169, 181, *see also* Jorge Luis Borges
Auerbach, Erich, 177
Augustine, 154
Austen, Jane, 174

Auster, Paul, 8, 106, 122, 123, 129, 130, 132, *see also* J. M. Coetzee: *Here and Now*
Austin, J. L., 209
Australia, 38, 40, 41, 42, 44, 149, 168, 169, 172, 175, 179, 180, 246, 248, *see also* Adelaide
literature of, 7, 9, 140, 148, 155, 169, 170, 171, 173, 179, 181, 244, *see also* Peter Carey, Ivor Indyk, Gail Jones, Nicholas Jose, Text Publishing, Patrick White
autobiography, 6, 10, 21, 25, 37, 92, 94–97, 142, 143, 144, 146, 148, 188, 222–23, 225, 226, 227–29, 231, 238, *see also* memoir
automatism, 51, 54, 126

Bach, Johann Sebastian, 94, 148, 153, 156, 187, 189, 190, 191, 192, 193, 196
Bakhtin, Mikhail, 152, 208, 215–16
Bal, Mieke, 29
ballet *see* dance
Barthes, Roland, 19, 34, 41, 49, 152, 155, 156, 157, 158, 160, 163, 188, 195, 196, 208, 210, 211, 222
Bataille, Georges, 164
Beckett, Samuel, 4, 6, 7, 9, 63, 64, 65, 68, 75, 77, 82, 112, 114–18, 129, 143, 147, 149, 152, 153, 157–58, 160, 189, 207, 239, 240, *see also* manuscripts
Murphy, 65
The Unnamable, 157
Waiting for Godot, 20, 115, 116, 117
Watt, 65, 153, 189, 223
Beethoven, Ludwig van, 190
Benveniste, Émile, 208
Bergson, Henri, 19, 190

Index

Bible, 2, 26, 52, 60, 61, 110, 177
Biko, Steve, 18, 19, 221, 241
biography, 3, 4, 11, 97, 223, 225, 227, 230, 240, *see also* autobiography, memoir
Blanchot, Maurice, 208
Bloom, Harold, 152, 208
Bolaño, Roberto, 174
Bonnard, Pierre, 77, 203
Booker Prize, 15, 171, 244, 245, 246
Booth, Wayne, 62
Borges, Jorge Luis, 148, 182
Bourdieu, Pierre, 235, *see also* literary field
Brink, André, 122, 145, 154, 243, 245
Brooks, Cleanth, 62
Buber, Martin, 154
Bultmann, Rudolf, 26, 154
Burchell, William, 35, 38, 40, 154, 223
Burgess, Yvonne, 55, 126
Burroughs, William, 240
Buzzati, Dino, 17
Byatt, A. S., 49, 62, 171

Campbell, Joseph, 54
Campbell, Roy, 154
Cape Colony, 30, 32, 39, 110
Cape Town, 15, 38, 39, 92, 95, 110, 114, 115, 121, 152, 189, 190, 191, 203, 210, 230, 237, 242
capitalism, 1, 3, 5, 40, 56, 59, 61, 155, 170, 171, 173, 181, 183, *see also* financial crisis
Carey, Peter, 155
Casanova, Pascale, 115, 171
Cassin, Barbara, 112–13
Cavafy, C. P., 16, 21
Celan, Paul, 181, 182
censorship, 8, 11, 90, 124, 143, 144–147, 150, 156, 196, 235, 241–42, 244–45, 246
Cervantes, Miguel de, 2, 52, 60, 148, 150, 153
Césaire, Aimé, 209
character, 2, 5, 41, 45–49, 53, 56–57, 62, 86, 89, 90, 127, 147, 157, 170, 172, 174, 188, 197, 199, 238, 239
Chatman, Seymour, 49
Chaucer, Geoffrey, 23
Chomsky, Noam, 212, 213
Cixous, Hélène, 207, 208
Coetzee, J. M.
    'Achterberg's "Ballade van de gasfitter":
        The Mystery of I and You', 109, 140
    'Confession and Double Thoughts',
        143–44, 158–59, 160, 162, 166, 233

'Die Skrywer en die Teorie', 139
'Eden', 7, 107–110
'Eight Ways of Looking at Samuel
    Beckett', 149
'He and His Man', 234, 238
'Hero and Bad Mother in Epic', 5, 53–54
'Homage', 8, 68, 147, 148, 151
'Into the Dark Chamber', 18, 36, 126, 144
'Jerusalem Prize Acceptance Speech', 33, 35, 150
'Lectura John M. Coetzee en Malba', 43
'Lies', 98
'Literatures of the South', 3, 31, 38, 42, 181
'Man's Fate in the Novels of Alex La
    Guma', 37
'Nevertheless, My Sympathies are with the
    Karamazovs', 123, 124, 126, 127, 134
'Remembering Texas', 69
'SA Authors Must Learn Modesty', 35, 43, 148, 243, 244
'Samuel Beckett and the Temptations of
    Style', 64–65, 67
'Samuel Beckett in Cape Town – An
    Imaginary History', 114–115, 116
'The Comedy of Point of View in Beckett's
    Murphy', 157–58, 239
'The English Fiction of Samuel Beckett', 4, 138, 153, 207, 212–13
'The First Sentence of Yvonne Burgess's
    The Strike', 55, 126
'The Novel Today', 8, 143, 166, 230, 237
'The Rhetoric of the Passive in English', 65, 67
'Truth in Autobiography', 143, 228–29
'What is a Classic?', 121, 148–49, 152–53, 156, 189–92
'Working with Translators', 1, 109, 112, 118–119, 120
'Writing in South Africa', 235
A Land Apart, 33, 122
A Posthumous Confession, 107
Age of Iron, 3, 6, 8, 9, 42, 70–76, 78, 82, 122, 123, 125, 126, 129, 131, 133–136, 147, 151, 192, 193, 211, 212, 216, 238, 239
Boyhood, 5, 22, 31, 35–37, 40, 94, 95, 96, 97, 106, 107, 141, 228
Coetzee Papers, 3, 4, 6, 10, 15, 26, 62, 71, 139, 142, 145, 148, 151, 198, 201, 208, 210, 211, 214, 221–27, 230–32, 235, 237, *see also under* manuscripts

Index

Index

190–91, 193, 195, 206–07, 223, 225–28

Cold War, 228

colonialism, 1, 3, 5, 18, 31, 33, 35, 39, 40, 42, 47, 50, 56, 67, 69, 70, 106, 110, 111–12, 116, 117, 124, 126, 131, 140–42, 150, 161, 168, 171, 174, 178, 183, 189, 197, 240, 243, *see also* apartheid, decolonization, imperialism, violence

composition, 4–5, 15–27, 29, 62, 65, 80, 139, 142, 146, 174, 200, 210–11, 221, 222, 225–27, 229–30

computing, 53, 65, 207, 241, *see also* automatism, 'Hero and Bad Mother in Epic'

confession, 71, 143, 144, 158, 164, 228, 229

consecration *see* cultural capital

consolation, 2, 4, 6, 64, 71, 72, 73, 74, 75, 77, 79, 82

context, 7, 9, 107, 176–77, 232
  historical, 5, 9, 18, 21, 27, 29–31, 32–33, 39–40, , 50, 71, 107–08, 116, 139, 140, 141, 142, 149, 168, 243
  textual, 87, 89, 93–94, 107, 113, 190, 244, 245

Cope, Jack, 247

Couto, Mia, 181

Culler, Jonathan, 208

cultural capital, 7, 9, 10–11, 64, 117, 170, 171–72, 173, 234–35, 246

dance, 9, 80, 81, 159, 164, 165, 166, 174, 183, 187, 188, 190, 191, 194–196, 197–199, *see also* Kenneth Macmillan, Norman McLaren

Dante Alighieri, 211

de Beauvoir, Simone, 19

de Man, Paul, 208

decolonization, 1, 24, 141, 209

deconstruction, 25, 208, 218

Defoe, Daniel, 7, 9, 31, 32, 33, 34, 36, 40, 143, 148, 155, 159, 162, 234, 238

dehumanization, 20, 47, 50, 58, 59, 69, 133, 165, 178

Deleuze, Gilles, 208

Derrida, Jacques, 21, 106, 137, 158, 208, 211, 212

dialogic, 124, 127, 207, 215–16

dialogue, 5, 8, 45, 49, 59, 60, 79, 106, 119, 122–33, 136, 142, 207, 215–17, 225, 239, 242

Diderot, Denis, 210

Disgrace (2008), dir. Steve Jacobs, 202–03

Dostoevsky, Fyodor, 7, 9, 26, 47, 52, 59, 61, 62, 94, 143, 148, 152, 153, 155, 158, 159, 162, 166, 215–16, 239

Du Plessis, Catherine Lauga, 104, 114

Duncan, Robert, 17

Duras, Marguerite, 240

Dust (1985), dir. Marion Hänsel, 202

Dutch, 7, 84, 103–06, 120, 140
  literature, 103, 105–07, *see also* Gerrit Achterberg, Marcellus Emants, Simon Vinkenoog

Eagleton, Terry, 208

Eco, Umberto, 208

Eliot, T. S., 7, 16, 17, 148, 190

Emants, Marcellus, 107

embodiment, 10, 89, 90, 170, 189, 194, 196, 203, 216, 217

English, 1, 12, 103, 104, 106, 107, 168, 172
  Australian, 39, 175, 183
  Irish, 115, 116
  South African, 111, 116

epistolarity, 8, 17, 98, 122, 123, 127–36, 137, 212, 214

Erasmus, Desiderius, 236

ethics, 66, 68, 72, 75, 77, 79, 82, 86, 142, 146, 162–63, 168, 180, 184, 187, 195–97, 206, 212, 218, 219, 226

existentialism, 26, 209

Fanon, Frantz, 209

Fauchery, Antoine, 40–42, 200

Faulkner, William, 148, 153

feminism, 154, 160–62

film, 9, 15, 23, 98, 176, 187, 188, 189, 191, 194–196, 197, 198, 201–203, 208, 212, *see also* Michelangelo Antonioni, *Dust, Disgrace*, Marion Hänsel, Werner Herzog, John Huston, Pier Paulo Pasolini, Satyajit Ray, *The Lives of Animals, The Muse*, Francois Verster, Orson Welles

financial crisis, 129

Fish, Stanley, 208

Flaubert, Gustave, 19, 26, 64, 70, 72, 147

Fludernick, Monika, 30, 32

focalization, 2, 5, 23, 35, 37, 57–61, 66, 75, 78, 79, 80, 87, 89, 119, 147, 176, 188, 190, 192, 195, 196, 197, 239

Index

Index

Lens, Nicholas, 10, 199–201
Leonie, Sergio, 174
Leroux, Etienne, 49, 62, 154
Les Troubadours du Roi Baudouin, 191
Lessing, Doris, 171
Levinas, Emmanuel, 212
liberalism, 18, 19, 21, 25, 146, 245
life-writing, 222, 231, see also autobiography, biography, confession, memoir
linguistics, 9, 62, 103, 118, 140, 155, 204, 208, 212, 218, see also Émile Benveniste, Noam Chomsky, Alexander von Humboldt, Roman Jakobson, George Lakoff, Benjamin Lee Whorf
literary field, 7, 49, 62, 168, 169, 178, 179, 227, 235, 243
literary prizes, 11, 169–173, 245, see also Booker Prize, Nobel Prize
    Büchner Prize, 181
    CNA Prize, 235, 243, 246
    Commonwealth Writers' Prize, 244
    Geoffrey Faber Memorial Prize, 15
    James Tait Black Memorial Prize, 15
    Jerusalem Prize, 35, 244
    Miles Franklin Prize, 171
    Neustadt International Prize, 247
    Prix Femina Étranger, 244
Louw, W. E. G., 154
Lukács, Gyorgy, 208

Mackellar, Dorothea, 44
MacKinnon, Catharine, 145
Macmillan, Kenneth, 195
Mandelstam, Osip, 145
manuscripts
    Beckett's, 4, 207, 223, 224
    Coetzee's, 4, 10, 15, 16, 19–20, 24, 26, 62, 79, 83, 210, 221, 222, 224–27
market, literary, 7, 9, 11, 85, 117, 152, 173, 201, 241–45
Márquez, Gabriel García, 148
Marx, Karl, 155, 208, 210
Mauthner, Fritz, 197
McLaren, Norman, 194–95, 198
Medvedev, Pavel, 208
Melville, Herman, 26, 149
memoir, 69, 94–96, 128
metafiction, 21, 24, 25, 34, 41, 68, 71, 85, 89, 118, 155, 158, 170, 171, 172, 176, 193, 197, 199, 200, 238
methodology, critical, 11, 48, 65, 67, 207, 222, 227, 230–32

Michael Kohlhaas see Heinrich von Kleist
migration, 3, 35, 37, 38, 41, 42, 149
Mikro, 119
milieu see setting
Miller, Arthur, 195
Miller, Henry, 240
Miller, J. Hillis, 25, 208, 211
Miller, Nancy K., 160–61
Millin, Sarah Gertrude, 145, 154
minimalism, 48, 49, 201
mis en abyme, 193–94, 197
mise en scène, 18, 30, 43
Mitchell, W. J. T., 188
modernism, 17, 77, 157
Montaigne, Michel de, 214
Mphahlele, Es'kia, 37
music, 9, 80, 187, 188, 189–94, 196, 231, see also Johann Sebastian Bach, Ludwig van Beethoven, Philip Glass, Ustad Vilayat Khan, Nicholas Lens, Les Troubadours du Roi Baudouin, opera, Franz Schubert
Musil, Robert, 16, 148

Nabokov, Vladimir, 148
Nagel, Thomas, 214
narration, 1, 4, 5, 17, 18, 23, 25, 41, 46, 53, 54–62, 63, 66, 69, 71, 78–79, 84, 95, 128, 134, 135, 146, 147, 148, 157, 175–77, 188, 190, 195, 201, 239, see also focalization
narratology, 46, see also Mikhail Bakhtin, Mieke Bal, Roland Barthes, Joseph Campbell, Seymour Chatman, Monika Fludernick, Gérard Genette, Vladimir Propp, Viktor Shklovsky
national literature, 9, 11, 30–31, 34, 42, 85, 116, 141, 170, 171, 173, 180, 243, 245, see also under Argentina, Australia, South Africa
nationalism, 9, 41, 44, 108, 169, 192
naturalism, 16, 55
neo-colonialism, 1, 31
neo-liberalism, 40
Neruda, Pablo, 182, 184
Netherlandic see Afrikaans, Dutch
New Criticism, 62
Nietzsche, Friedrich, 26, 151, 154, 156, 198, 209, 216
Nobel Prize in Literature, 93, 115, 116, 148, 171, 179, 234, 235, 238, 244, 245
nouveau roman, 15, 201, 240

Index

novel, the, 4, 6, 9, 15, 32, 40, 41, 46, 64, 66, 84, 87, 89, 154, 157, 159, 197, 203, 215, 245
Ntshona, Wintson, 32

Olson, Charles, 198
Ong, Walter, 19
opera, 9, 10, 80, 187, 189, 192, 193, 194, 197, 199–201, 203, see also Philip Glass, Nicholas Lens
opinion piece, 6, 92, 93, 94, 112–114, 214, 238
Opperman, D. J., 107

paraphrase, 47–48, 62
Pascal, Blaise, 26
Pasolini, Pier Paulo, 191, 193
Pasternak, Boris, 19
pastoral, 36, 37, 51, 52, 55, 98, 140–42, see also plaasroman
Paton, Alan, 119, 154
Paz, Octavio, 19
pedagogy, 9, 23, 47, 79, 115
performance, 3, 144, 189, 191, 193–94, 196–99, 234, 236, 238, 243, see also dance, music, opera, persona, theatre
persona, authorial, 3, 107, 127, 227, 234, 235, 238, 239, 246
philosophy, 9, 10, 66, 79, 88, 154, 156, 168, 180, 206–220
photography, 9, 40–42, 187, 188, 195–96, 199, 200, 201, 204, 241
plaasroman, 51, 52, 55, 56, 61, 62, 98, 141–42
place, 7, 29, 31, 35, 37, 39, 40, 42, 141, 142, 175, 179–80, 182
Plato, 144, 154, 206, 207, 211, 213, 215, 216
plot, 2, 5, 18, 21, 22, 26, 29, 45, 46–49, 53–54, 73, 77, 139, 174, 199
Poe, Edgar Allan, 171
poetry, 7, 21, 22, 29, 53–54, 87, 104, 105, 107, 109, 182, 191, 207
pornography, 58, 68, 145, 165, 166, 196, 226
postcolonial, 117, 118, 124, 141, 154, 170, 171, 180, 245
postmodernism, 71, 118, 154, 160, 222, 223
post-structuralism, 34, 171, 208
Pound, Ezra, 7, 17, 148, 151
prestige see cultural capital
Pringle, Thomas, 154
Propp, Vladimir, 53, 62
prosody, 5, 54, 66, 73, 74, 75, 108, 133

Proust, Marcel, 157
provincial, 1, 31, 32, 34–35, 38–39, 118, 148, 175, 179, 189, 190, 191, 243
provocation, 4, 8, 10, 21, 154, 188, 206, 209, 211, 214, 216, 218–220
psychology, 9, 67, 122, 127, 128, 155, 165, 208, 209, 211, 228, 240, see also Sigmund Freud, Arabella Kurtz
public sphere, 10, 11, 79, 179, 222, 228, 234, 235, 236, 238, 239
publishers see Ravan Press, Secker & Warburg, Text Publishing
publishing 11, 115, 171, 181, 228, 234, 239–244, 247

race, 18, 22, 36–37, 42, 56, 61, 66, 70, 116, 119, 120, 131, 135, 141–42, 145, 154, 160, 197, 221, 242, 244, 245, 247
Randall, Peter, 240–43
Ransom, John Crowe, 62
rape, 46, 56, 146, 195, 196
Ravan Press, 106, 240–44
Ray, Satyajit, 191
real, the, 9, 30–32, 40, 42, 43, 188, 195–97
realism, 5, 17, 21, 23, 30, 37, 41, 43, 56, 67, 71, 72, 83, 88–89, 174, 191, 193, 195, 196, 199, 213, 214, 217, 240
reciprocity, 3, 19, 20, 46, 50, 56, 130, 134, 143, 192
reviews, 11, 24, 25, 48, 63, 81, 82, 110, 129, 140, 143, 166, 171, 176, 177, 230, 243, 245, see also under J. M. Coetzee
rhetoric, 4, 5, 6, 61, 66, 87, 208, 216, 230, 236
Rhys, Jean, 155
Rich, Adrienne, 34, 160, 161, 162
Richardson, Samuel, 129
Ricoeur, Paul, 19, 121
Rilke, Rainer Maria, 148
Robbe-Grillet, Alain, 240
romanticism, 21, 188, 192, 193, 203
Roth, Philip, 55
Rousseau, Ina, 7, 107–09
Rousseau, Jean-Jacques, 143, 158, 193, 228–29
Rushdie, Salman, 237
Russian formalism, 62, 208, 210, 212

Sahlins, Marshall, 26
Said, Edward, 81
Sargent, John Singer, 76–77, 203
Sarraute, Nathalie, 240
Sartre, Jean-Paul, 154, 209

Index

Index

Cambridge Companions to ...

AUTHORS

Edward Albee edited by Stephen J. Bottoms

Margaret Atwood edited by Coral Ann Howells

W. H. Auden edited by Stan Smith

Jane Austen edited by Edward Copeland and Juliet McMaster (second edition)

Balzac edited by Owen Heathcote and Andrew Watts

Beckett edited by John Pilling

Bede edited by Scott DeGregorio

Aphra Behn edited by Derek Hughes and Janet Todd

Walter Benjamin edited by David S. Ferris

William Blake edited by Morris Eaves

Boccaccio edited by Guyda Armstrong, Rhiannon Daniels, and Stephen J. Milner

Jorge Luis Borges edited by Edwin Williamson

Brecht edited by Peter Thomson and Glendyr Sacks (second edition)

The Brontës edited by Heather Glen

Bunyan edited by Anne Dunan-Page

Frances Burney edited by Peter Sabor

Byron edited by Drummond Bone

Albert Camus edited by Edward J. Hughes

Willa Cather edited by Marilee Lindemann

Cervantes edited by Anthony J. Cascardi

Chaucer edited by Piero Boitani and Jill Mann (second edition)

Chekhov edited by Vera Gottlieb and Paul Allain

Kate Chopin edited by Janet Beer

Caryl Churchill edited by Elaine Aston and Elin Diamond

Cicero edited by Catherine Steel

J. M. Coetzee edited by Jarad Zimbler

Coleridge edited by Lucy Newlyn

Wilkie Collins edited by Jenny Bourne Taylor

Joseph Conrad edited by J. H. Stape

H. D. edited by Nephie J. Christodoulides and Polina Mackay

Dante edited by Rachel Jacoff (second edition)

Daniel Defoe edited by John Richetti

Don DeLillo edited by John N. Duvall

Charles Dickens edited by John O. Jordan

Emily Dickinson edited by Wendy Martin

John Donne edited by Achsah Guibbory

Dostoevskii edited by W. J. Leatherbarrow

Theodore Dreiser edited by Leonard Cassuto and Claire Virginia Eby

John Dryden edited by Steven N. Zwicker

W. E. B. Du Bois edited by Shamoon Zamir

George Eliot edited by George Levine and Nancy Henry (second edition)

T. S. Eliot edited by A. David Moody

Ralph Ellison edited by Ross Posnock

Ralph Waldo Emerson edited by Joel Porte and Saundra Morris

William Faulkner edited by Philip M. Weinstein

Henry Fielding edited by Claude Rawson

F. Scott Fitzgerald edited by Ruth Prigozy

Flaubert edited by Timothy Unwin

E. M. Forster edited by David Bradshaw

Benjamin Franklin edited by Carla Mulford

Brian Friel edited by Anthony Roche

Robert Frost edited by Robert Faggen

Gabriel García Márquez edited by Philip Swanson

Elizabeth Gaskell edited by Jill L. Matus

Edward Gibbon edited by Karen O'Brien and Brian Young

Goethe edited by Lesley Sharpe

Günter Grass edited by Stuart Taberner

Thomas Hardy edited by Dale Kramer

David Hare edited by Richard Boon

Nathaniel Hawthorne edited by Richard Millington

Seamus Heaney edited by Bernard O'Donoghue

Ernest Hemingway edited by Scott Donaldson

Homer edited by Robert Fowler

Horace edited by Stephen Harrison

Ted Hughes edited by Terry Gifford

Ibsen edited by James McFarlane

Henry James edited by Jonathan Freedman

Samuel Johnson edited by Greg Clingham

Ben Jonson edited by Richard Harp and Stanley Stewart

James Joyce edited by Derek Attridge (second edition)

Kafka edited by Julian Preece

Keats edited by Susan J. Wolfson

Oscar Wilde edited by Peter Raby

Tennessee Williams edited by Matthew C. Roudané

August Wilson edited by Christopher Bigsby

Mary Wollstonecraft edited by Claudia L. Johnson

Virginia Woolf edited by Susan Sellers (second edition)

Wordsworth edited by Stephen Gill

Richard Wright edited by Glenda R. Carpio

W. B. Yeats edited by Marjorie Howes and John Kelly

Xenophon edited by Michael A. Flower

Zola edited by Brian Nelson

TOPICS

The Actress edited by Maggie B. Gale and John Stokes

The African American Novel edited by Maryemma Graham

The African American Slave Narrative edited by Audrey A. Fisch

Theatre History by David Wiles and Christine Dymkowski

African American Theatre by Harvey Young

Allegory edited by Rita Copeland and Peter Struck

American Crime Fiction edited by Catherine Ross Nickerson

American Gothic edited by Jeffrey Andrew Weinstock

American Literature of the 1930s edited by William Solomon American

American Modernism edited by Walter Kalaidjian

American Poetry Since 1945 edited by Jennifer Ashton

American Realism and Naturalism edited by Donald Pizer

American Travel Writing edited by Alfred Bendixen and Judith Hamera

American Women Playwrights edited by Brenda Murphy

Ancient Rhetoric edited by Erik Gunderson

Arthurian Legend edited by Elizabeth Archibald and Ad Putter

Australian Literature edited by Elizabeth Webby

The Beats edited by Stephen Belletto

British Black and Asian Literature (1945–2010) edited by Deirdre Osborne

British Fiction: 1980–2018 edited by Peter Boxall

British Literature of the French Revolution edited by Pamela Clemit

British Literature of the 1930s edited by James Smith

British Romanticism edited by Stuart Curran (second edition)

British Romantic Poetry edited by James Chandler and Maureen N. McLane

British Theatre, 1730–1830, edited by Jane Moody and Daniel O'Quinn

Canadian Literature edited by Eva-Marie Kröller (second edition)

Children's Literature edited by M. O. Grenby and Andrea Immel

The Canterbury Tales edited by Frank Grady

The Classic Russian Novel edited by Malcolm V. Jones and Robin Feuer Miller

Contemporary Irish Poetry edited by Matthew Campbell

Creative Writing edited by David Morley and Philip Neilsen

Crime Fiction edited by Martin Priestman

Dracula edited by Roger Luckhurst

Early Modern Women's Writing edited by Laura Lunger Knoppers

The Eighteenth-Century Novel edited by John Richetti

Eighteenth-Century Poetry edited by John Sitter

Emma edited by Peter Sabor

English Dictionaries edited by Sarah Ogilvie

English Literature, 1500–1600 edited by Arthur F. Kinney

English Literature, 1650–1740 edited by Steven N. Zwicker

English Literature, 1740–1830 edited by Thomas Keymer and Jon Mee

English Literature, 1830–1914 edited by Joanne Shattock

English Melodrama edited by Carolyn Williams

English Novelists edited by Adrian Poole

English Poetry, Donne to Marvell edited by Thomas N. Corns

English Poets edited by Claude Rawson

English Renaissance Drama, second edition edited by A. R. Braunmuller and Michael Hattaway

English Renaissance Tragedy edited by Emma Smith and Garrett A. Sullivan Jr.

English Restoration Theatre edited by Deborah C. Payne Fisk

The Epic edited by Catherine Bates

Erotic Literature edited by Bradford Mudge

European Modernism edited by Pericles Lewis

European Novelists edited by Michael Bell

Fairy Tales edited by Maria Tatar

Fantasy Literature edited by Edward James and Farah Mendlesohn

Feminist Literary Theory edited by Ellen Rooney

Fiction in the Romantic Period edited by Richard Maxwell and Katie Trumpener

The Fin de Siècle edited by Gail Marshall

Frankenstein edited by Andrew Smith

The French Enlightenment edited by Daniel Brewer

French Literature edited by John D. Lyons

The French Novel: from 1800 to the Present edited by Timothy Unwin

Gay and Lesbian Writing edited by Hugh Stevens

German Romanticism edited by Nicholas Saul

Gothic Fiction edited by Jerrold E. Hogle

The Graphic Novel edited by Stephen Tabachnick

The Greek and Roman Novel edited by Tim Whitmarsh

Greek and Roman Theatre edited by Marianne McDonald and J. Michael Walton

Greek Comedy edited by Martin Revermann

Greek Lyric edited by Felix Budelmann

Greek Mythology edited by Roger D. Woodard

Greek Tragedy edited by P. E. Easterling

The Harlem Renaissance edited by George Hutchinson

The History of the Book edited by Leslie Howsam

Human Rights and Literature edited by Crystal Parikh

The Irish Novel edited by John Wilson Foster

Irish Poets edited by Gerald Dawe

The Italian Novel edited by Peter Bondanella and Andrea Ciccarelli

The Italian Renaissance edited by Michael Wyatt

Jewish American Literature edited by Hana Wirth-Nesher and Michael P. Kramer

Latin American Poetry edited by Stephen Hart

The Latin American Novel edited by Efraín Kristal

The Literature of the American Renaissance edited by Christopher N. Phillips

The Literature of Berlin edited by Andrew J. Webber

The Literature of the Crusades, Volume 1, edited by Anthony Bale

The Literature of the First World War edited by Vincent Sherry

The Literature of London edited by Lawrence Manley

The Literature of Los Angeles edited by Kevin R. McNamara

The Literature of New York edited by Cyrus Patell and Bryan Waterman

The Literature of Paris edited by Anna-Louise Milne

The Literature of World War II edited by Marina MacKay

Literature and Disability edited by Clare Barker and Stuart Murray

Literature and Science edited by Steven Meyer

Literature on Screen edited by Deborah Cartmell and Imelda Whelehan

Lyrical Ballads edited by Sally Bushell

Medieval English Culture edited by Andrew Galloway

Medieval English Literature edited by Larry Scanlon

Medieval English Mysticism edited by Samuel Fanous and Vincent Gillespie

Medieval English Theatre edited by Richard Beadle and Alan J. Fletcher (second edition)

Medieval French Literature edited by Simon Gaunt and Sarah Kay

Medieval Romance edited by Roberta L. Krueger

Medieval Women's Writing edited by Carolyn Dinshaw and David Wallace

Modern American Culture edited by Christopher Bigsby